P9-CSB-336

SOUTHERN STUFF

SOUTHERN STUFF

Down-home talk
and bodacious lore
from deep in the
heart of Dixie

Mildred Jordan Brooks

AVON BOOKS ◆ NEW YORK

I want to thank everyone who contributed to this book over the years, to note my heartfelt appreciation to my nonpareil typist, Chris Mazzuca, and most of all—for his enthusiasm and his invaluable help on *Southern Stuff*—my deepest gratitude to my editor, David Highfill.

SOUTHERN STUFF is an original publication of Avon Books. This work has never before appeared in book form.

AVON BOOKS
A division of
The Hearst Corporation
1350 Avenue of the Americas
New York, New York 10019

Copyright © 1992 by Mildred Jordan Brooks
Published by arrangement with the author
Library of Congress Catalog Card Number: 91-93007
ISBN: 0-380-76491-1

First Avon Books Trade Printing: February 1992

AVON TRADEMARK REG. U.S. PAT. OFF. AND IN OTHER COUNTRIES, MARCA REGISTRADA, HECHO EN U.S.A.

Printed in the U.S.A.

OPM   10 9 8 7 6 5 4 3 2 1

For my mother, Carrie Lee,
the Southerner who made me one,

For my husband, Brooke,
the greatest Damnyankee of them all,

For my daughter, Diana,
whom I made half a Southerner,

For my sister, Joan,
of the soft Southern voice,

For Cud'n Jim Bob,
who gave me the idea for this book,

and

For my fellow Southerners everywhere

Contents

Being Southern is like being Jewish—
it is both a culture and a religion.

Introduction

$\mathcal{Q}$uite some years ago, in a state of almost ecstatic anticipation, a young girl from North Carolina left on her maiden visit to New York City. On the first day her excitement was considerably diminished by a disconcerting discovery that both surprised and annoyed her. She found that, from Macy's to Bonwit Teller, from the Automat to the Oak Room at the Plaza, from Greenwich Village to the Bronx, no one listened to *what* she said, only *how* she said it.

After about thirty minutes of shopping in Macy's, she and her companion, a young lady of Virginia background, became aware that they were being followed. No matter which part of the store they went to, the same two middle-aged women were close behind. When finally the two girls turned to confront their hangers-on, they were stunned to find their withering stares met by broad smiles—the indulgent, patronizing kind of smile that some people reserve for overly cute children and childish old folks. "We hope youse don't mind," one said, "but we just love the way you goils tock."

Without another one of those words that the New Yorkers were so taken with, the two young girls spun on their heels and marched off. They had not come to New York to amuse, and they definitely were not amused.

Years after the Macy's episode and after living in numerous and scattered parts of the United States and traveling in foreign countries, it became apparent to me, once that young girl, that no one—absolutely no one—is indifferent to a Southern accent. I learned that many non-Southerners are charmed, that a fair number are envious, while no one—even those who claim to be revolted—is indifferent to it. So, I ask you, in all the world is there another language so intriguing, so beguiling, so warm and appealing, to so many different people as our American Southern? And "people" certainly includes us Southerners as well; we are notorious for loving to hear ourselves talk, and sometimes even admit it.

I am not a "professional Southerner." I do not display the Confederate flag on my house or my automobile bumper. I do not brag about family heroes who fought in "The War of Northern Aggression" (and almost won it); I do not boast about being eligible for the Daughters of the Confederacy or being a descendant of one of the founders of Jamestown; and I certainly do not carry on about the revered black nurse of my childhood who loved her white babies more than she did her own children.

However, I do have one fervent wish about the South. Before our cultural differences are all wiped out, and especially before the English language is completely homogenized by television, advanced education, routine foreign travel, and our one-world trend in general, I sincerely hope that we Southerners, in every conceivable way and through every possible medium, record for posterity our unique Southern speech. Which will explain why one Southern woman has traveled thousands of miles on Southern roads and spent many years of her life that she might compile this dictionary.

Soon after I began work on *Southern Stuff,* I said to my mother: "Mom, will you be sure to keep your ears open and save me any Southern expressions you overhear or that you use yourself?"

"Way-ul, Ah'll try, sugah, but you have to remembuh, Ah've been trave'lin' aroun' so much the las' twinny yeah's, Ah don't talk like those people much innymoah." (Most of her traveling had been in the Southern states, with Washington, D.C., her northernmost venture.)

She was convinced that she had practically no Southern accent, and she "distinctly knew" that she had never sounded like "some of these people aroun' heah who talk so slow and flat, Ah just wanna scream." She never sent me any words, either, for the simple reason that she never "heard" any, and I understood perfectly, because I had once been in those very same shoes.

When I was twenty-one years old, I moved from Richmond, Virginia, to the District of Columbia for the express purpose of studying acting with a well-known Washington teacher. For my second lesson there she had me work only on words with *g* endings. I didn't do too well, because I kept thinking I was pronouncing my *g*'s when I wasn't. Then we began with words spelled with *i*'s and *e*'s, my teacher insisting that I repeatedly pronounced *i* like *e*, and vice versa. "It is not 'foun'n *pin*,' "she said, "it is foun*tain pen—en—en—en.*" [See "the Great Vowel Shift" under "V"]

Then, when we left the *i*'s and *e*'s, we spent what seemed like an eternity on the word "naked," until finally when I was convinced I had it right—"Oh, shades of Stanislavsky!" my teacher cried. "It is not *nekkid*, girl, it is *naked*. It is naked spelled with an *a!*"

By this time I was beside myself with frustration. "I'm sorry," I told her, "but I did not say *nekkid* that time—as plain as day I said nekkid." But just then, as plain as day, and for the first time ever, I *heard* myself talking, and I knew I had said "nekkid" . . . What could I do? I broke into a big laugh and my teacher joined in.

I do not believe that all Southerners talk in the same, particular way, rather I think we speak in different ways throughout the various parts of the South. In the South there are dialects and shades of dialects. There is the thick-as-molasses drawl and the touch-of-honey accent, with all the varied ways of speaking in between. Yet there is no *one* Southern accent; there is no such thing as *a* Southern dialect. Our speech and our accents vary from state to state, even within a state.

Years ago, in a Greenville, S.C., boardinghouse that served ten people for lunch—what we called dinner then—a bright young college boy who sat on my left asked me if I would "please pass the leeeeee-munnnn." The word was so drawn out and the long *e* so accentuated that I actually thought he had used a foreign word. I had no idea what he had asked for until a woman opposite me caught my attention, then subtly gestured toward the bowl of lemon slices that rested on my right.

Of the ten people there that day, two were from Georgia, one from North Carolina, the others all native South Carolinians, and except for the college student who had recently come from an isolated rural section of South Carolina, all the rest of us pronounced the word "līmon." (In parts of Tennessee and Kentucky I have heard lemon pronounced as though it were spelled with an *a* instead of an *e*.)

I used to think that the genesis of a dictionary—in the old days called a wordbook—was the need for a particular collection of words and their definitions. Not entirely true. A dictionary is also born of love, the result of a long and incurable romance between the compiler and a language that is gentle and warm, eloquent and rich.

I've heard spoken somewhere in the South the majority of the entries that make up *Southern Stuff*. The exceptions are a few older and virtually extinct words and phrases that have been contributed by older persons, and then a small number that I have never heard spoken but that I have discovered in my reading of Southern literature.

If there seems to be an emphasis on mountain and rural speech, that is explained in part by the fact that many of the North Carolina people with whom I spent my childhood came originally from the Southern Appalachians. But the principal reason I have concentrated on the speech of the less literate is not because it is the most "ear-catching" of our language—which it is—but because it is our true folk speech, and therefore it is the part of our vocabulary that is most likely to disappear as the world shrinks and our different cultures become less individualistic.

To explain the locutions in the dictionary about which non-Southerners might remark: "That's not Southern. We use that in ———." Yes, that is true in a number of instances, but I have chosen to include these because of the distinctive way that Southerners employ these particular terms.

In addition, there are my "synthetic" words—locutions that are not found in a standard dictionary. They are coined by the combining or running together of two or more words to make one word, the way we Southerners do it. I have spelled these synthetic words phonetically, just as they sound to the ear.

I illustrate in a sentence the meaning and use of a particular word that shows what type of person uses a particular locution, such as "rural," "educated," or "mountain."

As an example, consider the word "Greensboro," the name of one of the older cities of North Carolina. While the educated or cultivated residents will pronounce it something close to "Greensburah," the rural or uneducated will call it "Greensbur," or, in some cases, "Grainsber." Just as in the hills of Georgia, North Carolina, and Kentucky, I have heard "tobacco" called "terbaccer," "terbaccy," and sometimes "baccy"; but in the cities of those states it is most often pronounced "tuhbaccuh."

Throughout this book, when the reader notices inconsistencies in the pronunciation and spelling of a particular word, I ask him or her (and shouldn't there be a word like "shim" to fit this need?) to remember that the South is a big South—it is roughly one-fifth the United States—and because of its expanse, our vocabulary and our accents are varied, just as they are in other regions of the U.S.A.

Varied? They are, indeed. Which leads me to point out three of our distinctly different Southern vernaculars. (To my deep re-gret—although this dictionary does offer a smattering—I have not had the time nor the opportunity to collect more.) They are: the arresting, unique, and Africa-influenced jargon of the Gullahs; the lilting, French-mixed, and charming parlance of the Cajun people; and the rich and remarkably apt language of the Southern blacks.

I wish to apologize for any omissions—unintentional, I assure you—of words, expressions, and sayings that might have been relevant to this book that I have failed to include. (To anyone sending those oversights to me, my undying gratitude!)

Last of all, let me say that if I didn't love Southerners and the South deeply, if I didn't talk like a lot of other Southerners I've known, I never could have done this book at all—would not have wanted to. And as much as I hope *Southern Stuff* will evoke a nostalgic pleasure in the Southern reader—as well as serve as an entertaining discovery for the non-Southern sampler—my more serious intent in compiling this book has been to help preserve a most distinctive part of our Southern culture—to record for future generations the way we (our forebears) used to talk.

—M. J. B.

A Dictionary of
Southern Words and
Pronunciation

But when he speaks, what elocution flows!
Soft as the fleeces of descending snows
The copious accents fall, with easy art;
Melting they fall, and sink into the heart.

—ALEXANDER POPE (BY WAY OF HOMER)

Abbreviations in This Work

adj	adjective
adv	adverb
conj	conjunction
contr	contraction
excl	exclamation
interj	interjection
n	noun
prep	preposition
pron	pronoun
q.v.	which see
v	verb

a-. A prefix much used in the ole days and still heard rurally and in the mount'ns. It's used for "strangthening" verbs and giving rhythm and balance to our speech. "He was a-comin' up the road a-grinnin' lak a chessy cat."

a, *prep.* Means "of." As in: "It was the time a day when her younguns always got kind a fretful."

ABC store. Where you buy your "buhbun in Vuhginyuh." ("ABC" stands for Alcoholic Beverage Control, a state-run agency that sells liquor in many Southern states.)

abide, *v.* Tolerate or bear. "In this classrum I simply will not countenance nor abide sluhvunly speech on the part of innywon."

aboot; abou-oot, *adv.* "Almost" in Vuhginyuh.* "No, you can't go oot to play 'cause it's aboot time for us to staht cleaning the hoose."

abroad, *adj.* [Ozarks] Outside the mountains. "Our younguns cain't wait to grow up so's they can go abroad and work in the flatlands."

ack; act, *v.* Behave. "Why don't you set up theah an' ack like you got good sense?"

acknowledge the corn. To confess to telling a lie or failing at something. "C'moan! With the evidence starin' you plum in the face, you may as well acknowledge the corn."

act like you're somebody. Have some self-respect, some dignity.

---

*This writer, who moved from North Carolina to Virginia as a young adult and lived there for several years, has yet to meet a Virginian who will agree that they pronounce "about," "out," and "house" any way except the accepted Webster's way. (There is a legitimate basis for this pronunciation, however: see "hoose.")

act ugly, *v.* Misbehave. "My ma would beat the livin' daylights out of me if Ah acted ugly when cump'ny came."

Adam's apple, *n.* The "larnyx" (but spelled "larynx"). It was named Adam's apple to remind us of the first time a man swallowed something handed to him by a woman.

addle, *v.* Confuse. "Looks like ever'time Ah get goin' good with mah work, he jes' delights in comin' in here to addle me."

admire, *v.* To revel in; to be pleasured by. "Fah mah suppuh Ah'd sure admire to have me a mess a turnup sallit an' a big hunk a cawn bread."

afred, *adj.* "Afraid" in Virginia, the Carolinas, and elsewhere. For example, "Senatuh Irvin of Nawth Ca'lina was ver' much afred that those Watuhgate scoundrels would get away with their skulduggery."

aftah whyul. Later on.

Ah, *pron.* First person singular. (Remembuh, "I" pronounced "Ah" did not start on the plantations, but was brought over from fashionable London by the early settlers. The dropped *r*'s and *g*'s of Southern speech also originated with the English nobility.)

ah. Are or or. "Ah you an' him goin', ah ain't you?"

ahdunt, *adj.* Warm, intense, passionate.

Ahkanzus, *n.* Often pronounced this way, with the accent on the "kan," except in Arkansas itself. (But there always has been a hassle about this. Way back in 1881 the Arkansas legislature appointed a special committee to try to decide on the correct pronunciation, and they agreed to make "Arkansa*w*" official. This didn't mean that people from out-a-state had to pay them any mind, though—and they haven't.)

ahm, *n.* One of the upper extremities of a human being.

ahmoanyuh, *n.* [Accent on the "ah-" in Vuhginyuh] Spirits of ammonia—what Southern belles used to take to keep from swoonin'. "Quick, before she faints, get her a dose of ahmoanyuh!"

ahmoanyuh coke, *n.* A "Co'-Cola with a squirt of ahmoanyuh"—very popular for curing headaches an' settling nerves.

ahnt, *n.* The Vuhginyuh correlative of uncle.

Ahtayah. I say to you; I tell you.

Ahtha, *n.* A man's name; like in, "King Ahtha, ah Ahtha Godfrey."

Ah-ont. I desire; I want.

Ah reckon. Means "yes." "C'n you sew up this hole in the seat of my pants real quick-like for me?" "Ah reckon."

Ahtic Suckle, **n.* "Sugah, it's cole up theah!"

aig, *n.* **1.** What you eat with "hayam." **2.** What you find "unduh a chicken"—if you're dumb enough to lift up a layin' chicken. **3.** The *raison d'être* of a hen; the production of aigs may well be the most magnanimous and self-sacrificing act ever performed by one animal for another.

ain't much. 1. Not doin' so well; feelin' poorly. "Ah'm worried about pore ole Aint Sally, she shore ain't been much lately." **2.** Not respectable; havin' little character. "Them Joneses down near the depot, they sure ain't much, are they?"

**Ahtic Suckle is the reminduh of anothuh instance when Southern talent an' courage were required to take care of things. That's when Admuhrul Retched E. Bud of Vuhginyuh accomplished the first-of-all airplane flight to the Nawth Pole, which he undertook, *despite* the hateful name of the place, to oblige the United States Navy. Later he explored Anahtica an' the South Pole—first again, of course—an' he stayed theah for ages, endurin' all sorts of hardships while doin' scientific resuch fah the U.S.A. (Well! You didn't expect him to settle an' work at the *Nawth* Pole, did you?—not even in the name of science, posterity, or country!)*

air. 1. *n.* Error. "Wun strike, wun air, wun man out." **2.** *v.* Are; as in "Air you going to work naow, er air you jes' gonna set ther like a bump on a log?" **3.** *adv.* Thither. "El, look up air at 'at air airplane!" **4.** *n.* Arrow. "Ah shot an air into the air . . ."

airy one. Not a fairy, nor an angel; it means "anyone" or "either."

al, *n.* Owl—that wise ole bird. (But he sure looks stupid, dud'n he?)

Alberta peach, *n.* Elberta, the variety most commonly grown in Dixie; or, generally speaking, *The* Georgia Peach.

alligator pear, *n.* The avocado was called this in the southern-most South until recently. ("Alligator" may derive from the fact that they both thrive in the same environment, but more likely it was because the rough skin of the avocado reminded someone of a "gator's" hide.)

all-overs, *n.* **1.** Jitters; nervousness; a feeling of unease. "Ah declare, ever since I saw that acci-dent, Ah've had the all-overs sah bayad." **2.** Underwear. "When I'se growin' up Ah had to weah them ole long, heavy all-ovuhs, when all the othuh girls were wearin' faincy drawuhs."

alple, *n.* A bribe for the teacher. [For some reason the mountaineers and old folks often put an extra *l* in "apple."]

alple ciduh, *n.* Apple cider, the champagne of the South.

Amaircun, *n.* American; a citizen of the United States [pronounced "Amurcan" by some Texans].

ambeer, *n.* Tobacco juice mixed with spittle. "The ole potbellied stove had been spit at so much, it looked lak it 'ud plum been painted with ambeer."

ambyoo-lance, *n.* Ambulance; a station wagon equipped with a bed for the sick.

amen cawnuh, *n.* Amen corner; a section near the pulpit of a church occupied by the most ardent an' audible of the worshipers.

anklets, *n.* Short socks worn by girls and women.

anour, *n.* An hour; sixty minutes.

ant; aint, *n.* Usually married to someone you call uncle. [Except in Vuhginyuh and, sometimes, South Carolina, where they say "ahnt."]

antic, *n.* A clown or joker. "That Pug Hollins! Always the antic, with never a serious thought in his head."

antigodlin, *adj.* Not plumb; askew. "You know the ole Cartuh house with the antigodlin roof?"

anxious, *adj.* Eager. ". . . as anxious as a preacher after chicken."

anyhow gone. Really, truly gone. "Whin a purty girl like that sets her mind on gettin' you, buddy, you are anyhow gone."

Appomatox, Surrenduh at. "A figment of the Nawthun imagination; one of the moah popular myths of Yankee folklore. What rilly happened was, ouah side declared a brief moratorium, an' just as expected, those Yankees nevuh came back."

Argon, *n.* Oregon, the state with no sales tax and lots of rain.

Arkansas toothpick. What Bowie knives used to be called in and around Arkansas.

arm-crooking, *v.* Act of toting leftovers from the house where a domestic works.

arn, *n.* Iron; one of the earliest wrinkle removers known to woman. [The culchuhed say "irne."]

arnge, *n.* **1.** An orange-flavored cold drink. "One ginger, one arnge, an' two Co'Colas." **2.** A citrus fruit, purportedly invented in Florida.

Arsh taters, *n.* Irish potatoes in the mount'ns an' country. And don't think the "Irish" isn't necessary—as many sweet taters as we eat, we have to differentiate.

arthur, *n.* Author, one who writes books, stories, or "po-try."

arthuritus, *n.* One of the oldest diseases known to man—*and* woman.

artis' pitcher, *n.* Not a picture taken with a camera, but a real man-made, hand-painted work of art.

asa spades. 1. Ace of spades. **2.** Something very black. "Ah'm skeered to go; it's black as the asa spades out there." **3.** The death card in fortune-telling.

ashamed, *adj.* Bashful; timid; embarrassed. "Don't be 'shamed to come in; ain't nobody gonna bite you."

Ashley and Cuppuh. [Spelled "Cooper"] Two small rivers that meet in Charleston, South Carolina, "to form the Atlantic Ocean" (if you listen to Charlestonians).

asparagrus, *n.* A slender, green, spear-shaped vegetable.

asprin; asburn, *n.* Aspirin, a pill for pain; the panacea of the South—except for the B.C. [q.v.] devotees.

assurance, *n.* [Black] Insurance. "Yes, ma'am! I mean to keep my burial assurance paid up even if I don't have a rag on my back or a mouthful in my belly."

ast; axed. Past tense of "ask."

asta. To have inquired of a female. "Ah asta, but she said no."

athalete, **n.* One who goes in for lots of exercise.

athist, *n.* **1.** A confirmed unbeliever. **2.** "One who puts no othuh god befoah hisse'f."

Attakapa Indians. [Pronounced "Tuckapaw"] Attakapa is a Choctaw word meaning "man-eater." It is said that long ago there were actually cannibals in Louisiana.

auta. Ought to; should.

audo-mow-beel, *n.* [Accent on the "mōw"] Fancy for car.

Aura-C, *n.* RC Cola, as in Nashville, Tennessee, and environs. "Ah'll have a Aura-C and bourbon with lots o' rocks."

A.W. After the War (of "Nawthun Agression," of course).

awedum, *n.* Autumn, when the leaves turn to gold.

awetoe, *n.* Auto; "motuhcah."

awfis, *n.* A workshop, or a room for conducting business.

awmi, *n.* Army; a whole bunch of "sojers" [q.v.]. "Sixteen years old, he joined the awmi and left home without even a fare-thee-well."

awmos', *adv.* Almost; nearly.

awready, *adv.* Previously; before.

awright, *adv.* Okay. As in "Awright awready!"

ax, *v.* To inquire. "Ax me no questions and Ah'll tale you no lahs." ["Ax," or "axe," was correct usage in Chaucer's time.]

---

*Athalete is one of those words that we Suthunuhs made more euphonious by addin' one of the *a*'s that we dropped from words like "vile," an' "rilly" (spelled "vial" and "really").

ax-ray pitcher, *n.* X-ray picture—proof positive that beauty *is* only skin deep.

Ayan, *n.* Ann, or Anne. "There was Ayan Sheridan, Ayan of Cleves, and Queen Ayan of England."

Ayatlayantah, *n.* "The personification of the spirit of the Civil Wah South—the pride of Gawjah. Ayatlayantah—the magnificent phoenix of the Wah Between the States, this brave little town, aftuh bein' bumbarded fah fawty days an' fawty nights, was then vuhchully bunned to the ground by that horrible ole Ginral Shuhman, only to rise again from its own ashes to become bigguh an' bettuh than evuh."

Ayud, *n.* Ed, an abbreviation of the male moniker Edward. Also, "the name of a loquashus equine televizhun star of old."

babsouse, *v.* Humorous for baptize.

Babtis, *n.* Baptist; a denomination, as opposed to Methdis, sometimes strongly.

Babtis pallet, *n.* A make-do bed spread on the floor (named, no doubt, by a member of an opposing denomination).

babtis poker, *n.* The card game Flinch. It consists of about a zillion cards—150 to be exact—and is quite different from the more familiar deck of cards.

back, *v.* To address an envelope. "Heah—you back this onvuh-lope fah me while Ah finish up mah lettuh."

back at. Back with. "I'll be right back at you."

back back, *v.* To drive in reverse; to move backward.

backbone, *n.* "We like it in ouah men, an' adoah it out of ouah hawgs—aftuh it's cooked, natchrully."

backdoor man, *n.* A man who leaves by the back door when the husband of his inamorata unexpectedly enters the front door.

backdoor trots, *n.* Diarrhea.

backhouse, *n.* A backyard toilet. "Where else would you put a thang lak that?"

back on your raisin', go. When you forget your humble beginnings, put on airs, an' get all biggety [q.v.]. "To go back on yore raisin' is a pretty serious charge if you're a Suthunuh."

back-seat person, *n.* A humble, unobstrusive sort of individual; a follower, not a leader.

bacon, *v.* To beckon; to summon by gesture.

bad boy, *n.* The devil.

bad disease, *n.* A disease sometimes contracted by naughty men who've been hanging out with bad women [q.v.].

bad place, *n.* Be good so you won't go there, 'cause, be assured, it *is* Hell.

bad woman, *n.* A low-down woman, like a "Jazzabel" or a prostitute.

bag, *v.* To beg; to implore; to ask for money.

bah-bah, *interj.* Bye-bye. "Bah-bah, s'long naow."

bahbuh, *n.* Barber; "one who cuts yore hay-uh."

baldface, *n.* Moonshine; inferior "likker."

bald-faced, *adj.* Clean-shaven.

ball-headed, *adj.* One with little or no hair.

ball iggle, *n.* Bald eagle, our national bird.

ballot, *n.* Ballad (absolutely nothing to do with voting). A "ballot" is a song that tells a story—usually a sad one.

banquette, *n.* A sidewalk in New Orleans.

bar, *n.* Bear. "Thar's chawklut bars an' polar bars."

Bare asprin, *n.* Bayer aspirin—not "nekkid" aspirin.

barl, *n.* A barrel; a container for holding monkeys and measuring fun.

barn, *v.* To be born; to come into existence.

barn door is open, your. [Kentucky] Means your fly is unzipped.

barnyard golf, *n.* The game of horseshoes or "hoss-shoe pitchin'."

bass-ackerds, *adj.* "That's whin you're doin' it all wrong; but what bettuh definition than the word itse'f?"

bawdy, *n.* Body; torso; "yore physical bein'."

bawi, *n.* Boy; a "man-chile."

bawx, *n.* Box; a six-sided receptacle, often made of "codbode."

B.C., *n.* A commercial headache powder, and next to aspirin in the hearts of most Southerners. (If you told a native of Dixie to go take a powder, most likely he'd reach "fah a B.C.—fah his headache, that is.")

Beal, *n.* Bill, nickname for William.

Beans, Beer, and Snuff Boys. Country singers who are on radio and TV programs sponsored by companies manufacturing these products.

beautiful nuisance, *n.* The kudzu vine. Remember how fast the beanstalk grew for Jack? Well, that's nothing compared to the kudzu vine! It's the scourge of the deep South, and if we didn't know differently, we'd swear it was a secret weapon that had been brought down from up yonder during the "War of Northern Aggression."

beauty mattress, *n.* [Uneducated] Any really good-quality mattress.

beck, *n.* Not the front.

before-hand person, *n.* One who is apt to be ahead of other people. "Callie always was a before-hand person. If somebody didn't hold her back, she'd try to get in the store before they got the doors unlocked."

behind name, *n.* [Louisiana] One's last name.

belly washer, *n.* "A grate big long tall drank o' sump'm—lak a Pepsi-Cola."

benasty, *v.* To make dirty. "I fell down in the mud and benastied myself."

benne seeds, *n.* Sesame seeds in South Ca'lina.

bibleback, *n.* A bible-spouting person; one obsessed with religion.

bible-thumper, *n.* **1.** A self-appointed preacher. **2.** Anyone who's always quoting or trying to "sell" the Scriptures.

bidness, *n.* **1.** Commercial dealings or trade. **2.** One's personal affairs. "I'd sure appreciate it if you'd keep your nose outa my bidness."

Big Bens, *n.* Any overalls.

big bug, *n.* A socially prominent individual; an "impahdunt" person.

Big D, *n.* That's Dallas, y'all, D-A-L-L-A-S, T-E-X-A-S—"down where the cotton-picking South ends and culture begins," as one diffident Dallasite so modestly phrased it.

Big Easy, *n.* "N' Awleans"; named that because of its so-called laid-back life-style.

biggety, *adj.* Enlarged with self-importance. "She's so biggety! Acts like she's the greatest thing since sliced bread."

big re-cess, *n.* Lunch period in grammar school.

bird-dog, *v.* To follow or to hound. "That Vernon Sykes! Don't you know he bird-dogged me all over town trying to get a date."

biscuit, pass the. When a Southerner says, "Pass the biscuit," he's not asking for one lil' biscuit, he means the whole great big plate of biscuits.

blackguard, *v.* To abuse with bad language. "That man's got a tongue! He's been blackguarding that pore little woman ever since he mare'd her."

blave, *v.* To believe; to have faith.

bleeder, country and western. A tear-jerking country and western ballad.

bless out. To tell someone off.

blockade, *n*. Moonshine—the liquid kind.

blong, *v*. To belong; to be the "propity" of.

bloodbound, *adj*. Predetermined by one's blood and genes. "With those kinfolks of his, looks like he was bloodbound to turn out bad."

bloon, *n*. Air surrounded by something solid to hold it in.

bluebelly, *n*. Yankee Civil War soldier. "Of course, sometimes we called them an entirely different color; it starts with *y*."

blue cat, *n*. A very large, bluish catfish from the Mississippi; when fried, it's a highly prized dish in Memphis and thereabouts.

blue john, *n*. Inferior-quality milk; skim milk.

Bluxie, *n*. A town in Mississippi. It's spelled Biloxi, but if you're in the know, you forget the *o*.

bobby-cue, *n*. Barbecue; meat roasted on a rack over hot coals— pork in most of the South, beef in Texas. (Southerners are very passionate about their "bobby-cue"; in fact, it well may be the national dish of the South.)

bob wire, *n*. Barbed wire; a hellish type of wire for building a prohibitive kind of fence. "He was so all-fired mean, he'd put a bob wire fence around a kindergarden playground."

bodacious, *adj*. **1.** Extraordinary or remarkable. **2.** Audacious. "I hired me some bodacious handyman today. He wouldn't even stop working long enough to catch his breath."

bodaciously, *adv*. Bodily; entirely. "He bodaciously beat the livin' daylights out'n thet bully."

bode, *n.* Food, meals, as in "rum an' bode"; what you get along with your room in a South Carolina boarding house.

body, *n.* A bodice or undershirt. "To keep warm, she had to wear a flannel body under her shirtwaist."

boffum. The two of them.

bottled-in-the-barn, *n.* Bootleg whiskey.

boudin, *n.* Blood sausage as made by the Cajuns of Louisiana. "Mon Dieu! If there's anything better than boudin, don't tell me 'bout it."

boughten, *adj.* Not "ho'made."

bounden duty. The meaning of this phrase is known by all married people; "othuhs are advised to bide their time in happy ignrunce."

boy, *n.* [Pronounced "bawi"] From cradle to grave, in one way or another, every Southern male is a "boy." "This boy I went with before I met your granddad can still read the paper and drive without glasses at eighty-six years old."

brag on. Southerners brag *on* something or someone, not *about*. "It embarrasses me when you brag on me like that."

breadbasket, *n.* The stomach; a depository for "vittles."

break her wing. In the olden days when a suitor put his arm around a girl and kissed her, he was said to "break her wing." "Yes suhree, I know what *you're* up to, Huhbut Beauregahd Swathmoah! You are plannin' to da-yance me out on that dahk vuhranduh an' break my wing, naow ahn't you?"

break in. What you do to new shoes.

breast baby, *n.* One who is still of nursing age.

briarhopper, *n.* A derogatory term for the Appalachian Mountain folks.

briar-patch chile, *n.* A child begotten out of wedlock; a base-born child.

brown-bag, *v.* To take one's bourbon, or other booze, along in a paper sack. "The worst thing about these ole dry-law states is, if you'd like to take in a Sat'dy night dance, or you jus' wanna go out an' have yourse'f a nice dinnuh, you either gotta brown-bag it, or else you gonna wind up sobuh as a judge an' boahd ha'f to death."

brownie, *n.* An ole-timey name for a penny.

brown jug, *n.* A biscuit with a hole punched in it and molasses poured in.

brush whiskey, *n.* Moonshine made way out in the woods.

bub, *n.* Bulb. "If you want electric lights, you gotta have bubs."

Bubba, *n.* The Southern correlative of Sister, and baby talk for Brother. "The trouble with Bubba is, that name can stick with a male forevermore."

bubbies, *n.* Breasts; especially small or newly budding breasts.

buckra, *n.* Black man's name for the white man.

bud, *n.* Bird. "If a Vuhginyun says he's goin' bud huntin', it dudn't mean he's goin' oot lookin' fah unopened baby roses. In othuh wuds, one in the hayand is worth any numbuh in the bush."

bud dawg, *n.* Bird dog; "created fah huntin' buds an' eatin' leftovah biscuit."

bug dust, *n.* Baloney; lies. "That story you're tellin' is pure bug dust an' you know it."

buhbun, *n.* Bourbon—the parlor name for "cawn likker."

buhleery, *n.* Bolero, a Spanish dance; also a type of short jacket.

buhzeer, *n.* Brassiere, "the buhzum friend of every girl."

bull fiddle, *n.* Bass fiddle.

Bull Run, the Battle of. Famous Civil War battle, also called Manasses. Leave it to the insensitive to give it, not only an indelicate name, but an erroneous one. But considering what the Yankees had in mind to do to us at both of these encounters, maybe it wasn't such a misnomer after all.

bum, *n.* Bomb; dynamite. "Yes siree, if he didn't make a ho'made bum and nearly blow the house up."

bumbershoot, *n.* An umbrella.

bumblefooted, *adj.* Like having two left feet; a clumsiness in walking.

Buminhayam, *n.* "The lodgest city in Alabayamah."

bun, *n.* Burn or bun. "There are sunbuns, cinnamon buns, an' buns worn in the hayuh."

burning a river. Dressed in one's best; ready for a special happening. "Whoo-ee, don't you look good! You're really burning a river today."

Burnt-tail Jenny, *n.* **1.** The wife of a will-o'-the-wisp. **2.** The wife of a jack-o'-lantern.

butternut boys. Pennsylvania troops dubbed the Confederate soldiers this because of their brownish homespun clothing, which took its color from an extract of the butternut tree. (This is what they wore when uniforms were no longer available.)

B.W. and A.W. To the rest of the world, time may be reckoned B.C. and A.D., but to the older Southerner, it was always B.W. and A.W.—"Before the War and After the War" (the Civil War, that is). [Mock Twain]

by-m-by, *adv.* "Soonuh or latuh."

C

cabbage patch, *n.* Where almost all Southern babies come from, especially before the sexual revolution. "Mama, where'd I come from?" "Why, honey, Daddy and I found you in a cabbage patch."

cad, *v.* To have taken; carried. "He cad me to town in his bran'-new cah—F.O.B. from Dee-troit."

ca-fay, *n.* [Accent on the first syllable] Restaurant.

cah, *n.* Car; an "audo-mow-beel."

cain't-see to cain't-see. [Mountain and rural] From before dawn to after dusk. "Them labor unions are awright if you ast me. They got a lot o' rights for us workin' folks. I know 'cause you're talkin' to somebody c'n still recollect when his ma and pa worked up there in the mill nigh on most o' their lives from cain't-see to cain't-see."

Cajuns, *n.* [Corruption of "Acadian"] The charming and fun-loving residents of Southern Louisiana, descendants of French-speaking people who were deported by the British in the mid-1700s from their homes and farms in eastern Canada.

They have maintained their own folk culture and are known for their piquant cuisine.

Cajun catsup, *n.* "Hot stuff"; tobasco and other pepper sauces.

calaboose, *n.* The jailhouse.

calamity, *n.* A white elephant; secondhand item; something you bought and wished you hadn't. "We better have us a yard sale and get rid of some of these calamities."

calculate, *v.* To think; to guess. "I calculate it's about ten more miles to Miz Owens's house."

Calinah, *n.* Carolina. "There's two of them—Nawth and Sooth."

call up, *v.* Southerners never just phone people—they call them *up*.

call up the house. Referring to a telephone call to someone at home. "He called up the house and we jawed for abut anour."

calvary, *n.* Cavalry. Used to be an important and desirable branch of the military. "Ah tell you, suh, mah grandfathuh was the most admired hossman in the U.S. Calvary."

camry, *n.* Camera. "His pitcher was took with Sally Belle's new Kodak camry."

ca-nell, *n.* Canal.

canidit, *n.* Candidate; one who runs for an "awfis."

canned cream, *n.* A euphemism for evaporated milk.

can't-hardlies, *n.* **1.** The all-overs [q.v.]. **2.** A bad case of impatience. "Birdie Mae couldn't half play Old Maid, she had the can't-hardlies so bad."

cape jessmin, *n.* Jasmine—a flower that would smell as over-poweringly sweet by any other name.

cap'm, *n.* Captain; an army officer who is above a lieutenant and below a major, and a naval officer who is above both of these.

carhouse, *n.* A garage.

carpet-bagger, *n.* A Northerner who went to the South after the War between the States for personal gain; that's what first inspired those famous words "Go home, Yank."

carry, *v.* **1.** To tote. **2.** As a courting term, it means "to escort." In other words, if your girl's name is Carrie, you carry Carrie to the dance.

carsodge, *n.* Corsage; "a bunch o' posies fuh wearin'."

cascade, *v.* [Black use, chiefly] To vomit; to throw up.

case, *n.* **1.** Someone who has a peculiar or unusual personality. "Boy, you're a real case, you know that?" **2.** A crush on someone. "Bill's got a big case on that new girl up the street."

case nickel, *n.* A five-cent piece, not five pennies.

cash money, *n.* Not checks, not bonds, not promises, but real cash in hand. "Jessie Mae bought herse'f a new Frigidaire [q.v.], and she paid for it with sure 'nuf cash money."

casket, *n.* Coffin. (Casket was more often used in the early 1900s.)

catamount, *n.* A wildcat [an abbreviated form of "cat of the mountain].

catawampus, 1. *n.* A horrendous imaginary animal. **2.** *adj.,* Askew. "Look at that carpet, all catawampus."

catching breaks. [Black] Taking odd or temporary jobs. (See "loafer's bench.")

catching disease, *n.* A contagious disease. "Why you shunnin' me? I ain't got no catchin' disease."

cavalry, *n.* Calvary; a hill near old Jerusalem.

cawfee, *n.* Coffee, an "early moanin' bevridge."

cawn, *n.* Corn. **1.** "Rosenears"; maize; cawn on the cob. **2.** "Cawn likker."

cawnuh, *n.* Corner; "wheah two walls meet."

cee-gar, *n.* Cigar; a great big brown "cigrette."

cee-ment, *n.* As in sidewalk.

cee-ment pond, *n.* A swimmin' pool.

cerny, *adv.* Without a doubt; certainly. "Cerny Ah lak black-eye peas an' ham hock, who dudn't?"

Champs Elysées of the South. Monument Avenue in Richmond, Virginia.

chanch, *n.* **1.** Chance; opportunity. **2.** A possibility of something happening. "He's got a chanch for the measles."

charlie, *n.* A cockroach in Dallas.

chat, *v.* To pay your respects by way of a little conversation. "I want to go over an' chat Miz Wilson before we leave."

chawed, *adj.* Vexed. "If you want to see Pa chawed, jus' let somebody make fun of his size."

cheer, *n.* Something you "set" on.

cherokee clay, *n.* The bone-white clay once imported from North Carolina by Wedgwood of England to be used for their fine stoneware.

chessy cat, *n.* The prissy say "Cheshire" cat.

chesterfield, *n.* A sofa in Virginia in a style inspired by Lord Chesterfield of England. "Don't forget to plump up the pillows on the chesterfield."

chicken hollerin' time. Early mornin' on the farm.

chicken, Suthun fried. "The most descecrated dish in the histry of our Suthun cuisine." See **Southern fried chicken**. (Aside to all Yankees: Listen, if y'all are gonna keep on committin' sacrilege against yard birds, if y'all insist on foulin' up fowls the way you bin doin', then do it unduh yo' own name, you heah? Don't call it *innythang Suthun!*)

chickry, *n.* Chicory. **1.** A flavoring for Louisiana coffee. **2.** A salad green.

chiggah, *n.* Chigger; a small red bug that you catch in the woods if you aren't careful.

chile, *n.* A youngun [plural: "chi'ren" or "chil'ren"].

chimley, *n.* Chimney. **1.** Entrance for Santy Claus. **2.** Exit for smoke.

chinch, *n.* A bedbug, a merciless mite that works under cover at night.

Chinese of the South. Because of their addiction to rice and ancestor worship, Charlestonians have been called this.

chinkie-pin, *n.* A small chestnutlike nut, the chinquapin.

chinnin', *v.* Talking to; gabbing with. "She's been chinnin' on the phone all mornin'."

chirk up, *v.* To cheer up and show some life.

chitlins, *n.* Chitterlings. The small intestines of a "hawg," and considered a *gas*tronomical delight by people with the intestinal fortitude to eat them.

chivaree, *n.* [Rural] A noisy, rustic, and often crude celebration by the guests at a wedding.

chiwoohwooh, *n.* A chihuahua. "You know the kind o' woman that walks around holdin' one of them nervous-actin' little chi-woohwoohs?"

Cholls, *n.* Charles. There's one in England who's next in line for the throne.

chuffy, *adj.* Short and stout.

chunk, *v.* To throw. (In some parts of the South they never throw stones, they chunk them, and the chunker usually calls a stone a rock.)

church, *v.* To be tried, chastised, or cut off from membership in a church. "He was churched for drinkin' blackber' wine and playin' cards on Sund'y."

cipher, *v.* **1.** To figure. **2.** To solve by pondering over. "Will y'all be quiet! How do you tink Ah'm ever gonna cipher out this groshry bill with all that racket goin' on?"

citified, *adj.* Showing sophistication; putting on the dog; dandified.

city chicken, *n.* A fancy veal and pork dish, originated as a substitute for chicken (when veal was cheap, no doubt), but considered better by the Louisianans who ate it.

clabbuh, *n.* The Southerner's yogurt; what Little Miss Muffet was eating when the mean old spider came along and scared her.

clabbuh cheese, *n.* Cottage cheese.

clabbering up to rain. Getting ready to cry, "puddlin' up."

clane, *adj.* Clean, not dirty.

claphat, *adj.* Hasty; frenetic. "She's so derned claphat, it makes me nervis jes' bein' around her."

clever, *adj.* Amiable; pleasant and good-natured. "Always a smile on her face an' just as clever as can be."

cloes, *n.* What you wear if you don't want to go naked. "There's Sunday cloes an' everyday cloes; store-boughten cloes an' ho'-made cloes; yo' ole cloes an' yo' good cloes."

closet drinker, *n.* A secret and sometimes hypocritical drinker, meaning that the liquor is kept hidden and sometimes even drunk in the closet. " 'Those Babtis ah the biggest closet drinkers of all,' said the Presbuhtearn to the Methdis."

coam, *n.* **1.** Cone, an edible holder for a hunk of ice cream. **2.** Comb, a miniature rake for the hair.

coal oil, *n.* Kerosene; "karseen oil."

coathouse, *n.* Where a South Carolinian goes to have his deed recorded.

cockaroach, *n.* A despised insect that's fond of warm climes and dark and dirty kitchens.

Co'-Cola, *n.* The nectar of the South; the Rebel's elixir. It invigorates, it nurtures (well, the soul, anyway), it inspires. It's not only a delight, it's a necessity, a "fix," a way of life, and a Southern heritage.

coffee cow, *n.* A sorry cow that doesn't give much more than enough milk for coffee.

coffee lace, *n.* A little bourbon in your coffee; an "efficacious eye-openuh."

cogitate, *v.* To think; to ponder over. "Pa sets thar cogitatin' while Ma's hoein' the corn."

cold slaw, *n.* Cabbage salad.

cole drank, *n.* A bottle of pop that's been chilled.

combinations, *n.* A garment for underwear that combines both top and bottom; a union suit. "You look like the rakin's and scrapin's of the earth settin' there playin' cards in your combinations."

comere, *v.* Come here. "Hey, comere a minute. Ah wanna tell you somethin'."

Confederate failure, *n.* How Southerners refer to the Battle of Gettysburg.

comfuhtuhble, *adj.* [Accent on the "tuh"] Comfortable; "being at ease" for some Virginians.

common, *adj.* Low, low-class—one of the worst things a Southerner can be.

congolene, *n.* [Black] A preparation for straightening the hair, consisting partly of lye, Vaseline, and soap.

conk, 1. *v.* [Black] To straighten the hair. **2.** *n.* Conch [Pronounced "conk"], a sea animal native to the Florida Keys.

conk-buster, *n.* [Black] **1.** Rotgut liquor. **2.** Something requiring much thought. **3.** A brainy or educated black person.

consenting age, *n.* Of marriageable age.

contrary, *v.* Oppose or annoy. "You jes' plain delight in contraryin' me."

convick, *n.* Convict; someone who's made such an "ass of hisself that the authorities have to dress him up in a striped suit like a zebra."

cood, *n.* Cud, what a cow chews.

coon's age, *n.* A considerable length of time.

cooter. 1. *n.* [Deep South] A turtle or a terrapin. **2.** *v.* To loiter or trifle around. "You're cooterin' away your time *and* mine."

copperhead, *n.* What the Yankees called other Northerners who sympathized with the South during the so-called "Civil" War.

copuhration, *n.* Corporation, a "bidness" concern.

corduroy road, *n.* A road made by laying saplings or boards across an existing road to prevent motorists from getting stuck in mud.

cork, *v.* To fill up crevices; to caulk.

corn cob, *n.* An accoutrement for an outhouse.

corn dodger, *n.* A primitive type of hard-baked cornbread. Supposedly named because if one was thrown at you, you'd better dodge.

corn oyster, *n.* A corn fritter with a mock oyster taste.

corn sqeezin's, *n.* Moonshine.

cotton, *v.* **1.** To like; to take to. **2.** To play up to. "Independent? Why, that man wouldn't cotton to the Queen of England if he thought it would get him the Star of India dymunt."

cotton gin, *n.* [The shortened version of "cotton engine"] Catherine Greene, widow of General Nathaniel Greene, is "responsible" for the invention of the cotton gin. She kept telling Eli

Whitney, a guest at her plantation, that he should make a cotton separator until he finally made one.

counter hopper, *n.* A store clerk.

counterpin, *n.* A bedspread.

countrified, *adj.* Hicky as heck.

country captain, *n.* A Southern adaptation of chicken curry, with the accent on the liberal use of tomatoes.

country mile, *n.* A considerable distance.

coupla, *n.* Two of anything.

count (your) mercies. Count your blessings.

cow-brute, *n.* A bull.

cowcatcher, *n.* Not a Southern word for cowboy; it's the front of a train "fah throwin' off cows an' othuh hindrances."

cowcumber, *n.* What the rural and uneducated used to call cucumbers. (Some people thought they were only fit for cows to eat.)

cow-pasture pool, *n.* Otherwise known as golf. [This term is allegedly of Texan derivation.]

cowpea, *n.* The black-eyed pea.

Cowtown, *n.* Fort Worth, Texas—a town that just barely, but oh-so-happily, managed to be Southern. Like Will Rogers said: "Where the West begins and Dallas peters out."

crack the winduh. To open a window slightly. "How 'bout crackin' that winduh a bit—it's gettin' mighty hot in heah."

cracker, *n.* A native of Florida and Georgia. (This may have originated from their fondness for cracked corn, specifically hominy grits.)

crap, *n.* [Mountain] Crop. A batch or a yield. "We got us a tremenjous big crap o' taters this year."

craunch, *v.* To chew noisily—what you do when you eat celery or green apples.

cream nut, *n.* The Brazil nut.

creases, *n.* Watercress or ground cress, a spicy green eaten boiled or in salads.

Creole cawfee, *n.* Coffee made of a very dark roast and containing 10 to 20 percent chicory, which gives it body. A sign outside one of the coffee houses in the old French market of "New Awlins" describes Creole coffee this way:

> *Black as the devil,*
> *Strong as death,*
> *Sweet as love,*
> *Hot as hell!*

critter, *n.* A creature, man or beast. Used most often in a sympathetic sense, as in "The pore critter. She ain't stop naggin' him since the day they jumped the broomstick [q.v.]."

Croatan, *n.* A person of mixed black, Indian, and white blood who is said to be a descendant of Sir Walter Raleigh's lost colony of Roanoke Island, N.C.

croker sack, *n.* A tow sack [from "crocus," a coarse kind of sacking cloth like gunny and burlap].

crook, *n.* One of the older terms for a prostitute.

crookedy, *adj.* Anything that twists and turns. "This is the crookedyest danged road I ever seed in my life."

crosseyeded, *adj.* That's a *bad* case of strabismus.

crumb snatcher, *n.* A baby or young chile. "Not in a family way again! Haven't they got enough crumb snatchers to feed?"

Cubah, *n.* Cuba, an island republic off the southern coast of Florida.

cud'n, *n.* Cousin, the son or daughter of an uncle or aunt; something that, for some strange reason, "Suthunuhs seems to have a lot more of than Nawthunuhs—cud'ns by the dud'ns."

cump'ny, *n.* Company; the visitors entertained by a Southern host.

cunsun, *n.* Concern; "a bidness firm; a copuhration."

curling, *n.* The complex inflections of speech and the wide range of vocal tones employed by the early Southern orators. Patrick Henry's "Give me liberty" speech is said to have brought this method to the pinnacle of perfection.

curtain lecture, *n.* What every husband dreads—a nagging or blessing out by one's spouse after a couple has, presumably, retired for the night. (This comes from the days of curtained and canopied beds.)

cush, *n.* **1.** Mush or gruel. **2.** A dish made from seasoned cornmeal dough, boiled in pot liquor. **3.** What dressing or stuffing—as in a chicken—used to be called.

cuppin, *n.* [Early North Carolina and environs] Cow pen.

Cuppuh, *n.* [Yankee orthography, C-o-o-p-e-r] A surname. "Mr. James Pockuh of Chollston told us all about Mr. Gahdun Cuppuh, the famous astronaut."

Cuppuh Rivuh, *n.* Cooper River. "Centuries ago two rivuhs threw their ahms aroun' the little peninsula that was to become known as Chollston, S.C., an' one of these streams was the Ashley an' the othuh, the Cuppuh." (Note: For years South Carolina children have been told that the "Ashley an' the Cuppuh met in Chollston to form the Atlantic Ocean." It's a theory that holds watuh as far as we're cunsunned.)

cushaw, *n.* A crooked-neck squash; the "neck punkin'."

cut a rusty. To show off; to play a prank. "Two dranks of that dandeline wine an' he wuz cuttin' all kinds of rusties."

cyard, *n.* A card in old Virginia. (Note: The use of the intrusive *y* is said to have become popular when the English people began imitating their then-king, who had a speech impediment.)

cyarn, *n.* Carrion; what buzzards eat.

cyarn crow, *n.* A buzzard.

Cyarter, *n.* "If Mr. J. C. had been elected fifty yeahs befoah he was, Vuhginyuns would have refuhhed to him as Prezdent Cyarter. Note: Cyarter (spelled "Carter") happened to be the name of one of the earliest and most prominent FFVs [q.v.]. For example, one Vuhginyun Cyarter was so rich—a mere three hundred thousand acres was only one asset—and lived in such regal style that he became known as King Cyarter." [See "cyard."]

cylinders of sin, *n.* Cigarettes; "coffin nails."

cymling, *n.* [Virginia chiefly] Summer squash.

dab'mport, *n.* Davenport; a couch or a sofa.

dad-gummit, *excl.* A euphemism for "damn it."

dad-shimed, *adj.* [Rural] Damned. "I'll be dad-shimed if it didn't snow in April!"

daily, life does get. Life does get burdensome. "Life do get daily!" said ole Uncle Joe as he leaned on his hoe looking bone-weary.

Damnyankee, *n.* Once considered to be the vilest creature on God's green earth, but now conceded to be of the human species. (Author Boyce House once reported that "the difference in a Yankee and a Damnyankee is that the Yankee has sense enough to stay where he belongs.")

dangersome, *adj.* "Messin' aroun' with a mar'ed woman can be a dangersome thang."

Darce Day. "A singuh an' a movie stah."

dark secrets, *n.* A delicious cookie—all full of dates and pecan goodies.

dast, *v.* Dare. "You don't dast go in that hainted house, I betcha."

dauncy, *adj.* Being overly fastidious or "mincy" about one's eating. "She's so dauncy about her eatin'—her little finger up in the air an' her pickin' over her food like it's dirdy."

Davis, Jefferson, *n.* President of the Confederate States of America, our Southern savior—for a short while.

dawg, *n.* Man's best friend.

Dayan, *n.* Short for Dayanel—as in the lion's den.

day and time. Any time at all. "I'm glad to see him inny day and time."

day-ud, *adj.* Unalive.

deah, *n.* "A tum of endeahment."

d'eat. To eat. "What you got good d'eat?"

declare, I, *excl.* Before the sexual revolution, Southern women did a lot of "declaring." "I declare! That's about the most awful thing I ever heard in my *entyah* life." After the revolution they became very daring and went to really strong expressions— things like "Drat it!" and "I'll be darned!"

declinin' chair, *n.* A reclining chair. "He jus' sets there in his declinin' chair an' does nothin' all day long."

deef, *adj.* Deaf. "Thet ole rock 'n' roll music will make you deef as a doorknob."

deppity, *n.* Deputy; an assistant sheriff.

despise, *v.* This word does not mean the same thing down South as it does to the rest of the English-speaking world—especially to Southern womanhood. It means to feel lukewarm about or, at its most intense, not to like something very much. "Ah simply loathe an' despise that boy. The last time he called me up, Ah didn't talk to him more'n forty-five minutes before I just came right out an' told him Ah had better things to do."

devil's own urine, *n.* "Dat ole debbil," alcohol.

devil's riding horse, *n.* A praying mantis.

devil's tramping ground, *n.* A bare circle of ground sur-rounded by a lush forest. It is said that the devil prowls there at night and that nothing green will grow there. (Tater Top Moun-tain, Near Siler City, N.C., is one of the Uwharries.)

Diddy-Wah-Diddy, *n.* A never-never land; a glorious place of plenty where "mouth-watering vittles like juicy poke roasts an' big ole chocklut cakes step right up an' jes' beg you: 'Eat me—please, eat me!' "

diggers; diggin's, *n.* Worms dug up to use in fishing.

Dimocrat, *n.* "Ah you a Dimocrat ah a dawg?" as one old governor of "Ahkansaw" used to put it.

ding-busted, *adj.* Concarned; damnable. "This ding-busted ole contraption is enough to make a preacher cuss."

dinners, *n.* A woman's breasts. "Her dress was cut so low, her dinners were about to fall out."

dip, *v.* To take snuff in the lip or jaw. "Do you dip?" doesn't mean "Are you fond of dunking chips in sour cream?"

dip stick, *n.* A brush (usually a chewed twig) used for dipping snuff.

diptheery, *n.* Diptheria, a catching disease that gives you a high fever and makes it hard for you to breathe.

dirdy, *adj.* Not clane.

dirty rice; dirdy rice, *n.* A pilau made of chicken giblets, rice, onions, garlic, and spices. The "dirty" comes from the color it takes from the giblets.

disconfit, *v.* [Mountains; old] To inconvenience; to put someone out. "Wal, I wouldn't mind eatin' me a bite with y'all if you shore it wouldn't disconfit you none."

disremember, *v.* To forget. "I disremember whether it wuz me or Sam who done it."

dite, *n.* [Long *i*] Self-inflicted starvation. "Don't tell me she's on one of them ole dites agin."

dividing line, *n.* The Mason and Dixon Line, once said to be "the dividing line between cold bread and hot biscuits."

Dixie, *n.* "Where the oranges and magnolias bloom, except when blighted by a blizzard from the land of Yankee Doodle"— Senator Bob Taylor of old Tennessee.

Dixie; Dixieland, *n.* How did the South get its nickname? Well, the most convincing evidence is that it came, loosely speaking, from a ten-dollar bill. The early nineteenth century in this country was a crazy kind of time: More and more territories were opening up, commerce was growing lickety-split, while at the same time there was no nationally organized or reliable banking system. With banks, states, even counties, able to issue notes as they chose, one can imagine the foul-up this caused and the lack of trust it set up in the citizens. People became increasingly wary, especially travelers who found themselves in strange new areas of the country. Which currency could be relied upon to be sound and negotiable anywhere? was the question everyone was asking. Traffic on the Mississippi was beginning to go great guns, and word spread that the bank to be trusted was the Banque des Citoyens of New Orleans. The word spread up and down the river grapevine: "Don't take nothin' but dixies." "Them dix notes are always good." "They'll take dixies anywhere, no questions asked." The Banque des Citoyens's most widely circulated bill was the ten-dollar denomination. It was printed in English on one side and in French on the reverse. To be expected, the French word *dix* was mispronounced by the English-speaking and mostly uneducated rivermen, and soon they began referring to that section of the U.S.A. as "the land of dixies." Hence, Dixie and Dixieland.

dō, *n.* Door; the thing you open and close to go in and out. ("Do" and "flo" for door and floor are not the result of an African influence brought over by slaves; instead this pronunciation was brought by early settlers from southern England, where it was then the literate and proper usage of the period.)

do, *n.* [Pronounced "doo"] A social get-together. "Peg and me went to a big do at the Babtis church yestiddy."

doctor book, *n.* A manual for practicing "home" medicine.

dogwood winter, *n.* A cold spell in early spring.

do-less, *adj.* Lazy; good for nothin'. "She really got herse'f a do-less man, didn't she?"

doney; doney-gal, *n.* [Mountain; old] A sweetheart. ("Doney" was also a synonym for "woman" in the old days. "Look! Two donies comin' up the road an' both of 'em toting younguns." One theory is that the word came originally from the Spanish *dona*.)

dooby, *n.* Pie filling baked without a crust. "Did you see that fat thang settin' stuffin' hisse'f with blackber' dooby, an' it jes' covered in cream?"

doodly-squat, *n.* The equivalent of nothing. "If you ast me, ain't none o' them worth doodly-squat."

dope, *n.* The "national" cole drink of the South—ouah beloved "Co'-Cola." (In the early days of Coca-Cola, there was a belief by some that it contained so much cocaine that it was not only narcotizing, but that it would eat up the dope "addict's" stomach.)

Some sixty-odd years ago, dopes, when ordered from a soda fountain, came in all flavors and varieties, and you simply weren't the cat's pajamas (the with-it type) if you asked for a plain dope. One always requested something extra in his Co'-Cola, such as a squirt of cherry, vanilla, or chocolate syrup, or maybe a squeeze of lemon, orange, or lime, and, most popular of all, a dash of ammonia. Of course, the dope lovers with real imagination became even fancier and began calling for such concoctions as a cherry-chocolate dope or lemon-vanilla dope. (Ammonia was always referred to just that way, never correctly as "spirits of ammonia." One's "need" for ammonia was presumed to indicate a show of sophistication, and to give evidence of a delicate nervous system.)

doreen, dorene, *n.* [1920s and '30s] A mirrored compact that holds powder.

double duck fit, *n.* High agitation. "When she heard that Hubert was gonna get married, I thought she would throw a double duck fit."

double harness, *n.* The state of matrimony.

dough-beater, *n.* A wife.

Dowling, Lt. Dick, *n.* The hero of the Battle of Sabine Pass, Tex. (Civil War). With only forty-two men, his company stalled sixteen thousand Union soldiers and took four hundred of them as prisoners. Dowling had been a Texas bartender.

down-go, *n.* Bad health; ill fortune. "Soon as I seen how much she'd fell off, I knowed she was on a real down-go."

downtown, *n.* Downriver in New Orleans.

down yonder. One of the points of a Rebel's compass; the other three are "up yonder, round yonder, and ovuh yonder."

dozens, play the. [Black] To throw off on or insult someone's parents. "Man, don't you come 'round here playin' them dozens with me 'cause ever'body knows my mama's a saint an' your mama ain't fit to wash my mama's feet."

drag the main. To ride up and down the main street of a town to check what's going on, to see who and what you can—one way of fighting small-town boredom.

drap, *n.* Drop. As one famous poet, Mr. S. T. Coleridge, *almost* put it: "Wadder, wadder everwher' an' not a drap to drink."

draw up, *v.* To shrink. "If this dress draws up even one fraction of an eench, I'll nevuh be able to get in it."

dreckly, *adj.* Directly; sometime or other. "Ah'll do it dreckly" usually means "whin Ah git good an' ready."

dreen, *v.* To drain. "If you'll dreen the wadder out o' the sink, I'll fix the dern thing."

dress, *v.* When a Southerner dresses a chicken, she's really undressing it; she's gettin' it ready for the pan.

dressin', *n.* Stuffing for a Rebel turkey.

drip pots, *n.* What you put around on the floor if it rains and your roof leaks.

drummer; drummer-man, *n.* A peddler; a traveling salesman.

drunk, *adj.* Though it's common knowledge that a Rebel is almost never at a loss for words, we do seem to have a superabundance of terms for describing a Southerner who has "had too much." Here are some of them: blotto; clobbered; cockeyed; dead to the world; full as a tick; glassy-eyed; half-crocked; half-shot; high as a Georgia pine; high as a kite; hung one on; juiced; juiced up; knocked for a loop; likkered up, all; lit; lit to the gills; lit up; lit up like a Xmas tree; loaded; looped; on a toot; out like a light; petrified; pie-eyed; pifflicated; pixilated; potted; snootful, has a; soused; stewed; tanked up; three sheets to the wind.

drunken dreamin's, *n.* DT's in "Gawjah" in early twentieth century.

dry cattle, *n.* [Rural Georgia] Maidens, especially young women who have never had children. "A cow dud'n give milk until after she's calved, does she?"

DT room, *n.* In the first bloom of liquor-making in Kentucky, many of its citizens became such enthusiastic supporters of the new product that it became necessary for "hoe-tels" and inns to maintain a special drying-out room for these loyal and public-spirited men.

dud'n, *contr.* As ole Aint Sally Hawkins would put it: "Dud'n she look purty in her new checkered shirtwaist?"

dumbfloundered, *adj.* Struck dumb; stunned. "It left her plum dumbfloundered when he said what he did."

dummern, *n.* [N.C. Mountains; old] A woman. "Nine dummerunses, but only two ole men showed up at meetin' last night."

dust, *n.* A smidgeon of something powdery. "Cain't even make gravy—ain't a dust o' flour left."

dymun; dymunt, *n.* Short for "diamond engagement ring"—variously defined as: **1.** The sparkling declaration of the triumph of woman over man; the prize that proclaims the woman the winner. **2.** Proof positive that woman is the smartest animal in the jungle. "Did you heah? Seymour give Jessie Mae her dymunt last night an' they ain't been goin' together but two months."

eah, *n.* Ear. "The bettuh to heah you with, my deah."

eah-bobs, *n.* Ornaments for the ears.

earpan, *n.* Eardrum.

easin' powduh; restin' powduh, *n.* A drug in the form of a powder for easing pain. "His pains let up considduhble since Doc Grubbs give him that easin' powduh." "B.C.'s an' Goodies are light easin' powduhs you can buy at the stoah."

east, *n.* Yeast. "No, east is not a direction; it's a dough expanduh."

easty, *adj.* Yeasty. "This bread tastes a lil' too easty fah me."

East Vuhginyuh, *n.* What West Virginia used to call Virginia to keep it in its place.

eater, *n.* Any fruit grown primarily to be eaten raw. "These here alples don't make much of a pie, but you'll never taste a better eater."

Eating Capital of the South, *n.* New Orleans—and a title it well deserves. It's been said that nowhere in the U.S.A. is the food so consistently good.

eatin' table, *n.* Not a table you eat, but the table where you eat—as distinguished from the cook table.

eau sucrée, *n.* [New Orleans area] A sugar and water mixture drunk after meals as a guard against dyspepsia.

eddaquit, *n.* [Accent on the "quit"] Etiquette.

egg bread, *n.* French toast in parts of South Carolina.

el, *interj.* Well. As in, "El, I will declare!"

electorial, *adj.* Electoral. Relating to one American college, the intellectual standards of which are not necessarily high.

element, *n.* The sky; the heavens. "The element sure looks threat'nin' this mornin'."

eleveners, *n.* [Old] Time out in the mornin' for refreshment. (Rumor has it that for eleveners, many Kentucky gentlemen chose bourbon over coffee.)

Elizabeth, Miss, *n.* [Black] Between friends when discussing a white female employer, "Miss Elizabeth" was employed as a secret code name; it was also used as a general term for referring to that category of employer. "Well, how were things at your Miss Elizabeth's today? Better than yesterday, I hope."

Ellick, *n.* Alec. A man's name. "Y'all remembuh Ellick Guinness in all those mahvelous Ainglish movies, don'tchu?"

ellum, *n.* Elm, a kind of tree and a popular name for city streets.

English peas, *n.* Green peas, as distinguished from the "black-ahed" kind, and as in peas and carrots.

epitaph, *n.* Insults; name-calling. "He wuz always throwin' epitaphs at me."

epizootics, *n.* Any disease of an indefinite nature. If an animal is off his feed, or ailing for no known reason, he has the epizootics. (Used humorously, also, in speaking of humans.)

et, *v.* Past tense of "eat." Conjugation: "I will eat pie today; I et pie yestiddy; I have et pie ev'ryday this week."

evenin', *n.* From twelve noon till suppertime; the period after supper is appropriately called night.

evengloam, *n.* Twilight. "Ah like to set on the porch at evengloam; it's a kind o' sad but nice time o' day."

everlastin', *n.* A kind of nonperishable flower, like the wood rose and the strawflower. "She had a vase full of the purtiest everlastin's."

everwhichaway, *adj.* In all directions; in a senseless, crazy, or confused way. "Whin he's drunk, he jumps in his ole Ford an' drives down the road everwhichaway but straight."

excape, *v.* To make a getaway.

exorb, *v.* To take up or in; as in "shock exorber."

exracise, *n.* What keeps one fit.

extry, *adj.* More'n you thought you'd get. "It's that lil' sump'm extry that counts."

eye-eatin', *v.* Gazing at with desire, or with extreme interest. "You've been eye-eatin' that girl ever since she set down there."

eyeballs, *n.* An object of pure delight or devotion. "That young-gun has been his eyeballs since the very day she come into this world."

eye-opener, *n.* A toddy or a shot of booze, especially first thing in the morning.

eyewinker, *n.* Eyelash. "Don't you just hate to git an eyewinker in your eye?"

face hurts. The condition of blushing. "Ever' time he sees Sallie Mae, his face hurts like innythang."

face whitenin', *n.* [Mountains and rural; old] Face powder.

fair to middlin', *adj.* Just so-so; not so hot.

fairy, *n.* Ferry. A big flat boat that takes you and your car across the river.

fais-dodo, *n.* An evening dance or party in the Cajun part of Louisiana. (Fais-dodo means "go to sleep." The entire family attended these shindigs, and naturally they had to get the babies bedded down before the serious dancing began.) "You know that Napoleon Arnaud? He just lives for the fais-dodo."

fambly, *n.* Family. **1.** The kinfolks living under one roof. **2.** All of one's blood kin.

faintified, *adj.* Feeling faint; a tendency toward fainting. "Delivuh me from a faintified kind o' female."

fangers, *n.* Fingers. Those little things dangling down at the end of your arms.

far, *n.* Fire; what you sit in front of when you're cold.

fard, *v.* Fired; that's when you suddenly have no job.

far in the hole! [See "far."] This was the traditional shout used by a moonshiner's lookout to give warning that the federal men were getting close; but if a human holler was going to be too risky, the watchman gave a bird call instead. "Whoo-ee! Whoo-ee, whoo-ee!" (Who? *Who!* W'y, them damn revenooers, who else?)

farplace, *n.* Fireplace, "the best place for a far; it's found at the bottom of a chimley."

fat back, *n.* White bacon, used as seasoning for pinto beans and cooked salad greens.

fault, *v.* Finding fault with. "One of those wimmin who faults her man no matter what he does."

faux, *n.* Mess-mates of knives. "Some table she set! We was missing one spoon and two faux."

favor, *v.* To resemble somebody. "That youngun sure favors his paw."

fawg, *n.* A low-lying cloud; a ground cloud.

feather-legged, *adj.* Weak in the legs. "That scared me so bad, it left me right feather-legged."

Febuwerry, *n.* The second month of the year.

feller, *n.* A girl's sweetheart; a beau.

fall off. To lose weight. "On a diet! W'y, if she falls off innymoah, you can use her hip bone fah a hat rack."

fernent, *prep.* **1.** Near; close to. **2.** Opposite, against. "It was fernent his principles to treat innyone thataway."

ferro, *n.* [Mountains] A locust or cicada.

fever worm, *n.* A caterpillar.

FFV, *n.* This stands for First Families of Virginia, or a member of one of those bloodlines. ("Don't think, howevuh, that there was evuh an FFV so tasteless an' so ungenteel as to refuh to himself, or any othuh Vuhginyun, in this mannuh—no mattuh how blue the blood.")

fill out. To get plump, especially in the right places.

fillin' station, *n.* Where you go to get your car filled up with gas and oil.

fim, *n.* You can't take a picture without fim in your camera.

fine-aired, *adj.* One who puts on airs. "Who does she think she is—actin' so fine-aired an' high-falutin'!"

finely, *adv.* At long last.

fireboard, *n.* A mantelpiece.

firebread, *n.* Bread made over an open fire. "He was brung up on firebread an' slouchy gravy [q.v.]."

fit, *v.* Past tense of "fight."

fitified, *adj.* [Mountain; old] Subject to having fits.

fitten, *adj.* Fit for; fitting; suitable.

fix, *v.* To *pre*pare, not *re*pair. (Yankees make breakfast; Southerners fix it.)

fixin' to. About to; gettin' ready to. "Ah'm fixin' to go to town."

flabbergab, *n.* A tale-bearer; a gossip.

flambaste, *v.* To bully, overwhelm, or frighten. "They didn't do no vylunce, just tried to flambaste ever'body."

flatfoot, *n.* [N.C. and around Galax, Va.—originally from the British Isles] This is a type of dance done in the mountains.

Flawduh, *n.* Florida, "a state moah Suthun than Gawjah, but only geographic'ly."

fleamale, *n.* A gal-dog who's infected with those insects.

flibbertygibbet, *n.* A silly, fluttering, restless young woman.

flip-floppy, *adj.* Careless, graceless, and indelicate in actions (said of a girl or woman).

flitter, *n.* A fritter or a pancake.

flō, *n.* Floor, the bottom part of a house, what you walk on.

flouncy, *adj.* Flip-floppy [q.v.]; a disdainful, rather vulgar way of acting or showing off. "She was loud an' flouncy."

flounder-house, *n.* This type of dwelling was unique to the older section of Alexandria, Va. The houses remind some of a flounder in that they are long, flat, and without windows on one side. (Window glass was very expensive due to the excessive English tax at that time.)

fly brush; fly bush, *n.* In the days before screens, these were waved over the dining table to shoo the flies away. Fly brushes were sometimes only a leafy tree branch, but usually they were made of strips of fringed newspaper fastened onto the end of a long stick. Sunday ones were sometimes made of white tissue paper, while the fanciest of all were fashioned from real peacock feathers.

flying cigar, the, *n.* An 1897 type of flying saucer (except it was shaped more like a cigar) that was reported to have been sighted by some leading citizens of Aurora, Tex. Although the occupants were immediately recognized as Martians, they did not scare the sighters for the simple reason that the space people were busy singing "Nearer, My God, to Thee" and giving away religious pamphlets.

flying room, *n.* [Mountains] An elevator.

Forth of Jew-ly. President Thomas Jefferson started this Independence Day celebration, then died on the same day fifty years later.

Fode, *n.* A car very popular in Georgia and South Carolina.

fō, *n.* "The number befo' five to innyone who walks the flo, but if you're one of those Southerners who says 'floah,' then the numbuh is 'foah.' "

foeman, *n.* Foreman—the boss-man.

foesight, *n.* Just the opposite of hindsight, but supposedly much better.

fokes, *n.* "In the South there are po' fokes and rich fokes, common fokes and nice fokes, strange fokes and ev'ryday fokes—all kinds o' fokes; but nevuh in the histry of Dixie have there been any fokes known as 'folk' or kinsfolk.' "

fooraw; foofooraw, *n.* A loud disturbance; a big commotion; a boisterous party.

foot it. To walk it.

foot-stamping, *n*. Southern females learn this about as soon as they become steady on their feet, and then it stands them in good stead for the rest of their lives. First they use it on Daddy for things like winning his support for talking Mother into letting the little angel stay up a half hour longer, then for inveigling him out of pocket change for an extra lollipop; soon they graduate into using it for bigger and better prizes. Foot-stamping is of untold aid in winning arguments with boyfriends and husbands, although since women's lib, it is not as necessary a device as it used to be.

Fort Liquordale, *n*. A nickname for Fort Lauderdale, because of its reputation as a playground.

fotched-on, *adj*. [Old] Put-on airs; newly richlike; brought in from another place. "Her an' them fotched-on airs of her'n!"

frand, *n*. Friend, not foe; or, as said in those immortal words: "A frand in need ain't much to fall back on, is he?"

fragrant weed, the, *n*. Tobacco.

frazzle, *n*. What you get worn to.

french disease, *n*. A polite name for syphilis.

frever, *adv*. That's always.

frigidaire, *n*. Any electric icebox.
"Margie-Ann got herse'f a new Frigidaire."
"Oh, she did? What kind?"
"A Kelvinator."

frizzle-frazzle, *n*. Prattle; frivolous chatter like "girl talk." "Miz Lucy Parmentier had a deep an' inquirin' mind an' she yearned for moah mental stimulation than was afforded by the frizzle-frazzle of her limited social circle."

froggish, *adj*. Combative; spoiling for a fight. "Soon as he takes a nip, he starts gettin' froggish."

frogstool, *n.* A toadstool.

frolic, *n.* A fun party in the old days.

frolic tune, *n.* [Mountain and rural] Music for a hoedown. "Frolic tunes are all right, but they don't give a body the satisfaction that a good ole hymn does."

front name, *n.* [Cajun] One's given name. "I know yo' front name, mah frand, but what's yo' behind name?"

front room, *n.* The "pahlah; the settin' room."

fum. 1. *adj.* Not flabby. **2.** *n.* A business concern.

funeralize, *v.* [Uneducated] To hold a funeral service. "I thought that preachuh would nevuh get through funeralizing. I nevuh got so tired of anything in my life—they made more commotion ovuh him than they did over Jesus Christ." [A verbatim quote from the conversation of a certain Southern female octogenarian.]

funichoor, *n.* Furniture, the main furnishings of a house.

funnin', *v.* Joking or teasing. "Aw, go on—you're just funnin' me."

funsies, *n.* Fun. "I didn't mean to scare you when I hollered—I was jus' doin' it for funsies."

fur piece, *n.* A long distance.

furriner, *n.* A Damnyankee; or anyone from the other side of the mountain.

fust. 1. *n.* First; as in "fust, second, thud." **2.** *adj.* "Befoah all othuhs."

fut, *n.* The termination of your leg.

g, the final. Yankees think it's incorrect when speaking to drop the final *g* in words like puddin(g) and goin(g). No way. This was the proper form used by the nobility and the educated classes of England and consequently was brought over here to America by the educated Southerner-to-be. (Not until around the time of World War II did the English start pronouncing the *g*, but not us Rebels. We believe in stickin' with what is right and proper.)

gah-ron-tee, *v.* Guarantee. A Cajun's way of assuring one of something. "Ah gah-ron-tee, that's the best gumbo ever you put tongue to."

galded, *adj.* Chafed; galled. "Pore little feller was apt to get galded between his chubby legs."

galloping liar, *n.* Someone who tells stories big and fast.

galry, *n.* Gallery; a front porch in parts of the Deep South, like South Carolina and Texas.

gardeen, *n.* A guardian.

garntee, *n.* Guarantee. "Don't you ever buy anythang expensive without getting your garntee with it."

gas, *v.* To indulge in excessive boasting or a lot of talk about nothing. "He'd stand there gassing all day if I was dumb enough to listen."

Gawjuh, *n.* [Soft *g*] Georgia, a state a little bit south and west of South Carolina, and with its residents, a state of mind.

Gawjuh ice cream. Hominy grits.

gayly; gaily, *adj.* [Mountains] In good spirits; well (in health). "You're feeling mighty gayly today, I'm glad to see."

Geeche, *n.* [From Ogeechee] **1.** A dialect spoken originally by Negro slaves who lived near the Ogeechee River in Georgia. The patois is a combination of English and African words. **2.** One who is a descendant of these people.

gee-un, *n.* Gin; a card game and type of rummy as played in Ayatlayantah, Gawjuh.

gee-tar; git-tar, *n.* Guitar, a stringed musical instrument. "You pluck a strang, you get plenny of twang."

geewahhawed, *adj.* Off center; not plumb. "Some coppentuh! Ah've nevuh seen anything he built yet that wasn't geewah-hawed."

gemmen, *n.* Gentlemen; wellborn, refined men.

gentle, *v.* To tame or make docile. "There's never been a woman too feisty for John Summers. A little gentling from him and they're putty in his hands."

gentleman's fever, *n.* In those dear, dead, hush-hush days (that we sincerely hope are beyond recall), this was the polite way of saying "venereal disease."

get-go, *n.* Power; energy. "That ole Model-T nevuh did have any get-go to it."

get-out, *n.* A superlative. "That boy is as smart as all get-out."

getting place. The getting place is where you get something when you don't want to tell where you got it. "Where'd you get a quarter, boy?" "Got it at the getting place." [William Faulkner]

getting ready. About to; getting in the mood to. (Getting ready means much more than just preparing to do something. For example, someone who's just sitting and looking out a window may very well be "getting ready" to go to work.)

Gettysburg; Gettysbug, *n.* The South's Gethsemane—July 1863. (When this writer lived in South Carolina, then later in Virginia, she never once heard anyone pronounce the *r* in Gettysburg.)

getup, *n.* An outfit of clothing and its accessories, especially an outlandish one. "My Lord in heaven, did you see that getup she had on? Why, they wouldn't even let her in a tacky party with that mess on."

giggle soup, *n.* An alcoholic drink, often illicit booze.

gin, *n.* Short for "engine," as in "cotton gin." (It didn't take Southerners long to shorten that one. They just never did cotton to unnecessary syllables.)

gin-u-wine, *adj.* Genuine; the real honest-to-goodness thing; not spurious, but authentic.

girly trick. "When she pulls the wool ovuh your eyes—tha's what you call a 'girly trick.' "

go back on your raising. When someone forgets his humble beginnings, puts on airs, and gets all biggety. (And believe you us, in the South, to go back on your raising, that's a pretty serious offense.)

godden, *n.* Garden, a miniature farm; a vegetable patch or flower plot.

go-down, *n.* A decline in health or fortune. "Grandpap's been on the go-down ever since the mule kicked him."

God's plenty, *n.* More than enough. "I couldn't eat another bite if you held a gun to my head. I have had a God's plenny."

go-fetcher, *n.* The Adam's apple. "Did you ever notice how his go-fetcher bobs up and down when he talks?" (The expression

"Adam's apple" comes from the legend that the forbidden fruit stuck in Adam's throat.)

goff, *n.* Cow-pasture pool [q.v.]. (The first golf club in America is said to have started in Charleston, S.C.)

goies, *n.* [Pronounced "go-ies"] The travel fever; flitting here and there and everywhere. "He'd a been a pretty good husband if he hadn't had such a bad case of the goies."

goll-darn; goll-dern, *n.* Two of our milder expletives which were invented for the use of small boys whose mothers were within hearing.

gollup, *n.* A quick, and often big, swallow of liquid.

gone goslin, *n.* A dead goose; a person whose fate is sealed. "You do that to me, bud, you're a gone goslin."

gonnies, ay. "Ay gonnies, I don't care if it harelips the South, I'm gunna do it!" ("Ay gonnies" is thought to be a euphemism for "By God.")

goober; goober pea, *n.* A ground nut. (And this doesn't mean a ground-up nut, but a nut that "growed" in the ground: the peanut.)

good again, as. Twice as good. "Umm, umm! This is as good again as last time."

good eating. Just that. "My, oh, my, these hawg jowls an' collard greens are sure good eatin'!" (It's been said that a Southerner never sells what he can eat, and a Yankee never eats what he can sell. Maybe that's one of the reasons we were once called the impoverished South.)

good-god bird, *n.* What a woodpecker was sometimes called in parts of the Carolinas. (Some woodpeckers have such a loud shriek that it is said to prompt an expression like: "Good God almighty, listen to that, willya!")

good heart, in. Having a positive spirit or attitude. "Yes, he was in real good heart yesterday."

Goodliest Land Under the Cope of Heaven, The. North Carolina. (And who's to argue with the two ecstatic Englishmen who said this way back in 1584?)

good moanin'. A greeting for early risers.

goody, *n.* An old word for "nut kernel." "Ma and me set up half the night picking out walnut goodies for the Christmas fruit-cakes."

goose drownder, *n.* A very hard rain; a near-flood.

goozle, *n.* Throat; or Adam's apple. "He near scared the goozle out of me."

gopher, *n.* A turtle in the deep South.

go-poke, *n.* A suitcase or grip.

gord, *n.* Guard. "In football it takes two gords to protect the one man who carries the ball."

gormy, *adj.* Sticky or smeary. "Who wants to pick up a youngun all gormy with butter and 'lasses?"

gourd dipper, *n.* A ladle made out of a scooped-out and dried-out gourd.

gracious plenty. A sufficiency; sometimes a plethora. "More turkey?" "No, ma'm! I have had a gracious plenny."

graffe, *n.* Giraffe; the camelopard; the tallest of all mammals. (The fights that giraffes have among themselves are called "necking." All that neck and no voice? Not true. Because their voices are so seldom heard, they are popularly supposed to be dumb, but actually they have voices that range from a low bellow to a hoarse bawl.)

Gragry, *n.* Gregory; a man's first name. ("Y'all remembuh Gragry Peck in *To Keel a Mockingbud*, don't you?")

grain, *adj.* Green, one of the secondary colors.

grain banes, *n.* Green beans. "First you let them liven up in cole wadder, then you strang 'em, you snap 'em (in about three pieces each), you throw in a couple slices of bacon, season 'em rale good, add a cup o' wadder, an' let 'em bile gently fah about thirty minutes. Hot a'mighty dern, are they good!"

grāmy, *v.* [Old] To annoy; to anger. "It gramies me whin he walks around with that silly grin on his face."

grandma, *n.* Low gear, especially in a truck. "We struggled all the way up the mount'n in grandma and thought we wouldn't make it."

Grant, Julia. If Useless—sorry, Ulysses—was fighting us in the name of abolishing slavery, why did Mrs. Grant hold on to *her* slaves?

granny doctor, *n.* [Mountain] Obstetrician.

granny woman, *n.* [Mountain] A midwife; a catch-woman [q.v.].

grape harbor, *n.* Grape arbor.

grass widder, *n.* Grass widow, one whose husband hasn't gone "up yonder—jes' gone with the wind."

graphophone, *n.* A gramophone; the closest thing to a hi-fi in the old days—a phonograph.

gravel, *v.* To vex; to embarrass. "It graveled him, the way they were throwing off on his friend."

Graveyard of the Atlantic. Because of the frequent storms that caused so many shipwrecks in the old days, the sea area around

Cape Hatteras and the Outer Banks of eastern North Carolina became known as this.

graveyard stew, *n.* Milk toast, so-called because it was often served to sick people.

gravy sponge, *n.* A buttermilk or baking powder biscuit.

grayhorse, *n.* [South Carolina] Sorghum and butter mixed together for sopping.

great balls of fire. An exclamation of wonder, amazement, or disbelief.

green apple quick step. What you get when you eat too many green apples or drink too much new cider.

green out. To cheat; to outdo. "Sure he's clever, but you better watch him or he'll green you out every time."

Greyhound Therapy. [Circa 1980s] That's when the homeless of Kentucky get a free bus trip to the emergency shelter in Lexington.

grinding rock, *n.* A whetstone.

gripe, *n.* [Yankees put an *a* where the *i* is.] **1.** Grape. "It takes a whole passel of these things to make one gallon of gripe wine, and scuppernong gripes making the greatest." (It is said that scuppernongs were first discovered—*after* the Cherokees did it, of course—by Sir Walter Raleigh. If he'd just thought to take some of them back to Queen Elizabeth, he probably could have had all the ships he wanted.) **2.** Grape soda pop. When somebody sends you to the store for "a gripe," he means a kind of cold drink.

grits, *n.* Georgia ice cream, or poi as made in Dixie; a farinaceous dish made of ground and dried corn and served with butter or gravy; a passionately loved breakfast food.

gritted bread, *n.* This was first made by the Indians—a kind of baked corn pudding made from freshly grated maize.

gritter, *n.* [Mountain] A grater.

grosher, *n.* Grocer.

gross, *v.* To complain; to grouse. "You got no business grossing about that."

ground nut, *n.* A goober pea; a pinder; a peanut.

ground, on the. [North Carolina] Not in jail or prison. "Call me a lawyer so I can get my feet back on the ground fast!"

ground pea, *n.* A peanut.

growing bones. [Black—heard in Richmond, Va.] Pregnant. "Girl, you're not growing bones again!"

grown to the chair. Signifies indolence. "I swear, he was so slow to move, I thought he'd grown to the chair."

GTT. Means "Gone to Texas." Back in the 1870s and 1880s, so many left their home states to seek their fortunes in Texas (the "Texas fever" had started as early as 1840) that it became common to find businesses closed with a sign on the door stating, "Gone to Texas." But later the migrations became so commonplace that the adventurers left signs that read simply, "GTT."

guinea squash, *n.* [Georgia] An old name for eggplant.

gull, *n.* A young female in the Old Dominion and in the Palmetto State.

gullah, *n.* **1.** One of a group of Blacks, descendants of slaves from western Africa, inhabiting the sea islands and coast districts of South Carolina, Georgia, and a small section of northeast

Florida. **2.** The dialect spoken by these people, which is a blend of English and the Liberian languages brought by the earliest slaves.

gulley jumper, *n.* A mountaineer; occasionally a farmer.

gulley washer, *n.* A hard rain.

gum, *n.* Not what you chew, but a trap for a small animal.

gumbo. A stew made of sundry vegetables, seasonings, and chicken, ham, or seafood, then thickened and given the desired "tackiness" by the use of okra or file (powdered young sassafras leaves) or both. A dish truly indigenous to America. It was probably first made in Louisiana, and is still one of their mainstays. (Gumbo, or gombo, is not only the term for the stew, it is also another word for okra; and both gumbo and okra are African words, of which, curiously enough, only a handful became a part of the American language.)

gungo. Going to go. "Are you gungo to the school shindig tonight?"

gunna. Going to. "Are you gunna eat now, or you wanna wait till the second table?"

gunny sack, *n.* A tow bag.

guvment, *n.* Government—"of the folks, by the folks, for the folks."

guy, *v.* To tease or to make fun of. "I just plain-out despise being guyed about my red hair."

gyneolatry, *n.* Gyneolatry as practiced in the Old South was characterized by a reverence for and an extravagant chivalry toward women. (Some have dared suggest—and they were no doubt *Yankees* who said it—that these beautiful sentiments sprang more from the male's attitude toward class and purity than from true romance and chivalry. What a ridiculous thought!)

gynt, *n.* [Pronounced "gīnt"] "A great big overgrowed felluh."

hack, *v.* To embarrass; to get someone's goat. "Boy, was he hacked when we caught him crocheting."

hafintwo. A Rebel never cuts anything in half; he always cuts it "hafintwo."

hail, *n.* Hell, the bad place; as in "The hail with you!"

haint; hant, *n.* A spirit; usually one that "skeers" you.

hair all over her head. Hair in disarray. "She looked like a wild woman—a dirty face and her hair all over her head."

hair to heel. From head to toe.

hairy worm, *n.* [Tennessee] A caterpillar.

hal, *v.* Howl. "Ever'body's heard a dawg hal."

half-moon pie, *n.* A circle of rich dough that has been filled with stewed fruit, folded over, and fried.

hambone, *n.* A slapping sort of rhythm-keeping, done by a person who bends forward and slaps his thigh back and forth with a relaxed hand.

hamfatter, *n.* An unskilled but flamboyant performer. "Ham" as in "ham actor." (This probably originated during minstrel show days and was perhaps a black expression.)

hand, *n.* Penmanship. "Goodness, you sure write a purty hand."

hanel, *n.* Handle; an object that you grab on to so you can use or open something. "How'm I gunna lift this go-poke [q.v.] with the hanel broke?"

Happy Pappy Program. [Mountain] The vernacular for government welfare programs during Hoover Time—the Great Depression. (What was great about it?)

hard cider, *n.* Fermented cider—the champagne of the South.

hark; harken, *v.* [Mountain] To listen. "It's best not to harken to lies."

haslet stew, *n.* The viscera of the hog—liver, heart, and lights—seasoned and stewed till done, with cornmeal dumplings cooked on top. (Lights is an old word for lungs.)

hauling freight, *v.* Going fast; moving with speed and determination. "Last time I saw Horace, he was hauling freight right out of town."

have up. To have arrested; to be summoned to court. "If she keeps slanderin' me, I'm gonna have her up for sure."

having the tree. That's when the Xmas presents are given out from under the tree. "They're funny people—they always have their Xmas tree on Xmas Eve morning."

hawn, *n.* Horn, a warning device sounded by the driver of a vehicle. "Just as I was going in the hoose, she passed in huh new Fode cah and honked huh hawn at me. I noticed on the back it said, 'Vuhginyuh is fah lovuhs.' "

hay-am, *n.* The thigh of a hind leg of a hog. "Nothing like fried hayam, aigs, red-eye gravy, and grits for breakfast—man, that's eatin'."

hayuh, *n.* Hair; those follicles on top of your head; your crowning glory.

head, *n.* [Old; rural] A person; an individual. "Two head come in the store early and robbed him 'fore he knowed what was goin' on."

headcheese, *n.* Ground-up hog's head, boiled, seasoned, then allowed to jell. The French give this a fancy name, *fromage de tête*, and serve it as a gourmet dish.

head rammer, *n.* A big shot in an organization or group. "Yeah, he's the head rammer of our American Legion post—has a say in everything we do."

head-wings, *n.* [Mountain; old] Ears of a human being.

heah, *v.* Hear; to perceive by listening.

heap, *n.* A large amount. "Heap" is a word Southerners would have a hard time doing without, but a "whole heap" is even more popular.

hear tell. To hear of or about. "I hear tell there's a boy over in Winston has a constant ticking in his head, and if you get near enough, he sounds just like a Big Ben alarm clock."

heartbeat, *n.* A moment. "For two days and nights it seemed to us that his death was only a heartbeat away."

heart history, *n.* The story of one's love life or romantic interests. "She told me her entire heart history at one sitting."

heartrendering, *adj.* Heartrending.

heat snakes, *n.* The waves of heat that one can see rising from pavement on a hot, sunny day.

he-balsam, *n.* Both a black and a red spruce tree.

hecack, *n.* A big disturbance; a free-for-all altercation.

he-cup, *n.* A belch in reverse.

heel taps, *n.* The last few drops in a whiskey glass. "Grandpa would wink at me, and when Mama left the room, he'd give me heel taps. 'Make a man of you, boy,' he'd say."

hee-um, *n.* Hymn; a religious song.

hellacious, *adj.* Severe; intense; causing much trouble or worry. "She gave me one hellacious cussing out."

helling, *v.* Raising hell. "He was always an' forever hellin' around."

hell I reckon. An affirmative exclamation. "Is she purty? Well, hell I reckon!"

hen apple, *n.* An egg.

hen fruit, *n.* A chicken's special gift to humankind.

hep, *v.* Help; to assist.

hernica, *n.* [Mountain and rural] A hernia.

he-row, *n.* A real first-class giant-killer; a man among men; a courageous and distinguished person.

herowine, *n.* A lady he-row.

herring, *n.* Hearing. Senator Sam Irvin presided over the Watergate "herrings," the legislative session held for the testimony of witnesses.

hibiscuit, *n.* [Children and uneducated] A hibiscus.

hickernut, *n.* A hickory nut.

hick'ry; hick'ry switch, *n.* A switch taken from a hickory tree.

hick'ry stick tea, *n.* A switching. "If you don't straighten up and behave, you're going to get a big dose of hick'ry stick tea, young man.

high and low. Everywhere you can think of; where a Rebel looks for something missing.

high on the hog. Living sumptuously. "They're broke by Mond'y, but I'll tell you, they sure live high on the hog ev'ry Sat'dy."

hightail, *v.* To travel fast; to rush off.

high up to picking cotton. [Georgia] Someone as high as a kite; inebriated.

hill, *n.* The back of one's foot.

hillbilly, *n.* Your chances of avoiding a fight with a mountaineer are much better if you don't use this word—especially if you're not a hillbilly—because, according to one old mountain adage, "There are two classes of people in the world, hillbillies and SOBs."

him, *n.* Hem; the bottom of your dress.

hippin, *n.* [From Old English "hipping cloth"] Pants for wee wee people; a diaper.

Hired, *n.* Howard, a man's name; as in Hired Hughes, the famous rich man, and Hired Baker, who was first a senator from Tennessee and then President Reagan's head rammer—his chief of staff.

hissy, *n.* A fit of anger; an "acting-up." By the time we got home, she was in a real hissy."

hit, *pron.* [Mountain and uneducated] Queen Elizabeth I used "hit" for "it," so can it be too wrong?

hit a-rainin', and. Means "on top of everything else." "What a day! He tore his pance on the way, we got to the picnic and found we'd forgot our lunch, Sissy fell down and hurt herse'f real bad, and hit a-rainin'."

hiwahyah, *n.* **1.** A salutation; an inquiry to someone's health. **2.** [Capitalized] The fiftieth state of the Union.

hobbyhorses, *n.* How we usually refer to a merry-go-round. "She simply could not wait to ride the hobbyhorses."

hockey, *n.* Defecation; usually used in talking to children and by children.

hoecake, *n.* Corn bread, originally cooked on a hoe and baked on the hearth or in the ashes.

hoedown, *n.* A lively, boisterous shindig with dancing.

hō-tell, *n.* A great big fancy rooming house.

hogback, *n.* A ridge of land shaped like a hog's back.

hoghead mush, *n.* The highly seasoned boiled meat from a hog's head with corn meal added, then chilled in a loaf pan till set. It is sliced and eaten cold or fried in bacon drippings.

hog heaven, *n.* Height of pleasure. "Jus' give him a poke bobby-cue san'wich, a Co'-Cola, a moon pie, and he's in hawg heaven."

hog-killing pie, *n.* [North Carolina] It's a pie made of stewed dried fruit, brown sugar, and butter, so-called because it was made to feed the hands at a hog killing.

hogleg, *n.* A six-shooter in the Ozarks.

holding dog, *n.* A small dog that's just right for holding in your lap.

hold your tater. Just you wait a while! "Naow," said the groceryman to the little boy who was hidden by the pickle barrel and whose voice was changing, "If you'll hold your tater, in about two shakes of a sheep's tail I'll be over there and wait on both of you."

holler and a whoop. Something that's close by. "Sure, I knowed ole man Cy Whitt. W'y, all his life he lived just a holler and a whoop from us." (In the old days, when there were no cars or telephones, hollering was the communication system used to keep in touch with one's neighbors.)

hollering contest, *n.* Not a kind of marital ruckus, but a hollering competition that's held once a year in Spivey's Corner, N.C., so expert hollerers can show off their whooping skills.

holt, *n.* A grip or a grasp on something. "You better git a holt of yourse'f, you know that?"

Holy City, the. Charleston, S.C., because of its nearly two hundred churches, some around three hundred years old.

ho'made, *adj.* Not store-bought, but made at home.

hominy, *n.* A food that is produced by inflating corn kernels, and which is sometimes referred to as "big hominy." The corn kernels are treated with lye to remove the husks, then boiled until they swell two to four times their original size—and oddly enough, eating this won't kill you.

hominy grits, *n.* "Little hominy" or grits; the breakfast delight of the South.

hominy snow, *n.* Snow that's in fine grains, like hominy grits.

hone, *v.* To long for. "There wasn't a day in the army that he didn't hone for home."

honking, *v.* Party-going, good-timing, or juking, as in a honky-tonk with honky music.

hoodoo, *n.* [Black and others] Voodoo.

hookworm hustle, *n.* The "hustle" part is pure sarcasm, for it means just the opposite—it is the slow, listless walk of the ener-vated and poorly fed. "They came down the road slow as molasses with the hookworm hustle."

hoojee, *n.* [Georgia] A hillbilly or a redneck.

hooraw, *n.* [Mississippi and others] Foolishness; baloney. "That's just a big bunch of hooraw he's talkin'."

hoose; hou-oose, *n.* A place of abode—room and bode, that is—in South Carolina and Virginia. [The pronunciation "hoose" is not incorrect, only obsolete. It was the right Old English way of pronouncing it when the word was spelled "hus." See "vowel shift."]

hoot al, *n.* Hoot owl; a living, breathing alarm clock that lives in a tree.

hoot al shift, *n.* An all-night work shift.

hootenanny, *n.* **1.** A thingamajig. **2.** A gathering with folk sing-ers and audience participation.

Hoover cart, *n.* A two-wheeled farm cart, usually pulled by a mule or a horse.

Hoover Time, *n.* The Great Depression; named in "honor" of Herbert Hoover.

hop, *n.* A planned but casual dance; a jump dance.

hoped, *v.* Past tense of "he'p" (help).

hoppergrass, *n.* A grasshopper.

hoppin' John, *n.* Black-eyed peas cooked with bacon fat, ham pieces, salt pork, or the like, and served over or mixed with steamed rice. It's the tradition for children to hop on one foot around the table before eating it, and it's considered a good-luck food for New Year's Day. As the saying goes, "For ev'ry black-eyed pea you eat on New Year's Day, during the year you'll get a dollar back." (When hopping John is warmed over the next day, it becomes skipping Jack.)

hoppytoad, *n.* A toad-frog.

hornyhead, *n.* A hornyhead chub—a type of fish. (It is called this because during the breeding season, the male's head grows hornlike protuberances.)

horseback guess, *n.* A rough guess.

horse quart, *n.* A *big* bottle of moonshine.

hose pipe, *n.* A rubber hose for watering, or for other uses.

hot, *n.* [South Carolina and Virginia] Heart, the seat of emotions and sensibilities. "In your hot you know he's right."

hot a-mighty damn. In this instance, "hot" is a euphemism for "God." "Hot a-mighty damn, but do you look goo-ood to-night!"

hots, *n.* Hot meals. "My ma served us three hots ever' day of our lives."

hot red boudin, *n.* A Cajun-type sausage, and the word "hot" is not taken lightly by the Cajuns. *Mais non!*

hot stuff, *n.* Tobasco and other hot pepper sauces—a staple on the tables of many Southerners.

hot 'un, *n.* A hot one, meaning a hot biscuit. "Take two hot 'uns, why doncha, and butter 'um while they're hot."

hot water tea, *n.* A mixture of boiling water, milk, and sugar; cambric tea. (This comes in right handy when you run out of tea bags *and* money.)

how come? Why? "How come you're nevuh 'round whin Ah needjuh?"

howdy; hi-dy. 1. *n.* A greeting. **2.** *v.* To greet. "It's very bad manners if somebody howdies you and you don't howdy back."

howsomever, *conj.* However. "He's a good-lookin' man, howsomever, he ain't the *best*-lookin' man I ever seen by a long shot."

huh, *n.* The possessive form of "she" in "Vuhginyuh, Sooth Carolina, and Gawjuh."

Huhbut, *n.* "A mayan's name, as in Victuh Huhbut and Huhbut Hoovuh."

huhry, *n.* Hastened movement. "In New York everybody seems to be in a huhry, but down here in Ayatlayantah, we jus' take ouah own sweet time."

huffy-mad, *adj.* Touchily and indignantly angry.

hunt, *v.* To look for. "What are you doing in the refrigerator?" "I'm hunting for sump'm good d'eat."

hump on, get a. Get busy; hurry up.

hung in the mouth. Hungry. "Boy, am I hung in the mouth—not a bite since breakfast."

hung the moon. Greatly admired; well thought of. "Her mother wasn't silly about her, but her daddy—well, he thought she hung the moon."

hurting in the breast, a. A sadness; a depression. "He left home over twenty years ago, but she's still got a hurtin' in the breast for him."

hush-mouthed, *adj.* Not revealing anything; keeping one's own counsel. "I swear, if he isn't the most hush-mouthed individual I ever met in my life!"

hut, *v.* To inflict pain.

hypmatize, *v.* Hypnotize. "I'm scared of him. He's got such funny eyes, I'm afraid he's gonna hypmatize me."

hymn bleeder, *n.* A country-music business term for one of the more dramatic hymn singers.

ice tea, *n.* To a Southerner this drink is second in importance only to Co'-Cola. (And in some areas they may even run neck and neck.)

ice pebbles, *n.* Hail.

idd'n. A contraction of "isn't." "Idd'n he the one? All dressed up and rarin' to go."

idee, *n.* A figment of the imagination; an idea. "W'y, the very idee—you sayin' a thang like that."

I don't care. Means "yes." (Southerners have been taught to be so polite and unaggressive that they find it difficult to come right out and say "yes." A child is asked if he would like a piece of "ho-made" fudge. He begins to salivate and struggles to keep his hand from shooting out to grab a handful. Just in time he gets hold of himself and he murmurs real demurelike, "I don't care." Then, of course, if it's a Southern hostess, she's just as polite and insists that he have at least three pieces.)

ignernce, *n.* Ignorance, the state of being "unidjicated."

I guess. I reckon. "It's about time for suppuh, idd'n it?" "I guess."

ill, *adj.* Not sick, but ill tempered. "Leave that baby alone till he wakes up good. You know he's ill as a hornet when he first gets up."

I'll be! This is an exclamation that leaves it up to one's audience to decide what the speaker should be (which is not too good an idea when you think of all the things worse than "I'll be dogged" that could be supplied).

imbom, *v.* Embalm; to preserve from decay. "Those Egyptians really knew how to imbom a dead body, didn't they?"

I'm here to tell you. You said it! Or you said a mouthful. "Is the cake good?" "Girl, I'm here to tell you!"

imitate, *v.* [Rural; old] To look like; to resemble. "He sure imitates his pa—he's the spittin' image, ain't he?"

impahdunt; impordant, *adj.* Important; noteworthy; significant.

in bed with the doctor. So sick the doctor had to be called in. "Is she sick? I should say she is! She's been in bed with the doctor all week."

indian turnip, *n.* That pretty little plant called, also, jack-in-the-pulpit.

Indy, *n.* It's the country that has the brown Indians, not the red.

infare, *n.* Wedding festivities hosted by the groom's family.

infernal revenue. The department of the government that charges you for working.

infuhmation, *n.* **1.** An inflamation. **2.** The "numbuh-givin' service" of a telephone company. **3.** Pus. "That boil is just full of infuhmation."

ingun; ingern, *n.* [Rural and mountain; old] Onion.

injun, *n.* **1.** A motor; a machine. **2.** [Capitalized] The original American as well as the original Southerner.

ink pen, *n.* What your teacher will let you write with after you master the pencil.

innerdoose, *v.* Introduce; to make acquainted; to bring to the knowledge of.

innersting, *adj.* No, not a burning sensation inside your body; it means to attract the attention of, or to arouse one's curiosity or interest. "That's one innersting story on daytime TV, that 'Love of Life' is."

inny, *adj.* One or another; this or that.

in reason. Means "within reason." "I know in reason he'll show up there tonight."

in-surance, *n.* [Accent on the "in"] The state of bein' in-sured.

in the road. Always going; forever gadding about. "I declare that is one restless human being. She's in the road *all* the time."

iotum, *n.* A teeny amount. "Don't you know by now that I do not care one iotum about your politics?"

Irish channel, *n.* A section of New Orleans that was heavily settled by the Irish.

Irish potatoes; arsh taters, *n.* (As distinguished from sweet potatoes) Southerners eat too many sweet potatoes to risk referring to Irish potatoes as just plain taters.

irne, *n.* The earliest wrinkle remover known to woman. ["Iron" is often pronounced "arn" in the mountains.]

ī-scream. [Accent on the *i*] A frozen dessert.

Itly, *n.* Where "rale Eyetalyuns" come from.

itty bitty, *adj.* Teenie weenie.

Ivins, *n.* [*I* as in "it"] Evans, a surname.

jackleg, *adj.* Makeshift. "I'm so sick of this old jackleg furniture!"

jakeleg, *adj.* An affliction brought on by drinking too much whiskey. "He's now on crutches with a jakeleg from all that mount'n dew he's been drinkin'."

jambalaya, *n.* **1.** A Louisiana rice dish made with seafood and/or meats and seasonings. **2.** A mixture. "Her house is just one big jambalaya of junk."

Jamestown weed, *n. Datura stramonium,* or tobacco. (In the early days of tobacco use, it was claimed that smoking would heal the gout, cure hangovers, and reduce fatigue and hunger.)

jamrock, *n.* One of the stones used in the facing of a fireplace. "Ever' jamrock in their fireplace she'd grubbed up from their own land."

janders, *n.* [Old] Jaundice. "He had the wust case of the yaller janders I ever seed in my life."

Januwerry, *n.* The first month of the year. "Did y'all know Januwerry the first is the birthday of every American race horse?"

jarfly, *n.* A locust; a cicada.

jar head, *n.* A mule in Southern hill country.

Jarry, *n.* A man's first name; as in Jarry Lewis and President Jarry Ford.

jasper, *n.* [Mountain] A fellow; a guy (not complimentary). "I never see them two jaspers there that they ain't up to some kind of devilment."

jaw, *v.* To gab at length, sometimes argumentatively. "They pretend to be friends, but all they ever do is jaw at each other."

Jaypan, *n.* It was people from there that bummed [q.v.] Pearl Harbor.

jealous, *adj.* Envious. "Sometimes I think she's jealous of the very food I put in my mouth."

Jeemie, *n.* The familiar form of "James," as in Jeemie Swaggart and Jeemie Cahter (but no comparison intended).

jell, *n.* Jail, a building with lots of bars but no booze; a small-time prison.

jellico weed, *n.* Angelica.

jell sale, *n.* Jail cell; a room without a view, furnished to "wanted" guests at taxpayers' expense.

jerp, *n.* [Mountain] A little bit. "You better put a jerp more salt in the collard greens."

Jerusalem artichoke, *n.* Nothing like t'other kind of artichoke, which is a thistle. (The Jerusalem artichoke is the tuber part of the sunflower stalk and is eaten cooked, but most often made into pickles. The cultivation of this food product was learned from the Indians.)

jessmin, *n.* The cape jasmine, and others of the species.

jevver. Did you ever. "Jevver see innythang lak it?"

jew. Did you. "Jew hear what I said?"

jewlarker; jularker, *n.* [Mountains; old] A sweetheart; a beau. "She's all dressed up fittin'-to-kill, waitin' for her jewlarker."

jewry, joolry, *n.* Gems and ornaments; adornments for the body—bracelets, necklaces, rings.

jibber jabber, *n.* Foolish talk.

jibbers, *n.* Saint Vitus's dance; chorea. (Superstition used to have it that it was caused from being fathered by a drunkard.)

jigamaree, *n.* [Alabama; Georgia] A thingamajig; a party with folk music.

jim, *n.* Gem.

jimber-jawed, *adj.* A jutting-out lower jaw. "I can't stand those jimber-jawed bulldawgs."

jine, *v.* [Old-timey] Join.

jinky board, *n.* [Probably from Gullah] A seesaw.

job, *v.* To jab. "Quit jobbing me with your elbow."

joggling board, *n.* A kind of "ho'made" springboard; sometimes a seesaw.

Jolie Blonde, *n.* Said to be the "national anthem" of the Cajuns of Louisiana.

johnnycake, *n.* A simple kind of corn bread.

johnny-jump-ups, *n.* Wild pansies.

johnny walkers, *n.* Stilts; tom-walkers [q.v.].

jonah, *n.* Someone who is jinxed; a loser. "That poor girl. She's been a jonah all her life."

jool, *n.* Jewel; a jim [q.v.].

joree. [Mountain; old] **1.** *n.* A chewink; a towhee. **2.** *v.* Jest with or at. "They're always joreeing him about his girl."

josie, *n.* [Mountain; old] A shiftlike dress.

journeycake, *n.* A johnnycake (so-called because it was often taken with someone who was going to be away from home for some time).

journey proud, *adj.* Pride in one's travels. "Those journey-proud people can bore you to death with their braggin'—not to mention their picture slides."

jower, *n. & v.* To argue; to quarrel. "Mr. Simpson and me had a jower over politics, but I don't like jawing with my neighbors."

joy-of-the-mountain, *n.* The trailing arbutus, a flower.

juberous; jubious, *adj.* Dubious; doubtful. "I'm juberous about ever'thang that lie'n jasper says."

jue, *n.* Due. "You'll git all that's jue you but not one cent more."

jughead, *n.* A jarhead; a mule.

juice harp, *n.* A jew's harp. An alleged musical instrument, juicy because it's held between the teeth while being played. The modulation of tone is produced by the varying amounts of juice available at the moment.

juke box, *n.* Nickelodeon; a music-playing box that requires coins.

juking, *v.* Going out to dance, or to have a good time at a club playing jukebox music; to go from one to another jukebox place.

juliper, *n.* [Mountain and rural] The juices and drippings from cooked meats; the Southerner's *au jus.* "If you spill the juliper, how're we gonna make gravy?"

Jul-you-ette, *n.* The "herowine" of Shakespeare's *Romeo and Juliet.*

jump, *n.* A very spirited dance for couples.

jump the broomstick. To get married; sometimes, to become engaged to be married. "Have yo' fun, boys, 'cause wunst you've jumped the broomstick, it'll be a diff'rent story."

june around. To work busily at an activity. "That house was a pigsty, but after Billie Jean juned around for a while, it looked like a million."

Juneteenth, *n.* For a long while June 19 was celebrated as Emancipation Day by Texas blacks because it wasn't until that day in 1865 that they learned of their emancipation.

Jurden; Jerdan, *n.* The old way of pronouncing the surname "Jordan."

Just cause, that's why. To a Southern female this is a full and definitive answer to anyone's "Why?"

kag, *n.* Southerners spell it k-e-g, but a great many of them pronounce it "kag."

kairseen; karseen, *n.* Kerosene; oil for the lamps of Kentucky and other points South.

keel, *v.* To end a life. "Keel, keel, keel—that's all I read about. You'd think this was Washington, D.C."

keen, *v.* A penetrating flash of the eyes. "That girl was mad as fire. She keened her eyes at me ever'time I opened my mouth."

keeping, *n.* Something held back or saved. "If you're gonna want light bread ever' whipstitch, then we gotta have us a keepin' of 'east."

keep the sifter going. [Rural and mountain] To keep enough flour in the house that there'll be enough bread to eat. "Sure cain't keep the sifter goin' if I cain't work."

Kentucky breakfast, *n.* "A big beefsteak, a quote o' buhbun, an' a houn' dawg." (If you wonder what the dog's for, he's there to eat the beefsteak.)

Kentucky kuhnul *n.* A territorial honorific, not a military title.

kernel, *n.* A small, firm lump under the skin; a hard swelling.

ketchin' a baby. Delivering a baby. "Innybody can ketch a baby—though it's usely a ketchwoman who does—but it's what to do with him aftuh he's ketched, is the problem."

ketchwoman; catchwoman, *n.* A midwife.

kick, *v.* To sting or hurt someone or something. "You keep messin' around there, one of them bees is gunna kick you."

kick the cat. To get angry. "Oh, don't pay her no never mind. She kicks the cat if you even look at her straight."

kill (a) duck dead. To wear a subject out; to finish something off. "Would you look at that empty pint! We sure killed that duck dead, didn't we?"

kilt, *v.* Murdered; gone, but not from natural causes.

kinfolks; kinpeople, *n.* (Never kin*s*folks) Why is it that Southerners seem to have more of these than Yankees do?

kissing cousin; kissin' cud'n, *n.* Any cousin you are fond enough of to kiss; all old friends who have come to be regarded as one of the family; and any longtime friend of the opposite sex that's so attractive you just have to kiss her. "During the Wah Between the States there was one moah kind of kissin' cud'n—it was inny friend who held the same political views as yore own. And that made for a heap of kissin' cud'ns!"

kittle, *n.* Kettle; tea kettle.

kittle tea, *n.* Hot water tea or cambric tea.

kiver, *n.* What you put over you when you're in bed and cold.

kiverlid, *n.* Coverlet; an old-fashioned, hand-loomed bedspread.

kiyutle, *n.* [Louisiana] A little dog.

knee baby, *n.* A baby big enough to sit on your knee, but still too little to play in the yard. [See "yard baby."]

knock-down-and-drag-out, *n.* A rowdy, brawling affair; a fight. "Boy, that was some knock-down-and-drag-out up at Seymour's last night."

knowledge box, *n.* [Mountains] The brain.

Know-Nothing Party. Sam Houston's party when he ran for governor of Texas; it was a secret and short-lived political party of the nineteenth century.

knucks, *n.* A game of marbles characterized by the unusual penalty paid by the loser: the winner gets to rap his opponent's knuckles or shoot a marble at them.

knucklebones, *n.* A pair of bones shaken in a way to carry a rhythm and used as a musical instrument.

kuhnul; colonel, *n.* **1.** An intermediate officer in the U.S. Army. **2.** A member of the nobility of Kentucky.

lackey-boy, *n.* [Mountain; old] A hired hand; an odd-job man for the farm.

ladder, *n.* **1.** What one usually hates to write but loves to receive—a letter. **2.** A run in the stockings.

laid off. Planned to or meant to. "I laid off to do it, but I just never got 'round to it."

laid up. Sick; gone to bed; infirm. "He was laid up all winter with the asthmy."

lagniappe, *n.* [Louisiana; pronounced "lan-yap"] A little something extra given to a customer by a tradesman; a small bonus; something for nothing. "When I bought the two-hundred-dollar coat, she threw in a silk scarf for lagniappe."

laig, lag, *n.* The appendage that terminates with the foot.

lamp oil; lamp ahl, *n.* Kerosene for the lamps of the America of yesteryear; coal oil.

lamp oil times. The olden days.

land-office business, *n.* A big turnover in business; lots of sales made. "Soon as our ad came out in the paper, we started doing a land-office business."

land of the trembling earth. The Okefenokee Swamp in Georgia—seven hundred square miles of wildlife and natural beauty, preserved for the sake of ecology and for the enjoyment of the public. (Yes, Yankees are admitted, too.)

land sake, for. A favorite expression of Southern women in older days. "Land sake, if that boy didn't eat ev'ry one of our biscuits!"

Lankorn, *n.* In Kentucky, where Abe Lincoln was born, that's how they said his name.

lap baby, *n.* A baby who's not yet reached the toddling stage.

larnyx, *n.* Larynx.

larrup, *n.* A blow. "His Daddy gave him a couple of good larrups across his bottom."

'lasses, *n.* Molasses; long sweetening [q.v.].

lass-go-trade; last-go-trade, *n.* Compliments exchanged between two people, with the one who initiated the exchange going last. "Boy, do I have a lass-go-trade for you!"

lassoo, *n.* Lasso.

lastiest, *adj.* The longest-lasting of all.

lasty, *adj.* Long-lasting. "The younguns' clothes you order from Sears's wish book are really lasty."

latch pin, *n.* [Old] A safety pin. "She was some pitiful youngun. I never seen her in my life that she was wearin' a pair o' shoes worth shucks, or her clothes wudn't helt together with latch pins."

lath open bread, *n.* [Mountain; old] A very "short" type of biscuit-bread that breaks into thin, flaky layers after it's baked.

latitudes of lovely languar. The South was described this way by Nathaniel P. Willis, a well-known nineteenth-century author and transplanted Yankee who had become captivated by the South. The "lovely languor," according to Willis, was one of the more compelling characteristics of the Southern belle.

lavaliered, *n.* Pre-pre-engaged. A college girl is lavaliered, then pinned, then engaged.

lavish, *n.* A plentiful amount. "That woman sure sets a lavish of food out for cump'ny."

law me, *interj.* A favorite utterance of older Southern ladies expressing consternation and surprise.

laying off, *v.* Nothing to do with horse bets or bookies; it means planning, intending. "I've been laying off to fix mah roof for over a year naow."

lay up. To lie with in the biblical sense. The expression is usually employed to describe the goings-on of an illicit affair.

leader, *n.* A tendon or muscle. "I woke up this moaning with the leaders in my neck stiff as all get-out."

lead pincil, *n.* "That sure ain't no fountain pin."

leather britches, *n.* String beans that are strung together with a darning needle and hung in a cool place to dry for winter use. After a soaking, they are cooked like fresh beans (a process adopted from the Indians).

learn, *v.* To teach. "I'm gonna learn you how to do this if it's the last thang I ever do."

leave, *n.* Let. "Leave me be, naow!"

leavins, *n.* What's left. "No, thank you, ma'am, but I don't take nobody's leavins!"

Lee, General Robert E. A major Southern diety and head of the Confederate forces in the War for Southern Independence. (At one time many Southerners were the namesakes of General Lee. By way of example: A certain dictionary writer's middle name is Lee, her mother's name was Carrie Lee, her father's first name, Lee; then she has cousins by the dozens named Lee, and an uncle whose given name was Robert E. Lee, in full.)

leggerns, *n.* Leggings.

lepud, *n.* Leopard, an animal that is famous for never changing his spots; but neither does the spotted hyena, the spotted eagle, nor the spotted bass, and do people go around talking about them?

lessee. Has nothing to do with a lease. Means "Let's see." "Lessee naow, what can we have good fah suppuh?"

lettuh. To give permission to a female. "Lettuh go, lettuh go, God bless huh!"

liberry, *n.* It has to do with books, not berries.

lible, *adj.* Likely; apt. "He's lible to fall in love if he keeps hangin' 'round that girl that way."

lickwish, *n.* A flavoring for candy and stuff; licorice.

liddle, *adj.* Little, not large.

lief, *adv.* Willingly; just as soon. "I'd as lief go as not, and a little rather."

lig, *n.* League. "You know, like the Junior Lig and the Lig of Nations."

light, *v.* To descend and rest; to come to a stopping point. "I *wish* you-all would light and come in," said the man to his friends passing by.

light bread, *n.* Yeast bread, as opposed to hot biscuits and cawn bread.

light a rag. To take off in a hurry. "When they told him his mama was coming down the street, boy, did he light a rag out o' there."

light-minded, *adj.* Foolish; without all one's marbles.

light out. Leave quickly. "Did you see her light out when she heard about the free samples they were givin' away at the A&P?"

like, *v.* To lack. "This soup likes salt and pepper."

like to. Almost. "She like to have had a fit when he winked at her."

lily-whites, *n.* The hands of a white person; especially delicate, cared-for hands. "You'll never find her with her lily-whites in a pan of dishwater."

limb-hit, *adj.* [Mountain and rural] Someone not "quite right"; mentally off. "It was plumb pitiful. One of their younguns limb-hit and another'n with a gimpy laig."

limbs, *n.* The southernmost extremities of a Southern lady.

limping Susan, *n.* An okra, rice, and chopped bacon pilau as made in South Carolina.

line, *n.* Lion, "a feeuhs jungle animal that weahs a big fuh collah, winnuh an' summuh."

linkister; also linkster and lingister, *n.* [Mountain] An interpreter for the Cherokee Indians of the Eastern Band in the Smokeys.

lint dodger, *n.* A cotton mill or textile worker; a lint head.

lint head, *n.* A lint dodger; occasionally called a "cotton tail."

lipstick lapper, *n.* A man who's fond of kissin' women; an overly ardent gentleman caller.

liquid assets, *n.* Spirits on hand; one's booze inventory. "Honey, don't you think we better check our liquid assets before the ABC store closes—see if we have enough buhbun for the weekend?" [See "ABC store."]

liquid dynamite, *n.* Raw, raw whiskey—"the kind that takes yo' breath an' puckers yo' innerds."

listen up. Pay attention. "You chi'ren quieten down now an' listen up to what I have to tell you."

lightern knot; lightern wood, *n.* Lightwood; any resinous wood used for kindling.

Little Bit, *n.* A popular nickname for a small person. "I swear, there goes Little Bit Parker with a package bigger'n she is."

Little Christmas, *n.* The epiphany—January 6. Still celebrated in eastern North Carolina and a few other areas where, sometimes, this is the principal observance of Christmas.

little colt's foot, *n.* A mountain plant: shortia.

little house, *n.* A privy.

little re-cess, *n.* [Accent on the "re"] A short recreational break in a school routine, as distinguished from "big re-cess," which is the longer period when lunch is eaten.

liver and lights. The liver and lungs from a freshly killed hog. (Cut up and stewed with seasonings, these make a favorite dish at hog-killing time.)

liver nips, *n.* [South Carolina] Beef liver, highly seasoned with onions, pepper, and other ingredients, then ground or minced.

loafers' bench, *n.* [Florida] A spot where unemployed black men sit, waiting and hoping to be picked up for a day's work.

loblolly, *n.* A lot of goo; or a big batch of unappetizing-looking food. "What is this big loblolly sitting here on the stove? I *hope* it's not our supper!"

locking eyeballs. A prolonged stare between two people. "Ah got so sick a-watchin' them lockin' eyeballs with each other that Ah just wisht he'd ask her fer a date an' git it over with."

lodge, *adj.* Of ample proportions.

lonesome-hearted, *adj.* Lonely; pensive; lonesome for a particular person. "All day long Ah was so lonesome-hearted, Ah was just on the vuhge of teahs."

long 'bout. Close to; nearly. "It was long 'bout tin o'clock whin her old cookstove started actin' up."

long bob, *n.* Describes the length of a hair styling.

long handles, *n.* Long underwear; union suit. "Ah decla-ah, he really embarrassed me when he came to the door in those ole long hannels."

long hungry, *adj.* Gluttonous. "Long Hungry Smith—he's been long hungry all his life."

long neck, *n.* A kind of bottle of beer that is taller rather than shorter, as contrasted with beer in a can.

long sweetening, *n.* Molasses and syrups, as distinguished from short sweetening, which is sugar.

lookie, *interj.* Used to call someone's attention to something. "Well, lookie here who's comin' down the road!" [Originally was "look you"]

loose, *adj.* Thin and watery; as in "loose grits."

loppered milk, *n.* A dessert made of clabber, sugar, cream, and nutmeg; bonnyclabber.

lost bread, *n.* French toast in Louisiana.

Lost Cause, the. "That War"; the Confederate Failure, as it was sometimes put.

Love and Desire. [Pronounced "Dee-zy-uh"] Two streets in New Orleans.

lovebug, *n.* The lovebug is a disease-carrying "insect" that can attack anyone at any time, but is most apt to strike its victim suddenly. The symptoms of the disease produced by the bite of this bug are many and varied, but common manifestations include: dizziness, delusions, euphoria, moodiness, dreaminess, palpitations of the heart, loss of sense of reality, fits of giggling, a sensation of floating, a tendency to star-gaze, and even a distortion of vision. (The latter helps to explain why the love object may look so much better to the one afflicted with the lovebug disease than to persons not involved.) This malady, designated L-O-V-E, is one of the oldest known to man—*and* woman—maybe more ancient even than arthritis, and like that affliction, is one of the most stubborn to treat. The duration of the disease can be anywhere from a day or so to many years, and the methods of treatment are nearly as diverse as are the symptoms. However, in severely persistent cases, there are only two sure cures—time or marriage—and sometimes it takes both.

love drops, *n.* [North Carolina] Not an aphrodisiac, but a type of cookie.

love feast, *n.* Just the opposite of what one might think; a religious service where food is served and eaten in an atmosphere of brotherly love. The Moravians of North Carolina are well-known for these observances.

love (someone's) neck. To hug someone's neck. "Come here, you purty lil' thang, an' love Grampa's neck."

love hole, *n.* A deep hole or a rut in a road that would cause a buggy to lurch and—they hoped—would throw two lovers together.

loveliest garden in the world. What the famous author John Galsworthy said about Magnolia Gardens in South Carolina (Near Charleston).

low, *v.* [Short for "allow"] To declare as one's opinion or intention. "He 'lowed as how he was gonna paint the barn tomarrah."

low cotton, in. In a depressed state; in bad circumstances.

low-down, *adj.* Common; trashy. "You cain't git much more low-down than them Gibbses. So common. And their grammar! I ain't never heard nobody murder the English language like they do."

low-rate, *v.* To slander, denounce, or depreciate. "I'm damned tired of you goin' around low-rating us, you hear that? Saying that Lester and me is common and that we're always pickin' a fight and don't pay our debts."

lug, *v.* To transport or carry an object with difficulty. (Southern women seldom simply move, take, or carry an object. Poor things, they are so delicate and tender that they have to lug everything—even a postcard from the post office—and *especially* if there's a man anywhere around.)

Lunchburg, *n.* The doughboys of World War I called Lynchburg, Va., this because of the Red Cross–sponsored canteens at the local railroad station.

lung fever, *n.* [Old] Pneumonia.

lusty, *adj.* [Old] Pregnant. "One babe in her arms and lusty with another."

Luziana, *n.* That's not the way Southerners spell it, but sure as shooting it's the way some of them say it.

machine, *n.* [Old] An automobile; a car. "I was proud as punch when Pa came driving up in our new machine."

mad. 1. *adj.* A word that a lot of Southerners didn't know there was a better one for—"angry"—until we learned it in school. **2.** *n.* Anger; temper. "Don't let your mad get the best of you."

Madison, Dolly. Truly the very first American hostess with the mostest. And a Southerner, of course.

magnolia cum laude. [Used facetiously] The most coveted honor that can be awarded a "Suthun" belle. "When it comes to those wide-eyed looks an' winnin' ways, she had already graduated magnolia cum laude before she was fourteen."

magruduses, *n.* Ingredients. "Be sure you got all the magruduses in that cake before you start mixing it."

mah, *adj.* The possessive form of the pronoun "Ah." "Ah picked up mah hat an' mah coat an' Ah lit out of that place."

main drag, *n.* The main street of a town; the street where all the action is. "Anne and I got all dressed up, then we drove up and down the main drag."

make light of. To make fun of; to ridicule. "He rilly likes to make light of people; he tries to make ever'body feel like two cents."

make (your) manners. To behave yourself; take care of the amenities. "Now, listen here, you be sure to make your manners when you get there."

make over. To make a fuss about someone or something. "I don't trust people who go out of their way to make over me."

male Hershey bar, *n.* [1930s] The kind with almonds.

mammy, *n.* "What ev'ry Suthun girl had—rich or poah—(according to *her*) when she gets far enough away from home."

mango, *n.* **1.** A bell pepper in Ohio. **2.** A tropical fruit known for its exotic flavor and abundant juice. (A person newly introduced to the mango asks an old Florida resident the best way to handle the juicy morsel. "Get a knife, disrobe, jump in the bathtub, peel, eat, then shower.")

manly state, in the. "In the spring when a young man's fancy lightly turns to thoughts of love"—and beyond—he's in "the manly state."

mared, *adj.* Not single, for better or for worse.

Marelan, *n.* Maryland, the state in which, it's said, Betsy Ross made our first flag.

mare's pee, *n.* Uncouth for beer.

marrying book, *n.* The bible.

marry North. One of the graver transgressions of a Southerner against his or her heritage, especially after the Civil War. "Shh! If you even mention huh name when huh fathuh's around, he gets in a reg'lar quivuh. Haven't you hud? On huh way back from Richmond the poor girl plum lost her head ovuh a Yankee, an' before you could say Jack Robinson, she married Nawth."

marvels, *n.* [Mountain and juvenile] Marbles.

mash, *v.* To press. Charming Southern gentleman to lady who stands between him and control panel in crowded elevator: "Would you be so kind as to mash six for me?"

Mason-Dixon Line. "The dividing line between cold bread and hot biscuit," said Governor Bob Taylor of old Kentucky; and "the dividing line between the men and the boys," said someone else. (And everyone knows on which side of the line the men were).

'mater, *n.* Love apple; tomato. "Nothin' better than a bacon an' 'mater samich with lots o' may'naise."

mayan, *n.* The correlative of "woman."

maypop, *n.* A field flower that children love to find because of the loud noise they make when squashed.

mean, *adj.* Mischievous. "He's a cute youngun, but he's mean as can be."

meanness, *n.* An epithet that means "the meanest one," or meanness personified. "Hey, Meanness, you're doin' ever'thing you can to make me mizzable, aren't you?"

measuring worm, *n.* When this tiny worm is found on clothing, because of the consistent way it inches itself along, it is said to be measuring the garment. "Look, there's a measuring worm on you, and if you don't knock it off, that means you'll get a new dress."

meat, *v.* [Old] To furnish with meat. "That big hawg, all butchered up, will near 'bout meat us all winter."

Mechlenburg Declaration of Independence. Written in Mechlenburg County, N.C., May 31, 1775, declaring that colony's independence from England over a year before the national proclamation of July 4, 1776.

meddling, *v.* Rummaging in something that doesn't concern you. "Why don't you quit meddlin' in my dresser drawers?"

meller, *adj.* Ripe, sweet, and/or soft; mellow. "If you take a bunch of good, solid pears from the tree, wrap 'em carefully in newspaper, pack 'em in a box, put 'em in a cool, dark place, they'll be meller and perfect for Christmas."

memory box, *n.* [Mountain] One's memory. "My memory box sure ain't what it wunst wuz."

Memphis, *n.* "Where the Old South and the New South Meet," where W. C. Handy wrote the first blues, where Elvis cut his first record, the biggest city in TINN-e-see, and a "Place of Good Abode."

Memphis martini, *n.* Gin with a wad of cotton in it. [Fred Allen]

mere, *n.* A looking glass.

Merry, *n.* A girl's name; as in Merry Pickford, Merry Tyler Moore, and Merry Jane.

mess, *n.* **1.** Enough of a particular food for a meal. "Gracious, I sure wish we had us a big mess o' turnip sallit." **2.** A character whose behavior is unusual, or who is a big pack of foolishness. "He's one big mess—he keeps us laughin' all the time."

Methdis, *n.* A member of the Methodist church.

Methodist pallet, *n.* A crude makeshift bed made on the floor.

Methusalum, *n.* Methuselah, a biblical character who lived to an overripe old age *(969 years old!).*

Mi-am-uh, *n.* An early pronunciation of "Miami," and still heard from older residents.

middlebuster, *n.* [Old] A double moldboard plough.

middlin', *adj.* So-so; about midway. "He's feelin' fair to middlin'."

middlins, *n.* Pieces of fatback (pork) with only touches of lean.

middlin' meat, *n.* Pork fatback with a streak of lean.

might could. Might be able to. "I might could go if I had me a couple more dollars."

minamal wage, *n.* The smallest wage the government allows.

mincy, *adj.* **1.** Ailing. "My ma has been kinda mincy all week." **2.** Picky in eating. "I declare, she's such a mincy eater, just watching her makes me lose my appetite."

mind, *v.* Means to remember. "Do you mind when was the last time we saw each other?"

mine, *n.* Brain; mental capacity. "He had one of the finest mines the world has ever known."

mingitis, *n.* Meningitis, a serious disease affecting the spinal cord.

minie ball, *n.* A rifle bullet much used during the War of Northern Aggression.

minnie, *n.* [Louisiana] A cat or kitten. [From Cajun *minette*]

mint julep, *n.* A spirituous drink, first made in the South. It consists of crushed fresh mint, a generous amount of bourbon, sugar, and lots of shaved ice, and ideally, is served in a silver cup. (To truly enjoy a mint julep, you need a magnolia tree in bloom, a palmetto fan, and a spacious verandah that faces South.)

minyou, *n.* Menu, a printed card that gives you fair warning of how much the vittles in a restaurant are gonna set you back.

mirate, *v.* [Uneducated and humorous] To show admiration. Like this: "Aftuh Ah'd mirated ovuh ev'ry stitch she had on, she was in a bettuh humor." [Frances E. Rose]

mirliton, *n.* What Louisianians call the chayote or the vegetable pear—a kind of squash.

Miss Agnes. A phrase used as an interjection to show surprise and relief, such as: "Oooh, Miss Agnes!"

Miss Anne, *n.* [Black] A general term that blacks used (widely at one time) among themselves to mean any white woman.

mis-chee-vous, *adj.* [Accent on the "chee"] Naughty; impish.

Missippi, *n.* *Maybe* Southerners get all four *s*'s in there. (Perhaps it's just difficult for the listener to detect them.)

Miss Priss, *n.* A title, often affectionate, given to a female who is being a bit too prim or acting fussily feminine. "Well, little Miss Priss! Look at her, all dressed up and purty as Princes Di."

mister, *n.* Husband. "Howdy, Mis Crutchfield. And how's your mister feelin' today?"

Mister Charlie, *n.* [Black] Any white man, or a particular one; not used in talking to a white man, but about him.

mistote, *v.* [Rural and uneducated] To miscarry a pregnancy.

misty-moist, *adj.* Damp weather. Like this: "It was so misty-moist outside, it made my new permanent fuzz up."

miyun, *n.* 1,000,000.

Miz, *n.* The title of a Southern married lady. (And we used it way before women's lib.)

Miz Dr.; Mrs. Doctor, *n.* The widely used title of a physician's wife in the early part of the twentieth century. ". . . And now I'd like to present to you, the president of our organization, Mrs. Dr. Best."

mizeries, miseries, *n.* Troubles, physical and otherwise. "She's really got the mizeries today."

mizery, *n.* Pain. "Man, I've got a mizery in my back that just won't quit."

mizzuble, *adj.* Feeling, or being, in an absolutely wretched condition.

mock. 1. *v.* To copy; to imitate or impersonate. "Mom, he keeps mocking me—copies everything I do and say." **2.** *n.* Mark. "On your mock, get set, go!"

mommick. 1. *n.* A mess; in complete disorder. "When she got through bakin' that ole cake, my kitchen was a mommick." **2.** *v.* [South Carolina] To mess something up; to disarrange a thing. "Don't you see you're botherin' that cat? Why don't you quit mommicking his fur that way?"

monkey blood, *n.* [Cajun] Mercurochrome.

mo'om pitcher, *n.* A picture show; movie.

Moon Pie, *n.* A very popular "store-boughten" cakelike sweet. A Moon Pie is not a pie at all, but a kind of confection consisting of three round vanilla-flavored cakelike cookies, held together by a marshmallow filling and covered—top, sides, and bottom—with a sweet milk-chocolate coating. Extremely popular in the South, these goodies are sometimes called Sweetie Pies in other parts of the country.

moonshine, *n.* The made-in-the-woods brand of corn liquor. "There's three kinds of moonshine: the hugging kind, the kind that makes you sing, and the kind that gives you fifteen fights to a pint." [Ray Hicks]

mooth, *n.* Mouth. A Virginian might tell you that eating too many black walnuts will give you a "soah mooth."

mor'n. A compound word meaning "more than." "Ah like cawfee mor'n tea."

morn gloam, *n.* [Mountain] The first light of morning.

morphadite, *n.* Hermaphrodite.

mosey, *v.* To move lazily and aimlessly about. "So aftuh we ate ouah grits 'n eggs we got dressed an' moseyed on down to the postawfis."

mosquito hawk, *n.* A dragonfly; also called "snake doctor."

mother-in-law of the army. San Antonio, because of its huge military establishment. "As everyone knows, wherevuh there's a lot of sojers, there's gotta be a whole heap of roe-mance—'speshly in the roe-mantic South."

mottah, *n.* Martyr, one who suffers gladly for posterity; a glorified masochist.

mought, *v.* [Uneducated] Might. "He mought do it, then he mought not."

mountain caviar, *n.* A steamed cabbage dish that is made with New Coke in place of water. (This recipe was originated by Mrs. Ham [Faye] Matthews of Chalybeate Springs, N.C.)

mountain dew, *n.* Moonshine.

mountain oysters, *n.* The testes of a hog or sheep when used for food; said to taste like oysters when fried.

mountain trumpet, *n.* A whittled cow's horn that you blow like a trumpet.

mountain wine, *n.* Said to be made of fishberries and jimson-weed—a revolting mixture—and drunk by people who can't afford a better alcoholic drink (This is probably a tall tale from mountain lore).

mouth organ, *n.* The harmonica.

mount'n; moun'n, *n.* Mountain in the "mount'ns."

mourner's bench, *n.* A seat near the church pulpit for sinners who are especially concerned about their souls and are ready to be saved.

much obliged. Often used for "thank you." "Much obliged for this fine suppuh you served us."

mudbugs, *n.* Crawfish in Louisiana.

mudcat, *n.* **1.** A flathead catfish. **2.** A nickname for a Mississippian.

muddle, *n.* A mess of a stew utilizing freshly caught fish, usually made by a man and eaten near the scene of the crime—the riverbank. Besides fish, it includes ingredients like salt pork, tomatoes, onions, and cracker crumbs.

mudhead, *n.* A Tennesseean.

mufflelata, *n.* [New Orleans] A large po'-boylike sandwich, containing a variety of meats and cheese served on Italian bread.

mule; mulekick, *n.* White lightning; rotgut.

muley cow, *n.* A hornless cow.

mulligrubs, *n.* The blues. "Just let her fail to hear from her boyfriend and she's got the mulligrubs all day."

mumbly-peg, *n.* A game played with a jackknife by throwing it and trying to make it stick in the ground.

musheroon; mushyroom, *n.* Mushroom. "You better be keerful. Them things can kill you if you get holt of the pizen kind."

mushmelon; mushmillion, *n.* [Mountain and rural] Cantaloupe. "Out in the country they used to slice up a mushmelon and serve it like a vegetable."

mushrat, *n.* Muskrat.

mush-tash, *n.* An adornment for the upper lip; a lipwig. "It's not for straining mush; it's a disguise for the upper lip."

my-naise; may-naise; ma-nez, *n.* Mayonnaise, what no Southern sandwich is complete without.

nabel, *n.* The navel, the core of one's being.

nacherly, *adv.* According to the "laws of nacher."

nair, *adj.* Narrow, not wide.

nanner, *n.* A yellow fruit, much relished in the raw and sometimes used in cooking; as in, "nanner puddin'."

naow, *adv.* At the present time.

nap, *n.* Nape. ". . . by the nap of the neck."

narrow face, *n.* A chicken. "I'll boil us up a pot o' beans and fry a couple of narrow faces for suppuh."

nary, *adj.* [Uneducated; old] Neither one nor the other. "Nary a youngun showed up for little Mary's birthday."

nasty, *n.* Visciousness; meanness. "That woman's sure got a lot o' nasty in her."

Natchez Trace, *n.* A once popular thoroughfare running from New Orleans to Nashville, a distance of about seven hundred miles.

navigate, *v.* To direct oneself on a course of action. "He was so pixilated from all that old Maude he'd been drinkin', he couldn't hardly navigate."

Nawfok, *n.* Norfolk, a seaport town in Virginia.

N'Awlins, *n.* The largest and most important city in Louisiana, and possibly the most charming and seductive city in the United States. Or, as Shakespeare *almost* said it, "Age cannot wither her, nor custom stale her infinite variety, other cities cloy the appetites they feed, but she makes hungry where most she satisfies." (Two notes of interest: Considering its size, New Orleans has the best restaurants in the country; and the Vieux Carré—

the old part of the city—is truly what it has been called, the "Little Paris of the New World.")

neah, *adj.* Near. (The Southern pronunciation of the word "near" makes sense, because it actually comes from the Old English *neah. Neah, nearra, niehst* of Old English became our nigh, near, next.)

necessary, *n.* An old word for privy.

needcessity, *n.* [Mountain] Necessity.

nekkid, *adj.* Naked, the state of undress; wearing only one's birthday suit.

Nero, My God, to Thee. Many a small child of the South had no idea that the correct word was "nearer."

nervis, *adj.* That's when you feel all-overish, skittish.

newasunce, *n.* Nuisance. Something annoying; a pest.

newfangled, *adj.* New-fashioned; fancy or "far-out." "Her and her newfangled ways!"

new ground, *n.* Ground recently plowed and ready for cultivation.

Newnited States, *n.* Used facetiously to define the United States after "That War" ended.

nice-nasty, *adj.* Overly nice; trying to be nice but making things worse. "Land sakes, was she nice-nasty! Her younguns always looked clean, but I swear to you, I've seen that woman wipe their noses with her dishrag."

nigh. 1. *adv.* Nearly. As the gracious old mountaineer said to his guest: "He'p yourse'f to the vittles, and take, take! Take blame nigh all." **2.** *adj.* Nearest. "Take the nigh road, go about a mile, and you'll see the old place." [Barbara Heck]

night to howl. Night to turn loose—to have a big time. (Perhaps this comes from the excited howling of dogs during a hunt.) "Ev'ry Sat'dy he gets dressed up and goes out, 'cause that's his night to howl."

ninny pie, *n.* The milk a baby gets from his mother's breast; loosely, the milk a baby is fed, from breast or bottle.

nip and tuck. With rapid alternations of favorable and unfavorable aspects. "Everything was always nip and tuck with those people, broke half the time and all sorts of bad luck. I was always scared they were going to starve to death."

no-count, *adj.* Worthless; good for nothin'. ". . . a sorry, no-count man."

no flies on. Being "with it"; having what it takes. "Boy, that Sarah Jean Jenkins sure don't have no flies on her."

nohow, *adj.* [A corruption of "anyhow"] "He don't have no sense nohow."

nome. A compound word meaning "no, ma'am." "Nome, no moah fah me—Ah've had a gracious plenny."

norate, *v.* To gossip; to spread rumors or scandal. "Ah'm tired of you norating around that Jess and Ah don't get along."

North Carolina caviar, *n.* The roe of the menhaden, a fish.

northside manners. If you observe this kind of manners in "Chollston," S.C., most likely you were to the manner born. (It all had to do with the unique architecture of the lovely town houses, most of which were close together, with their piazzas on the side facing south. "Northside manners" refers to the restraint practiced by the residents in not looking out their north-facing windows to spy on the activities of their neighbors.)

not right. Not bright; mentally off. "You only had to look at that poor gawking fellow to tell he was not right."

no never-mind. No attention; no concern. "Forget him! He sure paid you no never-mind, so why worry?"

nubbin, *n.* A small or imperfect ear of corn.

nubbin stretcher, *n.* Rain that makes the corn grow.

nucular bum, *n.* Nuclear bomb. "He looks like he wouldn't move even if somebody planted a nucular bum under him."

nun's sigh, *n.* A soufflé-type fritter that's "as light as a nun's sigh," first made by the Creoles of Louisiana.

nuss, *n.* Nurse, an angel of mercy in old Appalachia.

oahduh, *n.* What we try to bring out of chaos. As Judge Irvin said during the Watergate hearings: "Oahduh in the coatroom (courtroom)!"

oatenmeal, *n.* "Ver' good with milk an' sugah."

obleege, *v.* In days gone by, "oblige" was most often pronounced this way.

oddosity, *n.* An oddosity is more than odd; it is also a curiosity.

ofay, *n.* A white person to a black person.

okrie, *n.* Okra, a green and sometimes slimy vegetable.

Old Christmas, *n.* Until 1752, when the English calendar was revised, Christmas was celebrated on January 6. In some places in the South it is still observed, especially in Rodanthe, N.C., where Old Christmas has been celebrated for over two centuries.

old-lady freckles, *n.* Age spots. (As one might guess, these discolorations of the skin were given this chauvinistic name *before* women's lib—and it was probably a man who did it.)

old maid, *n.* If you wind up with the last of something, that makes you an old maid. "Uh oh, that was the last biscuit on the plate, so you're the old maid!"

old Satan's parfume, *n.* Mountain dew; moonshine.

old sour, *n.* A fermented Key lime and salt mixture, much utilized as a food enhancer by the South Florida cooks of years past.

ole, *adj.* Old, a term of affection, of pride, of tenderness, of approbation—a word indispensable to most Southerners. "Look at Ole Glory flyin' there!" "Well, lookie here, if this isn't my ole friend, Gladys." "These are the best ole beans I ever tasted."

on account of. Because; the reason why. "It's on account of what he said that I had to bless him out [q.v.]."

one, *n.* "One" is used to mean "one or the other." "You or Benson one has to do it."

one more. The "more" adds intensity to the word "one." "Man, oh man, that was one more purty girl I saw you with yesterday."

oot; ou-oot, *adv.* In a direction away from a Virginia interior. "If you go oot of this hoose, you'll be punished suhveahly."

opsit, *adj.* Across from; opposite.

opry, *n.* A drama that is sung instead of spoken, in which the male leading character keeps yelling, " 'No! No! No!' in a foreign language, all the time he's holdin' up the female star, who is slowly but surely sangin' herse'f to death."

ornery, *adj.* Hard to get along with; cantankerous.

ouah, *adj.* The possessive form of "we."

oughta. Ought to. "I felt like I oughta go for groshries, but Katie Marie said she'd go for me."

outen, *prep.* Out of. "You're not goin' outen this house till you learn some manners."

outen the light. [Georgia] Turn the light off. "Will you outen that light so I can go to sleep?"

outhouse, *n.* The little house behind the big house that has no plumbing.

out-magnolia, *v.* To be more Southern than. "No one can out-magnolia Betty Jean Baumgarner, speshly when she gets around a good-lookin' man. My lord, the sugah an' molasses just drippin' from her tongue till you'd think Scarlett O'Hara was theah in the flesh."

outside child; outsider, *n.* [Old-timey] A child born out of wedlock.

overhalls, *n.* A type of men's work clothes; spelled "overalls."

owl's head pistol. A cheap, inferior pistol.

oysterizer, *n.* Osterizer, one of those small electrical appliances that whips, beats, or chops food.

pack of foolishness. A lot of nonsense; someone who is given to jokes. "Get out of heah! You're nothin' but a pack of foolishness."

pah, *n.* Pie. "You want apple, cherry, lemon meringue, or a small piece of all three?"

paid woman, *n.* A prostitute. "Yes, sirree, he sure disgraced himself when he fell in love with that paid woman."

palate, *n.* Pilot, one who flies through the air with the greatest of help from aeronautical technology.

palpitators, *n.* Enterprising Southern women—*flat* women, we're talking about—wore falsies over a century ago. But bein' smart *and* being Southern (one and the same, of course), they chose the more poetic name "palpitators."

panther sweat, *n.* Rotgut whiskey.

Papa Noel, *n.* [Louisiana] Santa Claus.

paralyzed oath, *n.* The way some Texans swear to something, a bit insincerely perhaps. "Ah'll take a paralyzed oath that Ah'll nevuh take anothuh drank o' likker long as I live!" (Apparently the speaker hopes for a short life.)

parbreak, *v.* [Mountain] To vomit.

pareboil, *v.* Yankees parboil; Southerners pareboil.

Paris of the West. New Orleans.

pass and repass. To exchange only the amenities with someone. "We don't really know each other that well. Just pass and repass when we meet."

passel, *n.* A considerable number. ". . . 'bout ten hound dogs and a whole passel of younguns."

pass howdy. An exchange of greetings. "Even though we've never been introduced, we always pass howdy when we run across each other."

pass the time of day. To exchange a greeting and maybe a bit of news.

pass words. Verbally expressed hostility between people. "Ah'm mad as I can be at Mary Lee, but Ah'm not about to lower myself by passing words with her."

pastorium, *n.* A Protestant parsonage.

pattren, *n.* A pattern.

paunch, *n.* Punch, the drink of choice at "poddies an' weddin' receptions."

paw-paw, *n.* An old name for "papaya."

pea-can, *n.* A nut, not a vessel.

peacemaker, *n.* An oyster loaf (sandwich) that New Orleans husbands who were "tardy" in getting home took to their wives as a peace offering.

peach leather, *n.* A confection, made of fresh peach pulp and sugar; it is cooked, then dried in the sun. (The original idea is said to have come from the Indians of North Carolina.)

peach tree tea; peach tree medicine. A whipping administered with a switch from the peach tree.

pea popping, *n.* A gathering where the people shell peas in a partylike atmosphere.

peart, *adj.* Spirited; pert. "Sallie Ann looked right peart after Doc Morton dosed her up good."

pearten, *v.* To brighten up and become more sprightly.

peckerwood, *n.* A woodpecker.

peck on. To knock lightly, as at a door. "I pecked on her door, but she musta been out."

peculiar institution, *n.* Negro slavery in the United States was designated as this by plantation owner John C. Calhoun in 1830. (Too bad he didn't find it "disgraceful" as well, and fight to end it.)

p-doodle, *n.* Nothing or next to nothing. "You don't know p-doodle about playin' cards."

peek-through, *n.* [Louisiana] A peephole.

peeper, *n.* A frog that makes a peeping sound.

Pemberton, John Styth. He was an Atlanta pharmacist, and he made the first "Co'-Cola" syrup in 1886. He mixed this ambrosia in a three-legged iron pot in his own backyard and used an oar for a stirrer. It was first dispensed in its concentrated form as a tonic for nerves and stomach disorders, then became popular as a crackerjack cure for hangovers. A few years later some blessed soul added carbonated water to the salutary tonic and our revered Coca-Cola was born.

pendercitis, *n.* Inflammation of the appendix. "You keep swallerin' them grape seeds, you'll come down with pendercitis sure as you're settin' there a-chompin'."

Pepsi, *n.* A big Pepsi, one of the first belly washers [q.v.] to come on the market; it engendered many a Pepsi-Cola loyalist in the South.

pester, *v.* To bother persistently. "If you don't quit pestering me, there'll be no pitcher show for you this Sat'dy."

petticoat mirror, *n.* A cheval glass; a long, free-standing mirror necessary in the old days for inspecting one's petticoats.

phlegm dispenser, *n.* A toddy or eye-opener, especially first thing in the morning. "Ahem!" said the old Kentucky gentleman as he set his glass down on the breakfast table. "Theah's nothin' in the world like buhbun to cleah the throat *or* the brain, is theah?"

piazza, *n.* [Pronounced "pee-AH-za"] A porch in Charleston, S.C.

piccolo, *n.* A jukebox.

pick up. To gain weight. "You're jes' nicely filled out naow, but if you pick up inny moah, you're gunna be too fleshy."

piddle-diddle, *v.* To spend time aimlessly. "He'll piddle-diddle all day if you don't keep after him."

piddling, *v.* Messing around, accomplishing nothing.

pieback job, *n.* [Georgia; Florida] An easy, "sweet" job. "He's as lazy as a worm-eaten hound dog. He wouldn't even take a pieback job, no matter what it paid."

piece, *n.* An indefinite distance; a short distance. "He lives down the road a piece."

piece around. Get a little something from here, there, or wherever. "I didn't cook a thing yesterday. Just pieced around whenever I got hungry."

pieded, *adj.* [Old] Of variegated coloring. "She thought that little pieded pony was the purtiest creature God ever put on this earth."

pie plant, *n.* Rhubarb; not a fight, but an edible plant esteemed for pie-making.

piggin, *n.* A wooden vessel shaped like a pail, with a stave or two extending upward to serve as handles.

pig stand, *n.* A place to buy and eat barbecue.

pigtail stew, *n.* A concoction of pigtails, ears, feet, and sometimes spareribs and liver, all stewed up with salt and lots of pepper.

pilau; pilaf; purloo, *n.* [South Carolina and deep South] A rice dish, made with meat, seafood (or both), onions, sometimes other vegetables, and various seasonings. Very good and extremely popular.

piller, *n.* Pillow.

pin, *n.* Pen. "There are ballpoint pins and pigpins."

pincil, *n.* "What you write a lettuh with if you don't have a pin."

pinder, *n.* A goober pea, ground nut, ground pea, monkey nut, pindal, Indian earth-nut, peanut, or pinder.

pine bark stew. A fish stew made in South Carolina. (During the Revolutionary War when seasonings were not available, allegedly this was flavored instead by the tender roots of a pine tree and cooked over a pine-bark fire: hence its name.)

pīney, *n.* The peony.

pinto beans; pintoes, *n.* The favorite dried bean of North Carolina and some other parts of the South. (More beans than potatoes are eaten in North Carolina, and little did the older North Carolinians know that they were being brought up on a food with such an exotic name: *frijole.*)

pipginny, *n.* [Georgia] A pimple.

Piscopalian, *n.* A member of the Protestant "Piscopal" Church.

pitched off. Irate. "Ma got pitched off at Pa for layin' out all night an' gamblin'."

pitcher, *n.* Picture, what you take with a "camry."

pitcher show, *n.* Moving pictures.

pit-too-ee, *n.* [North Carolina; old] A chew of tobacco when it's wet from being chewed.

pixilated, *adj.* Drunk, or half-drunk.

pizen, *n.* [Old] Poison. "You call this moonshine? I call it pizen."

place, *n.* A small imperfection; a pimple or sore spot. "I see you have a place on your face. Are you bilious or did you scratch yourself or something?"

played out. Exhausted; worn out. "He's plum played out—working in the field in ninety-five-degree weather is enough to kill a horse, much less a man."

play-purty; play-pretty, *n.* A child's toy.

play the dozens. [Black] To slander or insult someone's parents. "Don't you come 'round here playin' them dozens on me. My mama better'n yo' mama inny day."

pleasure, *v.* To give pleasure. "It sure would pleasure me if you'd come visit us."

plague, *v.* To pester, annoy, or worry. "He was always plaguing her with threats of joining the army."

plum(b), *adv.* Downright; utterly. "These beans are plum good when you eat 'em with corn bread and lots of chow chow."

plum and nearly. Shortened version of "plum out o' town and nearly out o' the country." "Mr. Ben's new house is nice, but, my Lord, is it plum and nearly!"

plumgranite, *n.* Some Southerners mess "pomegranate" up this way, but a lot of Yankees have another way of bungling it: "pom-a-grant," they say.

plunder, *n.* [Old] Belongings of all kinds; baggage. "Lordy mercy, when I opened the door, there was Uncle George and all his plunder piled up on our doorstep."

poach, *n.* [Georgia; South Carolina] Porch, what you sit on when the day's work is done; a verandah.

po' boy; poor boy, *n.* A sandwich of heroic proportions as made in and around "New Awlins," a big feast of delectables, stuffed between prodigious lengths of crusty French bread. Submarines, hoagies, heroes, grinders—compared to po' boys, all these other complete-meal sandwiches are "po' eatin', we gah-ron-tee."

pocket handkerchief, *n.* A handkerchief.

pocket piece, *n.* [Florida] A half-pint bottle of whiskey; a bottle just right to fit in a man's back pocket.

pocosin, *n.* A swamp or marsh in parts of the South.

poison ivory, *n.* Poison ivy.

poke. 1. *n.* Any kind of bag; a paper sack. **2.** *n.* Pork; as in "poke roasts" and "poke chops." **3.** *v.* To dawdle; to move in a lazy way.

poke sallit; poke salad, *n.* The green sprouts of the pokeweed, cooked like turnip salad and said to act like a tonic on one's body.

poke stalks, *n.* Cooked and served like asparagus.

pokey, *n.* The calaboose; the jailhouse.

pokin beans, *n.* Pork and beans.

po-lice; pleece, *n.* [Accent on the "po"] If you pilfer, plunder, or drive drunk, one of these is likely to take you to jail.

polker, *n.* Poker, stud or draw.

pomegranate rattle, *n.* In olden days rattles for babies were made by drying pomegranates until the seeds rattled when shaken.

pon, *v.* To pawn. "They got so hard up she had to pon ev'ry piece of jew'ry she owned."

pond chicken, *n.* A big frog, because its hind legs when fried remind us of fried chicken.

ponder, *v.* To think about; contemplate. "I'd like to ponder over that some—have to study my mind 'fore I make a decision like that."

pone, *n.* **1.** Corn bread shaped in an oval. **2.** A lump or swelling.

Pontalbo, Baroness. The baroness, rumored to be the daughter of a nun, built an elegant structure in New Orleans that was said to be the first apartment house in the country. The building, still in excellent condition, has been in continuous use since 1850. Fronting on two different streets, the apartments overlook the Mississippi on one side and charming Jackson Square Park on the other.

pooched out. Distended. "She'd look right nice if she didn't have that pooched-out stomach."

poor-do, *n.* **1.** A measly something. "You're welcome to stay and eat with us if you can make out with poor-do." **2.** [Mountain] Scrapple.

poor man's chicken. Salt pork dipped in cornmeal and fried.

poor mouth. To plead poverty. "He was always crying poor mouth."

poppet, *n.* [Old] Doll.

popskull, *n.* Rotgut whiskey.

porch baby, *n.* One who's not yet old enough to be allowed in the yard alone.

pore, *adj.* The opposite of rich.

pork chopper, *n.* One who is put on a payroll as a favor, or in return for past services to a politician.

possum, *n.* What a surprise to a Southerner when he grows up to learn that the correct spelling is "opossum."

possum-poor, *adj.* That's when one is so poor, he's reduced to eating possum.

posy, *n.* A flower, or a bunch of flowers. "He never went courtin' without a posy for his girl."

potion, *n.* A part or a share; a serving of something.

pot likker; pot liquor, *n.* The liquid left in the pot after cooking vegetables, mainly greens. It's probably the only liquor in the South that's nonalcoholic, full of vitamins, good for you, and about as well liked as the other kind. It's great for drinking straight and perfect for dunking corn bread.

pound, *v.* To have a party at which each guest brings a pound of food for the honoree. "Soon as they move into their new house, we'll have to have a pounding."

pout, *v.* To punish someone by pouting. "After our little fuss, danged if that woman didn't pout me for two days."

President of Texas. It seems that Texas was too proud to start out with a mere governor; they wanted a president. General Sam Houston became their first, in 1836, and for a while they even had their own navy.

pressing club, *n.* For years in the South dry cleaning establishments were known as pressing clubs (no membership fee required).

presyterian, *n.* A bourbon highball that became popular in the 1950s. It was a shot of the South's favorite booze—bourbon—mixed with half ginger ale and half club soda.

prespiration, *n.* Genteel sweat.

pretty-by-night, *n.* A flower, the four-o'clock.

privy, *n.* An outhouse; the backhouse.

Professional Southerner, *n.* A Professional Southerner is a lot of things—none of them admirable and all of them boring. It can be anyone from the redneck who belches three times to each can of beer and who sports a Confederate flag on the bumper of his pickup, to the ultrarefined old gentlewoman who can't wait to tell you about being a descendant of one of the founders at Jamestown, and about her great-grandmother who was a "chahtuh membuh of the Daughtuhs of the American Revolution."

projeck, *v.* To mess around with; to bother a thing. "Listen, you're not to projeck with my personal propitty, you hear me?"

protracted meeting, *n.* A church revival that lasts for an extended period of time—a matter of days.

proud, *adj.* Happy or pleased. "Why, I'm right proud to see you!"

p-turkey, *n.* Practically nothing. "I near talked myself to death tryin' to entertain that woman, and she has yet to even say p-turkey to me."

puddle up, *v.* To be about to cry. "Good Gawd A-mighty, you can't say boo to that youngun that she dudn't puddle up."

puff, *v.* To swell with anger; to pout from indignation. ". . . sitting there all puffed up—mad as an old wet hen."

pulley bone, *n.* The wishbone of a fowl.

pull in your lip. A command to someone who's pouting.

pull-pit, *n.* Pulpit, the place from which the preacher delivers his sermon.

punkin, *n.* **1.** Pumpkin, and until a relatively short time ago, you wouldn't have heard a second "p" in a carload of Southern pumpkins. **2.** A playful word for a young child's buttocks.

punkin whiskey, *n.* A pumpkin stuffed with sugar, sealed, and left to ferment is said to produce "punkin whiskey."

pure-d satisfaction. Complete satisfaction. "I did it for the pure-d satisfaction of it."

purely, *adv.* Simply, or completely. "He just purely loved his grits an' gravy better'n anything."

purt nigh. Pretty near. "He purt nigh ate that whole damn chicken."

purty, *adj.* Pretty. (It's difficult for many Southerners not to transpose the *r* in that word.)

purty, *n.* Something pretty or of value. "I wouldn't take a purty for what my teacher said about me."

purty (pretty) in the face. "I can't say much for her shape, but she's right purty in the face."

purty up. To make a thing look better.

push, *n.* A gang; a crowd. "You mean that whole push is comin' here for suppuh?"

putt; put, *v.* Many Southerners like to rhyme this word with "hut." It means to bring an object to a place or a position. "Putt it there!" said the Rebel as he extended his hand.

put on. 1. *v.* To put on airs. **2.** *n.* Put-on; one who puts on airs. "She makes me sick. She's the biggest put-on I have ever seen in my life."

put-up sandwiches, *n.* Made-in-advance sandwiches.

pyore, *adj.* [Mountain; old] Pure, unsullied, flawless. ". . . as pyore as the driven snow."

quake and quail. To shake in one's shoes; to cower.

Q

quaker gun, *n.* A dummy gun or cannon, made of a log or some such object, placed and made to look from a distance like artillery; so-called because of the Quakers' opposition to war. (These were used with great success by the Confederates, especially by General Joseph E. Johnston at Centreville in July 1861, and by Brigadier General John Magruder at Yorktown in April 1862.)

quanity, *n.* Quantity, a number or amount of something.

quar, *n.* [Pronounce the *a* as in "bar"] Choir, a group of singers, especially a church "quar."

quare, *adj.* Peculiar. "He's as quare as a thirty-five-cent piece."

quarl, *n.* Quarrel; a disagreement.

quartee, *n.* [Louisiana; old] A white person of non-French descent.

quatette, *n.* Four folks together.

quern, *n.* [Old] A handmill for grinding food.

quid, *n.* A chew of tobacco.

quietus, *n.* **1.** To stop an action abruptly and completely. "He went looking at new automobiles, but Lee Ann put the quietus on that right quick." **2.** The calm that comes after death. "The quietus was on her and she had a look of perfect peace."

quile, *n.* A coil. "I swar, that danged snake looked jus' lak a quile o' rope layin' thar."

quill, *n.* [Old] A porcupine.

quill, *n.* A straw. "Much as she loves her Co'-Colas, you know she won't drink one without a quill."

quinch, *v.* To wince. "just utter his name and she'll quinch."

quinsy, *n.* A sore throat; tonsillitis.

quite, *adj.* Still; quiet. "When those chi'ren get quite like that, I'm always afraid they're up to somethin'."

quituate, *v.* To quit school; to drop out, Rebel style. "Dumb? You said it! I think he quituated from about the sixth grade."

quop, *v.* To throb. "If her bad tooth gave one more quop, she thought she'd kill herself."

quote, *n.* Quart; that is two pints or four cups or about twenty-two swigs.

r. "The educated Southerner has no use for an "r" except at the beginning of a word." [Mark Twain]

rabbit gum, *n.* A rabbit trap made from the hollow limb of a gum tree.

rabbit ridge, *n.* The wave that is made by pushing the side of the hand into the front of a man's hair.

rabbit tobacco, *n.* Webster's says it's the balsamweed, but to most Southern children it means that first pseudo cigarette they smoked behind the smokehouse (later, the garage), and behind Mother's back.

racket, *n.* "Will you cut out that racket? I can't hear myself think." (Somehow many Southerners prefer "racket" to "noise.")

racket store, *n.* [Circa 1900–1950] A five-and-ten type store.

racking, *v.* Jogging, or going at a slow trot.

rafle, *n.* [Various] Rifle; a shotgun.

raggedy, *adj.* Ragged; tattered.

ragtail, *adj.* Ragged, disheveled, and untidy. ". . . an old ragtail man livin' in a falling-down shack."

rah, *n.* Rye. "If it hadn't been for all tha rah whiskey and them bad women, no tellin' how fur that man coulda gone."

rain seed, *n.* Mottled clouds that threaten rain.

raise, *v.* What is done to hogs, flowers, and younguns; "chi'ren of culchued fam'lies ah reahed."

raise a breeze. To start an argument, a dispute, or to stir up some excitement.

raising, *n.* A bringing up. "Don't go back on your raisin'." (In the South, going back on one's raising is evidence of a major character flaw.)

raising sand. Cutting up; letting off steam; showing displeasure about something. "Now, don't get mad an' start raisin' sand again."

raisnut, *n.* [North Carolina; rare] Raisin.

raison, *n.* Cause; motive. "Just give me one good raison why you'd do such a thang."

Rajah, *n.* Roger, given name for a male. "There's the baseball hero, Rajah Hornsby, and there's the movie actuh, Rajah Moore."

rake over, *v.* To contemplate from all angles; to consider carefully.

rakings and scrapings. The lowest form of something or other. "How could you be seen with those people! Don't you know they are the rakin's an' scrapin's of this earth?"

ral; ole ral, *n.* [Old] Syphilis.

rale, *adj.* Real.

rale gin-u-wine. About as authentic as possible; "the rale thang." "For Christmas his Pa give him a rale ginuwine Barlow knife."

ramp, *n.* An onionlike plant grown—or found—chiefly in North Carolina and Tennessee. It is said to be more odoriferous than onions *and* garlic, and there are so many ramp lovers that Tennessee holds an annual ramp festival. "If Greta Garbo had known about ramp, she'd never have had that problem about privacy."

ramrod, *v.* To exert force and authority on. "He ramrodded the whole deal."

ramsack, *v.* To make a rough and surreptitious search; to ransack.

ramshack; ramshackelty, *adj.* Ramshackle. ". . . that ole gee-wahhawed [q.v.] house an' its ramshack furniture."

rang, *n.* Ring, a piece of jewelry shaped like a circle; an ornament for the finger.

rape, *n.* A green vegetable, a cross between broccoli and turnip greens.

Ra'ph, *n.* A man's name. Yankees pronounce it "Ralph" for some strange reason.

rapscallion, *n.* How the more polite Southerners used to refer to Yankee soldiers; that is, when they declined to describe them more graphically.

rare back. To rear back. "He rared back in his chair, showin' off an' actin' like a big man."

rassel, *v.* To wrestle. "They had a rasselin' match right there on Sally Virginia's front porch."

ratcheer. Not an antidepressant for rodents; it means "just at this place," short for "right here."

rattle (someone's) cage. To shock, or to upset someone. "When he sees the new Caddy she bought with *his money*, boy, will that rattle his cage."

rattling change, *n.* Pocket change.

rats, *n.* Rights; something you're entitled to; what's due you. "You gotta fight fah yo' rats, mah frand."

raver, *n.* A natural stream of water of considerable size, spelled r-i-v-e-r.

rawzum; rawzun, *n.* Resin. (Southern children used to chew tree resin and call it chewing gum.)

razoo, *n.* [Texas] A quick little trip or look-around. "We took a quick razoo around the neighborhood lookin' for our little dog."

reah. 1. *n.* The tail end of anything. "Do you *always* bring up the reah?" **2.** *v.* Cultured Southerners do this to their children, as compared with ordinary folks, who raise theirs.

rebel yell; rebel yale, *n.* The blood-curdling yell that scared the pants off Yankee soldiers.

receipt, *n.* A formula for cooking something. "May I have the receipt for your Lady Baltimore cake, please, ma'am?"

re-cess, *n.* [Accent on the "re"] Time out. Said to be the favorite "class" for most school children.

reckon, *v.* To guess; to suppose. "Ah reckon it's about time to start fixin' some vittles."

reckymember, *v.* [Rural and mountain; old] To remember. "It's been so long, I can't reckymember when I seen you last."

red, *n.* Chili in many parts of Texas and New Mexico. "What I wouldn't give right now for a big bowl of red and an ice-cold long neck [q.v.]"

reddish, *n.* A radish.

red eye, *n.* Rotgut likker.

red eye gravy. Made from fried ham drippings and water or coffee poured from the pot. "When that red eye boils up good, just try some on your grits an' your biscuit. Nothin' better!"

red light, *n.* A traffic light, whether it's red, green, or yellow at the time mentioned. "Naow, you be caiful, Puddin', when you come to that red light up theah. Don't you dayuh cross till it's turned grain."

red neck, *n.* Supposed to be the blue-collar or T-shirt-wearing man; but you shouldn't call one that unless you're prepared for a fight. (So-called because men who worked in the sun sometimes had sunburned necks.)

red nose, *n.* The blues. "You got the red nose again today? I tell you, that boy ain't worth it." (This comes from the fact that crying can cause the nose to turn red.)

refrigidaire, *n.* [Uneducated] Any electric refrigerator.

restrunt, *n.* A place where you can go and have ready-cooked vittles served to you—if you've got cash money.

retch, *adj.* That's when you have lots of money.

Retcherd; Retched, *n.* A man's name. "There's Little Retcherd, Retcherd the Lion-Hearted, and Retched Nixon."

reverent, *adj.* [Old] Undiluted and unadulterated. "I take both my coffee and my whiskey reverent."

revenooer, *n.* The nemesis of moonshiners; a revenue officer.

rheumatiz, *n.* [Old] Rheumatism. (Years ago arthritis was called rheumatism.)

rice and gravy. Said to be the favorite dish in Lake Charles, La. (They once thought of erecting a monument to that pièce de résistance.)

rice spoon, *n.* A very large spoon (over a foot long) used for serving only rice. It was once a must for the Charleston table, for in South Carolina, rice was often served twice daily.

rickety, *adj.* Shaky; weak; unsound. "Derned rickety old table!"

ridge runner, *n.* A briarhopper [q.v.]; a mountaineer.

riever; reaver, *n.* Thief. "That whole family is nothing but a bunch of low-down sneaking rievers."

riffle, *n.* Ripple. "I like to fish and watch the riffles in the wadder."

rīfle, *n.* A raffle. "They're holdin' another rifle at the Elks tonight."

rigamarow; rigamarole, *n.* (Southerners seem to think an extra *a* is needed in this word: rigmarole.) A foolish, rambling, drawn-out statement. "We had to listen to his whole dern rigamarow before he'd settle down."

rightly, *adv.* Really; truly; correctly. "I don't rightly know, chile, I don't rightly know."

right smart, *adj.* Quite a bit; a considerable amount. "I hate to tell you this, but I'm afraid your pore ole Gran'pa is a right smart sick."

right writing, *n.* What spelling was called once upon a time.

rile, *v.* To roil; to vex or stir up. "You ain't satisfied unless you got somebody all riled up, are you?" Or "Don't rile *that* woman!"

rilly, *adv.* Sure nuff; actually; really.

rimption, *n.* Plenty; a whole lot. "Ther's only a smidgen o' beans left, but ther's rimptions o' cabbage an' cawn bread."

rinch, *v.* [Mountain and rural] To rinse. "Rinch them clothes real good. If there's inny soap scum left in 'em, the culluhs won't be bright."

Rinctum Diddy, *n.* A variety of Welsh rarebit eaten around Danville, Va., among other places.

ringtail roarer, *n.* River gamblers and wagon drivers in the old days.

ringtail tooter; ringtail snorter, *n.* A fine and brave specimen of a man; or a man who attracts much attention. "Sure, I remember your daddy. He was one ringtail tooter as a young man."

rip, *n.* A low woman; a near-prostitute. "He's been laying up with some ole rip he took up with when the carnival come to town."

rippit, *n.* A noisy quarrel; a fistfight; a rough, boisterous party. "Let them two get together, it ends in a rippit ever' time."

riproar, *v.* To speak vociferously; to behave in a boisterous manner. "He come in here, made as a hornet, riproaring all over the place."

rip-roodle, *v.* To cut up; to romp; to hell around. "Ain't it 'bout time that you cut out all this rip-roodling and settled down, young feller?"

ripshin, *n.* A briar or briar bush. "Pull that ripshin off'n yore sleeve."

ripsnorting, *adj.* Acting bigger than life; something extreme in some way. "He's got hiself a knockout girl and a ripsnorting new automobile to drive her around in."

rip up the back. To destroy verbally. "I never had anyone talk to me the way she did—just ripped me up the back."

rising bread, *n.* Yeast bread, or light bread; not biscuits.

river sand, *n.* [Louisiana] Partly black blood. "He may have a little river sand in him, it looks like."

riz, *v.* [Old] Past tense of "rise." "The sun had already riz 'fore Pa woke up."

rizing, *n.* A swelling; a boil. "That youngun has a rizin' on her arm as big as a goose egg."

roach, *n.* A hairstyle that leaves the hair combed up and straight back. "He had real thick hair and he wore it in a roach."

rock, *n.* Anything from a pebble to a great big boulder. (A Southerner almost never casts a stone; he throws—or "chunks"—a rock.)

rococola, *adj.* The way someone once described the architecture of Atlanta (the home of Coca-Cola), implying that it was a rococco type with a uniquely Atlanta touch.

Rocky Mountain oysters. [Also called "lamb fries"] The testes of a lamb used as a food.

roebucks, *n.* False teeth. (Years ago false teeth were actually mail-ordered; for instance, through the Sears and Roebuck catalog.)

Roenoke, *n.* Not many Southerners put that *a* in "Roanoke" when they say it.

rogue, *n.* [Old] A thief. "That man's such a pure-out rogue, he'd steal the pennies off a dead man's eyes."

Rogue's Harbor and Redemptioner's Refuge. North Carolinians bitterly resented this description of their state as William Byrd of Virginia so flamboyantly put it. Probably just neighborly jealousy, they decided.

roller shade, *n.* Window shade.

Rolley, *n.* Raleigh, the capital city of North Carolina, named after Sir Walter Raleigh.

rollix, *v.* To philander; to revel. "He rollixed 'round the country till no decent girl would have him."

roosevelt, *n.* An outhouse (or privy) built by the WPA workers during Roosevelt's administration.

Roosevelt mules, *n.* Given by the federal government to impoverished farmers during the depression.

root soaker, *n.* A good, heavy rain.

roshnears; rosenears, *n.* Eating corn, as contrasted to corn grown for livestock; corn on the cob. [Short for "roasting ears"]

rotten egg, *n.* One who comes in last on a bet or in a competition. "Last one in the lake is a rotten egg!"

rowdy, *adj.* [Early 1900s] A jacket made of denim and usually worn with overalls. "That's no way to go courtin' a girl, in yore overhalls an' rowdy."

rubbige, *n.* Rubbish.

ruction, *n.* A fight; a commotion; a dispute. "As I always said, don't ever get into a ruction between a man an' his wife."

ruff, *n.* A roof in several parts of the South.

ruint, *adj.* Ruined. "Jezebel, she was a ruint woman."

rullick; ralic, *n.* An old, worn-out thing; a relic. "Did you see that hat she was wearin'? Where does she come up with a rullick like that?"

rum, *n.* Room. "A rum with a view" and "rum and board."

rumpus, *n.* A disagreement; an uproar. "There's always a rumpus when they play cards together."

running off, *n.* Diarrhea; green apple quick step [q.v.].

run over, *v.* To press quickly; a once-over with an iron. "Give me a minute so I can run over this dress right quick."

run with. Pal around with; go with. "Is he still running with that same tacky bunch?"

rustics, *n.* Capers, antics, escapades. "You and your rustics. I wish you'd get serious for a change, show a little dignity."

rusty, *n.* [Mountain] A show-off action. "You cut one of your rusties while we're visiting the Perkinses, boy, you'll catch what-for when we get home."

rusty gravy, *n.* [North Carolina] Gravy to which tomatoes have been added.

ruther, *adv.* Prefer to. "I'd ruther do it myse'f, Mammy."

sack, *n.* A paper bag; sometimes a cloth bag. (For some reason, or through habit, many Southerners prefer "sack" to "bag.")

sad cake, *n.* A cake that did not rise as it should have, therefore is heavy. "I pure-out cannot stand a sad cake."

saddleback house, *n.* A house with a roof shaped roughly like a saddle; the roof goes up from each side and peaks in the middle.

sad iron, *n.* An old-timey iron, very heavy, pointed at both ends, with a removable handle.

safe, *n.* An old-fashioned cabinet with perforated tin, or wire-mesh doors, for ventilation. They were used in the kitchen for the safekeeping of cooked foods.

sainter, *v.* [Tennessee; Kentucky] To saunter.

Salem, North Carolina. The Salem historians claim that early settlers there held the first Independence Day celebration in America—on July 4, 1783.

sallit, *n.* Salad; as in "turnup sallit."

salry, *n.* **1.** Celery, what one serves with olives or puts in chicken salad. **2.** Pay for doing one's job—salary.

samp, *n.* [From the Algonquin] A kind of coarse hominy; also, the cooked cereal made from samp.

sandbugger, *n.* A patty made from cooked potatoes, seasoned with onions, and fried.

sandlapper, *n.* [Ozarks] One from the flatlands or swamps instead of the mountains; a swamp angel.

sang, *n.* [Mountain] Ginseng, or sang, is an herb used as a demulcent in teas for drinking, or in lotions.

Sanna Claws; Santy Claus, *n.* Santa Claus.

sanwich; samich, *n.* Something to eat separating two pieces of bread.

sashay, *v.* **1.** To strut or glide as in square dancing. [Comes from *chasser,* French for "chase" or "drive"] **2.** To walk proudly and prissily. "Man alive, will you watch that purty thing sashaying down the street!"

sashiate, *v.* [Old] Sashay.

sass, *n.* Sauce; as in "apple sass."

sassperilly, *n.* [Mountain] Sarsaparilla. A tea, or "medicine," made from the root of the sarsaparilla plant and used to treat rheumatism and other ailments.

sassy, *adj.* High-spirited; impudent. "That's a family you don't mess with. Every one of 'em is fat an' sassy."

Sat'dy; Sairdy, *n.* Saturday—the live-it-up day of the week down South. "Come Sat'dy, man, I'm goin' to town—more ways than one."

Saturday-night special, *n.* A switchblade knife, and more recently an inexpensive handgun, used for protection and/or vindication.

saucer, *n.* In the old days, for many people a coffee cup was used to hold the coffee, but the saucer was utilized for cooling it, and for drinking. Whence comes: "It's already been saucered and blowed." (At one time "coffee saucers" were manufactured and used entirely independent of a cup. These coffee saucers were deeper than the common saucer.)

saucered and blowed. Cooled off and ready to drink, usually coffee or tea.

sawrite. Short for "it's all right."

say-so, *n.* [Cajun] An old wives' tale; a myth; a misconception perhaps. "You listen to all that crazy say-so Granny Ledoux tells, you be 'fraid to go sleep at night."

say uncle. To give up or give in. "He rasseled him to the ground and he didn't loosen his holt one time till Lester said uncle."

say what? [Black] What was that you said?

scairdy cat, *n.* One who's afraid.

scalawag, *n.* Those traitors who supported reconstruction after "The War."

scollet, *n.* **1.** A color; as "She woah a scollet ribbon in huh hayuh." **2.** [Capitalized] A girl's name; as in Scollet O'Hara.

scout, *v.* To elude or evade. "That low-down Lonnie Smith! He's been scoutin' the law ever since I knowed him."

scratchankle, *adj.* Worn-out; inferior; hardscrabble. "That ole scratchankle farm he's a-workin'—nobody could make a livin' on that."

scrimption, *n.* A little bit. "Ah awready feel like a stuffed toad, but Ah will have just a scription moah of that turkey dressin'."

scrollop, *n.* [Tennessee] A woman who's a combination slut and trollop.

scrooch; scroonch, *v.* To make yourself, or a thing, smaller. "Scrooch down in your seat so he won't see you."

scrouge, *v.* To crowd. "You-all are scrouging me right out of this bed."

scrunge, To sponge on. "Lookie here, you're too big a boy to be scrunging on your mama."

scrupulous, *adj.* Apprehensive. "Ever since my acci-dent, I've been a lil' bit scrupulous about gittin' in innybody's audomo-bile."

scuppernong, *n.* A grape of the muscadine variety. (The name comes from the Algonquin *Askuponong,* which means, literally, "at the place of the magnolias," and even the beauty of the phrase cannot match the deliciousness of the grape. It is said that scuppernongs were first discovered—after the Indians, of course—in North Carolina by Sir Walter Raleigh.)

scutter, *n.* Someone remarkable, either as a rascal or an expert. "He's a reg'lar scutter when it comes to politicking."

sech, *adj.* Such. "I have never seen sech a person!"

second-day dress, *n.* [Old] A dress for the bride to wear on the day after the wedding.

second joint, *n.* A euphemism for the thigh of a fowl. (Surely no one thinks that a Southern lady would say "thigh" or "leg" in mixed company.)

second table. At the second serving, or second table, is where and when children ate when the family had company. (That was one of the reasons children couldn't wait to grow up. At the second table one usually wound up with the gizzards, wings, and backs of the chicken, not to mention cold biscuits and gravy.)

seeve, *n.* A sieve.

serviette, *n.* A table napkin.

setter, *n.* **1.** A large bird dog trained for hunting. **2.** One's behind; what one sits on. "You sass me one more time and I'll warm your setter."

settin'-down work. Work that can be done while sitting. "Piecing quilts is my favorite settin'-down work."

setting room; sitting room, *n.* The room of a house that is truly the living room, in contrast to the parlor, which is used for special occasions only.

set-to, *n.* A small argument or misunderstanding. "Ah'm a bit annoyed with Mary Virginia. We had a little set-to last night about her always bein' late."

shackledy, *adj.* Rickety. A thing so run-down or weak that it's shaky.

shackling, *adj.* **1.** Lazy and shiftless. **2.** Shambling; loose-jointed. "That shackling walk and hanging lip—I swear that boy musta been behind the barn when the brains were passed out."

shakeguts, *n.* A wagon or horse-drawn vehicle when driven over rough roads.

Shakespayuh, *n.* The one and only Bard, the greatest writer of our Mother Tongue. "Shakespayuh was an authuh that the late Senatuh Sam Irvin was fond of quoting."

shaking fat, *n.* Fat on the body that shakes or trembles. "The girl is right purty in the face, but there's a heap o' shakin' fat on that body."

shanksprung, *adj.* Bow-legged. ". . . so shanksprung he couldn't stop a pig in a ditch with a net."

shaping food, *n.* Meats and starches, foods that become relatively compact in the digestive system.

shapings, *n.* [Mountain] Young, immature pea and bean pods. "Chinese snow peas, my foot. That ain't nothin' but a fancy name for shapin's, if you ast me."

shavetail, *n.* An untrained mule.

she-balsam, *n.* A variety of fir tree. (The "he-balsam" is a red or black spruce tree.)

she-crab, *n.* South Carolina is a place where females are never discriminated against when it comes to one of its favorite foods, she-crab soup. Not only is a he-crab avoided like a Yankee right after The War, but anyone who dares use a he-crab for soup is in danger of being shunned as a heathen and a traitor. For even a tomfool South Carolinian—if it's possible to imagine such a paradox—knows that it's the girl-crab that produces the "ikra" (the roe of the crab), and it's these eggs that give that heavenly flavor to the soup.

shed, *v.* To get rid of. "He got shed of a pile o' money in no time flat."

shellie beans, *n.* Shelled beans, taken from the overmature green or snap bean, to be cooked with the whole green beans.

Sherman, *n.* "Shuhman"—General William Tecumseh Sherman—a dirty seven-letter word in Georgia. (A barbaric but brilliant Yankee general, he was famous for his destructive march across the South toward the end of the Civil War.)

Sherman's sentinels, *n.* The chimneys left standing in the ruins of burned houses after Sherman's infamous march through Georgia.

Sherman, Texas, *n.* A town named for a general, all right, but a fine, upstanding, upright, real genuine Texas hero—General Sidney Sherman. It was cavalry General Sidney Sherman who helped Sam Houston get rid of that survigrous [q.v.] old Santa Anna at the Battle of San Jacinto.

shet, *v.* Shut, what one does to an open door if it's cold outside.

shimmy, *n.* A chemise.

shindy, *n.* **1.** An energetic dance; a hop. **2.** A caper.

shine around. To pursue romantically; to set one's cap for. "That fool better not come shining around my daughter."

shinnery, *n.* A dense and uncultivated growth on land. "This used to be a purty place—rose bushes an' nice flow'rs—but now it's all gone back to shinnery."

shinny. 1. *n.* Alabamian for "shine" (moonshine). **2.** *v.* To climb easily and quickly. "Good Gawd, he shinnied up that tree like a danged monkey."

shirtwaist, *n.* A woman's blouse.

shivaree, *n*. [A corruption of "charivari"] A crude, noisy sere-
nade for greeting purposes and the celebration of an event, such
as a country wedding.

shoe bread, *n*. A thin meat sandwich that can be concealed in
one's shoe and used for enticing a desirable hunting dog away
from home.

shooting arn; shooting iron, *n*. A gun in the mountains.

shore; sho; shuah, *adj*. For certain. "She was shore a fine
worman."

short pint, *n*. A half-pint of whiskey; a pocket piece [q.v.].

short sweetening, *n*. Sugar, as compared to "long sweetening,"
which is molasses or syrup.

shot, *adj*. Of less than average height; not tall.

shot-gun house, *n*. A narrow one-story house in which the
rooms (often only two) extend one behind the other.

shrimp mammy, *n*. A squid—called a shrimp mammy because
they are so often found in a catch of shrimp.

shrub, *n*. A kind of fruit punch, sometimes with vinegar added,
and once very popular in the South.

shuck, *v*. **1.** Past tense of "shake." "And then we all shuck
hands." **2.** To strip the husks off corn for cooking.

shuck juice, *n*. Corn liquor.

shucks, aw. A mild but often-used interjection.

shurf, *n*. Sheriff, the man who wears a shiny star and can sniff out
moonshine just by the way a car looks weighted-down in the
back.

shut-mouth, *adj*. Closemouthed.

shut of; shed of. Rid of; as in "Goree! I sure am glad to be shut of that shackledy ole bed."

shys, a case of the. Afflicted with severe bashfulness.

sick headache, *n*. That's a headache so bad, it makes you half-sick at your stomach, and sometimes sick all over. (Southern belles never have plain headaches. They have absolutely unbearable headaches, positively raging headaches, and perfectly killing headaches that "just won't stop." The more delicate the belle, the more apt she is to believe that sick always precedes the word "headache.")

sick time, *n*. The time for giving birth. "It was Lacy Ann's sick time and she didn't have hardly any clothes for the new baby."

sidegongling, *adj*. Tilted. "That picture is so sidegonglin', it makes me right queazy to look at it."

side meat, *n*. Salt pork from the side of a hog.

sideways, *n*. [Facetious for "suicide"] "She's always threatening to commit sideways when all she's asking for is a little attention."

signify, *v*. [Mostly Black use] **1.** To attempt to make an impression with pretended knowledge. "Don't you come around here signifying with me." **2.** To make sense; to be significant. "Man, that don't signify."

si-gonglin'; si-antigodlin', *adj*. Leaning to one side; out of plumb; sidegongling. ". . . an old si-gonglin' barn."

sign the book. To make a condolence call at a funeral home. "We're goin' over to the funeral parlor to sign the book."

silencer, *n*. A lid for a slop jar or chamber pot with an aperture about a fifth its size on one side, a device designed for silencing or reducing noise.

simmon, *n.* Persimmon, a fruit that is delicious when ripe, but that will turn your mouth "wrong-side outerds" if eaten when green. (Most Southern children of older generations never knew that a "per" was supposed to go before the "simmon.")

sing, *n.* **1.** A songfest. "On Sunday we're all going to an all-day sing." **2.** Ginseng.

single house, *n.* A style of Charleston, S.C., house that sits very close to the street, with a side and a wall facing the street, and the "front" and porch facing a side garden. The property is entered through a doorway in the wall. This design allows for greater privacy in the city.

sin-killer, *n.* A preacher, especially the hellfire-and-damnation kind.

sinus, got the. An attack of sinusitis. "Poor thing, he's got the sinus again."

si-reen, *n.* Siren. "It makes you feel so bad when you hear one of those ole si-reens, 'cause you know an am-bulance is on its way to pick up some pore soul."

Sister, *n.* [The Southern correlative of "Bubba"] The title for the eldest daughter of a family. (Females can grow to adulthood in the South and seldom hear their baptismal name spoken by the family.)

skeer, *v.* Scare; to frighten.

skin alive. To berate someone; to dress down.

skinny minute, *n.* A very short period of time. "Just you wait a damn skinny minute!"

skipping Jack, *n.* Leftover hopping John [q.v.] when warmed over.

slaunchways, *adj.* Slanting; on an angle; sidegonglin'.

slew, *n.* More than a few; a whole lot. "They got out o' their ole jalopy, an' here followin' them was a whole slew of runny-nosed, snaggle-toothed, ragtail younguns."

slick-faced, *adj.* Clean-shaven. "There's so many of those old beards around these days that it's right gratifying to see a slick-faced man."

slickry, *adj.* Slippery. "I'd like okra if it wasn't so slickry."

slickum, *n.* [North Carolina] A kind of dumpling cooked on top of stewed chicken.

slipperslide, *n.* A shoehorn.

slop jar, *n.* A bigger and taller chamber pot; a small-scaled, portable "toilet," oftentimes made of china.

slopping sugar. To apply effusive sweet talk, unrestrained flattery, or soft soap. "Oh, my Lord, they hate each othuh with a passion, and theah they were sloppin' sugah all ovuh each othuh."

slouchy gravy, *n.* Gravy made when there's no "real" meat to flavor it; it's made with fried fat back or bacon grease, flour, salt and pepper, and sometimes chopped onion.

slows, *n.* Slow of movement; laziness. "He has got the slows." [Abe Lincoln]

slud, *v.* Past tense of slide. "He slud into second base." [The matchless Dizzy Dean]

slut's wool, *n.* Those dust balls on the floor and under the bed.

smack-dab, *adj.* Exactly. "She threw the mess down smack-dab in the middle of the parlor."

smarts, *n.* Sassiness; impertinence. "That youngun has the smarts so bad, I can hardly stand to be around her."

smidgen, *n.* A tiny bit. "There's a smidgen of pie left."

smoothing iron, *n.* A flatiron, like the kind that was heated on the old cookstove.

smother, *v.* If a Southern cook smothers a chicken, she doesn't put a pillow over its head. The chicken is floured, seasoned, browned in fat, a small amount of water added, then covered and cooked over low heat until the meat is loosened from the bone; a delicious change from fried or baked chicken.

snakebit, *v.* Getting stuck in a deal; being defrauded. "I sure got snakebit when I bought that ole car."

snake doctor, *n.* The dragonfly; the snake feeder.

snake feeder *n.* Dragonfly.

snake fence, *n.* A worm fence or a Virginia fence, and all three of these are the zigzaggy kind like Abe Lincoln used to split rails for. They are built in segments of six to eight (in height) inter-locking rails.

snaps, *n.* Green beans. "We had snaps with roshnears steamed on top, an' oh, was that good!"

snip, *n.* A smart-alecky, low-class girl.

snowbird, *n.* [Florida] Someone from other climes who comes to Florida in the winter to take advantage of the warm weather. (This term is not applied to the paying tourists so much as to the temporary job seekers who sponge off the state's winter economy.)

snuck, *v.* Past tense of sneak.

snuff-ball, *n.* A dandelion puffball.

snuff queen, *n.* A country-and-western-music groupie (so-named because originally snuff companies were big advertisers on such programs).

soaker, *n.* A hot biscuit that's been buttered, sugared, and had hot coffee poured over it. (Before sophistication set in, Southern children used to love it.)

soamachine, *n.* A sewing machine, a dressmaker's helpmeet.

sob, *v.* [Mountain] To make wet, sobby. "If we sob up these papers, then they cain't ketch far [fire]."

S.O.B, *n.* Charleston, S.C., may be the only place in the world where one is proud to be called an S.O.B—"South of Broad" (Street). The residents there comprise a large part of Charleston's aristocracy.

sobby, *adj.* [Mountain] Soggy.

soda-pop moon, *n.* Moonshine bottled in "recycled" soft drink bottles.

sody, *n.* An old pronunciation of "soda."

sojer, *n.* Soldier. "There's something about a sojer that is fine, fine, fine."

Solid South, the. The states of the United States which had seceded before and immediately after the start of the Civil War and which, for a long time after the Reconstruction period began, voted a "solid" Democratic ticket.

some, *adv.* Somewhat. "He was some better last time I saw him."

some kind of. Very, or exceptionally. "This cherry pie is some kind of good!"

some kind of purty. Real, real pretty.

somerset, *n.* Somersault.

some sugar, *n.* Kisses. "Come here, buttercup, and give your daddy some sugar."

something happens, if. A euphemism for "if something bad happens." "If somethin' happens tonight after I leave, just phone me and I'll call the undertaker for you."

sonker, *n.* [North Carolina] An extra-deep fruit cobbler—usually made with the most plentiful fruit of the season, or the one on hand at the moment.

son-of-a-bitch bed, *n.* A crude bunk bed.

sooner, *n.* An untrained or mongrel dog. (Or, as it was once put by a North Carolina mountaineer: "A dawg that 'ud sooner do it in the house than in the yard.")

Sooth Ca'lina, *n.* The Palmetto State—a state of extreme beauty, both natural and man-made. (Charleston, for instance, has long been known for its grace and culture—for so long and to such an extent that in the eighteenth century it was known throughout America and Europe as "Little London.")

soothing syrup, *n.* Like paregoric, cough syrups, Castoria—any medication that eases or corrects an illness or a discomfort.

sop. 1. *n.* A gravy made from only the juices and fat of a fried meat, with water or coffee added, but no flour. (An irresistible sop is made from the drippings of fried ham and a half-cup or so of weak coffee. After it boils up good, it is ready to be sopped with buttermilk or a baking powder biscuit.) **2.** *v.* A way of eating without a fork, and the only way to eat molasses mixed with butter, and hot biscuits.

sopping good, *adj.* "Sopping good" is when a serving of food is so delectable that one can't bear to leave a drop, even if one must resort to sopping.

soption, *n.* A gravy, or sauce, or such. "Put a little more of that soption on my bobby-cue san'wich, please."

Sore-back, *n.* What North Carolinians used to call Virginians.

sorghum, *n.* A light-colored molasses which has a slight malty taste and is more delicate in flavor than the blackstrap variety. (Sopping sorghum is an old Southern custom.)

sot, *v.* Past tense of "sit."

sour bug, *n.* A gnat. (Gnats are called this because they are attracted to soured or fermented foods.)

Southern breakfast, *n.* A Co'-Cola and two asprin. (Or so it has been said; for without a Coke, many a Southern belle would think she'd had no breakfast.)

Southern coffee, *n.* [Louisiana] Southern coffee is usually of a darker roast and contains chicory, as opposed to Northern or regular coffee, which is chicory-free.

Southern-fried chicken, *n.* To begin with, it must be a Southern chicken, fried in a Southern pan, on Southern ground, by a Southern cook. There are as many ways of frying chicken as there are states in the Confederacy (well, *were*), but for chicken to be truly Southern-fried, several edicts must be followed. Commandment number one: A Southern chicken shall never be butchered into chunks so large and so unwieldy as quarters and halves. Southern fried chicken shall always be thoroughly disjointed—disjointed in the South meaning that the wing is taken from the breast, the breast cut in two pieces, the drumstick severed from the thigh, and the back, neck, heart, liver and gizzard treated and fried as separate and important parts of this revered delicacy. Commandment number two: If one vestige of blood shall be detected in the chicken when finally attacked by knife, fork, or tooth, then the offender, the cook, shall be chastised by the enforcement of a very old but effective law—she shall be rapped on the head with her own frying pan while a bagpiper pipes "The Bonnie Blue Flag," and the Stars and Bars fly at half-staff.

Southern gold, *n.* Peanuts (according to Georgia farmers). Earlier it was cotton that was called "Southern gold."

Southern hyperbole, *n.* Exaggeration for effect as uttered by Southern belles who believe they are telling the truth.

southernmost swill, *n.* An alcoholic concoction served in Florida that's made of gin, green coconut milk, and Key lime juice.

Southern woman, *n.* Southern woman is not so much a Venus's-flytrap disguised as a shrinking violet as she is a B-1 bomber mistaken for a butterfly. One of the things that annoys a Southern woman most is when, because of her soft voice and sweet manner, someone takes her for a dumbbell.

sowbelly, *n.* Salt pork.

spang, *adj.* Directly; exactly; completely. "Jes' think what 'ud happened if old William Tell hadn't hit that apple spang in the middle."

spare, *n.* Sparrow, a very small and common bird.

sparegus; sparagras, *n.* Asparagus.

sparkling light, *n.* A small, open kerosene lamp with a floating wick, used in the nineteenth century.

spasmodics, *n.* A kind of fit; an intense tizzy. "She was so shocked, we thought she was going to have the spasmodics."

speck, *n.* A little bit. "Not one speck of sense did that girl have."

spect, *v.* Short for "expect." "I spect so."

spell, *n.* **1.** A length of time. "Come and set a spell." **2.** An attack of some ailment; a noticeable reaction to an emotion. "She's about to have one of those spells again."

spicket, *n.* A faucet; a spigot.

spider, *n.* A cast-iron skillet. (In older times, spiders came with little legs so they could be set over an open fire.)

spitting image, *n.* Someone who looks just like someone else. "I declare to my soul, if he idn't the spittin' image of his daddy!" ["Spitting image" is said to be a corruption of "spirit and image."]

split the quilt. To get a divorce. "Those movie stars sure are quick to split the quilt, wouldn't you say?"

spoon bread, *n.* An absolutely and unbelievably luscious and mouth-watering type of corn bread, made and baked like a custard pudding and eaten with either a fork or a spoon. (A story once circulated around Richmond, Virginia, strongly hinted that the original recipe was transmitted directly from Mount Olympus to the mistress of an Old Dominion plantation. Once you've tasted this manna, the legend is easy to believe.)

spread it on. To brag or to put on airs. "Man, she can really spread it on thick, can't she?"

spring house, *n.* An early refrigerator. It was a tiny house built over a spring, with the water piped through in such a way that a trough filled with chilly running water, this process acting as a refrigerant for food stored in the trough.

spring onion, *n.* A green onion or scallion.

square, *adj.* Honest. "He's the squarest man you'll ever hope to meet."

squeze, *v.* ["Ez" as in "fez"] Past tense of "squeeze." "She squeze her big self into that little dress till I thought the seams were gonna pop."

squigly, *adj.* Weak; wavery. "Ever'time I see that girl, my knees go all squigly."

squinch, *v.* To squint. "If you'd get yourself some eyeglasses, you wouldn't have to squinch that way."

squinch al; squinch owl, *n.* Screech owl. (But don't they all squinch?)

squint-eyed, *adj.* Nearsighted. "I swear, that pore girl was so squint-eyed it looked like she was sashaying around with her eyes closed."

squshy, *adj.* Mushy or pulpy. "You've ruined the pintoes. You've cooked them till they're all squshy."

srimp, *n.* Shrimp in parts of Alabama and scattered places of the South.

stack cake, *n.* [Mountain] A layer cake.

staff of life, *n.* Bread. (Until fairly recently it was thought necessary to eat lots of bread to stay healthy. For instance, a child could be verging on obesity; still he was urged, "Eat your bread, hon. Don't you know bread is the staff of life?" Yes, many an unwanted biscuit has been stuffed down a Southern child's throat in an act of misguided kindness.)

Standing Peachtree, *n.* Atlanta, Georgia, when Atlanta was a little Indian village. Standing Peachtree later became Terminus; Terminus was changed to Marthasville, finally to become Atlanta.

start-nekkid, *adj.* Wholly bare. ". . . standing there in his birthday suit, start-nekkid."

State of Franklin, *n.* What Tennessee was called before it actually became a state in 1796. It was previously the western part of North Carolina.

statue; sling-statue, *n.* A game in which a person is spun round and round by another person, then turned loose and while still moving is abruptly ordered to freeze by the spinner yelling, "Statue!" The player is then judged on the artistic merit of his pose.

stemwinder, *n.* A remarkable person, animal, or object. "Man o' War! There was a real stemwinder of a horse."

step off the carpet. To get married. "I heard yesterday that Buster Caudle had stepped off the capret with Jessie Mae Hendrix."

stick one's head in. To enter a place briefly (at least with one's head) to give a brief greeting or a message. "On my way to church I stuck my head in at the Nelsons' to say hey."

stilted shoes, *n.* [Mountain] High-heeled shoes.

stir-off, *n.* A boiling of sugar cane to make molasses. "The stir-off took all day, but yielded us five gallons of top-notch 'lasses."

stir up, *v.* To agitate; to upset. "Now, don't go getting him stirred up by telling him about seein' Ab drunk."

stitch, *n.* An article of clothing.

stitch to (one's) back, not a. The condition of not owning one item of clothing.

stompers, *n.* Clodhopper shoes; heavy shoes.

stomping ground, *n.* One's home ground; one's favorite hangout or territory.

stone bruise, *n.* A sore spot on the bottom of the foot, the result of being bruised by stepping on a stone, or hard object, with the bare foot.

store-boughten, *adj.* Not made at home, but bought.

store-boughten air, *n.* An electric fan. "Last August I don't know what we would have done without our store-boughten air."

storify, *v.* To tell a story; to make up a story; to exaggerate an incident.

story, *n.* A euphemism for a lie; however, a story told by an unpopular person is never a story, but always a lie.

stove, *v.* [Mountain] To jab. "Danged if he didn't miss the ice cubes and stove the ice pick right through my new dishpan."

stove-up, *adj.* Stiff and sore from physical exertion, punishment, or an ailment. "By gum, all I did yestiddy was to rake that little bit of yard out there, and today I'm all stove-up."

strak, *n.* Strike. "Two on, three balls, two straks, two men out."

strawberrying, *v.* Going on a strawberry-picking jaunt.

street, *n.* A sidewalk. "He wouldn't walk on the street like he should, but he insisted on marching off right in the middle of the road."

string, *v.* [Country] To play a stringed musical instrument. "Can you play the banjo?" "I string a little, but I ain't no Chet Atkins, I can tell you that."

stringing clothes, *v.* Hanging clothes on a clothes line.

stripe-ed, *adj.* With stripes. "He wore a checkerdy shirt an' a stripe-ed suit."

struggle buggy, *n.* A jocular name for the early Fords.

study, *v.* To think; to contemplate; to be concerned with. "He went around with his head in the clouds and wasn't studyin' nobody or nothin'."

study one's mind. To think things over carefully in order to make a decision, or to come to a conclusion. "I got to study my mind before I jump into innything that iffy."

stuffing and stringing. Being self-indulgent by eating one's fill, then going out in search of pleasure or diversion. "All you ever do or wanna do is just stuff and string."

stump, *v.* Real Southerners rarely stub their toes, they usually "stump" them.

suck-back preacher, *n.* A preacher who, for emphasis, sharply and frequently sucks back his breath after delivering a phrase.

suck-egg, *adj.* Mean; base. "He's as mean as a suck-egg mule."

suckle, *n.* Circle; something that goes round and round with no beginning or end.

sugar, *n.* A kiss. "Come here, sweetie pie, and give your mama some sugah."

sugarbetes, *n.* [Uneducated] Diabetes.

sugar bread, *n.* A slice of bread and butter sprinkled with sugar.

sugar egg, *n.* A sweet treat for children, made by pouring hot, overcooked maple syrup into a blown-out eggshell. After cooling, the sugar granulates, the shell is removed, and the result is a sugar egg.

sugar foot, *n.* A term of endearment.

sugar-head, *n.* Top quality moonshine whiskey. (When shaken, true sugar-head will produce a beading—a circle of tiny bubbles that form at the top—and this bead serves as proof of excellence in sugar-head; proves, too, that the liquor has not been watered, since diluted sugar-head will not bead.)

sugar-head lit. Drunk; high as a Georgia pine from tippling on sugar-head.

sugar mouth, *n.* Honied, flattering, persuasive talk; sweet talk. "Go out with him if you must, but beware of the sugar mouth 'cause he really lays it on thick."

sugar-tit, *n.* Sugar tied in a cloth to be sucked by a baby; an "edible" pacifier.

suhpeeny, *n.* A subpoena.

suhsīdy, *n.* The rich, fashionable, socially prominent members of a community. "Lord, when Malvina got home from Miz Fillmore's tea yesterday, she acted just like she'd been inducted into high suhsidy."

Sultana, *n.* The *Titanic* of the South. When this Mississippi River steamboat exploded outside of Memphis, Tennessee, in 1865, more people were lost than on the *Titanic.* There were 1,513 missing when the *Titanic* went down in 1912, but forty-seven years earlier, 1,547 people were lost in the *Sultana* tragedy.

summers, *adv.* Somewhere. "Where'd he go? I don't know—he went summers."

sump'm; somethin', *pron.* Something.

sun ball, *n.* [Mountain] Sun. "The sun ball was droppin' behind Eagle Mount'n 'fore I ever got my canning done."

Sunday best, *n.* A person's best clothes; what one reserves for wearing to church.

Sunday-go-to-meeting clothes. One's Sunday best.

sure-nuff, *adj.* Actual; "ginuwine." "She was a sure-nuff movie actress."

survigrous, *adj.* [The superlative of "vigrous"] Very active and enterprising; sometimes, rambunctious. "He was sech a survigrous baby, he plumb wore his skinny lil' mama out."

susprise, *n.* [Occasionally heard in North Carolina.] Surprise.

swage, *v.* To assuage; to lessen in severity. "The risin' on his arm had swaged down some durin' the night."

swaller-pipe, *n.* [Mountains; old] Gullet; esophagus.

swamp angel, *n.* A person living in a swamp area; a swamper; a sandlapper.

swamp cabbage, *n.* [Florida and Lower South] Hearts of palm. (In Florida and Georgia hearts of palm used to be boiled and eaten like cabbage.)

swamp dew, *n.* Mississippi moonshine.

swamper, *n.* One from the swamps; a swamp angel.

swamp mucker, *n.* One living in the low country of Georgia and South Carolina.

swamp seed, *n.* Rice.

sweet'art, *n.* Sweetheart. ("Sweetheart" was originally "sweet-ard," with the "-ard" ending made use of in the same way as in coward and laggard.)

sweet'arting; sweethearting, *v.* Courting; wooing. "When he gets spruced up like that, you can just bet he's goin' sweet'ar-tin'."

sweet bub, *n.* The petal-like, aromatic bud of the strawberry shrub, also called the Carolina allspice; the longer the "bub" is held in one's hand, the sweeter it smells.

sweetening, *n.* Something eaten in place of a regular dessert, like toast and jelly. "Seems like I have to have a little sweet'nin' of some kind after ev'ry meal."

sweet gum, *n.* A twig from the sweet gum tree makes the most desirable brush for snuff dippers; and in older days, these twigs, after being chewed to soften and to spread the fibers, were used for cleaning the teeth when toothbrushes were not affordable.

sweet Lucy, *n.* Rotgut whiskey in Texas.

sweet milk, *n.* Fresh milk, in contrast to buttermilk. (In many areas of the South, because buttermilk is such a popular beverage, one must specify which milk one is ordering.)

sweetmouth, *n.* [Alabama] A flaked ice treat that is flavored with a colored syrup.

sweet tater, *n.* Sweet potatoes have long been a favorite food of the South. (To attest to this popularity is the fact that the largest sweet potato auction market in the world is in Tabor City, N.C., where each year they honor their beloved tuber by celebrating the Carolina Yam Festival.)

swig. 1. *n.* A swallow, or a big gulp of a liquid. **2.** *v.* A way of drinking moonshine or other liquids.

swimp, *n.* [Cajun and other parts of deep South] Shrimp.

swinge, *v.* To singe. "Swingeing a chicken is the quickest way to get rid of pinfeathers."

swivet, *n.* A state of nervous agitation; a major tizzy. "She was in a swivet for one whole month before her wedding."

swoard, *n.* [The *w* strongly pronounced] A big, very sharp, knifelike weapon with an extralong blade, used for fighting duels before shooting irons were invented.

swultry, *adj.* Hot and humid; sultry. "No wonder he got in trouble. Down there in the swultry tropics with all them warm-blooded sloe-eyed females shining up to him."

tac tac, *n.* [Cajun; pronounced "tock tock"] Popcorn.

tacky, *adj.* **1.** There is no other word to take its place, no exact synonym, but it means something like dowdy or ridiculous in manner or dress, or too much of the wrong thing. "She was the tackiest thing. Those high-heeled run-over shoes, that frizzy hair with all those little bows, that ratty ole fur piece, and a beaded dress, right in the middle of the day!" **2.** A gauche way of behaving. "Everything she did was just plain tacky." (Until a few years back, non-Southerners had no idea what this word meant, and it was never heard except when spoken by a Southerner. Then Hollywood picked it up, and now it's being exploited by the entire English-speaking world. Oh, well, imitation is the sincerest form of flattery.) **3.** A cooking term meaning "sticky."

tacky, *n.* **1.** A poor-white person. **2.** A sorry horse. "If that isn't one pitiful sight—that poor ragtail tacky riding an old broken-down tacky."

tail twister, *n.* The person who keeps things moving; one who gets things done. "He was the tail twister in that organization. Wudn't for him, nothin' would get done."

take, *v.* The study of some subject or activity. "Do you play the piano?" "Oh, yes, I take from Miz Hankins."

take and. A receipt direction. Old receipts started out, "You take and . . ." Like this: "You take and mix one cup flour with a half cup lard, then you take and measure . . ." and so on.

take and rake. [Mountain and rural] Means to serve yourself with food and start eating. "You don't have to be shamefaced 'bout eatin' at our place. Take and rake plenny now."

take company. [Old] To begin a courtship. "She had taken company with the most eligible bachelor in town."

take in. To begin, as school or church. "What time does school take in where you go?"

take in after. To chase. "Whoo-ee! Did you see how the poe-lice took in after that car?"

take it hard. To show a lot of grief over a death or a loss of some kind. "Did Miz Reese take it hard at the cemetery?" "Honey, I declare I thought she was going to jump right in the grave with him."

take on. To make a big fuss over, or to act show-offy about something. "She took on something awful about what he said."

takes a good picture. If someone takes a good picture, it doesn't mean he handles a camera well, but that he's photogenic.

take sick. To come down with a disease or an ailment. "That woman takes sick ev'ry whipstitch."

tal, *n.* Towel. "For her birthday she got three bath tals, three han' tals, and two wash rags—all matchin'."

tale; tayuhl, *n.* [Mountain and other] An idle or malicious report. "That ornery varmint! He's got a tale to tell about ever'-body."

tale-bearer, *n.* A gossip.

talk, *v. & n.* Yankees say it dictionary-proper, "tok," but Southerners like the "l" in it.

talking mess, *v.* Talking nonsense. "You're just talking mess and you know it."

tall cotton, *n.* A thing of quality. "When you're with that lady, honey, you are in *tall* cotton."

tamareen, *n.* Tambourine.

tanglefoot, *n.* Rotgut whiskey.

tar, *n.* You must have four of these on the wheels of your audo-mow-beel.

Tarheel, *n.* A North Carolinian. (One story is that this nickname comes from the Revolutionary War era. Cornwallis's men were said to have crossed a North Carolina river into which tar had been poured, and came out with tar on their heels. The more logical explanation, however, is that it followed naturally because of all the tar, pitch, and turpentine produced there.)

tarpeter, *n.* [A corruption of "torpedo"] A plaything familiar to Southern boyhood of yore. The tar used for keeping railroad ties in repair was picked up, shaped into what they thought a torpedo would look like, and used for their games of warfare.

ta ta. [From baby talk] What Southern parents say to their babies to teach, or to remind them to say, "Thank you."

tater, *n.* Potato. This tuberous plant comes in two varieties—Irish and sweet. Taters aren't only for eating, though; they're nature's own best stopper for the spout of an oil can.

tater trap, *n.* One's mouth. "If you don't shut yore big tater trap, boy, you're gonna be in big trouble."

Taxas, *n.* They spell their state "Texas," but a lot of them call it "Taxas." (No wonder Texans are so cosmopolitan; after all, since 1685 they've been under the jurisdiction or influence of France, Spain, Mexico, the Republic of Texas, the Confederacy, and the United States. And it's understandable why Texans are so proud—what other state once had its own president? Not to mention the facts that Dallas has long been a center of culture in this country, and that the state is loaded with colleges and universities.)

teacherage, *n.* A residence for the teachers of a particular school.

tea towel, *n.* Towels that are used for drying dishes, especially the fancy towels.

tear up. To destroy verbally; to get the best of someone. "You better watch out what you say to him. He can tear you up with a word and a look."

tear up (one's) stomach. To upset one's stomach; to cause diarrhea. "Them raw peanuts I et, on top of that bait o' Brunswick stew—man, is my stomach tore up today."

teddy, *n.* A woman's one-piece undergarment—usually dainty— and what Southern belles called their "shimmies" (chemises) years ago. "What a trousseau! A dozen or moah hayan-made teddies, jus' full of tucks an' trimmed in yods an' yods of impoahted lace and ribbon."

tee-niney, *adj.* Tiny.

tee-toncy, *adj.* Teenie weenie. "I'll have just a tee-toncy piece."

Tennessee quick step, *n.* [Civil War term] Diarrhea. (During the Civil War, whiskey was a standard treatment for this condition.)

tetch, *v. & n.* [Old] Touch.

tetched in the head. Crazy or feeble-minded.

tetchous; tetchy, *adj.* Sensitive; touchy. "Them tetchous people get on my nerves. I don't want to be around anybody I have to handle with kid gloves."

ten-cent hopes, *n.* Small expectations; not much to look forward to.

terbaccy, *n.* [Mountain and rural] Tobacco.

terms of endearment, Southern. Southerners love their food as much as each other, and nowhere is this more apparent than in their terms of endearment. Here's a short list: buttercup, dumplin', honey, honey bun, honey bunch, honey child, honey pot, lamb, lambkin, lollipop, puddin', puddin' pie, punkin, punkin head, sugah, sugah doodle, sugah candy, sugah foot, sugah pie, sugah plum, sweet, sweet'art, and sweetie pie.

terrified fever, *n.* [Black; old] Typhoid fever.

tetter, *n.* Various skin diseases, eczema for one; blisters and pimples.

Texas fever, *n.* This was the "disease" that prompted people to go to Texas in search of their fortunes, beginning about 1830.

Texas tea, *n.* Black gold; oil.

Texmex, *n.* A person of Mexican blood who was born in Texas.

thank-ye-ma'am, *n.* [Old] A deep hole or rut in the road; a love hole [q.v.] (A thank-ye-ma'am is said to have been called that because the constant jolting of a carriage caused a male rider to have to apologize continuously to a lady companion, then to thank her when she acknowledged his regrets. That was truly the age of courtesy.)

That War, *n.* How Southerners usually spoke of the War Between the States after the fact.

the. Years ago "the" preceded the name of most diseases, especially in the speech of the common folks. An individual was afflicted with the asthma, the rheumatism, the bad disease, et cetera.

thee-ay-ter, *n.* [Accent on the "ay"] An auditorium for the presentation of plays and other performances.

thick, *adj.* Chummy; intimate. "If you ask me, those two are getting mighty thick."

think on (it). To consider or contemplate a matter. "Now, wait a minute. I'm gonna have to think on that for a bit."

thin-minded, *adj.* Forgetful, or not up to snuff mentally. "She was so thin-minded, she was liable to forget her own name."

this here; this year. This. "This year thang is drivin' me crazy."

thoogh, *prep., adv., adj., n.* Through. "When he's thoogh with what he's doin', we'll go up and say hello."

thow, *v.* Throw. "Oh, man, could Dizzy Dean thow that baseball!"

three cheers, *n.* Seats for three people.

three hots, *n.* Three hot meals a day—often with hot, freshly baked bread with each meal. "I don't worry too much about nothin', so long as I've got a ruff over my head an' three hots a day."

three-M diet, *n.* Meat (fatback), meal (corn), and molasses—the standard and traditional diet of the old Southern frontier. (It was also true of the more deprived people during the Great Depression, and the cause of much pellagra.)

throw off on. Make fun of; to belittle, or speak disparagingly of. (To quote a North Carolina woman who drew the envy of some of her neighbors when President and Mrs. Lyndon Johnson chose to visit with her and her family in 1964: "We've been talked at, talked to, talked about, and throwed off on.")

thud, *adj.* As in "fust, secont, thud, and home!"

thunderbucket, *n.* A chamber pot; a slop jar.

thunderation, *n.* A euphemism for damnation; a mild imprecation.

tickled, *adj.* Pleased; happy. "I'm tickled to see you."

tickler, *n.* [Kentucky] A narrow bottle holding a half-pint; it was said to be "just enough to tickle the palate."

tight, *n.* A tight spot. "He was in a tight again."

tight-butted pants, *n.* Tight-fitting pants.

timberhead talk, *n.* When the men sat on the stanchion (also called the timberhead) of the Mississippi River barges to chat between towing jobs, that was said to be timberhead talk.

time, *n.* One's turn to do something, as in playing a game. "Oh, is it my time?"

time, *n.* Wages. "He got so mad, he quit right on the spot—didn't even ask for his time."

Tin-a-see, *n.* They know how to spell it there—Tennessee—and they also know how they want to say it.

ting-a-ling, *n.* [Cajun] A percussion musical instrument, the triangle.

tinpins, *n.* Tenpins, a game similar to bowling.

tin-tin. Fifty minutes to eleven.

tin willy, *n.* [Early 1900s] Canned corn beef.

tippling house, *n.* A saloon.

tip the jug. To drink intoxicating beverages. "Ain't a man in that family that don't love tipping the jug."

tippy-toe, *v.* To walk softly or gingerly; to walk on the toes. "Tippy-toe in there and see if the baby's asleep."

tisik; tizzik, *n.* [Old] Asthma.

tizzy, *n.* A lot of excitement over practically nothing. "One cross word to her and she's in a regular tizzy."

toad-floater, *n.* A hard rain.

toad-strangler, *n.* A gulley-washer; a powerful heavy rain.

tobacco juice, *n.* **1.** The brown fluid expelled by a grasshopper as a defense mechanism. **2.** A mixture of human spittle and tobacco essence.

to-do, *n.* A party or social function; a big hullabaloo.

toddick, *n.* A tiny amount. "All the stores closed and not a toddick of salt in the house."

togather, *adv.* Southerners spell it with two *e*'s, but they usually say "togather."

tolable, *adj.* Tolerable; how one feels if he feels neither good nor bad.

tomar; tomarrah, *n.* The day after today; the day that "never comes."

tomfool, *n. and adj.* A total fool.

tomthumb, *n.* [North Carolina] A sausage stuffed in a chitterling (chitlin) casing.

tom-walkers, *n.* Stilts.

tongue wagging. 1. *v.* Talking excessively. **2.** *adj.* "Pore man, he's got a real tongue-waggin' wife."

toot, *n.* An insignificant amount. "He wasn't worth a toot." "I don't give a toot!"

toothache tree, *n.* The prickly ash. The seeds and bark of this tree were used by people of the seacoasts of North Carolina and Virginia to brew a toothache remedy. (The leaves were said to smell like those of orange trees.)

tooth doctor, *n.* A dentist.

toothsome, *adj.* [Old-timey] Good to the taste.

top cow, *n.* [Ozarks and others] A bull.

tossel, *n.* A Southern tassel; a bunch of threads or cords tied together at one end and used as a hanging ornament for clothing and house furnishings.

tote, *v.* [Belgian Congo: "to pick up"] To carry. (To Southerners, "tote" seems to mean something more than "carry"; to tote a thing seems to indicate that more effort was involved.) "She was pitiful—havin' to tote all those heavy groshries all the way from the groshry store."

tother. The other. "I don't care which one I have—one's as good as tother."

totings, *n.* Leftovers that servants used to take home from the "big house" where they worked.

touch you! That's a reply (sometimes sincere, sometimes not) to someone who has done or said something supposedly remarkable. [Shortened from "Just let me touch you"]

tourister, *n.* [Mountain] A tourist; an outsider.

tourist's glasses, *n.* [Mountain] Sunglasses.

tow sack; tow bag, *n.* A gunnysack; a bag made from jute or burlap.

trade, *v.* To shop; to buy things. "We've traded at Bass's groshry store as long as I can remember."

traipse, *v.* To tramp doggedly about; to wander. "They traipsed all over town looking for some excitement."

train-left, *adj.* To have missed a train. "Bein' train-left is the most let-downes' feelin' in the world."

trash, *n.* If one is trash, one just isn't anybody; one is as common as corn bread.

trash mouth, *n.* Dirty or coarse language or subject matter. "Don't come around me talking that trash mouth, 'cause I want no truck with you."

trashy, *adj.* About the worst thing a Southerner can be; low, low class.

Traveller, *n.* The aristocrat of all horses—the beloved steed of Marse Robert E. Lee.

tree molasses, *n.* Maple syrup.

trifling, *adj.* No-account; shiftless. "Those Lesters up there, they always were a trifling bunch of people." (A person who is trifling is often trashy, as well.)

tromple, *v.* To trample.

truck, *n.* Association; dealings. "We'll have no truck with that vermin."

true fact, *n.* A "true" fact is somehow truer than a plain fact.

Truly Civil War, When the War Between the States Became a. The noblest gesture ever tendered a Rebel by a Yankee was when General Grant had the delicacy not to request General Lee's sword at Appomatox. On that historic day even a Southerner had to admit that General Grant's deportment was altogether sensitive, generous, compassionate, and impeccable. In fact, General Ullysses S. Grant lived his finest hour on April 9, 1865.

trumpery, *n.* Junk. "A closet full of trumpery, that's all it is."

trumpery room, *n.* A junk room.

trying the lard. To render pork fat.

tuckered; tuckered out, *adj.* Worn out; exhausted. "Climb Eagle Nest Mountain! Lord mercy, I'd be tuckered 'fore I got started good." "He was just plum tuckered out."

tump, *v.* To tilt or turn over. "She stumped her toe and the bucket tumped over."

tune heister, *n.* [Mountain] A musician. "You go to Nashville, 'bout ev'ry other guy you meet claims to be a tune heister."

tune up, *v.* Getting ready to cry. "She's been blue for a week—tunes up to cry if you just look at her."

turble, *adj.* Terrible. "The war was a turble time for ever'body."

turkle, *n.* [Mountain and rural] Turtle.

turn, *n.* **1.** A load of something. ". . . a big turn of groceries." **2.** Personality. "There was a real pleasant turn to her."

turn, *v.* To sour or go bad. "When the baby threw his bottle on the floor, I knew the milk had turned."

turn out, *n.* A gathering of people for an event.

turn over. To not "turn over" is to sleep soundly. "You certainly slept good last night. I don't think you even turned over."

turn the pan off. Means to "turn the fire (heat) off under the pan."

turnup sallit; turnip salad, *n.* Turnip tops that have been cooked, usually with cured pork fat.

turpentime, *n.* Turpentine.

tush; tesh, *n.* A tooth that protrudes, or that extends noticeably out of line.

twang (someone's) buds. To titillate the taste buds. "Lord, does that country ham and grits look good! They sure twang my buds."

twarge, *prep.* [Old] Toward. "Twarge dark he'll use'ly go up to Mr. Willet's and set around the store for a spell."

twict, *adv.* Twice. "Oncet, twict, three times . . ."

twidget, *n.* A girl or woman of low class and low morals.

twinkles, *n.* [Mountain] Pine needles. (They "twinkle" when stepped on.)

twixt; betwixt, *adv.* Between.

U

udduh. 1. *v.* Utter, to make vocal sounds. **2.** *n.* Udder. Mammary gland of a cow.

ugly, *adj.* The word "ugly" is a remonstrance that a Southerner hears from infancy on. A child born in the South is supposed to hear no ugly, see no ugly, and above all, *act* no ugly, ever. "Now, children, if one of you acts the least bit ugly when our comp'ny comes, well, you know what to expect." "Mama! Mama! Bubba's talkin' ugly again. He said 'darn you' to me."

ujinctum, *n.* [Old] A hell-like place. "If he doesn't mend his ways, he's headed straight for the ujinctum."

umbrella, *n.* A bumbershoot; a parasol.

umparr, *n.* The person or persons present at sports contests to call the plays and argue with the players.

Uncivil War, *n.* "That War" (as fought by the other side).

undentify, *v.* [Unschooled] To identify.

underbody, *n.* **1.** A woman's lightweight undershirt. **2.** A corset cover.

underminded, *adj.* Two-faced; devious. "He was the most underminded man I ever met."

understandings, *n.* Human feet as a foundation. (Someone with big feet is said to have a "good understanding.")

under the jail. "The penitentiary is too good for him. For what he did, he should be put under the jail."

unfitten, *adj.* Not fit for a particular purpose.

U-ninted States, *n.* "Well, *naow* they're u-ninted."

unthoughted, *adj.***1.** Spontaneous; natural; impromptu. "It was a purely unthoughted speech, but one of the finest you could ever hear." **2.** Thoughtless; unkind. "That was a very unthoughted thing you just said."

uppity, *adj.* Snobbish; having a superior manner.

upscuddle, *n.* A quarrel. "That was some upscuddle going on across the street last night."

uptown, *adj.* [Black] **1.** All decked out; looking special. "Man, look at those shiny shoes and that sharp new suit. Boy, you are uptown tonight." **2.** [New Orleans] Upriver.

uptown lady, *n.* A woman who is, or pretends to be, wealthy, refined, social, and sophisticated. "She thought she was a real uptown lady, but not in my estimation, she wudn't."

urging, *n.* Urge. "I had the strongest urgin' to slap his face."

used to could. Once was able to. "I used to could run a mile an' not git one bit breathy."

Useless Grant. Well, we didn't name him that. His own Yankee neighbors did it, and *before* the war. We did help right much to perpetuate it, though.

usings, *n.* Something kept for one's own use. "Yeah, we raise a heap o' hawgs, but us bein' so partial to poke, we still don't have much to sell after we've cured up our own usin's."

usuns, *pron.* [Mountain and rural; archaic] Us. "Rain or shine, usuns never miss Sund'y meetin'."

uv coas. Of course; certainly; sure enough.

valentime, *n.* What your sweetheart sends you on February the fourteenth.

vals, *n.* Vowels. "Aye, ee, ah, owe, yew, an' wunst in a while, wah."

vapors, *n.* A hysterical nervous state or a fainting fit that afflicts the more dramatic Southern belles. (This is what Great-Aunt Sarah, when young, used to get a case of if she wanted to get out of taking care of a disagreeable task, or when she wanted to impress a man with her fragility and femininity. It went out of style when men caught on.)

varmint, *n.* Any mean and bothersome thing; Yankees in Civil War times; a wild or troublesome animal.

vascinator, *n.* A fascinator; a head scarf.

vasty, *adj.* Immense; expansive. "After livin' in a vasty place like these here mount'ns, how'm I ever goin' to tolerate bein' cooped up in the city?"

veg-uh-tuh-ble, *n.* [Virginia; accent on the "tuh"] Edible plants.

verclose veins, *n.* Abnormally distended blood vessels (to people who quituated school too young).

very well. [Accent on the "very"] Means "fairly well." "I feel *very* well, thank you." ("Very" is not used as an intensive here, but in a conditional way.)

vestes, *n.* [Old; mountain] Vests. "Did you know that vestes are comin' back in fashion?"

vicy versy. [Mountain] One way or t'other.

viduck, *n.* Viaduct (not a gourmet dish featuring a web-footed fowl).

vigrous, *adj.* Vicious; fierce; mean. "You couldn't pay me to have one of them pit bulls. They are vigrous animals, they are." "That is one more vigrous female Odell Simms got hise'f hitched up with."

vile, *n.* A small glass or plastic container, often used for medicines; a vial. "She swallered a whole vile of sleepin' pills tryin' to commit sideways, and I swear she didn't even get sleepy."

vinegar pie. There are two kinds of vinegar pie: One is filled with a toothsome chesslike mixture that is very subtly flavored with cider vinegar; the other is a unique affair, the filling made of beaten eggs, vinegar, sugar, butter, chopped raisins, and spices.

violent water, *n.* Panther sweat; bad whiskey.

virgin Coke, *n.* [Circa 1920s–1930s] A Coke with a dash of cherry-flavored syrup.

Virginia Dare. The first white child born in America, in 1587. A North Carolina county was named for her.

vittles, *n.* Food for people. "I swear to you, she'd spend our last red cent on vittles, and not a drop o' likker in the house."

voider, *n.* A small receptacle used to help in clearing a table. With a brush, crumbs and ashes are swept from the tablecloth into the voider. (This is also called a "silent butler.")

volleydo, *n.* [New Orleans] A swing or merry-go-round.

volunteer, *n.* Plants grown from seeds not planted or tended in the usual way, but transported and dropped by birds or the wind. "That ole volunteer corn dudn't amount to a tinker's damn."

vomick, *v.* To throw up.

vow, *v.* In the kinder, gentler days of the South, ladies used to "vow" all over the place. "Ah vow your pa can't see the forest for the squirrels. If he brings innymore of these varmints in here for me to skin and cook, Ah don't know what Ah'll do."

vowel shift, the great. This was a major change in the pronunciation of English that began soon after Chaucer's time. Vowels were switched around—like "i" for "e," "e" for "a," "ou" for "oo." We Rebels didn't cotton to the idea much, though, so we still pronounce a lot of words the same way Mr. Geoff Chaucer did. Examples: "hoose" for "house" (Virginia and South Carolina); "pin" for "pen" (more or less throughout the South); "fer" for "far" (Mountains). And all the time this big sound to-do was going on, our ancestors pretty much held on to the same old spelling (called "right writing" then) that Mr. Bill Caxton, the first English printer, had used, and that's the reason English is often pronounced one way and spelled another.

vylun, *n.* Violin, a stringed instrument played with horsehairs.

wadder, *n.* Water. "Wadder, wadder, ever'whar, but not a drop to drink," as it may have gone had Samuel Taylor Coleridge written of an ancient mountaineer (from North Carolina) rather than an "Ancient Mariner."

wahnid, *v.* Wanted.

wagging tongue, *n.* A garrulous or gossipy person is said to have a wagging tongue.

waiter, *n.* **1.** [Old] A male attendant or usher at a wedding. **2.** A serving tray.

wait on. To wait for. "She's slow as 'lasses. Ever'wher we go, I gotta stop an' wait on her."

walking-around money, *n.* Money in your pocket to be used for immediate expenses.

walk out with. [Old] A courting practice. "He's got it bad. He's walked out with her most ev'ry night this week."

wampy-jawed; whomper-jawed, *adj*. A jaw that is out of line or protrudes.

wan, *n*. Wine. "There's sherry, pote, dandeline, and then there's that bubbly stuff."

wanna. Want to. "I don' wanna, but I gotta."

warm (his) britches. To give a spanking or whipping.

warnut, *n*. [Mountain and rural] Walnut. "Ainglish warnuts don't hold a light to our good ole black warnuts."

warsh, *n*. To cleanse with soap and "wadder."

Warshington, *n*. [Mountains mainly] The United States capitol.

washing powders, *n*. Soap or detergent powder.

wasp's nest bread, *n*. [Old] Light bread; "rising" bread; yeast bread. "My ole womern better not give me inny o' that ole wasp's nest bread—I'm a hot biscuit man myse'f."

watch your mouth. Be careful what you say.

water (wadder) works, *n*. [Black] The urinary system.

waving fence, *n*. A zigzag fence.

way-ul. 1. *n*. Well. "Hope you don't never fall in one." **2.** *interj*. As in "Way-ul, way-ul!"

weak trembles. A shakiness of one's body. "That old dog scared her so bad, she had the weak trembles all day."

well house, *n*. An old-timey "refrigerator"; a little house built near the well which contained a trough that was kept filled with cold water and in which food was kept cool. (When there was no well house, the well bucket itself was lowered partially into the water, holding perishables like milk and butter.)

went to. Started; began. "When he said no, she went to cryin' like huh little hot would break."

werman, *n.* [Mountain] Woman.

Wesort, *n.* One of a group of racially mixed people—Indian, white, and black—who live in Southern Maryland.

West by-God Virginia, *n.* Jocular for West Virginia.

Wes' Vuhginyuh, *n.* Would you believe the state of "Kana-wha"? That's what West Virginia almost decided to call itself when it separated from Virginia. Although it became the thirty-fifth state in 1863, the "West" part of its name never kept them from acting and sounding pretty darned Southern.

whangdoodle, *n.* An imaginary creature, shaped and described according to the purpose and the imagination of the individual telling a story. A whangdoodle can be scary, comic, or even lovable, but it is most often on the fierce side.

whar; wher, *adv.* "Where" in some parts of the South.

what-for, *n.* A chastisement or blessing out. "She really gave me the what-for when I got home last night."

what's (her) face. What's her name?

what is (something) doing (someplace)? Means "why." "What is that hat doing on that bed?" "Nothing that I can see—just lying there behaving itself."

what you say! [Black] An expression of surprise and/or agreement at what one is hearing.

wheel bar, *n.* A wheelbarrow.

where the woodbine twineth. Sleepyland. "Five more min-utes of rocking and the baby will be where the woondbine twineth."

which nor whether. One way or the other; indifference to something. "She didn't care which nor whether about what people thought."

whiffle dust, *n.* Magic dust that one sprinkles secretly near his quarry to insure that he'll get what he desires.

whipstitch, *n.* A small amount of time.

whistlebritches, *n.* A small boy dressed up in a mature style.

whistler's walk, *n.* A well-worn path connecting the cookhouse area with the living quarters of a plantation. Slaves carrying food from the kitchen were required to whistle as they hurried along, preventing them from sampling the dishes bound for the master's table. (In those days kitchens were often built apart from the main house as a fire prevention measure.)

white bacon, *n.* Fat back; salt pork.

white-eye, *v.* To be overcome from heat prostration, or some other condition, until one is near fainting, causing one's eyes to roll back. "I saw her white-eyeing and caught her before she fell."

white lightning, *n.* Moonshine whiskey.

white tiger, *n.* White lightning.

who-all. Who. "Who-all's goin' to the babtizin'?"

whole hawg (hog), *n.* The limit; all the way. "He decided to go whole hawg and eat the entire pie."

whomp up. To stir up, or throw things together. "He could whomp up a roe-mance between two dead people."

whoop and a holler. [See "holler and a whoop."]

who you are, remember. This is a warning from a parent or other relative that means to keep your dignity, "act like you're somebody," and, above all, uphold the family's standing; for pride (justified or not) is an outstanding characteristic of the Southerner's persona.

whup, *v.* To whip.

whyn't. A contraction for "why don't." "Whyn't you go an' stop pesterin' me?"

widder-woman, *n.* A woman whose husband has died.

widowmaker, *n. & adj.* Any dangerous or risky contraption or action that could cause a woman to become a widow. "Is Evel Knevil still pullin' those widowmaker stunts of his?"

wildcat, *n.* Lousy liquor; violent water.

wild oats, *n.* An old North Carolina name for wild rice. (Wild rice is not a true rice, but is the seed of a particular kind of marsh grass.)

windershiel, *n.* [Tennessee] Windshield. For keeping the wind and suicidal bugs out of a motorist's face.

wirehouse, *n.* Warehouse; a big building used for storage.

wise and masterly inactivity. This is the way wise old John C. Calhoun described the South's inclination not to hurry.

wish book, *n.* A mail-order catalog. "Soon's the new Montgumry Ward wish book gets here, Ma says I can order me a new Sund'y-go-to-meetin' dress."

witch water, *n.* The visible heat waves that rise up from a paved road on a burning-hot sunny day.

with squirrel. [Ozarks] In a family way. "Don't tell me that Jessie Mae's with squirrel *agin!*"

witness tree, *n.* A tree marked by a surveyor to indicate a certain distance or a boundary.

wobbles, *n.* Misgivings; butterflies in one's stomach. "She was purty as a pitcher in her weddin' dress, but oh, lordy, did she have a bad case of the wobbles.

women in white shrouds. [Mountain] Nurses.

womern, *n.* Old mountain talk for "woman."

woodcock, *n.* A once popular Louisiana dish which was a rarebit containing no woodcock, just as Welsh rabbit (or rarebit) contains no rabbit.

wood's-colt, *n.* [Mountain] An illegitimate child; an outsider [q.v.].

woolhat, *n.* A small-scale farmer of South Carolina, Georgia, and Florida, who wore a broad-brimmed woolen hat year-round and who took a fierce interest in politics. He was neither educated nor sophisticated, but anybody who wanted to win an election knew to pay him a little attention and a lot of respect.

won't. Wasn't. "It won't botherin' me none, whut he said."

word, *adj.* Distressed or perplexed. "I just wish to my soul he wouldn't sit around lookin' so word all the time."

wordbook, *n.* What you are eyeballing this very minute—a dictionary.

working medicine, *n.* A laxative.

worryation, *n.* [Mountain] Worry; vexation. "Nothin'—absolutely nothin'—is worth all the worryation I'm goin' through."

worth, *prep.* What's the price of? "How much are your eggs worth today, Miz Higgins?"

worth shucks, not. No-account; of no value. "He gave me his old Ford, but I tell you, it's really not worth shucks."

WPA. "We Poke Around," "We Piddle Around"; these two things are what people joked that WPA stood for. (That was the Work Projects Administration, a federal employment program instituted during the Great Depression.)

writermarouster, *n.* A court order of eviction; a notice to vacate a property. "When we got home that evening there was a writermarouster on our door."

wrongside outerds. Wrong side out.

wrop, *v.* [Mountain] Wrap.

wunst, *adj.* Upon a time. [Old for "once"]

w'y, yea-us. Southern for *mai oui.*

x. An *x* is a figure used to represent several things: a signature for the uneducated; a symbol for marking spots; a great big kiss.

Xmas gift! What people go around yelling at each other on Xmas morning, the tradition being that whoever shouts it first is supposed to get a present from the slower speaker. ("Xmas" is a shortened form of "Christmas." Many people object to this usage on the grounds that *x* stands for "unknown quantity," and therefore "takes Christ out of Christmas." Fiddle-dee-dee. In this instance *x* actually means Christ; we borrowed it from the Greeks.)

yale, *n.* Yell, a sudden cry or scream.

y'all; you-all, *pron.* Means "all of you." It is used in speaking to two or more people, never to just one person except by Damnyankees trying to be cute, or who don't know any better. Besides, "you all" is sanctioned by biblical use (Job 17:10). (Grammatically speaking, "y'all" is known as the "generous plural"; so is Yankee "youse," rural and mountain "you-uns," and the interesting "mongst-ye," which used to be heard in coastal North Carolina and Virginia.)

y'all come. An invitation meaning "All of you come to see us."

yaller. [Old] **1.** *adj.* Describing a color mindful of a ripe lemon. **2.** *n.* The yolk of an "aig."

yaller janders, *n.* A disease of the liver; jaundice.

yam, *n.* The yam is not a true sweet potato, and is of inferior quality to the sweet potato. Yet the terms "yam" and "sweet potato" are used interchangeably in the South—with one exception: for some unknown reason, when sweet potatoes are candied below the Mason and Dixon line, they invariably become "yams." (Sweet potatoes have long been a favorite food of Southerners, indeed, often serve as the mainstay of a Rebel's diet. To attest to this is the fact that the largest sweet potato auction market in the world is at Tabor City, N.C., where each year they honor their beloved tuber by celebrating the Carolina Yam Festival.)

yam, *v.* [Black] To eat. "You sit there yamming and I do all the work."

Yankee, *n.* A euphemism for Damnyankee; a dirty six-letter word.

Yankee shot you, where the. A Southerner's navel. An example: It's summer and the cute-as-a-speckled-pup porch baby toddles over to Gran'pa. Gran'pa smiles fondly, chucks the teensy youngun under the chin, then points to the small belly button peeping out from under the wee shirt. "Oh, what do I see? I see where the Yankee shot ya."

yarb, *n.* [Mountain and rural] Herb.

yarb woman, *n.* There are still yarb women (and men) who make their livings, "sich as they are," picking and selling the mountain herbs. The "yarbs" are bought by drug houses and by spice and herb purveyors.

yard egg, *n.* A hen egg found in the yard and, compared to a nest egg, considered by some to be a bit less desirable for the breakfast table.

yard baby, *n.* That's when a youngun is big enough to play in the yard if someone keeps "eyeballing" him from a "winduh" to see that he's all right. (This same child started out in life as a teensie-weensie "breast baby," became a "lap baby," was next a "knee baby," graduated to "porch baby," then felt real proud and grown-up when he finally made it to the yard.)

yard bird, *n.* A chicken.

yearling girl, *n.* [Georgia] A somewhat immature and still inexperienced young girl.

years, *n.* [Mountain and rural; old] What one hears with; headwings.

yes-siree Bob. A very definite "yes."

yessum. Yes, ma'am. "Yessum, thank you. I sure would like a piece of cake."

yestiddy, *n.* The day before today.

yonder, *adj.* At an indefinite distance—in the South, a *very* indefinite distance. If it's "over yonder," that can mean anything from six feet to sixty miles from the person speaking; if it's "out yonder," that can be out in his front yard or across the ocean;

but, man, when he says "up yonder," he can be talking about the starling in his plum tree as well as that place in the sky he's hoping to go to when he dies.

yore, *pron.* Your, as in "Yore new Sund'y dress is mighty purty. Did you order that outen the Montgumry Ward wish book?"

youngun, *n.* A Southern young person; often one who has fewer advantages than one who's called "chile."

yourn, *pron.* "It hain't mine, it's yourn."

youth-and-old-age, *n.* The zinnia—a flower that doesn't smell one bit like a posy should smell.

you-uns, *pron.* [Mountain; old] You-all.

you welcome. Southerners seldom bother with the "are."

yurling, *n.* Yearling; a baby cow or deer.

zast, *n.* Zest. A love of life; gusto.

zaybruh, *n.* A horse dressed up in stripes like a convict.

zeerow, *n.* A ring around nothing; a circle filled with naught.

zinc, *n.* [Virginia; Louisiana] A sink; a water basin.

Zine, *n.* Zion. On a hill far away, in Jerusalem, the site of Solomon's Temple and the City of David; the Promised Land.

Southern Sayings

(She) looks like an accident that started out to happen. Someone or something that's a big mess.

. . . all of hell and half of Georgia. That's a whole bunch of people. "Boy, howdy, I believe all of hell and half of Georgia was out there."

The Almighty made (her) as ugly as He could, then He set (her) up on a mud fence and tried to scare (her) to death. That's someone as ugly as homemade sin and who's probably aware of it.

. . . as alone as a Catholic at a Baptist convention.

. . . doesn't amount to a puddle of warm spit. [A favorite saying of Vice President John N. Garner]

There must have been an angel flying past. Said when someone is suddenly seized by a little chill or tremor.

. . . got a bad cat on the line. Someone to be aware of; someone threatening or dangerous.

Go bang your head against the wall. To heck with you!

(He) was not behind the barn when the brains were passed out. Said of a person who has an extra share of gray cells.

. . . batting his eyes like a toad-frog in a hailstorm.

(It) beats picking cotton. Having a good time; or having it better, or easier, than expected.

(That) takes the whole biscuit. "Well, if that don't beat all."

(He was) blinking (his) eyes like a fox when he sees daylight.

. . . blown up like a toad. 1. To be silently angry; to be pouting. **2.** To have a distended stomach from overeating or indigestion.

. . . like two bobcats in a croker sack. That's a lot of action.

(I wasn't) born on crazy creek. "I'm not stupid."

(He was) born tired and raised lazy. About as unenterprising and no-account as one can get.

(Did you) come to borrow a coal of fire? What's your hurry?

. . . has the brains of a roach in a bathtub.

. . . has a brain no bigger than a June pea.

(His) britches are riding high. A condition of being immodestly proud, or of acting high and mighty. "His britches are ridin' mighty high since he landed that new job down at the cotton mill."

(You're) burning green wood for kindling. Working against all odds; to perform futilely.

If you get burnt, (you) got to sit on the blister. For those who are tired of: "If you make your bed, you must lie in it."

. . . busier than a cat in a roomful of rocking chairs.

. . . busier than a one-eyed cat watching three mice.

(He's) got bidness [business] on the street. That's having very important matters to take care of outside the home.

. . . as busy as a bee in a tar bucket.

. . . **as busy as a fly in a molasses jar.**

. . . **as busy as a man with one hoe and two rattlesnakes.**

. . . **as busy as two coons fighting in a croker sack.**

. . . **like buying a pig in a poke.** Something unseen whose true value is uncertain.

. . . **can't see for looking.** That's when someone makes such a big to-do of looking that he forgets what he's looking for.

. . . **no more chance than a pig in a dog race.**

(I) don't chew (my) tobacco but once. 1. Someone who doesn't make the same mistake twice. **2.** Saying that a word to the wise should be sufficient.

Church ain't over till the fat lady sings. Means that it ain't over till it's over.

. . . **clean as a hound's tooth.**

(He's) going to clean your plow. He's going to straighten you out.

. . . **as cold as 'lasses in January.** From someone who remembers going out on a cold morning to draw a jug full of molasses stored in the barn.

. . . **as cold as a well-digger's toe.**

His comb was getting red. Said of a male thinking of a female in a "physical" way. "His comb was gittin' red fer Widder Brown even a-fore his pore sick wife had taken off for heaven."

(A rooster's comb is said to turn red when the fowl is in an amorous state.)

. . . as common as cornbread. 1. Someone really low-class. **2.** An overabundance of something.

. . . as common as pig tracks. About as low as can be imagined.

(He's) so conceited that God Almighty's overcoat wouldn't make (him) a vest.

. . . (one) coon you can't tree. Someone too smart to be caught or outdone.

Your cotton is below the price. That's telling a female that her slip (petticoat) is showing.

. . . till the cows come home. That's a *long* time. "If I wait for him to finish what he's tryin' to do, I'll be waiting till the cows come home."

. . . like a cow on crutches. Someone awkward and clumsy; the depth of gracelessness. "She's got a right purty face, but I swear to you, that girl's got a walk like a cow on crutches."

(He) would crawl on broken glass through Hell for (her). That's love and devotion in the extreme.

. . . as crazy as a betsy-bug. 1. Describing a person who behaves in a foolish, frenetic way. **2.** Someone insane.

. . . as crazy as a bullbat.

. . . as cross as a bar [bear] with two cubs and a sore tail.

. . . to cut the tail off the dog. To make a long story short.

. . . as dark as a sleeping bear's dream.

. . . as dark as a stack of black cats.

. . . darker than a wolf's mouth.

It's so dark in here, all we need is a little organ music and some flowers.

. . . as depressing as a homecoming at the orphanage.

The devil's beating his wife. That's when it's raining and the sun is shining.

(He's) digging (his) grave with (his) teeth. Overeating and/or eating an unhealthy diet.

. . . as discouraged as a rice planter up a salt river.

It ain't the dog in the fight, it's the fight in the dog.

(That old) dog won't hunt. That idea is no good; that's not going to work.

I don't care what you call me as long as you call me for supper. Someone who is not quick to take offense.

Don't come around selling me those wolf tickets, 'cause I'm not buying. A woman's answer to a man who is trying to sweet-talk her. [Georgia; Pinkie Chatman]

Don't pay me any sunshine, 'cause I might cloud up and rain anytime. Means that one is wasting one's time in trying to butter someone up.

Don't put that washing out, 'cause it ain't clean. An untrue story; malicious gossip.

She's got her dress tail caught on a bedpost. A female who is tied down with responsibilities or by domination. (Origin: In the old days parents would put a bedpost on a child's dress tail to keep the child from wandering off, or to keep it from blowing away in a storm.)

. . . drinking that mash and talking that trash. Drunken drivel. "All they're ever interested in doing on a Sat'dy night is to drink that mash an' talk that trash."

. . . as drunk as a skunk at a moonshine still.

. . . as dry as an old maid's kiss.

. . . so dry here, you have to prime yourself to spit.

. . . like a duck after a june bug. That's a *fast* move.

. . . as dumb as a bucket of rocks.

(He's) so dumb, (he) couldn't count to twenty without taking off (his) shoes.

. . . as easy as selling watermelons on June-teenth [q.v.].

. . . as easy as sneaking dawn past a rooster. Not a chance.

(It's) like eating crawfish—There isn't any pretty way to do it.

(She) eats so much, it makes (her) po' [poor] to tote it. Explaining someone who has a voracious appetite, yet remains thin.

(He) has enough money to burn a wet mule.

It's enough to make a dog laugh.

Everywhere I turn, there's a barbwire fence. Facing constant obstacles and hard luck.

(Her) eyes bugged out like a tromped-on bullfrog.

. . . a face like forty miles of bad road. That is *ugly*. "She looked like an old rip with a face like forty miles of bad road."

. . . a face like a mule eating briars. To frown painfully.

. . . as fast as Forty going North. ("Forty" was a crack train that used to highball it between the South and the North. The route originated in Atlanta and went to New York. [Of course, it came back—who'd want to stay up there? And naturally, it was expected to travel much faster on the way up. You know how those Yankees are about hurrying.])

. . . faster than a rooster after a june bug.

(She's) so fat, (she's) in (her) own way. That *is* fat.

(I) feel like (I'm) a day late and a dollar short.

. . . feeling like a turkey in young corn. Elated over one's good fortune.

(He) felt like a poor boy at a frolic. That's feeling pretty forlorn and left out.

(He) has to fight them off with a wet tow sack. Someone who's irresistible to the opposite sex.

. . . as fine as frog hair. Describing a person's physical condition, or the quality of a thing. "Ah'm feelin' fine as frog hair this morning."

It's like trying to fix something that ain't broke. What someone said about the "Co'-Cola Cump'ny" when they made the "mistake" of bringing out the New Coke.

(She's) got flies up (her) nose. Because a stuck-up person is said to have his nose in the air, there's the possibility of flies getting up there.

. . . too frail to send out in a high wind.

If you fried (her) for a fool, you'd be wasting your fat. Someone hopelessly foolish.

. . . as full as a June goat.

. . . ain't had so much fun since the hogs et [ate] my little brother. A saying originating from someone with a macabre sense of humor.

. . . raises more fuss than a weasel in a henhouse.

Glory to God and General Grant! A saying among Southern blacks after the War Between the States.

(I'm) going to tell (her) head a mess. Going to tell someone off.

. . . go to the well with (him). To support someone with a project, or in a time of need. "He'd gone to the well with Jim many a time, but now that he needed Jim, where was he?"

(We) got what the bear grabbed at. Nothing; nothing was realized for one's efforts.

. . . like Grant took Richmond. 1. Means the obvious: an all-out attack on something or someone. **2.** A successful conquest. "What a ball game! We took them like Grant took Richmond."

(It's) the greatest thing since 7 Up. Something remarkable or exciting.

(It's) the greatest thing since sliced bread. (To appreciate this expression, just consider the time when a housewife had to bake and slice bread three times a day for a large family.)

She had so much green paint on her eyelids, I thought her gallbladder had done busted. [Jerry Clower]

(He's) so green, if it was springtime, the cows would eat (him) up. Inexperienced; naive.

(He) grew up with a ring around (his) nose. That's someone who's used to drinking straight from the fruit jar; to the moonshine born.

(He) was grinning like a mule eating thistles.

She wore her hair up on her head. Referring to an upswept hairdo.

. . . as happy as a dead hog in a mud hole. Not a care in this world.

. . . as happy as a dead pig in the sunshine.

. . . as happy as if (he) had good sense. Implying that if the person referred to had good sense, he wouldn't be that happy.

. . . if it harelips the South. Regardless of the consequences. "If it harelips the South, I'm going to have to give that woman a piece of my mind."

(I) hate (her) worse than wolf pizen [poison]. "I hate that ole store-boughten bread worse than wolf pizen."

(His) heart thumped like a tired mule's.

. . . from hell to breakfast. For an indefinite length of time; for a long time. "If it takes from hell to breakfast, I'm gonna see to it that that dawg is housebroke."

(He) felt like (he) was in Hell with the lid screwed down. That's sheer, unadulterated misery; in a no-win situation. "Working in the hosiery mill in August was like being in hell with the lid screwed down."

Let the hide go with the hair. Be that as it may; to heck with it all.

. . . higher than a Georgia pine. Tipsy from that ole devil 'shine.

. . . higher than a hawk's nest. Indicates high spirits. "Just a mere hello from him left her feeling higher than a hawk's nest."

(It was) like hitting a pretty girl in the face with a shovel. A desecration; an act of vandalism; a gauche lapse of taste.

Hold it in the road. To keep calm and steady; to stay on the right course (probably comes from the early days of teaching someone to drive a car). "Listen, my friend, Ah know you got your troubles, but you just hold it in the road for a lil' while longer an' ever'thing's gonna be awright."

leaking honey like an overflowing bee-tree. Someone putting on a sticky-sweet act.

I hope to kiss a tadpole! An exclamation of surprise or incredulousness.

I'll be the horse's head and you be yourself. [Louis Armstrong]

. . . as hot as the Fourth of July.

. . . as hot as an ignoramus in Hell writing a love letter and trying to spell.

. . . hotter than a two-dollar pistol on Saturday night.

(He's) so hungry, (his) backbone and navel shook dice to see which one was going to have the first bite.

(He's) so ignorant that when (he) tells you howdy, (he's) told you about all (he) knows.

(She's) in (her) own way. Said of people who are so big or fat or awkward that they seem to get in their own way. "What a pity. That poor girl is so fat, she looks like she's in her own way."

. . . as independent as a hog on ice.

(You) can't insult me, I'm too ignorant. The speaker is implying that he's immune to insults, especially when considering the source.

It's none of your beeswax, cornbread, and shoe tacks. A childish way of saying, "It's none of your business."

. . . **as jumpy as a frog in heat.**

(He's) the kind of person who would charge hell with a bucket of water.

(She) didn't know where (her) head was. 1. A flibbertigibbet. **2.** A mentally confused person.

(He's) leading (his) ducks to a bad market. Someone on his way to trouble.

. . . **leave a big gap in the hedge.** Suggesting the loss of something. "When they moved away, it sure left a big gap in our hedge."

(Who) licked the red off of your candy?

(She really) put a lid on (my) jar. To dash someone's hopes; to stop a plan or action abruptly.

(He'd) lie on credit if (he) knew (he) could cash it in for truth. An inveterate liar.

Life do get daily. [Black; Mississippi] Bemoaning the routine, the mundane, or the trials and tribulations of everyday living.

Liquor talks loud when it's loose from the jug.

(I) look forward to that with as much pleasure as a good case of cholera.

(He) looked as guilty as a suck-egg hound.

(He) looked like (he'd) been drug through a brush heap back'ards. Someone completely disheveled.

. . . looking like a poor boy at a frolic.

(He) looks like (he's) been rode hard and put away wet. A tired and dedraggled sight.

(She) looks like a sick chicken on a hot rock. (Was this Scarlett O'Hara after Ashley Wilkes gave her his final no?)

(She) looked like the small end of nothing whittled down to a fine point. How low can one get?

(She) looks like (she) was sent for and couldn't go and then went and wasn't wanted. That's persona non grata, sure nuff.

(She) looked like forty miles of bad road.

That's a lost ball in high weeds. A helpless, if not impossible, situation.

(He's) so low, (he) could walk under a trundle bed with a top hat on.

. . . mad as a rooster in an empty henhouse.

. . . mad as an old wet hen.

You can't make pound cake out of manure.
[Ferrol Sams]

(She) could make the old feel young and the poor feel rich. That's the epitome of charm and personality.

(My) mama didn't raise a stupid child. "Don't pull that one on me; I'm too smart."

. . . mean as a bee-stung dog.

(He's) so mean, (he'd) cut you up in small pieces and send you to the undertaker collect.

(He's) so mean, (he) must have been suckled by a wolf with four tits and holes punched for more.

. . . mean as a suck-egg dog.

. . . mean enough to bite a snake.

(He's got) so much money, some of it has gone to bed. Much more money than a person can use.

. . . more (fun or pleasure) than the law allows.

(His) mouth ain't no prayer book. Indicating that someone can't be trusted or isn't truthful.

(I) don't let (my) mouth say nothing (my) head can't stand. Saying nothing insincere, or that one can't live up.

(His) mouth was going like a cotton gin in picking time.

. . . as natural as dignity to a cat.

. . . as nervous as a whore in church.

(You're) nicer than you are ugly. A classic left-handed compliment.

. . . **as noisy as a mule in a tin barn.**

. . . **not room enough to cuss a cat without getting hair up your nose.**

(She's) not the only oyster in the stew.

(We) had oatmeal for breakfast, cornmeal for dinner, and miss-a-meal for supper. [John Griffin] This was said to be depression fare in the South.

(I'm) not going to pay (you) any sunshine, 'cause (you) might cloud up and rain anytime.

. . . **paint (his) back porch red.** To give someone a spanking.

Who peed on your Pop Tart? [Kentucky; Ohio; B. J. Foster] Said to someone who's out of sorts.

(They) picked (him) before he was ripe. Someone unusually short or undersized. "That Mickey Rooney! Even though they did pick him before he was ripe, he sure wound up with a lot o' talent."

. . . **play a tune on the seat of one's pants.** To administer a whipping or a spanking.

(You) can play with my dog, (you) can play with my wife, but (you'd) better leave my gun alone. [Texas]

(He) was so pore [poor] and thin, (he) had to lean up against a sapling to cuss.

Wonder what the poor folks are doing? A remark made when someone is reveling in some unexpected pleasure or unaccustomed luxury.

. . . too poor to paint and too proud to whitewash. Whitewash was what poor people used instead ˜ paint. It is white clay—and free. It is simply dug up from the ground.

(He) poured (me) back in the jug. To be put in one's place. The peremptory silencing of a person. "Soon as I opened my mouth to speak, man, did he pour me back in the jug."

. . . prettier than a striped snake.

. . . as pretty as a baby's smile.

. . . as pretty as a silver dollar.

That puts the lid on the jar. 1. To complete a project. **2.** To make a mess of something. "Boy, you really put the lid on the jar when you laughed at his sister."

. . . putting the big pot in the little one. That's big doings in anticipation of a coming event.

(He) has all the qualities of a dog except that of faithfulness.

(She) radiates love like a King heater.

(He) has a rag on every bush. A man who pays attention to many females, or has a lot of them on the string.

(I'd) rather listen to (him) talk than go to the bank. Indicating a spellbinding speaker.

. . . rattle the dishes and fool the cats. To prepare and eat a meager meal.

. . . rougher than a night in jail in South Georgia.

. . . like a rubber-nosed woodpecker in a petrified forest. A real lesson in futility.

(He) looked sadder than a hog in a bathtub.

Don't come selling me them wolf tickets, 'cause I ain't buying. [Black; Georgia] A woman's reply to a man trying to sweet-talk her.

(She) doesn't have sense enough to bell a buzzard. (Sense enough? But really, wouldn't it be pretty dumb to *want* to bell a buzzard?)

(You'd) have to shake the sheets to find (him). That's someone with a really slight build.

(He) can shoot the grease right out of a biscuit without breaking the crust. Describing a sharpshooter par excellence.

. . . sip sorrow with a teaspoon. "If you insist on keeping on your sinful path, I'm afraid you'll end up sipping sorrow with a teaspoon."

(He's) so skinny, (he) could take a shower bath in a double-barrel shotgun.

(He was) so skinny, (he) was nothing but breath and britches.

(He's) so skinny, it would take two of (him) to throw a shadow.

Well, slap the dog 'n' spit in the fire! An exclamation expressing surprise and wonderment.

. . . slick as a puppy's belly. In fine shape; a fine specimen of something or other.

(He's) as slick as owl manure on a glass doorknob. An individual to beware of.

(He's) slicker than a bucket of boiled okra. 1. One who cons people. **2.** A slippery object or surface.

(She) slings a nasty ankle. A first-rate dancer.

. . . slopping sugar all over each other. 1. Friends or acquaintances who are being verbally and profusely flattering. **2.** Heavy kissing or necking.

. . . as slow as grass growing. "Look at him poking along. I swear he's slower than grass growing."

(She) has a smile that'll blind your eyes and break your heart.

. . . as sociable as a basket of kittens.

. . . as Southern as tobacco, as cotton and peanuts and red-eye gravy. [Representative Hale Boggs paid this compliment to Lady Bird Johnson]

. . . more Southern than Atlanta. Sugah, that *is* Suthun!

Sparrows get just as hungry as robins and eagles. We all have the same needs.

(He'd) spit in a wildcat's eye. Alluding to someone who is either exceptionally brave, daring, or just plain foolhardy.

. . . put spit on the apple. To make things nicer.

. . . staying one day ahead of yesterday. That's the slowest kind of progress. "The way things are, I'll be lucky if I can stay just one day ahead of yesterday."

Somebody just stepped on your grave. Said to someone who suddenly and involuntarily shivers. ("Grave" refers to one's future burial site.)

(She) couldn't stop a pig in a ditch. Someone who is quite bowlegged.

. . . as straight as a martin ever went to his gourd. (In parts of the South, gourds are used for martin's nests. A hole is cut in one side of the gourd, then the gourd is hung in a tree.)

(He's) stronger than Adam's off ox. (Anyone ever wonder what an *off* ox is? In a team, the animal farthest from the driver is the off one.)

. . . as stubborn as a pump handle.

(She's) a sturdy oak with magnolia blossoms all the year long. A woman of both character and beauty.

(They) ate supper before (they) said grace. A pregnancy before marriage. "Huh uh! Looks like they ate supper before they said grace."

(She) swallowed a watermelon. That's when someone is visibly pregnant. "Umm, sure looks like she swallowed a waddermelon, dudn't it?"

(He'd) swap you out of your rheumatism if you'd sit still. Referring to a sharp trader.

(She's) so sweet, (she) would melt like a caramel in a man's mouth.

(He) got (his) tail in a crack. In a tight place; in a complicated situation.

(You) just take that up the road and dump it. "Don't give me that baloney."

That takes the whole biscuit! "Well, if that don't beat all!"

(He) could talk a bone away from a dog. The last word in persuasiveness.

(You're) talking to Noah about the flood. Being told something one already knows far too well.

. . . as thick as mud in the Mississippi Delta and hit a-rainin'. [James R. Winfree]

(I ain't) had time enough to pick a peach. That's when one is really pressed for time.

That's like taking time to shuck a nubbin. Something not worth the effort.

. . . took off like a new Ford.

. . . tough as nails and rough as a cob.

. . . traveling in tall cotton. In contact with someone, or something, of rare quality; being in fine company

. . . **trotting down to Hell on a fast horse in a porcupine saddle.**

(That's) trouble waiting for a ride.

If it ain't the truth, you can cut me up for catfish bait.

(That's) like trying to put a pair of panty hose on a wildcat.

(He's) about twelve cookies short of a dozen. Describing someone who's not too bright.

. . . **as ugly as homemade sin.**

(He) was so ugly, (he'd) make a freight train take a dirt road.

. . . **up the creek without a paddle.** In a peck of trouble.

. . . **all vines and no taters. 1.** A blowhard; a phony. **2.** A very light and insubstantial meal.

(It's) like wading in water backwards. Referring to an overwhelming problem.

(He) wants it like a hog wants slop. That's salivating time.

There are more ways to kill a hound than choke him on hot butter. There must be a simpler solution, or an alternative.

. . . as welcome as a bastard at a family reunion.

. . . as welcome as a whore in church.

Go whistle up a stump. To heck with you!

(You're) not just whistling Dixie. You're telling the truth; you're telling it like it is.

. . . as wide-awake as a hoot owl.

(He) was willing to wash (her) feet and drink the water. He was sure "bit" by the lovebug [q.v.]. "I swan, I believe that boy'ud be willin' to wash her feet an' drink the wadder."

(He's) got the world in a jug and the stopper in (his) hand. He's got it "made."

. . . not worth a milk bucket under a bull.

(He) was worth (his) weight in wildcats. Someone to be reckoned with; a person of superior worth. "When it comes to backbreaking work, that boy is worth his weight in wildcats."

(She) was wound up tighter than a two-dollar watch. Someone near the breaking point, or in a state of high anxiety.

(She) was the most wrote-about girl in the boys' bathroom. [Georgia; Louise Pattterson] "Honey, that ain't no reputation a'tall. In fact, a Suthun girl who's dropped to that level might just as well pack up and move North."

You know what the governor of South Carolina said to the governor of North Carolina? This is a popular toast that is given before downing an alcoholic drink in many parts of the South. The answer: "It's a long time between drinks."

Southern Hyperbole

The Unintentional Lies
Told in the Name of Truth
by a Southern Woman

$\mathcal{S}$OUTHERN HYPERBOLE IS A TRAIT LEARNED AT MOTHER'S KNEE, a characteristic taken in with mother's milk. It is the stretched, strained, enhanced, expanded, enlarged, embroidered, amplified, magnified, and sometimes awesome truth as told by Southern women. It is a peculiarity never recognized by the individual involved, therefore never questioned; consequently, it becomes second nature and a way of life with even the most inherently honest female.

Yes, Southern femininity is given to the extravagant phrase, the exaggerated comparison; she adores the superlative as she spurns the understated; weak and passive words are beneath her notice, while the intensives give her life purpose and meaning. In other words, with a Dixie belle—verbally speaking—it is all or nothing.

How it began, there is no way of knowing, but start it did— originally, of course, with great, great, great, great-grandmothers —and became firmly entrenched as a unique characteristic of our Southern heritage. Could it have begun when ladies of the first isolated plantations found themselves too much deprived of the companionship of their peers, and like lonely children, learned to feed upon their own imaginations, to manufacture their own drama? Or did it perhaps commence when the first Southern man placed the first Southern woman on a pedestal? (After all, being on a pedestal is an unnatural position, for one has been removed from the commonplace.)

This is mere speculation, of course, but the fact remains that there evolved a unique and unprecedented entity known as South- ern Woman—a singular personality, complex and convoluted beyond analysis—with the distinguishing aspect of that persona being her myriad uses of her mother tongue. And "mother" tongue is most aptly employed here, because Southern Woman has edited, augmented, and embellished the English language in ways to make it the essence of woman: feminine, powerful, mysterious.

For the non-Southerner, however, an understanding of Southern hyperbole can only be realized through example, and to that end a variety of illustrations are offered here.

Let us begin with the word *like*, a word missing from Southern Woman's vocabulary. "Ah absolutely love and adoah Co'-Colas. But those othuh cole drinks—shoee-ee! Ah just pure-out loathe and despise those ole imitations, don't you?" She either loves something or she despises it. Feeble words serve no purpose in her speech.

This tender being cannot carry or take an object anywhere at any time. Absolutely not! Items like stamps and postcards are "lugged home from the post office"—which, incidentally, is always "about fifty miles" from her house. Everything she lifts "weighs a ton," and the small paper sack that she "drags" home from the grocery store has put an "awful strain" on her back.

Did you ever know a Southern girl who had a slight headache? Never. How could she? Because when a Southern female's head aches, it absolutely kills her. Just as this same female's shoes are never just a bit uncomfortable. Positively not. "These shoes have totally and undoubtedly *ruined* mah feet."

When a daughter of Dixie catches a bit of a cold, she quickly vows, "*Ah am sick enough to die,*" and if, in response, someone asks her why she doesn't see a doctor, she replies, "To tell you the truth, Ah'm scared to, 'cause Ah just know he'll tell me Ah have pneumonia." And why wouldn't this fragile creature expect to come down with a bad pulmonary infection? Isn't her physical constitution uniquely delicate, and doesn't that leave her much more sensitive than the ordinary person to changes in the temperature? This also explains why she is "freezing absolutely to death" when commoners have noticed only a faint chill in the air; and it's the reason for her "sweltering the whole livelong summuh," though it was the mildest kind of season.

And sleep. To Southern Womankind, there is something decidedly indelicate about sleep. Consequently, the twenty minutes or so that a Dixie belle may spend awake during the night, she describes this way: "It was just *awful!* Ah did not close my eyes the whole en-ty-ah night."

At least once a week a Southern girl has occasion to vow, "Ah have nevuh been so insulted in all mah born days!" while just as often she runs into a slight and not much liked acquaintance to whom she exclaims: "Ah don't believe Ah have evuh been so glad to see anyone as Ah am you!" When this same belle grows a little older, any male she at one time had a five-minute flirtation with becomes "a boy Ah was once almost engaged to."

When a man fails to treat a Southern daughter of Eve in a manner short of chivalrous, he is denounced something like this: "Did you evuh meet such a cad in your whole livelong *life?* Whey, he dudn't have one *ounce* of breedin'. And let me tell you this, for his sake Ah sinsairuhly hope that mah daddy or mah bubba *nevuh* find out how he behaved toward me this day." However, when this same Southern doll decides to turn on the *real* charm—that knock-out punch reserved for males only—watch out! That's when you keep your sons, your husband, and your father out of reach. Her modus operandi can take any direction, maybe even go this way: "Did Ah tell you that you have absolutely the most devastating smile Ah have evuh seen on a human being? Ah sweah, it's like a burst of sunshine aftuh a week of rainy weathuh, and every time Ah see it, Ah just go weak all ovuh." The man who hears this may be so young that his mouth is still glittering with braces, or so old that his eager smile displays twin rows of store-bought porcelain, but whoever he is, after being hit with this ammunition, chances are he's a gone goose.

Then there's the old tried-and-true approach that a Southern woman is so fond of. It's called the Indirect Attack, and it's probably been in practice since Virginia Dare's mother had to use it on an Indian brave to save herself on Roanoke Island. It works something like this:

"If Ah tell you something nice someone said about you, will you promise not to become *too* conceited?" She gives him her most appealing baby-doll gaze as she poses this momentous question.

"Cross my heart and hope to die," he lies, all a-twitter.

"Well, someone told me that in *huh* opinion, you positively have the manliest manner, the greatest physique, and the finest mind of any man she had *evuh* met."

"No kidding! Well, that's great to hear. But who was it told you that?"

"Well, na-ow—" her drawl becomes more pronounced as she

devises"—shall we just say that a little bird told me, and let it go at tha-yat?"

"Okay." He's grinning as if he has just been granted knighthood. Not that he doesn't know who the little bird is; what he doesn't know is how firmly and finally that little bird has him caged.

The Southern woman, especially after her enshrinement—that is, BECOMING A MOTHER—seems to feel the need to languish, to be surrounded by an aura of delicate health. Perhaps this helps to further enslave her husband and offspring—to keep them in line. Though she may be as strong as a sumo wrestler, and her robust looks give every indication that she will outlive her husband by twenty years, to hear her tell it, she is never quite well.

"Mama, how do you feel today?"

Mama, putting on her suffering but saintly expression as she looks wanly into the distance: "Oh, you know, hon. Ah nevuh really feel good anymoah."

"What hurts you today, Mama?"

"Oh, you know, dahlin'. Mah usual headache, and that little female problem Ah have. But don't worry about me, sugah. It's just something your mama has to learn to live with. You know, dumplin', we all have ouah crosses to beah, and Ah'm sure Ah'll be able to beah mine."

With many Southern females, it seems it is beyond the bounds of possibility to be direct. It is as if in doing so, they are committing a serious breach of etiquette.

"What do you think about ouah walking down to the drugstore and getting a Coke?" (Both of these blossoming young belles know that this is where the most attractive boys hang out.)

"Well, Ah don't know. Would you like to?"

"Ah really don't care. Ah suppose Ah do if you do."

"Well, Ah don't know. It's up to you, Mary Lou, *if* you think you'd like to."

As with sleeping, the Southern woman is convinced that it is indelicate to let anyone know she likes to eat. In addition, she has been taught never to accept an invitation to food unless she is strongly urged. (The prescribed number of times to demur before accepting seems to be three.)

Meet Melanie Sue and Sarah Frances, two young ladies who are longtime friends:

"Melanie Sue, you must try a piece of Mama's 'melt-in-your-mouth-light-as-a-feathuh' chocolate cake."

"Oh, no! But thank you very much."

"Are you sure? You know Mama makes the very best chocolate cake in the whole city of Ayatlayantah."

"Ah know. Ah know she does, but really, Ah don't believe Ah could eat a bite."

"Melanie Sue, you *love* chocolate cake—you know you do!"

"Of coas Ah do. Who dudn't? But you know what a small appetite Ah have always had, Sarah Frances."

"Certainly Ah do. An' you have that gawjuss figure to prove it, but you wouldn't want Mama's feelings hurt, now would you, Melanie Sue?"

"Well . . . in that case . . . but just the *teeniest* little slice, though."

With that she finally feels justified in picking up her fork, and very daintily but quite seriously begins to devour the huge piece of chocolate delight that's been set before her.

A Southern woman finds it almost impossible to accept a compliment without depreciating the thing praised. It's as though she considers it immodest to admit that she possesses something really nice. (Or could it be because she feels that nothing is truly good enough for her?)

"What a lovely dress you're wearing."

"You think so? Ah guess it looks pretty good, *considering* it was such a bargain."

Or: "You have a beautiful home—perfectly charming!"

"Well, thank you . . ." She looks around to find something to disparage. "But this old carpeting—we really should do something about it."

Or: "That is a stunning engagement ring. One of the most beautiful I have ever seen."

"Oh, thank you . . ." The newly betrothed studies her ring and then polishes it on her skirt. "But Ah do wish he had gotten something not quite so large."

But for goodness sake! Why go on like this? Surely by now everyone—even the Yankees—has a very good idea what Southern hyperbole is all about. Besides, a certain writer finds that she is absolutely and totally exhausted. In fact, she has never been so tired in her whole entire life. In addition to that, she didn't get one wink of sleep last night, has not eaten a bite all day long, not to mention her poor little fingers, which are swollen to a fare-thee-well from so much hard typing.

Most pressing of all, though, is what happened when the stone fell out of her diamond engagement ring and landed on her foot. There's a bone broken, she feels absolutely sure, and she really should be on her way to the hospital right this minute, only she just knows that when she does go, she will wind up being put in a cast from hip to toe.

Oh, well! We all have our crosses to bear, and being one of that rare breed—SOUTHERN WOMAN—she's confident that *somewhere* she'll find the strength to shoulder hers. And with lots more courage than most—naturally.

OXFORD WORLD'S CLASSICS

WINESBURG, OHIO

SHERWOOD ANDERSON was born in 1876 in Camden, Ohio, and grew up in Clyde, Ohio, which was to become the Winesburg of his most famous book. After serving briefly in the Army during the Spanish–American War, he moved to Chicago, where he pursued a career in advertising and business. Trying to write fiction in private, and increasingly torn between the conflicting demands of his outer and inner lives, he suffered a nervous collapse which led, in 1912, to his legendary walkout from the office of the business which he headed, and his determination to live the life of a writer. After several unsuccessful books, his *Winesburg, Ohio* appeared in 1919 and brought him wide recognition. The tales in *Winesburg*, as well as those in several other story collections which he published later, strongly influenced the direction of the modern short story. Following the commercial success of his novel *Dark Laughter* in 1925, he moved to Marion, Virginia, and became a townsman once again, owning and editing the town's two newspapers, one Democratic and the other Republican. In the 1930s his focus shifted to the industrial South, where in novels like *Beyond Desire* (1932) and *Kit Brandon* (1936) he pondered the impact of machine civilization upon the lives of Americans, an issue which engrossed him throughout his career. He died of peritonitis on a trip to South America in 1941. His earlier autobiographical works such as *A Story Teller's Story* (1924) and *Tar: A Midwestern Childhood* (1926) were supplemented by the posthumous publication of *Sherwood Anderson's Memoirs* (1942).

GLEN A. LOVE is Professor of English at the University of Oregon. He is the author of *New Americans: The Westerner and the Modern Experience in the American Novel*, *Babbitt: An American Life*, and other works on American literature.

OXFORD WORLD'S CLASSICS

For over 100 years Oxford World's Classics have brought readers closer to the world's great literature. Now with over 700 titles—from the 4,000-year-old myths of Mesopotamia to the twentieth century's greatest novels—the series makes available lesser-known as well as celebrated writing.

The pocket-sized hardbacks of the early years contained introductions by Virginia Woolf, T. S. Eliot, Graham Greene, and other literary figures which enriched the experience of reading. Today the series is recognized for its fine scholarship and reliability in texts that span world literature, drama and poetry, religion, philosophy and politics. Each edition includes perceptive commentary and essential background information to meet the changing needs of readers.

OXFORD WORLD'S CLASSICS

SHERWOOD ANDERSON

Winesburg, Ohio

Edited with an Introduction by
GLEN A. LOVE

OXFORD
UNIVERSITY PRESS

OXFORD
UNIVERSITY PRESS

Great Clarendon Street, Oxford OX2 6DP

Oxford University Press is a department of the University of Oxford.
It furthers the University's objective of excellence in research, scholarship,
and education by publishing worldwide in

Oxford New York

Athens Auckland Bangkok Bogotá Buenos Aires Calcutta
Cape Town Chennai Dar es Salaam Delhi Florence Hong Kong Istanbul
Karachi Kuala Lumpur Madrid Melbourne Mexico City Mumbai
Nairobi Paris São Paulo Singapore Taipei Tokyo Toronto Warsaw

with associated companies in Berlin Ibadan

Oxford is a registered trade mark of Oxford University Press
in the UK and in certain other countries

Published in the United States
by Oxford University Press Inc., New York

Editorial matter © Glen A. Love 1997

The moral rights of the author have been asserted

Database right Oxford University Press (maker)

First published as a World's Classics paperback 1997
Reissued as an Oxford World's Classics paperback 1999
Reissued 2008

British Library Cataloguing in Publication Data

Data available

Library of Congress Cataloging in Publication Data
Anderson, Sherwood, 1876–1941.
Winesburg, Ohio / Sherwood Anderson; edited with an introduction by Glen A. Love.
(Oxford world's classics)
1. Ohio—Social life and customs—Fiction. 2. City and town life—Ohio—Fiction.
3. Anderson, Sherwood, 1876–1941. Winesburg, Ohio. 4. City and town life in literature.
5. Ohio—In literature. I. Love, Glen A., 1932– . II. Title. III. Series.
PS3501.N4W578 1997 813'.52—dc20 96–24338

ISBN 978-0-19-954072-3

9

Typeset by Pure Tech India Ltd, Pondicherry
Printed in Great Britain by
Clays Ltd, St Ives plc

CONTENTS

INTRODUCTION

IN his book of loosely related short stories, *Winesburg, Ohio*, Sherwood Anderson made his most important contribution to modern American—and world—literature. Although a handful of his other tales, for example, 'I Want to Know Why', 'I'm a Fool', 'The Egg', and 'Death in the Woods', may individually represent a higher artistic achievement than any single story in *Winesburg*, still the book has a collective power which is greater than the sum of its parts. It has had an enormous influence on succeeding generations of writers. It restructured the course of the American short story, turning that genre from its O. Henry emphasis upon plot to its capacity for illuminating the emotional lives of ordinary people. For these and other reasons, *Winesburg, Ohio* remains today as an important part of America's imaginative record.

Winesburg is one of those rare works that have their own aura. We know the book so well that even if we don't know it, we know it. Lionel Trilling, many years ago in a generally disparaging essay on Anderson, called attention to this almost palpable quality of *Winesburg*: not just a book but 'a personal souvenir'. Trilling goes on to describe it from its outside, in the old Modern Library edition with its 'brown oilcloth binding, the coarse paper, the bold type crooked on the page'. 'Dreadfully evocative,' he concludes, as if the physical presence of the book itself were somehow enough to objectify his resentment of its hurtful appeal. And yet, he allows, 'as for the *Winesburg* stories themselves, they are as dangerous to read again, as

I am grateful to the journal *American Literature* for permission to draw from my 'Winesburg, Ohio and the Rhetoric of Silence' (Mar. 1968; copyright by Duke University Press) in this introduction.

paining and puzzling, as if they were old letters we had written or received'.[1]

It is this odd double quality of Anderson's stories, their almost aching personalness, together with the sense that they also touch the deepest springs of common human sympathy, that seems to hold us as readers. This reverberation inward and outward suggests the presence of myth in *Winesburg* and others of the author's best works, and the conception of Anderson as American mythopoeist has long been a centre of interest for critics.[2] *Winesburg* inevitably calls up phrases of interiority, of the buried life, of essences, of seeing beneath surfaces, of cutting to the bone. Edmund Wilson, Jr. may have given this strange invasive quality its most powerful metaphor when he wrote of Anderson's work, 'we are at once disturbed and soothed by the feeling of hands thrust down among the deepest bowels of life—hands delicate but still pitiless in their exploration'.[3]

The quality of doubleness extends into Sherwood Anderson's life as well. Born in 1876 into a growing and often poverty-stricken rural Ohio family, he seems to have cast his own parents, a loud-mouthed but ineffectual father and a quietly mysterious but insightful mother, into the figures of Tom and Elizabeth Willard, the mismated parents of George Willard, the young central character of *Winesburg*. Moving from town to town, the Anderson family spent Sherwood's formative years, from about 1883 to 1896, in Clyde, Ohio, the background for the fictional Winesburg, although Anderson would later claim both that the characters were drawn from his small-town boyhood and that they were portraits of fellow-roomers in a Chicago boarding-house. Later, Anderson

---

[1] Lionel Trilling, 'Sherwood Anderson', in Ray Lewis White (ed.), *The Achievement of Sherwood Anderson* (Chapel Hill: University of North Carolina Press, 1966), 214.

[2] David D. Anderson, 'Anderson and Myth', in David D. Anderson (ed.), *Sherwood Anderson: Dimensions of his Literary Art* (East Lansing: Michigan State University Press, 1976), 121–41.

[3] Edmund Wilson, Jr., '*Many Marriages*', *The Dial*, 74 (Apr. 1923), 400.

became an advertising writer and a successful businessman, married and with children of his own. At the same time, beneath this Babbitt-like exterior, he lived his own buried life, privately writing novels and short stories. Finally, in 1912 at the age of 36, he suffered a nervous collapse and, in a legendary gesture, walked out of the paint factory of which he was general manager to become an 'artist'. Though the walkout from business was not so final and dramatic as the legend would have it—Anderson continued to rely upon ad-writing to support himself long after his symbolic revolt—he did indeed begin to realize his ambition to become a writer. After coming out with two less-than-successful novels and a volume of poetry, he published *Winesburg, Ohio* in 1919 at the age of 43, and became famous. Other story collections followed, as well as more novels, non-fiction, and plays. He remained a productive writer until his death in 1941, but *Winesburg* stands as his one truly great book.

Its stories, along with a handful of others, have led following generations of writers to consider Anderson an essential spiritual ancestor. William Faulkner wrote of him: 'He was the father of my generation of American writers and the tradition of American writing which our successors will carry on. He has never received his proper evaluation. Dreiser is his older brother and Mark Twain the father of them both.'[4] Faulkner and Ernest Hemingway, both to become Nobel Prize recipients, were, as William L. Phillips has described them, Anderson's 'prize pupils',[5] and his line of influence reaches down to the present, wherein writers like John Updike, Raymond Carver, and Joyce Carol Oates have all paid homage to Anderson's arresting experiments in style and subject. *Winesburg, Ohio* is linked with a group of similar works, including Sarah Orne Jewett's *The Country of the Pointed Firs*, Jean Toomer's

[4] William Faulkner, interview, 'The Art of Fiction XII', *Paris Review*, 12 (Spring 1956), 46.

[5] William L. Phillips, 'Sherwood Anderson's Two Prize Pupils', in White (ed.), *The Achievement of Sherwood Anderson*, 202–10.

Cane, Hemingway's *In Our Time*, and Faulkner's *Go Down, Moses*, to which John Crowley has called our attention as forming an important American genre: a collection of stories concerning a central character, and coalescing as something closer to a novel.[6]

Just as Anderson helped to shape the writing of his followers, so his own craft in *Winesburg* was influenced by the works he read and admired, like Ivan Turgenev's *A Sportsman's Sketches* (1847–51) and George Borrow's tales of gypsy life in England, *Lavengro* (1851) and *The Romany Rye* (1857). In these writers, as in American writers like his fellow mid-American Mark Twain, Anderson seems to have found the same note of concern for ordinary lives which is seen in the *Winesburg* tales. From Gertrude Stein's new fictional techniques in such works as *Three Lives* (1909) and *Tender Buttons* (1914), Anderson found inspiration for his own stylistic experimentation with sound and rhythm. And in the free verse poems of Edgar Lee Masters's *Spoon River Anthology*, published in 1915 while Anderson was beginning to write the *Winesburg* tales, Anderson must have experienced his own shock of recognition. A friend loaned him the *Spoon River* book, and Anderson read it through excitedly in a single night. Masters's poems, epitaphs of people buried in a Midwestern town cemetery in which the dead confess their secret sins, frustrations, and broken dreams, provided Anderson with a record of quite literally buried lives which seemed to validate his own vision and may have helped him shape his emerging stories.

Anderson's early published works, the big, sprawling novels *Windy McPherson's Son* (1916) and *Marching Men* (1917), and the shapeless prose poems of *Mid-American Chants* (1918), strike chords which are wonderfully concentrated in *Winesburg*: the threatening sense of loss in much of modern life, the sickness of machine civilization, the difficulty of

---

[6] John W. Crowley, 'Introduction', in John W. Crowley (ed.), *New Essays on Winesburg, Ohio* (Cambridge University Press, 1990), 14–15.

human communication, the alienation of men from women and of both from the earth. In *Winesburg*, Anderson began thinking small—narrowing and deepening his focus, distilling the conflicts which engrossed him into a successful form, a series of stories about a boy approaching maturity in an American small town, a boy whose life is touched by the truths of the frustrated and warped grotesques who wear the masks of his kindred townspeople. The linear development of the earlier novels, emphasizing character development, control of plot, and an encompassing view of subject, is rejected in *Winesburg* in favour of a revelation of thoughts and feelings through symbolic setting and gesture. The Winesburg subjects, both town and townspeople, undergo through Anderson's technique an arrestment and isolation, like the figures on Keats's urn. The tales are presented in a series of highly charged scenes, disquieting but also peculiarly airless, as if taking place under a Plath-like bell-jar. Their effect is cumulative rather than progressive. Alfred Kazin has praised the stories as 'moments' of revelation, but they are set in the larger moment of the book itself.[7] That moment is, historically, the watershed moment of American history, occurring in the early 1890s, the period in which the book is set. This divide, made famous by Frederick Jackson Turner and his interpretation of American history, is commonly seen as marking the end of the Western frontier and the point at which the balance in America shifts from a nation primarily rural and agrarian to one that is increasingly urban and industrial.

The 'Revolt from the Village' label of scandalous realism which *Winesburg* wore during the years following its publication is little noticed today. A characteristic 1919 review claimed that the book would 'shatter forever what remains of the assumption that life seethes most treacherously in cities and that there are sylvan retreats where the days pass from

---

[7] Alfred Kazin, *On Native Grounds* (Garden City, NY: Doubleday, 1956), 169.

harvest to harvest like an idyll of Theocritus'.[8] It remained for V. F. Calverton, Maxwell Geismar, Malcolm Cowley, and others to correct the book's early reputation, and today it seems apparent that Anderson turned back, in *Winesburg*, to the cornfields and the village of his youth because they represented the sort of ordered, natural world where love and communication were possible. Throughout his career, the return to the village, not the revolt from it, was to become the characteristic journey of Anderson's idealized self.

This is not to say that there is no realistic component in the descriptions of town and townspeople in *Winesburg*. The sociological background in the novel may not be extensive, but it is essential, as critic William V. Miller argues.[9] Anderson's glimpses into the social life of rural Midwestern towns scarcely resemble the exhaustive examination of a Sinclair Lewis, whose *Main Street*, published in 1920, only a year after *Winesburg*, matches closely the common conception of realism as a fairly straightforward depiction of contemporary social life. We should not be surprised that *Winesburg, Ohio*, a title which seems to promise a slice of Midwestern realism, opens with a prologue called 'The Book of the Grotesque', which leads the work off into a new direction. *Main Street* invites interesting comparison and contrast with *Winesburg* and with Anderson's published statements on realism. Anderson's concentration upon interior life is the realm of anti-realism, or, as critic David Stouck persuasively argues, expressionism, the motivation for which Stouck finds in a letter Anderson wrote to Ben Huebsch, his first publisher: 'there is within every human being a deep well of thinking over which a heavy iron lid is kept clamped,' and it is the writer's task to release that well-spring.[10] But the most important

[8] M. A., 'A Country Town', *New Republic*, 19 (25 June 1919), 257.

[9] William V. Miller, 'Sherwood Anderson's "Middletown": A Sociology of the Midwestern States', *Old Northwest*, 15 (Winter 1991/2), 245–59.

[10] David Stouck, 'Anderson's Expressionist Art', in Crowley (ed.), *New Essays on Winesburg, Ohio*, 28.

effect of Anderson's modernist treatment of this buried life is that it becomes not a retreat into solipsism, but a world which we all have in common.

In the setting of *Winesburg*, in the fields and farms and the rounds of town life, are to be found the sources of the book's evocation of lost worth. Through the setting is expressed the essential unity of country life, linked to the cycle of crops, to the weather and the slow turning of the seasons. Here is a pastoral world organic and yet impervious to time. Its calmness and stillness suggest a self-sufficiency full of promise and latent with meaning. Balanced against this green world are threatening, disintegrative forces. Implicitly, there is the city, which stands on the horizon of Winesburg's scenes and events, and sometimes intrudes in episodes of the characters' lives. Always it is an emblem of irresistible progress and forces of change which threaten to alter forever the life of the town. It 'watches from the shadows | And coughs when you would kiss,' like W. H. Auden's personification of Time. It has attracted smart young village boys like Ned Currie, and it has turned back queer souls like Enoch Robinson and Doctor Parcival, just as it has accepted only the perfect, uniform apples from the Winesburg orchards, which

have been put in barrels and shipped to the cities where they will be eaten in apartments that are filled with books, magazines, furniture, and people. On the trees are only a few gnarled apples that the pickers have rejected. . . . One nibbles at them and they are delicious. Into a little round place at the side of the apple has been gathered all of its sweetness. One runs from tree to tree over the frosted ground picking the gnarled, twisted apples and filling his pockets with them. Only the few know the sweetness of the twisted apples. ('Paper Pills')

The twisted apples are, of course, the 'grotesques' of *Winesburg*'s prologue, 'The Book of the Grotesque'. There, the narrator tells of an old writer who dreams that all the men and women he had known had become grotesques. 'The grotesques were not all horrible. Some were amusing, some almost beautiful, and one, a woman all drawn out of shape, hurt the old man by her grotesqueness. When she passed he made a noise like a small dog whimpering'. The narrator goes on to explain the old writer's idea of grotesqueness, saying that when the world was young, people formed truths out of the errant and vague thoughts of the world.

The old man had listed hundreds of truths in his book. I will not try to tell you of all of them. There was the truth of virginity and the truth of passion, the truth of wealth and of poverty, of thrift and of profligacy, of carefulness and abandon. Hundreds and hundreds were the truths and they were all beautiful.

And then the people came along. Each as he appeared snatched up one of the truths and some who were quite strong snatched up a dozen of them.

It was the truths that made the people grotesques. The old man had quite an elaborate theory concerning the matter. It was his notion that the moment one of the people took one of the truths to himself, called it his truth, and tried to live his life by it, he became a grotesque and the truth he embraced became a falsehood.

The stories which follow would seem to present illustrations of the theory of a self-imposed grotesqueness, but such is not always the case. Irving Howe, in his book on Anderson, sees a contradiction in that the grotesqueness of the characters in the stories is less a result of their 'wilful fanaticism' than of their 'essentially valid resistance' to external forces. [11] Another reading, that of Robert Dunne, claims that 'in most of the *Winesburg* tales the characters look back first at moments early in their lives when they began practicing their tightly held ideals and when they reached a certain decisive moment when they could have adjusted their fixed plans but did not'. [12] Another view would centre upon the 'young thing within', which, the narrator tells us, saved the old writer from grotesqueness

[11] Irving Howe, *Sherwood Anderson* (New York: William Sloane, 1951), 107.
[12] Robert Dunne, 'Beyond Grotesqueness in *Winesburg, Ohio*', *Midwest Quarterly*, 31 (Winter 1990), 181.

himself. This interpretation would underscore the healing power of sexuality and art as they are presented in 'The Book of the Grotesque'.[13] Still another reading, one which is developed more fully in the following pages, finds the grotesques victims of their inability to communicate with others, an inability rooted in the failure of words themselves. Readers continue to find in 'The Book of the Grotesque' a brilliant example of Anderson's fictional method, less than systematic and yet at the same time compelling.

The grotesques—twisted apples, unfit for the fashionable cities—provide an explicit counterforce to the natural self-sufficiency of the setting, from which they are cut off almost as completely as from the urban world on the horizon. The silence of many of them, while it is a measure of their twisted sweetness, their significance, is not the purposeful, cornfield silence of their surroundings, but rather a threatening muteness, stretched taut over a great pressure to communicate. While they are likely to remain almost wordless until the moment at which they spill out their 'truth', a few, at the other extreme, sputter uncontrollably, like Joe Welling in 'A Man of Ideas', who cannot restrain himself when caught up in one of his own schemes: 'Words rolled and tumbled from his mouth. . . . Pouncing upon a bystander he began to talk'. Doctor Parcival in 'The Philosopher' is another compulsive talker, who watches from his office window until he sees George Willard alone in the newspaper office where he works, then hurries in to tell the boy his tales. Later, in self-disgust, he says, 'What a fool I am to be talking'. A common failing of all the grotesques is suggested in the plight of Enoch Robinson in 'Loneliness', who 'wanted to talk, but he didn't know how'. Thus both the mute grotesques and the sputtering grotesques manifest a sickness which is in conflict with the quiet and

---

[13] A. Carl Bredahl, 'The Young Thing Within: Divided Narrative and Sherwood Anderson's *Winesburg, Ohio*', *Midwest Quarterly*, 27 (Summer 1986), 422–37.

benign setting. The verbal incapacity of these figures who cannot love, who cannot draw comfort from their surroundings, is suggestive of their crippling inner wound. One recalls Irving Howe's description of Faulkner's *Light in August* as a work which 'resembles an early Renaissance painting—in the foreground a bleeding martyr, far to the rear a scene of bucolic peacefulness, with women quietly working in the fields'. [14]

From the precarious equilibrium of these forces—rural permanence threatened by encroaching city, placid setting opposed by tortured inhabitants, the urge to communicate thwarted by verbal incapacity—is created the aura of charged stillness which characterizes the tales. The first paragraph of the opening story, 'Hands', quickly sets forth the elemental conflicts:

[1] Upon the half decayed veranda of a small frame house that stood near the edge of a ravine near the town of Winesburg, Ohio, a fat little old man walked nervously up and down. [2] Across a long field that had been seeded for clover but that had produced only a dense crop of yellow mustard weeds, he could see the public highway along which went a wagon filled with berry pickers returning from the fields. [3] The berry pickers, youths and maidens, laughed and shouted boisterously. [4] A boy clad in a blue shirt leaped from the wagon and attempted to drag after him one of the maidens who screamed and protested shrilly. [5] The feet of the boy in the road kicked up a cloud of dust that floated over the face of the departing sun. [6] Over the long field came a thin girlish voice. [7] 'Oh, you Wing Biddlebaum, comb your hair, it's falling into your eyes,' commanded the voice to the man, who was bald and whose nervous little hands fiddled about the bare white forehead as though arranging a mass of tangled locks.

This opening, like the beginnings of all memorable fictions, is a microcosm of the strengths of what is to come: in this case, a portrait of an incommunicative grotesque, both defined and opposed by suggestive details of landscape and human com-

[14] Irving Howe, *William Faulkner: A Critical Study* (New York: Random House, 1952), 64.

munity. The concealed artifice of Anderson's apparently art-
less style is worth a closer look here. One notices that the
opening two sentences, both describing Wing Biddlebaum,
are, in the grammatical term, periodic, with the main clause
arrived at only after those details of scene—the half-decayed
veranda and the field seeded for clover but gone to weeds—
which suggest and prepare the reader for the half-ruined life
and blighted hopes of Wing, the subject of the main clauses.
The first action attributed to him ('walked nervously up and
down') presages his timidity and the repetitive nature of his
behaviour. In the second sentence, the reader's attention is
turned from Wing toward the object of his gaze, the wagon-
load of young berry-pickers. They are, of course, an extension
of the felicitous landscape, their easy and uninhibited physi-
cality etched against Wing's mute isolation, a contrast heightened by a change in grammatical structure in the next
sentences (3–5) given over to the berry-pickers. Now, main
clauses are shifted to the beginning of the sentences to form a
'normal' word order. The sentences become loose, rather than
periodic, and the presentation flows into a more direct,
straightforward narration, freed from the heavy subordination
and the symbolic details which marked the opening sentences
describing Wing.

Anderson's choice of the archaic 'youths and maidens' in
sentence 3 suggests an idealized, even mythical, landscape,
but the brief glimpse of innocence is dimmed by the cloud of
dust across the sun and by a taunting cry from one of the the
girl berry-pickers, a cry which carries our attention back to the
figure on the veranda. In shifting attention back to Wing (6),
Anderson reintroduces the periodic sentence with which
Wing has previously been identified, again opening with a
prepositional phrase, and again echoing the earlier suggestive
detail of the field gone to weeds. In both sentences 6 and 7,
normal word order is again set aside to encompass an appro-
priate attitude toward Wing. Subjects and verbs are reversed
('came a...voice', 'commanded the voice') so that Wing is

made passive, one to whom things happen—and have happened. Unlike the youths and maidens who laugh and shout, scream and protest, and even command, Wing remains silent, his behaviour repetitive and acquiescent. He can only watch, or listen, or pace up and down, or fiddle with his hands in a series of compulsive and perhaps ominous movements.

As the story develops, Wing's hands increasingly draw our attention. They seem ready to give him away, fluttering nervously, aimlessly, alarmingly. 'He wanted to keep them hidden away and looked with amazement at the quiet inexpressive hands of other men who worked beside him in the fields, or passed, driving sleepy teams on country roads.' These quiet, inexpressive hands announce their oneness with the natural setting, while Wing's hands are associated with images of futility and frustration, as when they are compared to 'the beating of the wings of an imprisoned bird'. The recurring presence of *hands* throughout not only this story but many of the stories suggests other opportunities for the inquiring reader to consider Anderson's use of images in establishing patterns of meaning and unity throughout the *Winesburg* stories. To pursue the imagery of hands, one thinks of the knob-like knuckles of Doctor Reefy in 'Paper Pills', which resemble the gnarled and twisted apples rejected by the pickers; or the bleeding hand of Reverend Curtis Hartman in 'The Strength of God'; or Kate Swift's sharp little fists, in 'The Teacher', beating, in frustration, upon her pupil, George Willard. Many such patterns underpin the stories, as Walter B. Rideout points out.[15] Anderson's use of light and darkness, of windows, of dreams, of countless subjects may repay close reading in ways often unanticipated, since the author often invests his images and physical details with intimations of the inner lives of his characters.

[15] Walter B. Rideout, 'The Simplicity of *Winesburg, Ohio*', in David D. Anderson (ed.), *Critical Essays on Sherwood Anderson* (Boston: G. K. Hall, 1981), 146–54.

The gulf between dream and reality in Wing Biddlebaum's life establishes still another tension in the story. Wing advises George Willard to close his ears to the 'roaring of the voices', to begin to dream, and his own ideal is expressed as a dream:

Out of the dream Wing Biddlebaum made a picture for George Willard. In the picture men lived again in a kind of pastoral golden age. Across a green open country came clean limbed young men, some afoot, some mounted upon horses. In crowds the young men came to gather about the feet of an old man who sat beneath a tree in a tiny garden and who talked to them.

The dream is one of perfect communication among human beings, set, significantly, in a 'pastoral golden age'. The Socratic instructor of youth is Wing's idealization of his own former role as teacher. But, like the contrast between Wing's inhibitions and the easy sensuality of the youths and maidens, the dream of a revered teacher is placed against the nightmarish incidents of his actual life, in which, like Socrates, he had been attacked as a corruptor of youth. A victim of homophobia in the town where he had been teaching as a young man, he had been run out after being beaten by the saloon-keeper father of one of the students, and later nearly lynched. Anderson's treatment of these events—the saloon-keeper's rage, his hard fists, the insect-like scurrying of the children, the rain, the darkness, and the stick and balls of mud which are thrown at the screaming figure of the terrified school-teacher—emphasizes sharply the opposition between the ugly reality of misunderstanding and the ideal of perfect communication, and between the agonizingly repressed and isolated grotesque and a setting of freedom, innocence, and love.

Besides serving as an ironic opposite to the inner state of the grotesques of Winesburg, the natural world occasionally provides the needed resolution and solace. Both of the latter functions are seen in 'The Untold Lie', in which Ray Pearson is saddened by the autumn beauty of the Winesburg country-side. His sordid little cabin, his scolding wife, a crying child—

all are brought into sharp relief by the lovely autumn twilight. 'All the low hills were washed with color and even the little clusters of bushes in the corners by the fences were alive with beauty.' Overcome by the splendour of the natural world and the squalour of his own life, he tears off his old tattered overcoat and runs across a field shouting protests 'against his life, against all life, against everything that makes life ugly'. Yet it is also the beauty of the autumn setting which results in a rare moment of contact between Ray and a younger man with whom he is working: 'There they stood in the big empty field with the quiet corn shocks behind them and the red and yellow hills in the distance, and from being just two indifferent workmen they had become all alive to each other. Here, the empty, quiet fields serve to dissolve momentarily the barrier of incommunicability which surrounds the men, and a brief but genuine awareness takes place. The silent moment becomes Ray Pearson's 'truth', while his unspoken advice to the younger man at the story's conclusion he dismisses as merely an untold lie.

George Willard, in whom Wing Biddlebaum and many of the other grotesques find the opportunity for verbal release, is, in a sense, the *genius loci* of the Winesburg landscape, the attendant spirit of the town. He provides a kind of synecdoche for the village, standing, Janus-like, between innocence and experience, youth and maturity, rural past and urban future. Many of the grotesques seem to sense the boy's connection with the spirit of life in the village, and they reach out for contact through him. That he also harbours feelings of loneliness and inadequacy seems not to occur to them; whether or not he actually shares in the aura of hope and life which interfuses the natural setting becomes less important than their belief that he does. Elmer Cowley imagines to himself that George 'belonged to the town, typified the town, represented in his person the spirit of the town' ('"Queer"'). Seth Richmond envies George's apparent link with the town and its people. Similarly, Wing Biddlebaum does not think of himself as a part of Winesburg although he has lived there twenty years, but with George Willard he finds the solace of human contact. 'With a kind of wriggle, like a fish returned to the brook by the fisherman, Biddlebaum the silent began to talk, striving to put into words the ideas that had been accumulated by his mind during long years of silence' ('Hands').

In his position as confidant to the grotesques, and hence as a counterforce to the loneliness and verbal failure which isolates them, George Willard's identification with the ameliorative aspects of the setting is further reinforced. He is the human, and thus communicable, manifestation of the same spirit which must remain deaf and dumb in the natural world. This is not to say that he is patriarchal or wise beyond his years. He is a believable character, possessed by the lusts and self-doubts of youth, whom Anderson is careful never to allow to become too good or all-knowing.

Feminist readings of *Winesburg*, in this respect, have recently added important insights into our understanding of George Willard and the other characters. Nancy Bunge and Claire Colquitt, for example, have demonstrated how exploitation is the defining element in nearly all the love relationships in the stories.[16] George is a participant in this exploitation, as is revealed in the stories 'Nobody Knows' and 'An Awakening'. Near the end of the book, in 'Sophistication', George Willard may be seen as coming to a new awareness, with Helen White, of the possibility for companionable love, but the awareness may be too little and too late to overcome the permeating impression of the rest of the book that there is no way for women to construct satisfying lives for themselves. This sense of women's sexual and emotional frustration drives some of *Winesburg's* most powerful stories, including

---

[16] Nancy Bunge, 'Women in Sherwood Anderson's Fiction', in Anderson (ed.), *Critical Essays on Sherwood Anderson*, 242–9; Claire Colquitt, 'Motherlove in Two Narratives of Community: *Winesburg, Ohio* and *The Country of the Pointed Firs*', in Crowley (ed.), *New Essays on Winesburg, Ohio*, 73–87.

'Mother' and 'Death' (about Elizabeth Willard); 'Surrender' (about Louise Bentley); 'Adventure' (about Alice Hindman); and 'The Teacher' (about Kate Swift). At the same time, Anderson may also be recognized for his insights into these women's lives; Sally Adair Rigsbee notes that 'few other modern male writers have been able to convey with such loving sensitivity the hurt women bear or to advocate as openly as Anderson does that the relationships of men and women should be equal'.[17]

In the matter of stylistic innovation, *Winesburg, Ohio* reveals interesting links with modernist experimentation of the time. Along with Willa Cather's 'unfurnishing' of the novel and Ernest Hemingway's 'iceberg theory', based upon the analogy that the dignity of movement of an iceberg results from nine-tenths of it being underwater,[18] Anderson, too, is deeply involved in techniques which leave the important things unsaid. Anderson's technique in this regard is to call attention, as narrator, to the inability of words to convey meaning satisfactorily. In 'Hands' he professes his inadequacy to the task of describing Wing's hands, saying, 'It is a job for a poet'; later, he says of Wing's sensitivity as a teacher, 'And yet that is but crudely stated. It needs the poet there'. This same refrain— the call for a 'poet', one whose godlike powers of communication will pierce the inexpressible mystery—sounds through the book, lending greater poignancy to the state of incommunicability in which both narrator and characters find themselves.

Describing Joe Welling, the narrator gropes for the right comparison: 'He was like a tiny little volcano that lies silent for days and then suddenly spouts fire. No, he wasn't like that— he was like a man who is subject to fits . . .' ('A Man of Ideas').

[17] Sally Adair Rigsbee, 'The Feminine in Winesburg, Ohio', *Studies in American Fiction*, 9 (1981), 242.

[18] See Glen A. Love, '*The Professor's House*: Cather, Hemingway and the Chastening of American Prose Style', *Western American Literature*, 24 (Winter 1990), 295–311.

Or, in portraying Wash Williams in 'Respectability', the teller backtracks to correct himself: 'I go too fast. Not everything about Wash was unclean. He took care of his hands'. Sometimes the narrator seems almost to give up before the impossibility of his task as in 'The Untold Lie', when he says of Ray Pearson, 'If you knew the Winesburg country in the fall and how the low hills are all splashed with yellows and reds you would understand his feeling'. Or, again, in the introductory 'Book of the Grotesque', the voice fumbles for a time with several similes about the old writer, then concludes, 'It is absurd, you see, to try to tell you what was inside the old writer...'. These repeated confessions of verbal inadequacy encourage the reader to doubt the power of words and serve to intensify the verbal failures which occur between the characters in the stories.

These failures are, of course, seen most readily in the dearth of verbal communication between characters. As the tales unfold, the act of speech becomes strained and frustrated almost beyond endurance. The verbs tell this most dramatically. Characters do not simply speak; they cry, they stammer, or mutter, or sputter, or ultimately are altogether silent. Perhaps the most characteristic and important verb in the book is 'whispered'. The soliloquy-like oral discourse in *Winesburg* is further emphasized by the high number of reflexive pronouns following verbs of speech ('said aloud to himself', 'muttered to himself', etc.). Verbs which express the normal give and take of discourse, such as 'answered', 'replied', and 'responded', are almost totally absent in *Winesburg*. The unusually high proportion of verbs of strained communication seems to permeate the texture of the entire work. The aura of loneliness and frustration in *Winesburg*, which every reader notices, must, to a great degree, radiate outward from advice unheard or unheeded, from words shouted to empty fields and sky, or whispered in lonely rooms.

Anderson's pastoral vision, which led him in *Winesburg* to turn from what he had come to regard as the shrill disorder of industrialism back to the country town of his youth, was, in an important sense, valid after all. Winesburg was the right place for love, the proper setting for human communication although, as the stories reveal, it may not occur there. 'Many people must live and die alone, *even* in Winesburg', concludes one of the tales ('Adventure'; italics added). Thus, the leave-taking of George Willard in the book's final episode gathers more than ordinary significance. 'Departure' is not really a story at all, but a protraction and savouring of the meaning of Winesburg for the city-bound youth, and a suggestion of the place's enduring value. On the final morning, George arises early and walks one last time on Trunion Pike, the road leading from the village out into the country. In his silent farewell to Winesburg, Anderson completes the pastoral frame begun in the opening paragraph of 'Hands', the first story. Here he expands earlier descriptions of setting into a diapason of countryside and seasons, reinforcing the bond between the young man and the natural world, reasserting his significant silence, his 'organic' nature, in contrast to the static quality of the grotesques.

Paradoxically, the lesson of purposeful, cornfield silence which George takes from his natural surroundings may be the beginning of the means by which the walls of thwarted communication which surround the grotesques will be finally broken down. He may become the hoped-for connector be-tween these tortured souls and the great world. Filled with his vague dreams, he is inevitably drawn to the city, where, im-mersed in that destructive element, he gives promise of be-coming the artist whose heightened understanding and whose craft of language may counteract the limitations of words, the one who, as Edwin Fussell says, will become the spokesman for all of the grotesques, whose 'fragmentary wisdom' he now possesses.[19]

---

[19] Edwin Fussell, '*Winesburg Ohio*: Art and Isolation', *Modern Fiction Studies*, 6 (Summer 1960), 110. For a questioning of the equating of George

And the sort of artist which George will become has been suggested all along. It is found in the book's dedication to Anderson's mother, the silent but insightful one, 'whose keen observations on the life about her first awoke in me the hunger to see beneath the surface of lives'. It is found in the narrator's expression of his craft in 'The Book of the Grotesque': 'The thing to get at is what the writer or the young thing within the writer was thinking about.' It is heard in Kate Swift's advice to George to 'know what people are thinking about, not what they say,' an admonition Anderson later repeated to his own son, John, when the young man was considering becoming a writer.[20] It is, in short, the sort of credo which is indistinguishable from Anderson's own self-conception as a writer. He presents us, finally, with an important paradox, the artist who is, at bottom, sceptical of his medium: distrustful of words, he is nevertheless driven to their use, not only to record his scepticism, but also to attempt a communication which even at its best cannot approach the power of non-words, the more perfect communication which lies wrapped within purposeful silence.

If this seems to suggest for the reader in a postmodern present something like a collapse of meaning and a retreat into interiority, then a further pondering of *Winesburg, Ohio* may be in order. Thomas Yingling argues from such a postmodernist perspective that the book shows Anderson attempting to shore up for his own age a great 'shibboleth' of nineteenth-century American culture, 'the notion that the commonality of life is grounded in some "universal" experience or quality of life (i.e., that beneath such negligible differences as class, ethnicity, race, and gender, we are all somehow "the same").... But even if we grant that it exists, we must also

Willard with the narrator of *Winesburg*, see Marcia Jacobson, '*Winesburg, Ohio* and the Autobiographical Moment', in Crowley (ed.), *New Essays on Winesburg, Ohio*, 53–72.

[20] *The Portable Sherwood Anderson*, ed. Horace Gregory (New York: Viking Press, 1949), 595.

insist that the "universal" is not the same as the "collective." [21]
Yingling's deconstructive reading of *Winesburg* brings to the
front what is certainly an issue of enduring, as well as contemporary, significance. What is the fate of a *Winesburg,
Ohio*, or any classic from the past, if contemporary ideological
tests are applied to such works, which are then almost inevitably found wanting? Can the common roots of experience
survive the gender and culture wars of the present and the
future?

That the basic universality of human nature can be dismissed as an outworn notion, or that cultural differences
have completely overridden nature in the determination of
human behaviour—these are assumptions which are increasingly questioned today. [22] We seem to have more in common as
human beings, as possessors of an undeniable human nature,
than the proponents of difference would allow. Though we
continue to suffer individually or collectively, our sufferings
and our silences may still unite us. Because the universal
underlies the collective, great works from the past continue
to speak meaningfully to us. The Andersonian artist in *Winesburg* does not dissolve into interiority, but lives to touch the
universal sympathy in which our shared differences are recognized. The responses of many readers through the years
who have found *Winesburg, Ohio* a moving and engrossing
experience suggest that the book will not go gently into that
good night of elegy and retrospective, but that it will continue
to hold its place in the conflictive present and future.

[21] Thomas Yingling, 'Winesburg, Ohio and the End of Collective Experience', in Crowley (ed.), *New Essays on Winesburg, Ohio*, 114.

[22] For a thorough examination of these issues in the present century, see
Carl N. Degler, *In Search of Human Nature: the Decline and Revival of
Darwinism in American Social Thought* (New York: Oxford University
Press, 1991).

NOTE ON THE TEXT

Winesburg, Ohio was first published in 1919 by B. W. Huebsch. Anderson had written most of the stories three years earlier, during late 1915 and early 1916, and had seen several of them published in little magazines before the appearance of the collected tales in book form in April 1919. The first printing, as Anderson scholar William L. Phillips discovered, may be identified by the incorrect use of 'lay' for 'lie' on line 5 of p. 86, an error corrected in the second and subsequent printings. Phillips, Ray Lewis White, and Robert Dunne have cited other errors in early printings, many of which were carried over into the Modern Library Edition of Boni and Liveright, which first appeared in 1922, still using the original plates.[1] The editorial work and typography on these plates left much to be desired. All other editions until Malcolm Cowley's Viking Press edition of 1960, which corrected most of these errors, were reproduced from these original plates.

This Oxford edition of *Winesburg, Ohio* is based upon the 1919 edition. As in Cowley, typographical errors, misused apostrophes, and usage errors have been silently emended, and the spelling of characters' names (Winney's Dry Goods Store, Aunt Callie, Tom Sinnings, Ned Winters, Hern's Grocery, Mrs. Kate McHugh, Wacker's Cigar Store, Wesley Moyer, Turk Smollet) has been made consistent.

The present edition differs from Cowley in several respects. Whereas Cowley adds thirty-seven commas intended to clarify meaning, this edition adds only five, in cases where the original punctuation is clearly in error. Cowley changes one

---

[1] For an overview of the bibliographical history of *Winesburg*, see Robert Dunne, 'A Need for a Critical *Winesburg, Ohio*', *Papers of the Bibliographical Society of America*, 84 (1990), 303–4.

verb from 'were' to 'was', which is here left unchanged, as a proper use of the subjunctive mood ('Godliness, Part Two', para. 3, penultimate sentence). Cowley misses one incorrect variant of the name Sinnings ('Mother', para. 4; p. 41, line 24 in Cowley's Compass Edition). Finally, this edition corrects one substantial error which remains in Cowley, and in nearly all other editions. That error is in the word 'carelessness' as one of the pairs of opposed truths mentioned by the old writer in the introductory 'Book of the Grotesque' (para. 12). The correct word is 'carefulness'. This is the word in the Newberry Library manuscript and in the early magazine version of the story, and it is the word that makes sense in the passage.

SELECT BIBLIOGRAPHY

Selected Anderson Works

Poor White (New York: B. W. Huebsch, 1920).

The Triumph of the Egg (New York: B. W. Huebsch, 1921).

Horses and Men (New York: B. W. Huebsch, 1923).

A Story Teller's Story (New York: B. W. Huebsch, 1924).

Sherwood Anderson's Notebook (New York: Boni and Liveright, 1926).

Perhaps Women (New York: Horace Liveright, 1931).

Death in the Woods (New York: Liveright, 1933).

Kit Brandon (New York and London: Charles Scribner's Sons, 1936).

Sherwood Anderson's Memoirs (New York: Harcourt, Brace, 1942).

The Sherwood Anderson Reader, ed. Paul Rosenfeld (Boston: Houghton Mifflin, 1947).

The Portable Sherwood Anderson, ed. Horace Gregory (New York: Viking, 1949).

Certain Things Last: The Selected Short Stories of Sherwood Anderson, ed. Charles E. Modlin (New York: Four Walls Eight Windows Press, 1992).

Letters

Letters of Sherwood Anderson, ed. Howard Mumford Jones and Walter B. Rideout (Boston: Little, Brown, 1953).

Sherwood Anderson: Selected Letters, ed. Charles E. Modlin (Knoxville: University of Tennessee Press, 1984).

Biography

Sutton, William A., *The Road to Winesburg: A Mosaic of the Imaginative Life of Sherwood Anderson* (Metuchen, NJ: Scarecrow Press, 1972).

Townsend, Kim, *Sherwood Anderson* (Boston: Houghton Mifflin, 1987).

Criticism

Anderson, David D. (ed.), *Sherwood Anderson: An Introduction and Interpretation* (New York: Holt, Rinehart & Winston, 1967).

——(ed.), *Sherwood Anderson: Dimensions of His Literary Art* (East Lansing: Michigan State University Press, 1976).

Anderson, David D. (ed.), *Critical Essays on Sherwood Anderson* (Boston: G. K. Hall, 1981).

Burbank, Rex, *Sherwood Anderson* (New York: Twayne, 1964).

Campbell, Hilbert H., and Modlin, Charles E. (eds.), *Sherwood Anderson: Centennial Studies* (Troy, NY: Whitston, 1976).

Crowley, John W. (ed.), *New Essays on Winesburg, Ohio* (Cambridge University Press, 1990).

Geismar, Maxwell, *The Last of the Provincials: The American Novel, 1915–1925* (Boston: Houghton Mifflin, 1943).

Howe, Irving, *Sherwood Anderson* (New York: William Sloane, 1951).

Love, Glen A., '*Winesburg, Ohio* and the Rhetoric of Silence,' *American Literature*, 40 (1968), 38–57.

Mellard, James M., 'Narrative Forms in Winesburg, Ohio', *PMLA* 83 (1968), 1304–12.

Papinchak, Robert Allen, *Sherwood Anderson: A Study of the Short Fiction* (New York: Twayne, 1992).

Phillips, William L., 'How Sherwood Anderson Wrote *Winesburg, Ohio*', *American Literature*, 23 (1951), 7–30.

Rideout, Walter B. (ed.), *Sherwood Anderson: A Collection of Critical Essays* (Englewood Cliffs, NJ: Prentice-Hall, 1974).

Small, Judy Jo, *A Reader's Guide to the Short Stories of Sherwood Anderson* (New York: G. K. Hall, 1994).

Taylor, Welford D., *Sherwood Anderson* (New York: Ungar, 1977).

Updike, John, 'Twisted Apples', *Harper's Magazine*, 268 (Mar. 1984), 95–7.

Weinstein, Arnold, 'Anderson: The Place of *Winesburg, Ohio*', in *Nobody's Home* (New York: Oxford University Press, 1993), 91–107.

White, Ray Lewis, *Winesburg, Ohio: An Exploration* (Boston: Twayne, 1990).

—— (ed.), *The Achievement of Sherwood Anderson: Essays in Criticism* (Chapel Hill: University of North Carolina Press, 1966).

—— *The Merrill Studies in Winesburg, Ohio* (Columbus, Ohio: Charles E. Merrill, 1971).

Bibliography

Sheehy, Eugene P., and Lohf, Kenneth A., *Sherwood Anderson: A Bibliography* (Los Gatos, Calif.: Talisman Press, 1960).

White, Ray Lewis, *Sherwood Anderson: A Reference Guide* (Boston: G. K. Hall, 1977).

A CHRONOLOGY OF
SHERWOOD ANDERSON

1876 Born in Camden, Ohio on Sept. 13, the third of seven children of Irwin and Emma Smith Anderson.

1883 Anderson family moves to Clyde, Ohio, the setting for *Winesburg, Ohio*, where Sherwood spends his childhood and teenage years.

1895 Mother dies aged 42, precipitating a breakup of the family.

1896 Arrives in Chicago where he works at various unskilled labouring jobs.

1900 Completes high school at Wittenberg Academy in Springfield, Ohio, and moves to Chicago, where he accepts a job as advertising solicitor. Later, he writes advertising copy and begins to move up in the business world.

1904 Marries Cornelia Lane of Toledo, Ohio. The marriage produces three children in the next seven years.

1907 Moves with family to Elyria, Ohio, to head a roof and paint supplies business. Begins writing to find himself.

1912 In November suffers a nervous breakdown and walks out of his Elyria office, an action symbolically ending his life as traditional businessman and family head.

1913 Moves back to Chicago to resume job as advertising copywriter, while also writing fiction.

1915 Publishes 'The Book of the Grotesque' and 'Hands' in *Masses* magazine. Writes about half of the *Winesburg* stories.

1916 Divorces Cornelia and marries nonconformist Tennessee Mitchell. Publishes his first novel, *Windy McPherson's Son*.

1917   Publishes second novel, *Marching Men*.

1919   *Winesburg, Ohio* is published and receives uneven reviews.

1920   *Poor White*, dealing with the industrialization of the Midwestern farming country, and perhaps Anderson's best novel, is published.

1921   Meets and encourages young Ernest Hemingway in Chicago. Goes to Europe, meets Gertrude Stein and James Joyce. Publishes *The Triumph of the Egg*, a collection of stories.

1923   Publishes *Many Marriages* (novel) and *Horses and Men* (stories).

1924   Divorces Tennessee and marries Elizabeth Prall. Meets and advises young William Faulkner in New Orleans. Publishes *A Story Teller's Story* (memoir).

1925   Publishes *Dark Laughter*, his one financially successful novel, and buys a small farm near Marion, Virginia.

1926   Builds 'Ripshin', a home, on the Virginia land. Publishes *Sherwood Anderson's Notebook* (essays) and *Tar: A Midwestern Childhood* (fanciful autobiography).

1929   Publishes *Hello Towns!*, a collection of his Marion newspaper writings.

1931   Publishes *Perhaps Women*, essays and sketches on women as possible saviours in modern life.

1932   Divorces Elizabeth. Publishes *Beyond Desire*, which, like much of his work in the 1930s, concerns labour troubles in Southern cotton-mill towns.

1933   Marries Eleanor Copenhaver, a social activist from a prominent Marion family. Publishes *Death in the Woods* (stories).

1936   Publishes *Kit Brandon* (novel).

1941 Dies from peritonitis, Mar. 8, at Colón, in the Panama
      Canal Zone, while on a trip to South America.

1942 *Sherwood Anderson's Memoirs* published posthu-
      mously.

WINESBURG, OHIO

A Group of Tales of
Ohio Small Town Life

THE TALES AND THE PERSONS

THE BOOK OF THE GROTESQUE

THE writer, an old man with a white mustache, had some difficulty in getting into bed. The windows of the house in which he lived were high and he wanted to look at the trees when he awoke in the morning. A carpenter came to fix the bed so that it would be on a level with the window.

Quite a fuss was made about the matter. The carpenter, who had been a soldier in the Civil War, came into the writer's room and sat down to talk of building a platform for the purpose of raising the bed. The writer had cigars lying about and the carpenter smoked.

For a time the two men talked of the raising of the bed and then they talked of other things. The soldier got on the subject of the war. The writer, in fact, led him to that subject. The carpenter had once been a prisoner in Andersonville prison and had lost a brother. The brother had died of starvation, and whenever the carpenter got upon that subject he cried. He, like the old writer, had a white mustache, and when he cried he puckered up his lips and the mustache bobbed up and down. The weeping old man with the cigar in his mouth was ludicrous. The plan the writer had for the raising of his bed was forgotten and later the carpenter did it in his own way and the writer, who was past sixty, had to help himself with a chair when he went to bed at night.

In his bed the writer rolled over on his side and lay quite still. For years he had been beset with notions concerning his heart. He was a hard smoker and his heart fluttered. The idea had got into his mind that he would some time die unexpectedly and always when he got into bed he thought of that. It did not alarm him. The effect in fact was quite a special thing and not easily explained. It made him more alive, there in bed, than at any other time. Perfectly still he lay and his body was old and not of much use any more, but something inside him

was altogether young. He was like a pregnant woman, only
that the thing inside him was not a baby but a youth. No, it
wasn't a youth, it was a woman, young, and wearing a coat of
mail like a knight. It is absurd, you see, to try to tell what was
inside the old writer as he lay on his high bed and listened to
the fluttering of his heart. The thing to get at is what the writer,
or the young thing within the writer, was thinking about.

The old writer, like all of the people in the world, had got,
during his long life, a great many notions in his head. He had
once been quite handsome and a number of women had been
in love with him. And then, of course, he had known people,
many people, known them in a peculiarly intimate way that
was different from the way in which you and I know people.
At least that is what the writer thought and the thought
pleased him. Why quarrel with an old man concerning his
thoughts?

In the bed the writer had a dream that was not a dream. As
he grew somewhat sleepy but was still conscious, figures
began to appear before his eyes. He imagined the young
indescribable thing within himself was driving a long procession of figures before his eyes.

You see the interest in all this lies in the figures that went
before the eyes of the writer. They were all grotesques. All of
the men and women the writer had ever known had become
grotesques.

The grotesques were not all horrible. Some were amusing,
some almost beautiful, and one, a woman all drawn out of
shape, hurt the old man by her grotesqueness. When she
passed he made a noise like a small dog whimpering. Had
you come into the room you might have supposed the old man
had unpleasant dreams or perhaps indigestion.

For an hour the procession of grotesques passed before the
eyes of the old man, and then, although it was a painful thing to
do, he crept out of bed and began to write. Some one of the
grotesques had made a deep impression on his mind and he
wanted to describe it.

At his desk the writer worked for an hour. In the end he wrote a book which he called "The Book of the Grotesque." It was never published, but I saw it once and it made an indelible impression on my mind. The book had one central thought that is very strange and has always remained with me. By remembering it I have been able to understand many people and things that I was never able to understand before. The thought was involved but a simple statement of it would be something like this:

That in the beginning when the world was young there were a great many thoughts but no such thing as a truth. Man made the truths himself and each truth was a composite of a great many vague thoughts. All about in the world were the truths and they were all beautiful.

The old man had listed hundreds of the truths in his book. I will not try to tell you of all of them. There was the truth of virginity and the truth of passion, the truth of wealth and of poverty, of thrift and of profligacy, of carefulness * and abandon. Hundreds and hundreds were the truths and they were all beautiful.

And then the people came along. Each as he appeared snatched up one of the truths and some who were quite strong snatched up a dozen of them.

It was the truths that made the people grotesques. The old man had quite an elaborate theory concerning the matter. It was his notion that the moment one of the people took one of the truths to himself, called it his truth, and tried to live his life by it, he became a grotesque and the truth he embraced became a falsehood.

You can see for yourself how the old man, who had spent all of his life writing and was filled with words, would write hundreds of pages concerning this matter. The subject would become so big in his mind that he himself would be in danger of becoming a grotesque. He didn't, I suppose, for the

* See 'Note on the Text'.

same reason that he never published the book. It was the young thing inside him that saved the old man.

Concerning the old carpenter who fixed the bed for the writer, I only mentioned him because he, like many of what are called very common people, became the nearest thing to what is understandable and lovable of all the grotesques in the writer's book.

WINESBURG, OHIO

HANDS

UPON the half decayed veranda of a small frame house that stood near the edge of a ravine near the town of Winesburg, Ohio, a fat little old man walked nervously up and down. Across a long field that had been seeded for clover but that had produced only a dense crop of yellow mustard weeds, he could see the public highway along which went a wagon filled with berry pickers returning from the fields. The berry pickers, youths and maidens, laughed and shouted boisterously. A boy clad in a blue shirt leaped from the wagon and attempted to drag after him one of the maidens who screamed and protested shrilly. The feet of the boy in the road kicked up a cloud of dust that floated across the face of the departing sun. Over the long field came a thin girlish voice. "Oh, you Wing Biddlebaum, comb your hair, it's falling into your eyes," commanded the voice to the man, who was bald and whose nervous little hands fiddled about the bare white forehead as though arranging a mass of tangled locks.

Wing Biddlebaum, forever frightened and beset by a ghostly band of doubts, did not think of himself as in any way a part of the life of the town where he had lived for twenty years. Among all the people of Winesburg but one had come close to him. With George Willard, son of Tom Willard, the proprietor of the new Willard House, he had formed something like a friendship. George Willard was the reporter on the *Winesburg Eagle* and sometimes in the evenings he walked out along the highway to Wing Biddlebaum's house. Now as the old man walked up and down on the veranda, his hands moving nervously about, he was hoping that George Willard would come and spend the evening with him. After the wagon containing the berry pickers had passed, he went across the field through the tall mustard weeds and climbing a rail fence peered anxiously along the road to the town. For a moment he stood thus, rubbing his hands together and looking up and down the road, and then, fear overcoming him, ran back to walk again upon the porch on his own house.

In the presence of George Willard, Wing Biddlebaum, who for twenty years had been the town mystery, lost something of his timidity, and his shadowy personality, submerged in a sea of doubts, came forth to look at the world. With the young reporter at his side, he ventured in the light of day into Main Street or strode up and down on the rickety front porch of his own house, talking excitedly. The voice that had been low and trembling became shrill and loud. The bent figure straightened. With a kind of wriggle, like a fish returned to the brook by the fisherman, Biddlebaum the silent began to talk, striving to put into words the ideas that had been accumulated by his mind during long years of silence.

Wing Biddlebaum talked much with his hands. The slender expressive fingers, forever active, forever striving to conceal themselves in his pockets or behind his back, came forth and became the piston rods of his machinery of expression.

The story of Wing Biddlebaum is a story of hands. Their restless activity, like unto the beating of the wings of an imprisoned bird, had given him his name. Some obscure poet of the town had thought of it. The hands alarmed their owner. He wanted to keep them hidden away and looked with amazement at the quiet inexpressive hands of other men who worked beside him in the fields, or passed, driving sleepy teams on country roads.

When he talked to George Willard, Wing Biddlebaum closed his fists and beat with them upon a table or on the walls of his house. The action made him more comfortable. If the desire to talk came to him when the two were walking in the fields, he sought out a stump or the top board of a fence and with his hands pounding busily talked with renewed ease.

The story of Wing Biddlebaum's hands is worth a book in itself. Sympathetically set forth it would tap many strange, beautiful qualities in obscure men. It is a job for a poet. In Winesburg the hands had attracted attention merely because of their activity. With them Wing Biddlebaum had picked as high as a hundred and forty quarts of strawberries in a day. They became his distinguishing feature, the source of his fame. Also they made more grotesque an already grotesque and elusive individuality. Winesburg was proud of the hands of Wing Biddlebaum in the same spirit in which it was proud of Banker White's new stone house and Wesley Moyer's bay stallion, Tony Tip, that had won the two-fifteen trot at the fall races in Cleveland.

As for George Willard, he had many times wanted to ask about the hands. At times an almost overwhelming curiosity had taken hold of him. He felt that there must be a reason for their strange activity and their inclination to keep hidden away and only a growing respect for Wing Biddlebaum kept him from blurting out the questions that were often in his mind.

Once he had been on the point of asking. The two were walking in the fields on a summer afternoon and had stopped to sit upon a grassy bank. All afternoon Wing Biddlebaum had talked as one inspired. By a fence he had stopped and beating like a giant woodpecker upon the top board had shouted at George Willard, condemning his tendency to be too much influenced by the people about him. "You are destroying yourself," he cried. "You have the inclination to be alone and to dream and you are afraid of dreams. You want to be like others in town here. You hear them talk and you try to imitate them."

On the grassy bank Wing Biddlebaum had tried again to drive his point home. His voice became soft and reminiscent, and with a sigh of contentment he launched into a long rambling talk, speaking as one lost in a dream.

Out of the dream Wing Biddlebaum made a picture for George Willard. In the picture men lived again in a kind of pastoral golden age. Across a green open country came clean-limbed young men, some afoot, some mounted upon horses. In crowds the young men came to gather about the feet of an old man who sat beneath a tree in a tiny garden and who talked to them.

Wing Biddlebaum became wholly inspired. For once he forgot the hands. Slowly they stole forth and lay upon George Willard's shoulders. Something new and bold came into the voice that talked. "You must try to forget all you have learned," said the old man. "You must begin to dream. From this time on you must shut your ears to the roaring of the voices."

Pausing in his speech, Wing Biddlebaum looked long and earnestly at George Willard. His eyes glowed. Again he raised the hands to caress the boy and then a look of horror swept over his face.

With a convulsive movement of his body, Wing Biddlebaum sprang to his feet and thrust his hands deep into his trousers pockets. Tears came to his eyes. "I must be getting along home. I can talk no more with you," he said nervously.

Without looking back, the old man had hurried down the hillside and across a meadow, leaving George Willard perplexed and frightened upon the grassy slope. With a shiver of dread the boy arose and went along the road toward town. "I'll not ask him about his hands," he thought, touched by the memory of the terror he had seen in the man's eyes. "There's something wrong, but I don't want to know what it is. His hands have something to do with his fear of me and of everyone."

And George Willard was right. Let us look briefly into the story of the hands. Perhaps our talking of them will arouse the poet who will tell the hidden wonder story of the influence for which the hands were but fluttering pennants of promise.

In his youth Wing Biddlebaum had been a school teacher in a town in Pennsylvania. He was not then known as Wing Biddlebaum, but went by the less euphonic name of Adolph Myers. As Adolph Myers he was much loved by the boys of his school.

Adolph Myers was meant by nature to be a teacher of youth. He was one of those rare, little-understood men who rule by a power so gentle that it passes as a lovable weakness. In their feeling for the boys under their charge such men are not unlike the finer sort of women in their love of men.

And yet that is but crudely stated. It needs the poet there. With the boys of his school, Adolph Myers had walked in the evening or had sat talking until dusk upon the schoolhouse steps lost in a kind of dream. Here and there went his hands, caressing the shoulders of the boys, playing about the tousled heads. As he talked his voice became soft and musical. There was a caress in that also. In a way the voice and the hands, the stroking of the shoulders and the touching of the hair were a part of the schoolmaster's effort to carry a dream into the young minds. By the caress that was in his fingers he expressed himself. He was one of those men in whom the force that creates life is diffused, not centralized. Under the caress of his hands doubt and disbelief went out of the minds of the boys and they began also to dream.

And then the tragedy. A half-witted boy of the school became enamored of the young master. In his bed at night he imagined unspeakable things and in the morning went forth to tell his dreams as facts. Strange, hideous accusations fell from his loose-hung lips. Through the Pennsylvania town went a shiver. Hidden, shadowy doubts that had been in men's minds concerning Adolph Myers were galvanized into beliefs.

The tragedy did not linger. Trembling lads were jerked out of bed and questioned. "He put his arms about me," said one. "His fingers were always playing in my hair," said another.

One afternoon a man of the town, Henry Bradford, who kept a saloon, came to the schoolhouse door. Calling Adolph Myers into the school yard he began to beat him with his fists. As his hard knuckles beat down into the frightened face of the schoolmaster, his wrath became more and more terrible. Screaming with dismay, the children ran here and there like disturbed insects. "I'll teach you to put your hands on my boy, you beast," roared the saloon keeper, who, tired of beating the master, had begun to kick him about the yard.

Adolph Myers was driven from the Pennsylvania town in the night. With lanterns in their hands a dozen men came to the door of the house where he lived alone and commanded that he dress and come forth. It was raining and one of the men had a rope in his hands. They had intended to hang the schoolmaster, but something in his figure, so small, white, and pitiful, touched their hearts and they let him escape. As he ran away into the darkness they repented of their weakness and ran after him, swearing and throwing sticks and great balls of soft mud at the figure that screamed and ran faster and faster into the darkness.

For twenty years Adolph Myers had lived alone in Winesburg. He was but forty but looked sixty-five. The name of Biddlebaum he got from a box of goods seen at a freight station as he hurried through an eastern Ohio town. He had an aunt in Winesburg, a black-toothed old woman who raised chickens, and with her he lived until she died. He had been ill for a year after the experience in Pennsylvania, and after his recovery worked as a day laborer in the fields, going timidly about and striving to conceal his hands. Although he did not understand what had happened he felt that the hands must be to blame. Again and again the fathers of the boys had talked of the hands. "Keep your hands to yourself," the saloon keeper had roared, dancing with fury in the schoolhouse yard.

Upon the veranda of his house by the ravine, Wing Biddlebaum continued to walk up and down until the sun had disappeared and the road beyond the field was lost in the grey shadows. Going into his house he cut slices of bread and spread honey upon them. When the rumble of the evening train that took away the express cars loaded with the day's harvest of berries had passed and restored the silence of the summer night, he went again to walk upon the veranda. In the darkness he could not see the hands and they became quiet. Although he still hungered for the presence of the boy, who was the medium through which he expressed his love of man, the hunger became again a part of his loneliness and his waiting. Lighting a lamp, Wing Biddlebaum washed the few dishes soiled by his simple meal and, setting up a folding cot by the screen door that led to the porch, prepared to undress for the night. A few stray white bread crumbs lay on the cleanly washed floor by the table; putting the lamp upon a low stool he began to pick up the crumbs, carrying them to his mouth one by one with unbelievable rapidity. In the dense blotch of light beneath the table, the kneeling figure looked like a priest engaged in some service of his church. The nervous expressive fingers, flashing in and out of the light, might well have been mistaken for the fingers of the devotee going swiftly through decade after decade of his rosary.

PAPER PILLS

HE was an old man with a white beard and huge nose and hands. Long before the time during which we will know him, he was a doctor and drove a jaded white horse from house to house through the streets of Winesburg. Later he married a girl who had money. She had been left a large fertile farm when her father died. The girl was quiet, tall, and dark, and to many people she seemed very beautiful. Everyone in Winesburg wondered why she married the doctor. Within a year after the marriage she died.

The knuckles of the doctor's hand were extraordinarily large. When the hands were closed they looked like clusters of unpainted wooden balls as large as walnuts fastened together by steel rods. He smoked a cob pipe and after his wife's death sat all day in his empty office close by a window that was covered with cobwebs. He never opened the window. Once on a hot day in August he tried but found it stuck fast and after that he forgot all about it.

Winesburg had forgotten the old man, but in Doctor Reefy there were the seeds of something very fine. Alone in his musty office in the Heffner Block above the Paris Dry Goods Company's Store, he worked ceaselessly, building up something that he himself destroyed. Little pyramids of truth he erected and after erecting knocked them down again that he might have the truths to erect other pyramids.

Doctor Reefy was a tall man who had worn one suit of clothes for ten years. It was frayed at the sleeves and little holes had appeared at the knees and elbows. In the office he wore also a linen duster with huge pockets into which he continually stuffed scraps of paper. After some weeks the scraps of paper became little hard round balls, and when the pockets were filled he dumped them out upon the floor. For ten years he had but one friend, another old man named John

Spaniard who owned a tree nursery. Sometimes, in a playful mood, old Doctor Reefy took from his pockets a handful of the paper balls and threw them at the nursery man. "That is to confound you, you blithering old sentimentalist," he cried, shaking with laughter.

The story of Doctor Reefy and his courtship of the tall dark girl who became his wife and left her money to him is a very curious story. It is delicious, like the twisted little apples that grow in the orchards of Winesburg. In the fall one walks in the orchards and the ground is hard with frost underfoot. The apples have been taken from the trees by the pickers. They have been put in barrels and shipped to the cities where they will be eaten in apartments that are filled with books, magazines, furniture, and people. On the trees are only a few gnarled apples that the pickers have rejected. They look like the knuckles of Doctor Reefy's hands. One nibbles at them and they are delicious. Into a little round place at the side of the apple has been gathered all of its sweetness. One runs from tree to tree over the frosted ground picking the gnarled, twisted apples and filling his pockets with them. Only the few know the sweetness of the twisted apples.

The girl and Doctor Reefy began their courtship on a summer afternoon. He was forty-five then and already he had begun the practice of filling his pockets with the scraps of paper that became hard balls and were thrown away. The habit had been formed as he sat in his buggy behind the jaded grey horse and went slowly along country roads. On the papers were written thoughts, ends of thoughts, beginnings of thoughts.

One by one the mind of Doctor Reefy had made the thoughts. Out of many of them he formed a truth that arose gigantic in his mind. The truth clouded the world. It became terrible and then faded away and the little thoughts began again.

The tall dark girl came to see Doctor Reefy because she was in the family way and had become frightened. She was in that condition because of a series of circumstances also curious.

The death of her father and mother and the rich acres of land that had come down to her had set a train of suitors on her heels. For two years she saw suitors almost every evening. Except two they were all alike. They talked to her of passion and there was a strained eager quality in their voices and in their eyes when they looked at her. The two who were different were much unlike each other. One of them, a slender young man with white hands, the son of a jeweler in Winesburg, talked continually of virginity. When he was with her he was never off the subject. The other, a black-haired boy with large ears, said nothing at all but always managed to get her into the darkness where he began to kiss her.

For a time the tall dark girl thought she would marry the jeweler's son. For hours she sat in silence listening as he talked to her and then she began to be afraid of something. Beneath his talk of virginity she began to think there was a lust greater than in all the others. At times it seemed to her that as he talked he was holding her body in his hands. She imagined him turning it slowly about in the white hands and staring at it. At night she dreamed that he had bitten into her body and that his jaws were dripping. She had the dream three times, then she became in the family way to the one who said nothing at all but who in the moment of his passion actually did bite her shoulder so that for days the marks of his teeth showed.

After the tall dark girl came to know Doctor Reefy it seemed to her that she never wanted to leave him again. She went into his office one morning and without her saying anything he seemed to know what had happened to her.

In the office of the doctor there was a woman, the wife of the man who kept the bookstore in Winesburg. Like all old-fashioned country practitioners, Doctor Reefy pulled teeth, and the woman who waited held a handkerchief to her teeth and groaned. Her husband was with her and when the tooth was taken out they both screamed and blood ran down on the woman's white dress. The tall dark girl did not pay any attention. When the woman and the man had gone the doctor smiled. "I will take you driving into the country with me," he said.

For several weeks the tall dark girl and the doctor were together almost every day. The condition that had brought her to him passed in an illness, but she was like one who has discovered the sweetness of the twisted apples, she could not get her mind fixed again upon the round perfect fruit that is eaten in the city apartments. In the fall after the beginning of her acquaintanceship with him she married Doctor Reefy and in the following spring she died. During the winter he read to her all of the odds and ends of thoughts he had scribbled on the bits of paper. After he had read them he laughed and stuffed them away in his pockets to become round hard balls.

MOTHER

ELIZABETH WILLARD, the mother of George Willard, was tall and gaunt and her face was marked with smallpox scars. Although she was but forty-five, some obscure disease had taken the fire out of her figure. Listlessly she went about the disorderly old hotel looking at the faded wall-paper and the ragged carpets and, when she was able to be about, doing the work of a chambermaid among beds soiled by the slumbers of fat traveling men. Her husband, Tom Willard, a slender, graceful man with square shoulders, a quick military step, and a black mustache, trained to turn sharply up at the ends, tried to put the wife out of his mind. The presence of the tall ghostly figure, moving slowly through the halls, he took as a reproach to himself. When he thought of her he grew angry and swore. The hotel was unprofitable and forever on the edge of failure and he wished himself out of it. He thought of the old house and the woman who lived there with him as things defeated and done for. The hotel in which he had begun life so hopefully was now a mere ghost of what a hotel should be. As he went spruce and businesslike through the streets of Winesburg, he sometimes stopped and turned quickly about as though fearing that the spirit of the hotel and of the woman would follow him even into the streets. "Damn such a life, damn it!" he sputtered aimlessly.

Tom Willard had a passion for village politics and for years had been the leading Democrat in a strongly Republican community. Some day, he told himself, the tide of things political will turn in my favor and the years of ineffectual service count big in the bestowal of rewards. He dreamed of going to Congress and even of becoming governor. Once when a younger member of the party arose at a political conference and began to boast of his faithful service, Tom Willard grew white with fury. "Shut up, you," he roared, glaring about.

"What do you know of service? What are you but a boy? Look at what I've done here! I was a Democrat here in Winesburg when it was a crime to be a Democrat. In the old days they fairly hunted us with guns."

Between Elizabeth and her one son George there was a deep unexpressed bond of sympathy, based on a girlhood dream that had long ago died. In the son's presence she was timid and reserved, but sometimes while he hurried about town intent upon his duties as a reporter, she went into his room and closing the door knelt by a little desk, made of a kitchen table, that sat near a window. In the room by the desk she went through a ceremony that was half a prayer, half a demand, addressed to the skies. In the boyish figure she yearned to see something half forgotten that had once been a part of herself recreated. The prayer concerned that. "Even though I die, I will in some way keep defeat from you," she cried, and so deep was her determination that her whole body shook. Her eyes glowed and she clenched her fists. "If I am dead and see him becoming a meaningless drab figure like myself, I will come back," she declared. "I ask God now to give me that privilege. I demand it. I will pay for it. God may beat me with his fists. I will take any blow that may befall if but this my boy be allowed to express something for us both." Pausing uncertainly, the woman stared about the boy's room. "And do not let him become smart and successful either," she added vaguely.

The communion between George Willard and his mother was outwardly a formal thing without meaning. When she was ill and sat by the window in her room he sometimes went in the evening to make her a visit. They sat by a window that looked over the roof of a small frame building into Main Street. By turning their heads they could see, through another window, along an alleyway that ran behind the Main Street stores and into the back door of Abner Groff's bakery. Sometimes as they sat thus a picture of village life presented itself to them. At the back door of his shop appeared Abner Groff with a stick or an empty milk bottle in his hand. For a long time there was a feud between the baker and a grey cat that belonged to Sylvester West, the druggist. The boy and his mother saw the cat creep into the door of the bakery and presently emerge followed by the baker who swore and waved his arms about. The baker's eyes were small and red and his black hair and beard were filled with flour dust. Sometimes he was so angry that, although the cat had disappeared, he hurled sticks, bits of broken glass, and even some of the tools of his trade about. Once he broke a window at the back of Sinnings' Hardware Store. In the alley the grey cat crouched behind barrels filled with torn paper and broken bottles above which flew a black swarm of flies. Once when she was alone, and after watching a prolonged and ineffectual outburst on the part of the baker, Elizabeth Willard put her head down on her long white hands and wept. After that she did not look along the alleyway any more, but tried to forget the contest between the bearded man and the cat. It seemed like a rehearsal of her own life, terrible in its vividness.

In the evening when the son sat in the room with his mother, the silence made them both feel awkward. Darkness came on and the evening train came in at the station. In the street below feet tramped up and down upon a board sidewalk. In the station yard, after the evening train had gone, there was a heavy silence. Perhaps Skinner Leason, the express agent, moved a truck the length of the station platform. Over on Main Street sounded a man's voice, laughing. The door of the express office banged. George Willard arose and crossing the room fumbled for the doorknob. Sometimes he knocked against a chair, making it scrape along the floor. By the window sat the sick woman, perfectly still, listless. Her long hands, white and bloodless, could be seen drooping over the ends of the arms of the chair. "I think you had better be out among the boys. You are too much indoors," she said, striving to relieve the embarrassment of the departure. "I thought I

would take a walk," replied George Willard, who felt awkward
and confused.

One evening in July, when the transient guests who made
the New Willard House their temporary homes had become
scarce, and the hallways, lighted only by kerosene lamps
turned low, were plunged in gloom, Elizabeth Willard had
an adventure. She had been ill in bed for several days and her
son had not come to visit her. She was alarmed. The feeble
blaze of life that remained in her body was blown into a flame
by her anxiety and she crept out of bed, dressed and hurried
along the hallway toward her son's room, shaking with exaggerated fears. As she went along she steadied herself with her
hand, slipped along the papered walls of the hall and breathed
with difficulty. The air whistled through her teeth. As she
hurried forward she thought how foolish she was. "He is
concerned with boyish affairs," she told herself. "Perhaps he
has now begun to walk about in the evening with girls."

Elizabeth Willard had a dread of being seen by guests in the
hotel that had once belonged to her father and the ownership
of which still stood recorded in her name in the county court-
house. The hotel was continually losing patronage because of
its shabbiness and she thought of herself as also shabby. Her
own room was in an obscure corner and when she felt able to
work she voluntarily worked among the beds, preferring the
labor that could be done when the guests were abroad seeking
trade among the merchants of Winesburg.

By the door of her son's room the mother knelt upon the
floor and listened for some sound from within. When she
heard the boy moving about and talking in low tones a smile
came to her lips. George Willard had a habit of talking aloud to
himself and to hear him doing so had always given his mother
a peculiar pleasure. The habit in him, she felt, strengthened
the secret bond that existed between them. A thousand times
she had whispered to herself of the matter. "He is groping
about, trying to find himself," she thought. "He is not a dull
clod, all words and smartness. Within him there is a secret

something that is striving to grow. It is the thing I let be killed in myself."

In the darkness in the hallway by the door the sick woman arose and started again toward her own room. She was afraid that the door would open and the boy come upon her. When she had reached a safe distance and was about to turn a corner into a second hallway she stopped and bracing herself with her hands waited, thinking to shake off a trembling fit of weakness that had come upon her. The presence of the boy in the room had made her happy. In her bed, during the long hours alone, the little fears that had visited her had become giants. Now they were all gone. "When I get back to my room I shall sleep," she murmured gratefully.

But Elizabeth Willard was not to return to her bed and to sleep. As she stood trembling in the darkness the door of her son's room opened and the boy's father, Tom Willard, stepped out. In the light that streamed out at the door he stood with the knob in his hand and talked. What he said infuriated the woman.

Tom Willard was ambitious for his son. He had always thought of himself as a successful man, although nothing he had ever done had turned out successfully. However, when he was out of sight of the New Willard House and had no fear of coming upon his wife, he swaggered and began to dramatize himself as one of the chief men of the town. He wanted his son to succeed. He it was who had secured for the boy the position on the *Winesburg Eagle*. Now, with a ring of earnestness in his voice, he was advising concerning some course of conduct. "I tell you what, George, you've got to wake up," he said sharply. "Will Henderson has spoken to me three times concerning the matter. He says you go along for hours not hearing when you are spoken to and acting like a gawky girl. What ails you?" Tom Willard laughed good-naturedly. "Well, I guess you'll get over it," he said. "I told Will that. You're not a fool and you're not a woman. You're Tom Willard's son and you'll wake up. I'm not afraid. What you say clears things up. If being a newspaper

man had put the notion of becoming a writer into your mind
that's all right. Only I guess you'll have to wake up to do that
too, eh?"

Tom Willard went briskly along the hallway and down a
flight of stairs to the office. The woman in the darkness could
hear him laughing and talking with a guest who was striving to
wear away a dull evening by dozing in a chair by the office
door. She returned to the door of her son's room. The weakness had passed from her body as by a miracle and she stepped
boldly along. A thousand ideas raced through her head. When
she heard the scraping of a chair and the sound of a pen
scratching upon paper, she again turned and went back
along the hallway to her own room.

A definite determination had come into the mind of the
defeated wife of the Winesburg Hotel keeper. The determination was the result of long years of quiet and rather ineffectual
thinking. "Now," she told herself, "I will act. There is something threatening my boy and I will ward it off." The fact that
the conversation between Tom Willard and his son had been
rather quiet and natural, as though an understanding existed
between them, maddened her. Although for years she had
hated her husband, her hatred had always before been a
quite impersonal thing. He had been merely a part of something else that she hated. Now, and by the few words at the
door, he had become the thing personified. In the darkness of
her own room she clenched her fists and glared about. Going
to a cloth bag that hung on a nail by the wall she took out a long
pair of sewing scissors and held them in her hand like a dagger.
"I will stab him," she said aloud. "He has chosen to be the voice
of evil and I will kill him. When I have killed him something
will snap within myself and I will die also. It will be a release
for all of us."

In her girlhood and before her marriage with Tom Willard,
Elizabeth had borne a somewhat shaky reputation in Winesburg. For years she had been what is called "stage-struck" and
had paraded through the streets with traveling men guests at

her father's hotel, wearing loud clothes and urging them to tell her of life in the cities out of which they had come. Once she startled the town by putting on men's clothes and riding a bicycle down Main Street.

In her own mind the tall dark girl had been in those days much confused. A great restlessness was in her and it expressed itself in two ways. First there was an uneasy desire for change, for some big definite movement to her life. It was this feeling that had turned her mind to the stage. She dreamed of joining some company and wandering over the world, seeing always new faces and giving something out of herself to all people. Sometimes at night she was quite beside herself with the thought, but when she tried to talk of the matter to the members of the theatrical companies that came to Winesburg and stopped at her father's hotel, she got nowhere. They did not seem to know what she meant, or if she did get something of her passion expressed, they only laughed. "It's not like that," they said. "It's as dull and uninteresting as this here. Nothing comes of it."

With the traveling men when she walked about with them, and later with Tom Willard, it was quite different. Always they seemed to understand and sympathize with her. On the side streets of the village, in the darkness under the trees, they took hold of her hand and she thought that something unexpressed in herself came forth and became a part of an unexpressed something in them.

And then there was the second expression of her restlessness. When that came she felt for a time released and happy. She did not blame the men who walked with her and later she did not blame Tom Willard. It was always the same, beginning with kisses and ending, after strange wild emotions, with peace and then sobbing repentance. When she sobbed she put her hand upon the face of the man and had always the same thought. Even though he were large and bearded she thought he had become suddenly a little boy. She wondered why he did not sob also.

In her room, tucked away in a corner of the old Willard House, Elizabeth Willard lighted a lamp and put it on a dressing table that stood by the door. A thought had come into her mind and she went to a closet and brought out a small square box and set it on the table. The box contained material for make-up and had been left with other things by a theatrical company that had once been stranded in Winesburg. Elizabeth Willard had decided that she would be beautiful. Her hair was still black and there was a great mass of it braided and coiled about her head. The scene that was to take place in the office below began to grow in her mind. No ghostly worn-out figure should confront Tom Willard, but something quite unexpected and startling. Tall and with dusky cheeks and hair that fell in a mass from her shoulders, a figure should come striding down the stairway before the startled loungers in the hotel office. The figure would be silent—it would be swift and terrible. As a tigress whose cub had been threatened would she appear, coming out of the shadows, stealing noiselessly along and holding the long wicked scissors in her hand.

With a little broken sob in her throat, Elizabeth Willard blew out the light that stood upon the table and stood weak and trembling in the darkness. The strength that had been as a miracle in her body left and she half reeled across the floor, clutching at the back of the chair in which she had spent so many long days staring out over the tin roofs into the main street of Winesburg. In the hallway there was the sound of footsteps and George Willard came in at the door. Sitting in a chair beside his mother he began to talk. "I'm going to get out of here," he said. "I don't know where I shall go or what I shall do but I am going away."

The woman in the chair waited and trembled. An impulse came to her. "I suppose you had better wake up," she said. "You think that? You will go to the city and make money, eh? It will be better for you, you think, to be a business man, to be brisk and smart and alive?" She waited and trembled.

The son shook his head. "I suppose I can't make you understand, but oh, I wish I could," he said earnestly. "I can't even talk to father about it. I don't try. There isn't any use. I don't know what I shall do. I just want to go away and look at people and think."

Silence fell upon the room where the boy and woman sat together. Again, as on the other evenings, they were embarrassed. After a time the boy tried again to talk. "I suppose it won't be for a year or two but I've been thinking about it," he said, rising and going toward the door. "Something father said makes it sure that I shall have to go away." He fumbled with the door knob. In the room the silence became unbearable to the woman. She wanted to cry out with joy because of the words that had come from the lips of her son, but the expression of joy had become impossible to her. "I think you had better go out among the boys. You are too much indoors," she said. "I thought I would go for a little walk," replied the son stepping awkwardly out of the room and closing the door.

THE PHILOSOPHER

DOCTOR PARCIVAL was a large man with a drooping mouth covered by a yellow mustache. He always wore a dirty white waistcoat out of the pockets of which protruded a number of the kind of black cigars known as stogies. His teeth were black and irregular and there was something strange about his eyes. The lid of the left eye twitched; it fell down and snapped up; it was exactly as though the lid of the eye were a window shade and someone stood inside the doctor's head playing with the cord.

Doctor Parcival had a liking for the boy, George Willard. It began when George had been working for a year on the *Winesburg Eagle* and the acquaintanceship was entirely a matter of the doctor's own making.

In the late afternoon Will Henderson, owner and editor of the *Eagle*, went over to Tom Willy's saloon. Along an alleyway he went and slipping in at the back door of the saloon began drinking a drink made of a combination of sloe gin and soda water. Will Henderson was a sensualist and had reached the age of forty-five. He imagined the gin renewed the youth in him. Like most sensualists he enjoyed talking of women, and for an hour he lingered about gossiping with Tom Willy. The saloon keeper was a short, broad-shouldered man with peculiarly marked hands. That flaming kind of birthmark that sometimes paints with red the faces of men and women had touched with red Tom Willy's fingers and the backs of his hands. As he stood by the bar talking to Will Henderson he rubbed the hands together. As he grew more and more excited the red of his fingers deepened. It was as though the hands had been dipped in blood that had dried and faded.

As Will Henderson stood at the bar looking at the red hands and talking of women, his assistant, George Willard, sat in the

office of the *Winesburg Eagle* and listened to the talk of
Doctor Parcival.

Doctor Parcival appeared immediately after Will Henderson had disappeared. One might have supposed that the
doctor had been watching from his office window and had
seen the editor going along the alleyway. Coming in at the
front door and finding himself a chair, he lighted one of the
stogies and crossing his legs began to talk. He seemed intent
upon convincing the boy of the advisability of adopting a line
of conduct that he was himself unable to define.

"If you have your eyes open you will see that although I call
myself a doctor I have mighty few patients," he began. "There
is a reason for that. It is not an accident and it is not because I
do not know as much of medicine as anyone here. I do not
want patients. The reason, you see, does not appear on the
surface. It lies in fact in my character, which has, if you think
about it, many strange turns. Why I want to talk to you of the
matter I don't know. I might keep still and get more credit in
your eyes. I have a desire to make you admire me, that's a fact.
I don't know why. That's why I talk. It's very amusing, eh?"

Sometimes the doctor launched into long tales concerning
himself. To the boy the tales were very real and full of meaning. He began to admire the fat unclean-looking man and, in
the afternoon when Will Henderson had gone, looked forward
with keen interest to the doctor's coming.

Doctor Parcival had been in Winesburg about five years. He
came from Chicago and when he arrived was drunk and got
into a fight with Albert Longworth, the baggageman. The fight
concerned a trunk and ended by the doctor's being escorted to
the village lockup. When he was released he rented a room
above a shoe-repairing shop at the lower end of Main Street
and put out the sign that announced himself as a doctor.
Although he had but few patients and these of the poorer
sort who were unable to pay, he seemed to have plenty of
money for his needs. He slept in the office that was unspeakably dirty and dined at Biff Carter's lunch room in a small

frame building opposite the railroad station. In the summer
the lunch room was filled with flies and Biff Carter's white
apron was more dirty than his floor. Doctor Parcival did not
mind. Into the lunch room he stalked and deposited twenty
cents upon the counter. "Feed me what you wish for that," he
said laughing. "Use up food that you wouldn't otherwise sell. It
makes no difference to me. I am a man of distinction, you see.
Why should I concern myself with what I eat."

The tales that Doctor Parcival told George Willard began
nowhere and ended nowhere. Sometimes the boy thought
they must all be inventions, a pack of lies. And then again he
was convinced that they contained the very essence of truth.

"I was a reporter like you here," Doctor Parcival began. "It
was in a town in Iowa—or was it in Illinois? I don't remember
and anyway it makes no difference. Perhaps I am trying to
conceal my identity and don't want to be very definite. Have
you ever thought it strange that I have money for my needs
although I do nothing? I may have stolen a great sum of money
or been involved in a murder before I came here. There is
food for thought in that, eh? If you were a really smart newspaper reporter you would look me up. In Chicago there was a
Doctor Cronin who was murdered. Have you heard of that?
Some men murdered him and put him in a trunk. In the early
morning they hauled the trunk across the city. It sat on the
back of an express wagon and they were on the seat as unconcerned as anything. Along they went through quiet streets
where everyone was asleep. The sun was just coming up over
the lake. Funny, eh—just to think of them smoking pipes and
chattering as they drove along as unconcerned as I am now.
Perhaps I was one of those men. That would be a strange turn
of things, now wouldn't it, eh?" Again Doctor Parcival began
his tale: "Well, anyway there I was, a reporter on a paper just as
you are here, running about and getting little items to print.
My mother was poor. She took in washing. Her dream was to
make me a Presbyterian minister and I was studying with that
end in view.

"My father had been insane for a number of years. He was in an asylum over at Dayton, Ohio. There you see I have let it slip out! All of this took place in Ohio, right here in Ohio. There is a clew if you ever get the notion of looking me up.

"I was going to tell you of my brother. That's the object of all this. That's what I'm getting at. My brother was a railroad painter and had a job on the Big Four. You know that road runs through Ohio here. With other men he lived in a box car and away they went from town to town painting the railroad property—switches, crossing gates, bridges, and stations.

"The Big Four paints its stations a nasty orange color. How I hated that color! My brother was always covered with it. On pay days he used to get drunk and come home wearing his paint-covered clothes and bringing his money with him. He did not give it to mother but laid it in a pile on our kitchen table.

"About the house he went in the clothes covered with the nasty orange colored paint. I can see the picture. My mother, who was small and had red, sad-looking eyes, would come into the house from a little shed at the back. That's where she spent her time over the washtub scrubbing people's dirty clothes. In she would come and stand by the table, rubbing her eyes with her apron that was covered with soap-suds.

"'Don't touch it! Don't you dare touch that money,'" my brother roared, and then he himself took five or ten dollars and went tramping off to the saloons. When he had spent what he had taken he came back for more. He never gave my mother any money at all but stayed about until he had spent it all, a little at a time. Then he went back to his job with the painting crew on the railroad. After he had gone things began to arrive at our house, groceries and such things. Sometimes there would be a dress for mother or a pair of shoes for me.

"Strange, eh? My mother loved my brother much more than she did me, although he never said a kind word to either of us and always raved up and down threatening us if we dared so much as touch the money that sometimes lay on the table three days.

"We got along pretty well. I studied to be a minister and prayed. I was a regular ass about saying prayers. You should have heard me. When my father died I prayed all night, just as I did sometimes when my brother was in town drinking and going about buying the things for us. In the evening after supper I knelt by the table where the money lay and prayed for hours. When no one was looking I stole a dollar or two and put it in my pocket. That makes me laugh now but then it was terrible. It was on my mind all the time. I got six dollars a week from my job on the paper and always took it straight home to mother. The few dollars I stole from my brother's pile I spent on myself, you know, for trifles, candy and cigarettes and such things.

"When my father died at the asylum over at Dayton, I went over there. I borrowed some money from the man for whom I worked and went on the train at night. It was raining. In the asylum they treated me as though I were a king.

"The men who had jobs in the asylum had found out I was a newspaper reporter. That made them afraid. There had been some negligence, some carelessness, you see, when father was ill. They thought perhaps I would write it up in the paper and make a fuss. I never intended to do anything of the kind.

"Anyway, in I went to the room where my father lay dead and blessed the dead body. I wonder what put that notion into my head. Wouldn't my brother, the painter, have laughed, though. There I stood over the dead body and spread out my hands. The superintendent of the asylum and some of his helpers came in and stood about looking sheepish. It was very amusing. I spread out my hands and said, 'Let peace brood over this carcass.' That's what I said."

Jumping to his feet and breaking off the tale, Doctor Parcival began to walk up and down in the office of the *Winesburg Eagle* where George Willard sat listening. He was awkward and, as the office was small, continually knocked against things. "What a fool I am to be talking," he said. "That is not my object in coming here and forcing my acquaintanceship upon you. I have something else in mind. You are a reporter just as I was once and you have attracted my attention. You may end by becoming just such another fool. I want to warn you and keep on warning you. That's why I seek you out."

Doctor Parcival began talking of George Willard's attitude toward men. It seemed to the boy that the man had but one object in view, to make everyone seem despicable. "I want to fill you with hatred and contempt so that you will be a superior being," he declared. "Look at my brother. There was a fellow, eh? He despised everyone, you see. You have no idea with what contempt he looked upon mother and me. And was he not our superior? You know he was. You have not seen him and yet I have made you feel that. I have given you a sense of it. He is dead. Once when he was drunk he lay down on the tracks and the car in which he lived with the other painters ran over him."

*

One day in August Doctor Parcival had an adventure in Winesburg. For a month George Willard had been going each morning to spend an hour in the doctor's office. The visits came about through a desire on the part of the doctor to read to the boy from the pages of a book he was in the process of writing. To write the book Doctor Parcival declared was the object of his coming to Winesburg to live.

On the morning in August before the coming of the boy, an incident had happened in the doctor's office. There had been an accident on Main Street. A team of horses had been frightened by a train and had run away. A little girl, the daughter of a farmer, had been thrown from a buggy and killed.

On Main Street everyone had become excited and a cry for doctors had gone up. All three of the active practitioners of the town had come quickly but had found the child dead. From the crowd someone had run to the office of Doctor Parcival who had bluntly refused to go down out of his office to the dead child. The useless cruelty of his refusal had passed unnoticed. Indeed, the man who had come up the stairway to summon him had hurried away without hearing the refusal.

All of this, Doctor Parcival did not know and when George Willard came to his office he found the man shaking with terror. "What I have done will arouse the people of this town," he declared excitedly. "Do I not know human nature? Do I not know what will happen? Word of my refusal will be whispered about. Presently men will get together in groups and talk of it. They will come here. We will quarrel and there will be talk of hanging. Then they will come again bearing a rope in their hands."

Doctor Parcival shook with fright. "I have a presentiment," he declared emphatically. "It may be that what I am talking about will not occur this morning. It may be put off until to-night but I will be hanged. Everyone will get excited. I will be hanged to a lamp-post on Main Street."

Going to the door of his dirty little office, Doctor Parcival looked timidly down the stairway leading to the street. When he returned the fright that had been in his eyes was beginning to be replaced by doubt. Coming on tip-toe across the room he tapped George Willard on the shoulder. "If not now, some-time," he whispered, shaking his head. "In the end I will be crucified, uselessly crucified."

Doctor Parcival began to plead with George Willard. "You must pay attention to me," he urged. "If something happens perhaps you will be able to write the book that I may never get written. The idea is very simple, so simple that if you are not careful you will forget it. It is this—that everyone in the world is Christ and they are all crucified. That's what I want to say. Don't you forget that. Whatever happens, don't you dare let yourself forget."

NOBODY KNOWS

LOOKING cautiously about, George Willard arose from his desk in the office of the *Winesburg Eagle* and went hurriedly out at the back door. The night was warm and cloudy and although it was not yet eight o'clock, the alleyway back of the *Eagle* office was pitch dark. A team of horses tied to a post somewhere in the darkness stamped on the hard-baked ground. A cat sprang from under George Willard's feet and ran away into the night. The young man was nervous. All day he had gone about his work like one dazed by a blow. In the alleyway he trembled as though with fright.

In the darkness George Willard walked along the alleyway, going carefully and cautiously. The back doors of the Winesburg stores were open and he could see men sitting about under the store lamps. In Myerbaum's Notion Store Mrs. Willy the saloon keeper's wife stood by the counter with a basket on her arm. Sid Green the clerk was waiting on her. He leaned over the counter and talked earnestly.

George Willard crouched and then jumped through the path of light that came out at the door. He began to run forward in the darkness. Behind Ed Griffith's saloon old Jerry Bird the town drunkard lay asleep on the ground. The runner stumbled over the sprawling legs. He laughed brokenly.

George Willard had set forth upon an adventure. All day he had been trying to make up his mind to go through with the adventure and now he was acting. In the office of the *Winesburg Eagle* he had been sitting since six o'clock trying to think.

There had been no decision. He had just jumped to his feet, hurried past Will Henderson who was reading proof in the print shop and started to run along the alleyway.

Through street after street went George Willard, avoiding the people who passed. He crossed and recrossed the road.

When he passed a street lamp he pulled his hat down over his face. He did not dare think. In his mind there was a fear but it was a new kind of fear. He was afraid the adventure on which he had set out would be spoiled, that he would lose courage and turn back.

George Willard found Louise Trunnion in the kitchen of her father's house. She was washing dishes by the light of a kerosene lamp. There she stood behind the screen door in the little shed-like kitchen at the back of the house. George Willard stopped by a picket fence and tried to control the shaking of his body. Only a narrow potato patch separated him from the adventure. Five minutes passed before he felt sure enough of himself to call to her. "Louise! Oh Louise!" he called. The cry stuck in his throat. His voice became a hoarse whisper.

Louise Trunnion came out across the potato patch holding the dish cloth in her hand. "How do you know I want to go out with you," she said sulkily. "What makes you so sure?"

George Willard did not answer. In silence the two stood in the darkness with the fence between them. "You go on along," she said. "Pa's in there. I'll come along. You wait by Williams' barn."

The young newspaper reporter had received a letter from Louise Trunnion. It had come that morning to the office of the *Winesburg Eagle*. The letter was brief. "I'm yours if you want me," it said. He thought it annoying that in the darkness by the fence she had pretended there was nothing between them. "She has a nerve! Well, gracious sakes, she has a nerve," he muttered as he went along the street and passed a row of vacant lots where corn grew. The corn was shoulder high and had been planted right down to the sidewalk.

When Louise Trunnion came out of the front door of her house she still wore the gingham dress in which she had been washing dishes. There was no hat on her head. The boy could see her standing with the doorknob in her hand talking to someone within, no doubt to old Jake Trunnion, her father.

Old Jake was half deaf and she shouted. The door closed and everything was dark and silent in the little side street. George Willard trembled more violently than ever.

In the shadows by Williams' barn George and Louise stood, not daring to talk. She was not particularly comely and there was a black smudge on the side of her nose. George thought she must have rubbed her nose with her finger after she had been handling some of the kitchen pots.

The young man began to laugh nervously. "It's warm," he said. He wanted to touch her with his hand. "I'm not very bold," he thought. Just to touch the folds of the soiled gingham dress would, he decided, be an exquisite pleasure. She began to quibble. "You think you're better than I am. Don't tell me, I guess I know," she said drawing closer to him.

A flood of words burst from George Willard. He remembered the look that had lurked in the girl's eyes when they had met on the streets and thought of the note she had written. Doubt left him. The whispered tales concerning her that had gone about town gave him confidence. He became wholly the male, bold and aggressive. In his heart there was no sympathy for her. "Ah, come on, it'll be all right. There won't be anyone know anything. How can they know?" he urged.

They began to walk along a narrow brick sidewalk between the cracks of which tall weeds grew. Some of the bricks were missing and the sidewalk was rough and irregular. He took hold of her hand that was also rough and thought it delightfully small. "I can't go far," she said and her voice was quiet, unperturbed.

They crossed a bridge that ran over a tiny stream and passed another vacant lot in which corn grew. The street ended. In the path at the side of the road they were compelled to walk one behind the other. Will Overton's berry field lay beside the road and there was a pile of boards. "Will is going to build a shed to store berry crates here," said George and they sat down upon the boards.

*

When George Willard got back into Main Street it was past ten o'clock and had begun to rain. Three times he walked up and down the length of Main Street. Sylvester West's Drug Store was still open and he went in and bought a cigar. When Shorty Crandall the clerk came out at the door with him he was pleased. For five minutes the two stood in the shelter of the store awning and talked. George Willard felt satisfied. He had wanted more than anything else to talk to some man. Around a corner toward the New Willard House he went whistling softly.

On the sidewalk at the side of Winney's Dry Goods Store where there was a high board fence covered with circus pictures, he stopped whistling and stood perfectly still in the darkness, attentive, listening as though for a voice calling his name. Then again he laughed nervously. "She hasn't got anything on me. Nobody knows," he muttered doggedly and went on his way.

GODLINESS

A TALE IN FOUR PARTS

PART ONE

THERE were always three or four old people sitting on the front porch of the house or puttering about the garden of the Bentley farm. Three of the old people were women and sisters to Jesse. They were a colorless, soft-voiced lot. Then there was a silent old man with thin white hair who was Jesse's uncle.

The farmhouse was built of wood, a board outer-covering over a framework of logs. It was in reality not one house but a cluster of houses joined together in a rather haphazard manner. Inside, the place was full of surprises. One went up steps from the living room into the dining room and there were always steps to be ascended or descended in passing from one room to another. At meal times the place was like a beehive. At one moment all was quiet, then doors began to open, feet clattered on stairs, a murmur of soft voices arose and people appeared from a dozen obscure corners.

Beside the old people, already mentioned, many others lived in the Bentley house. There were four hired men, a woman named Aunt Callie Beebe, who was in charge of the housekeeping, a dull-witted girl named Eliza Stoughton, who made beds and helped with the milking, a boy who worked in the stables, and Jesse Bentley himself, the owner and overlord of it all.

By the time the American Civil War had been over for twenty years, that part of Northern Ohio where the Bentley farms lay had begun to emerge from pioneer life. Jesse then owned machinery for harvesting grain. He had built modern barns and most of his land was drained with carefully laid tile drain, but in order to understand the man we will have to go back to an earlier day.

The Bentley family had been in Northern Ohio for several generations before Jesse's time. They came from New York State and took up land when the country was new and land could be had at a low price. For a long time they, in common with all the other Middle Western people, were very poor. The land they had settled upon was heavily wooded and covered with fallen logs and underbrush. After the long hard labor of clearing these away and cutting the timber, there were still the stumps to be reckoned with. Plows run through the fields caught on hidden roots, stones lay all about, on the low places water gathered, and the young corn turned yellow, sickened and died.

When Jesse Bentley's father and brothers had come into their ownership of the place, much of the harder part of the work of clearing had been done, but they clung to old traditions and worked like driven animals. They lived as practically all of the farming people of the time lived. In the spring and through most of the winter the highways leading into the town of Winesburg were a sea of mud. The four young men of the family worked hard all day in the fields, they ate heavily of coarse, greasy food, and at night slept like tired beasts on beds of straw. Into their lives came little that was not coarse and brutal and outwardly they were themselves coarse and brutal. On Saturday afternoons they hitched a team of horses to a three-seated wagon and went off to town. In town they stood about the stoves in the stores talking to other farmers or to the store keepers. They were dressed in overalls and in the winter wore heavy coats that were flecked with mud. Their hands as they stretched them out to the heat of the stoves were cracked and red. It was difficult for them to talk and so they for the most part kept silent. When they had bought meat, flour, sugar, and salt, they went into one of the Winesburg saloons and drank beer. Under the influence of drink the naturally strong lusts of their natures, kept suppressed by the heroic labor of breaking up new ground, were released. A kind of crude and animal-like poetic fervor took possession of them.

On the road home they stood up on the wagon seats and shouted at the stars. Sometimes they fought long and bitterly and at other times they broke forth into songs. Once Enoch Bentley, the older one of the boys, struck his father, old Tom Bentley, with the butt of a teamster's whip, and the old man seemed likely to die. For days Enoch lay hid in the straw in the loft of the stable ready to flee if the result of his momentary passion turned out to be murder. He was kept alive with food brought by his mother who also kept him informed of the injured man's condition. When all turned out well he emerged from his hiding place and went back to the work of clearing land as though nothing had happened.

*

The Civil War brought a sharp turn to the fortunes of the Bentleys and was responsible for the rise of the youngest son, Jesse. Enoch, Edward, Harry, and Will Bentley all enlisted and before the long war ended they were all killed. For a time after they went away to the South, old Tom tried to run the place, but he was not successful. When the last of the four had been killed he sent word to Jesse that he would have to come home.

Then the mother, who had not been well for a year, died suddenly, and the father became altogether discouraged. He talked of selling the farm and moving into town. All day he went about shaking his head and muttering. The work in the fields was neglected and weeds grew high in the corn. Old Tom hired men but he did not use them intelligently. When they had gone away to the fields in the morning he wandered into the woods and sat down on a log. Sometimes he forgot to come home at night and one of the daughters had to go in search of him.

When Jesse Bentley came home to the farm and began to take charge of things he was a slight, sensitive-looking man of twenty-two. At eighteen he had left home to go to school to become a scholar and eventually to become a minister of the Presbyterian Church. All through his boyhood he had been what in our country was called an "odd sheep" and had not got on with his brothers. Of all the family only his mother had understood him and she was now dead. When he came home to take charge of the farm, that had at that time grown to more than six hundred acres, everyone on the farms about and in the nearby town of Winesburg smiled at the idea of his trying to handle the work that had been done by his four strong brothers.

There was indeed good cause to smile. By the standards of his day Jesse did not look like a man at all. He was small and very slender and womanish of body and, true to the traditions of young ministers, wore a long black coat and a narrow black string tie. The neighbors were amused when they saw him, after the years away, and they were even more amused when they saw the woman he had married in the city.

As a matter of fact, Jesse's wife did soon go under. That was perhaps Jesse's fault. A farm in Northern Ohio in the hard years after the Civil War was no place for a delicate woman, and Katherine Bentley was delicate. Jesse was hard with her as he was with everybody about him in those days. She tried to do such work as all the neighbor women about her did and he let her go on without interference. She helped to do the milking and did part of the housework; she made the beds for the men and prepared their food. For a year she worked every day from sunrise until late at night and then after giving birth to a child she died.

As for Jesse Bentley—although he was a delicately built man there was something within him that could not easily be killed. He had brown curly hair and grey eyes that were at times hard and direct, at times wavering and uncertain. Not only was he slender but he was also short of stature. His mouth was like the mouth of a sensitive and very determined child. Jesse Bentley was a fanatic. He was a man born out of his time and place and for this he suffered and made others suffer. Never did he succeed in getting what he wanted out of life and he did not know what he wanted. Within a very short time after he came home to the Bentley farm he made everyone there a little afraid of him, and his wife, who should have been close to him as his mother had been, was afraid also. At the end of two weeks after his coming, old Tom Bentley made over to him the entire ownership of the place and retired into the background. Everyone retired into the background. In spite of his youth and inexperience, Jesse had the trick of mastering the souls of his people. He was so in earnest in everything he did and said that no one understood him. He made everyone on the farm work as they had never worked before and yet there was no joy in the work. If things went well they went well for Jesse and never for the people who were his dependents. Like a thousand other strong men who have come into the world here in America in these later times, Jesse was but half strong. He could master others but he could not master himself. The running of the farm as it had never been run before was easy for him. When he came home from Cleveland where he had been in school, he shut himself off from all of his people and began to make plans. He thought about the farm night and day and that made him successful. Other men on the farms about him worked too hard and were too tired to think, but to think of the farm and to be everlastingly making plans for its success was a relief to Jesse. It partially satisfied something in his passionate nature. Immediately after he came home he had a wing built on to the old house and in a large room facing the west he had windows that looked into the barnyard and other windows that looked off across the fields. By the window he sat down to think. Hour after hour and day after day he sat and looked over the land and thought out his new place in life. The passionate burning thing in his nature flamed up and his eyes became hard. He wanted to make the farm produce as no farm in his state had ever produced before and then he wanted something else. It was the indefinable hunger within that made his eyes waver and that kept him always more and more silent before people. He would have given much to achieve peace and in him was a fear that peace was the thing he could not achieve.

All over his body Jesse Bentley was alive. In his small frame was gathered the force of a long line of strong men. He had always been extraordinarily alive when he was a small boy on the farm and later when he was a young man in school. In the school he had studied and thought of God and the Bible with his whole mind and heart. As time passed and he grew to know people better, he began to think of himself as an extraordinary man, one set apart from his fellows. He wanted terribly to make his life a thing of great importance, and as he looked about at his fellow men and saw how like clods they lived it seemed to him that he could not bear to become also such a clod. Although in his absorption in himself and in his own destiny he was blind to the fact that his young wife was doing a strong woman's work even after she had become large with child and that she was killing herself in his service, he did not intend to be unkind to her. When his father, who was old and twisted with toil, made over to him the ownership of the farm and seemed content to creep away to a corner and wait for death, he shrugged his shoulders and dismissed the old man from his mind.

In the room by the window overlooking the land that had come down to him sat Jesse thinking of his own affairs. In the stables he could hear the tramping of his horses and the restless movement of his cattle. Away in the fields he could see other cattle wandering over green hills. The voices of men, his men who worked for him, came in to him through the window. From the milkhouse there was the steady thump, thump of a churn being manipulated by the half-witted girl, Eliza Stoughton. Jesse's mind went back to the men of Old Testament days who had also owned lands and herds. He remembered how God had come down out of the skies and talked to these men and he wanted God to notice and to talk to him also. A kind of feverish boyish eagerness to in some way achieve in his own life the flavor of significance that had hung over these men took possession of him. Being a prayerful man he spoke of the matter aloud to God and the sound of his own words strengthened and fed his eagerness.

"I am a new kind of man come into possession of these fields," he declared. "Look upon me, O God, and look Thou also upon my neighbors and all the men who have gone before me here! O God, create in me another Jesse, like that one of old, to rule over men and to be the father of sons who shall be rulers!" Jesse grew excited as he talked aloud and jumping to his feet walked up and down in the room. In fancy he saw himself living in old times and among old peoples. The land that lay stretched out before him became of vast significance, a place peopled by his fancy with a new race of men sprung from himself. It seemed to him that in his day as in those other and older days, kingdoms might be created and new impulses given to the lives of men by the power of God speaking through a chosen servant. He longed to be such a servant. "It is God's work I have come to the land to do," he declared in a loud voice and his short figure straightened and he thought that something like a halo of Godly approval hung over him.

*

It will perhaps be somewhat difficult for the men and women of a later day to understand Jesse Bentley. In the last fifty years a vast change has taken place in the lives of our people. A revolution has in fact taken place. The coming of industrialism, attended by all the roar and rattle of affairs, the shrill cries of millions of new voices that have come among us from over seas, the going and coming of trains, the growth of cities, the building of the interurban car lines that weave in and out of towns and past farmhouses, and now in these later days the coming of the automobiles has worked a tremendous change in the lives and in the habits of thought of our people of Mid-America. Books, badly imagined and written though they may be in the hurry of our times, are in every household, magazines circulate by the millions of copies, newspapers are everywhere. In our day a farmer standing by the stove in the store in his village has his mind filled to overflowing with the words of other men. The newspapers and the magazines have pumped him full. Much of the old brutal ignorance that had in it also a kind of beautiful childlike innocence is gone forever. The farmer by the stove is brother to the men of the cities, and if you listen you will find him talking as glibly and as senselessly as the best city man of us all.

In Jesse Bentley's time and in the country districts of the whole Middle West in the years after the Civil War it was not so. Men labored too hard and were too tired to read. In them was no desire for words printed upon paper. As they worked in the fields, vague, half-formed thoughts took possession of them. They believed in God and in God's power to control their lives. In the little Protestant churches they gathered on Sunday to hear of God and his works. The churches were the center of the social and intellectual life of the times. The figure of God was big in the hearts of men.

And so, having been born an imaginative child and having within him a great intellectual eagerness, Jesse Bentley had turned wholeheartedly toward God. When the war took his brothers away, he saw the hand of God in that. When his father became ill and could no longer attend to the running of the farm, he took that also as a sign from God. In the city, when the word came to him, he walked about at night through the streets thinking of the matter and when he had come home and had got the work on the farm well under way, he went again at night to walk through the forests and over the low hills and to think of God.

As he walked the importance of his own figure in some divine plan grew in his mind. He grew avaricious and was impatient that the farm contained only six hundred acres. Kneeling in a fence corner at the edge of some meadow, he sent his voice abroad into the silence and looking up he saw the stars shining down at him.

One evening, some months after his father's death, and when his wife Katherine was expecting at any moment to be laid abed of childbirth, Jesse left his house and went for a long walk. The Bentley farm was situated in a tiny valley watered by Wine Creek, and Jesse walked along the banks of the stream to the end of his own land and on through the fields of his neighbors. As he walked the valley broadened and then narrowed again. Great open stretches of field and wood lay before him. The moon came out from behind clouds, and, climbing a low hill, he sat down to think.

Jesse thought that as the true servant of God the entire stretch of country through which he had walked should have come into his possession. He thought of his dead brothers and blamed them that they had not worked harder and achieved more. Before him in the moonlight the tiny stream ran down over stones, and he began to think of the men of old times who like himself had owned flocks and lands.

A fantastic impulse, half fear, half greediness, took possession of Jesse Bentley. He remembered how in the old Bible story the Lord had appeared to that other Jesse and told him to send his son David to where Saul and the men of Israel were fighting the Philistines in the Valley of Elah. Into Jesse's mind came the conviction that all of the Ohio farmers who owned land in the valley of Wine Creek were Philistines and enemies of God. "Suppose," he whispered to himself, "there should come from among them one who, like Goliath the Philistine of Gath, could defeat me and take from me my possessions." In fancy he felt the sickening dread that he thought must have lain heavy on the heart of Saul before the coming of David. Jumping to his feet, he began to run through the night. As he ran he called to God. His voice carried far over the low hills. "Jehovah of Hosts," he cried, "send to me this night out of the womb of Katherine, a son. Let thy grace alight upon me. Send me a son to be called David who shall help me to pluck at last all of these lands out of the hands of the Philistines and turn them to Thy service and to the building of Thy kingdom on earth."

GODLINESS

PART TWO

DAVID HARDY of Winesburg, Ohio was the grandson of
Jesse Bentley, the owner of Bentley farms. When he was
twelve years old he went to the old Bentley place to live. His
mother, Louise Bentley, the girl who came into the world on
that night when Jesse ran through the fields crying to God that
he be given a son, had grown to womanhood on the farm and
had married young John Hardy of Winesburg who became a
banker. Louise and her husband did not live happily together
and everyone agreed that she was to blame. She was a small
woman with sharp grey eyes and black hair. From childhood
she had been inclined to fits of temper and when not angry she
was often morose and silent. In Winesburg it was said that she
drank. Her husband, the banker, who was a careful, shrewd
man, tried hard to make her happy. When he began to make
money he bought for her a large brick house on Elm Street in
Winesburg and he was the first man in that town to keep a
manservant to drive his wife's carriage.

But Louise could not be made happy. She flew into half
insane fits of temper during which she was sometimes silent,
sometimes noisy and quarrelsome. She swore and cried out in
her anger. She got a knife from the kitchen and threatened her
husband's life. Once she deliberately set fire to the house, and
often she hid herself away for days in her own room and would
see no one. Her life, lived as a half recluse, gave rise to all sorts
of stories concerning her. It was said that she took drugs and
that she hid herself away from people because she was often so
under the influence of drink that her condition could not be
concealed. Sometimes on summer afternoons she came out of
the house and got into her carriage. Dismissing the driver she
took the reins in her own hands and drove off at top speed
through the streets. If a pedestrian got in her way she drove

straight ahead and the frightened citizen had to escape as best he could. To the people of the town it seemed as though she wanted to run them down. When she had driven through several streets, tearing around corners and beating the horses with the whip, she drove off into the country. On the country roads after she had gotten out of sight of the houses she let the horses slow down to a walk and her wild, reckless mood passed. She became thoughtful and muttered words. Sometimes tears came into her eyes. And then when she came back into town she again drove furiously through the quiet streets. But for the influence of her husband and the respect he inspired in people's minds she would have been arrested more than once by the town marshal.

Young David Hardy grew up in the house with this woman and as can well be imagined there was not much joy in his childhood. He was too young then to have opinions of his own about people, but at times it was difficult for him not to have very definite opinions about the woman who was his mother. David was always a quiet orderly boy and for a long time was thought by the people of Winesburg to be something of a dullard. His eyes were brown and as a child he had a habit of looking at things and people a long time without appearing to see what he was looking at. When he heard his mother spoken of harshly or when he overheard her berating his father, he was frightened and ran away to hide. Sometimes he could not find a hiding place and that confused him. Turning his face toward a tree or if he were indoors toward the wall, he closed his eyes and tried not to think of anything. He had a habit of talking aloud to himself, and early in life a spirit of quiet sadness often took possession of him.

On the occasions when David went to visit his grandfather on the Bentley farm, he was altogether contented and happy. Often he wished that he would never have to go back to town and once when he had come home from the farm after a long visit, something happened that had a lasting effect on his mind.

David had come back into town with one of the hired men. The man was in a hurry to go about his own affairs and left the boy at the head of the street in which the Hardy house stood. It was early dusk of a fall evening and the sky was overcast with clouds. Something happened to David. He could not bear to go into the house where his mother and father lived, and on an impulse he decided to run away from home. He intended to go back to the farm and to his grandfather, but lost his way and for hours he wandered weeping and frightened on country roads. It started to rain and lightning flashed in the sky. The boy's imagination was excited and he fancied that he could see and hear strange things in the darkness. Into his mind came the conviction that he was walking and running in some terrible void where no one had ever been before. The darkness about him seemed limitless. The sound of the wind blowing in trees was terrifying. When a team of horses approached along the road in which he walked he was frightened and climbed a fence. Through a field he ran until he came into another road and getting upon his knees felt of the soft ground with his fingers. But for the figure of his grandfather, whom he was afraid he would never find in the darkness, he thought the world must be altogether empty. When his cries were heard by a farmer who was walking home from town and he was brought back to his father's house, he was so tired and excited that he did not know what was happening to him.

By chance David's father knew that he had disappeared. On the street he had met the farm hand from the Bentley place and knew of his son's return to town. When the boy did not come home an alarm was set up and John Hardy with several men of the town went to search the country. The report that David had been kidnapped ran about through the streets of Winesburg. When he came home there were no lights in the house, but his mother appeared and clutched him eagerly in her arms. David thought she had suddenly become another woman. He could not believe that so delightful a thing had happened. With her own hands Louise Hardy bathed his tired young body and cooked him food. She would not let him go to bed but, when he had put on his nightgown, blew out the lights and sat down in a chair to hold him in her arms. For an hour the woman sat in the darkness and held her boy. All the time she kept talking in a low voice. David could not understand what had so changed her. Her habitually dissatisfied face had become, he thought, the most peaceful and lovely thing he had ever seen. When he began to weep she held him more and more tightly. On and on went her voice. It was not harsh or shrill as when she talked to her husband, but was like rain falling on trees. Presently men began coming to the door to report that he had not been found, but she made him hide and be silent until she had sent them away. He thought it must be a game his mother and the men of the town were playing with him and laughed joyously. Into his mind came the thought that his having been lost and frightened in the darkness was an altogether unimportant matter. He thought that he would have been willing to go through the frightful experience a thousand times to be sure of finding at the end of the long black road a thing so lovely as his mother had suddenly become.

*

During the last years of young David's boyhood he saw his mother but seldom and she became for him just a woman with whom he had once lived. Still he could not get her figure out of his mind and as he grew older it became more definite. When he was twelve years old he went to the Bentley farm to live. Old Jesse came into town and fairly demanded that he be given charge of the boy. The old man was excited and determined on having his own way. He talked to John Hardy in the office of the Winesburg Savings Bank and then the two men went to the house on Elm Street to talk with Louise. They both expected her to make trouble but were mistaken. She was very quiet and when Jesse had explained his mission and had gone on at some length about the advantages to come through having the boy out of doors and in the quiet atmosphere of the old farmhouse, she nodded her head in approval. "It is an atmosphere not corrupted by my presence," she said sharply. Her shoulders shook and she seemed about to fly into a fit of temper. "It is a place for a man child, although it was never a place for me," she went on. "You never wanted me there and of course the air of your house did me no good. It was like poison in my blood but it will be different with him."

Louise turned and went out of the room, leaving the two men to sit in embarrassed silence. As very often happened she later stayed in her room for days. Even when the boy's clothes were packed and he was taken away she did not appear. The loss of her son made a sharp break in her life and she seemed less inclined to quarrel with her husband. John Hardy thought it had all turned out very well indeed.

And so young David went to live in the Bentley farmhouse with Jesse. Two of the old farmer's sisters were alive and still lived in the house. They were afraid of Jesse and rarely spoke when he was about. One of the women who had been noted for her flaming red hair when she was younger was a born mother and became the boy's caretaker. Every night when he had gone to bed she went into his room and sat on the floor until he fell asleep. When he became drowsy she became bold and whispered things that he later thought he must have dreamed.

Her soft low voice called him endearing names and he dreamed that his mother had come to him and that she had changed so that she was always as she had been that time after he ran away. He also grew bold and reaching out his hand stroked the face of the woman on the floor so that she was ecstatically happy. Everyone in the old house became happy after the boy went there. The hard insistent thing in Jesse Bentley that had kept the people in the house silent and timid and that had never been dispelled by the presence of the girl Louise was apparently swept away by the coming of the boy. It was as though God had relented and sent a son to the man.

The man who had proclaimed himself the only true servant of God in all the valley of Wine Creek, and who had wanted

God to send him a sign of approval by way of a son out of the womb of Katherine, began to think that at last his prayers had been answered. Although he was at that time only fifty-five years old he looked seventy and was worn out with much thinking and scheming. The effort he had made to extend his land holdings had been successful and there were few farms in the valley that did not belong to him, but until David came he was a bitterly disappointed man.

There were two influences at work in Jesse Bentley and all his life his mind had been a battleground for these influences. First there was the old thing in him. He wanted to be a man of God and a leader among men of God. His walking in the fields and through the forests at night had brought him close to nature and there were forces in the passionately religious man that ran out to the forces in nature. The disappointment that had come to him when a daughter and not a son had been born to Katherine had fallen upon him like a blow struck by some unseen hand and the blow had somewhat softened his egotism. He still believed that God might at any moment make himself manifest out of the winds or the clouds, but he no longer demanded such recognition. Instead he prayed for it. Sometimes he was altogether doubtful and thought God had deserted the world. He regretted the fate that had not let him live in a simpler and sweeter time when at the beckoning of some strange cloud in the sky men left their lands and houses and went forth into the wilderness to create new races. While he worked night and day to make his farms more productive and to extend his holdings of land, he regretted that he could not use his own restless energy in the building of temples, the slaying of unbelievers and in general in the work of glorifying God's name on earth.

That is what Jesse hungered for and then also he hungered for something else. He had grown into maturity in America in the years after the Civil War and he, like all men of his time, had been touched by the deep influences that were at work in the country during those years when modern industrialism was being born. He began to buy machines that would permit him to do the work of the farms while employing fewer men and he sometimes thought that if he were a younger man he would give up farming altogether and start a factory in Winesburg for the making of machinery. Jesse formed the habit of reading newspapers and magazines. He invented a machine for the making of fence out of wire. Faintly he realized that the atmosphere of old times and places that he had always cultivated in his own mind was strange and foreign to the thing that was growing up in the minds of others. The beginning of the most materialistic age in the history of the world, when wars would be fought without patriotism, when men would forget God and only pay attention to moral standards, when the will to power would replace the will to serve and beauty would be well-nigh forgotten in the terrible headlong rush of mankind toward the acquiring of possessions, was telling its story to Jesse the man of God as it was to the men about him. The greedy thing in him wanted to make money faster than it could be made by tilling the land. More than once he went into Winesburg to talk with his son-in-law John Hardy about it. "You are a banker and you will have chances I never had," he said and his eyes shone. "I am thinking about it all the time. Big things are going to be done in the country and there will be more money to be made than I ever dreamed of. You get into it. I wish I were younger and had your chance." Jesse Bentley walked up and down in the bank office and grew more and more excited as he talked. At one time in his life he had been threatened with paralysis and his left side remained somewhat weakened. As he talked his left eyelid twitched. Later when he drove back home and when night came on and the stars came out it was harder to get back the old feeling of a close and personal God who lived in the sky overhead and who might at any moment reach out his hand, touch him on the shoulder, and appoint for him some heroic task to be done. Jesse's mind was fixed upon the things read in newspapers and magazines, on fortunes to be made almost without effort by shrewd men who bought and sold. For him the coming of the boy David did much to bring back with renewed force the old faith and it seemed to him that God had at last looked with favor upon him.

As for the boy on the farm, life began to reveal itself to him in a thousand new and delightful ways. The kindly attitude of all about him expanded his quiet nature and he lost the half timid, hesitating manner he had always had with his people. At night when he went to bed after a long day of adventures in the stables, in the fields, or driving about from farm to farm with his grandfather he wanted to embrace everyone in the house. If Sherley Bentley, the woman who came each night to sit on the floor by his bedside, did not appear at once, he went to the head of the stairs and shouted, his young voice ringing through the narrow halls where for so long there had been a tradition of silence. In the morning when he awoke and lay still in bed, the sounds that came in to him through the windows filled him with delight. He thought with a shudder of the life in the house in Winesburg and of his mother's angry voice that had always made him tremble. There in the country all sounds were pleasant sounds. When he awoke at dawn the barnyard back of the house also awoke. In the house people stirred about. Eliza Stoughton the half-witted girl was poked in the ribs by a farm hand and giggled noisily, in some distant field a cow bawled and was answered by the cattle in the stables, and one of the farm hands spoke sharply to the horse he was grooming by the stable door. David leaped out of bed and ran to a window. All of the people stirring about excited his mind, and he wondered what his mother was doing in the house in town.

From the windows of his own room he could not see directly into the barnyard where the farm hands had now all assembled to do the morning chores, but he could hear the voices of the men and the neighing of the horses. When one of the men laughed, he laughed also. Leaning out at the open window, he looked into an orchard where a fat sow wandered about with a litter of tiny pigs at her heels. Every morning he

counted the pigs. "Four, five, six, seven," he said slowly, wet-
ting his finger and making straight up and down marks on the
window ledge. David ran to put on his trousers and shirt. A
feverish desire to get out of doors took possession of him.
Every morning he made such a noise coming down stairs
that Aunt Callie, the housekeeper, declared he was trying to
tear the house down. When he had run through the long old
house, shutting doors behind him with a bang, he came into
the barnyard and looked about with an amazed air of expec-
tancy. It seemed to him that in such a place tremendous things
might have happened during the night. The farm hands
looked at him and laughed. Henry Strader, an old man who
had been on the farm since Jesse came into possession and
who before David's time had never been known to make a
joke, made the same joke every morning. It amused David so
that he laughed and clapped his hands. "See, come here and
look," cried the old man, "Grandfather Jesse's white mare has
torn the black stocking she wears on her foot."

Day after day through the long summer, Jesse Bentley
drove from farm to farm up and down the valley of Wine
Creek, and his grandson went with him. They rode in a
comfortable old phaeton drawn by the white horse. The old
man scratched his thin white beard and talked to himself of his
plans for increasing the productiveness of the fields they
visited and of God's part in the plans all men made. Sometimes
he looked at David and smiled happily and then for a long time
he appeared to forget the boy's existence. More and more
every day now his mind turned back again to the dreams that
had filled his mind when he had first come out of the city to
live on the land. One afternoon he startled David by letting his
dreams take entire possession of him. With the boy as a
witness, he went through a ceremony and brought about an
accident that nearly destroyed the companionship that was
growing up between them.

Jesse and his grandson were driving in a distant part of the
valley some miles from home. A forest came down to the road

and through the forest Wine Creek wriggled its way over stones toward a distant river. All the afternoon Jesse had been in a meditative mood and now he began to talk. His mind went back to the night when he had been frightened by thoughts of a giant that might come to rob and plunder him of his possessions, and again as on that night when he had run through the fields crying for a son, he became excited to the edge of insanity. Stopping the horse he got out of the buggy and asked David to get out also. The two climbed over a fence and walked along the bank of the stream. The boy paid no attention to the muttering of his grandfather, but ran along beside him and wondered what was going to happen. When a rabbit jumped up and ran away through the woods, he clapped his hands and danced with delight. He looked at the tall trees and was sorry that he was not a little animal to climb high in the air without being frightened. Stooping, he picked up a small stone and threw it over the head of his grandfather into a clump of bushes. "Wake up, little animal. Go and climb to the top of the trees," he shouted in a shrill voice.

Jesse Bentley went along under the trees with his head bowed and with his mind in a ferment. His earnestness affected the boy who presently became silent and a little alarmed. Into the old man's mind had come the notion that now he could bring from God a word or a sign out of the sky, that the presence of the boy and man on their knees in some lonely spot in the forest would make the miracle he had been waiting for almost inevitable. "It was in just such a place as this that other David tended the sheep when his father came and told him to go down unto Saul," he muttered.

Taking the boy rather roughly by the shoulder, he climbed over a fallen log and when he had come to an open place among the trees, he dropped upon his knees and began to pray in a loud voice.

A kind of terror he had never known before took possession of David. Crouching beneath a tree he watched the man on the ground before him and his own knees began to tremble. It seemed to him that he was in the presence, not only of his grandfather but of someone else, someone who might hurt him, someone who was not kindly but dangerous and brutal. He began to cry and reaching down picked up a small stick which he held tightly gripped in his fingers. When Jesse Bentley, absorbed in his own idea, suddenly arose and advanced toward him, his terror grew until his whole body shook. In the woods an intense silence seemed to lie over everything and suddenly out of the silence came the old man's harsh and insistent voice. Gripping the boy's shoulders, Jesse turned his face to the sky and shouted. The whole left side of his face twitched and his hand on the boy's shoulder twitched also. "Make a sign to me, God," he cried, "here I stand with the boy David. Come down to me out of the sky and make Thy presence known to me."

With a cry of fear, David turned and shaking himself loose from the hands that held him, ran away through the forest. He did not believe that the man who turned up his face and in a harsh voice shouted at the sky, was his grandfather at all. The man did not look like his grandfather. The conviction that something strange and terrible had happened, that by some miracle a new and dangerous person had come into the body of the kindly old man, took possession of him. On and on he ran down the hillside sobbing as he ran. When he fell over the roots of a tree and in falling struck his head, he arose and tried to run on again. His head hurt so that presently he fell down and lay still, but it was only after Jesse had carried him to the buggy and he awoke to find the old man's hand stroking his head tenderly, that the terror left him. "Take me away. There is a terrible man back there in the woods," he declared firmly, while Jesse looked away over the tops of the trees and again his lips cried out to God. "What have I done that Thou doest not approve of me," he whispered softly, saying the words over and over as he drove rapidly along the road with the boy's cut and bleeding head held tenderly against his shoulder.

SURRENDER

PART THREE

THE story of Louise Bentley, who became Mrs. John Hardy and lived with her husband in a brick house on Elm Street in Winesburg, is a story of misunderstanding.

Before such women as Louise can be understood and their lives made livable, much will have to be done. Thoughtful books will have to be written and thoughtful lives lived by people about them.

Born of a delicate and overworked mother, and an impulsive, hard, imaginative father, who did not look with favor upon her coming into the world, Louise was from childhood a neurotic, one of the race of over-sensitive women that in later days industrialism was to bring in such great numbers into the world.

During her early years she lived on the Bentley farm, a silent, moody child, wanting love more than anything else in the world and not getting it. When she was fifteen she went to live in Winesburg with the family of Albert Hardy who had a store for the sale of buggies and wagons, and who was a member of the town board of education.

Louise went into town to be a student in the Winesburg High School and she went to live at the Hardys' because Albert Hardy and her father were friends.

Hardy, the vehicle merchant of Winesburg, like thousands of other men of his times, was an enthusiast on the subject of education. He had made his own way in the world without learning got from books, but he was convinced that had he but known books things would have gone better with him. To everyone who came into his shop he talked of the matter, and in his own household he drove his family distracted by his constant harping on the subject.

He had two daughters and one son, John Hardy, and more than once the daughters threatened to leave school altogether. As a matter of principle they did just enough work in their classes to avoid punishment. "I hate books and I hate anyone who likes books," Harriet, the younger of the two girls, declared passionately.

In Winesburg as on the farm Louise was not happy. For years she had dreamed of the time when she could go forth into the world, and she looked upon the move into the Hardy household as a great step in the direction of freedom. Always when she had thought of the matter, it had seemed to her that in town all must be gaiety and life, that there men and women must live happily and freely, giving and taking friendship and affection as one takes the feel of a wind on the cheek. After the silence and the cheerlessness of life in the Bentley house, she dreamed of stepping forth into an atmosphere that was warm and pulsating with life and reality. And in the Hardy household Louise might have got something of the thing for which she so hungered but for a mistake she made when she had just come to town.

Louise won the disfavor of the two Hardy girls, Mary and Harriet, by her application to her studies in school. She did not come to the house until the day when school was to begin and knew nothing of the feeling they had in the matter. She was timid and during the first month made no acquaintances. Every Friday afternoon one of the hired men from the farm drove into Winesburg and took her home for the week-end, so that she did not spend the Saturday holiday with the town people. Because she was embarrassed and lonely she worked constantly at her studies. To Mary and Harriet, it seemed as though she tried to make trouble for them by her proficiency. In her eagerness to appear well Louise wanted to answer every question put to the class by the teacher. She jumped up and down and her eyes flashed. Then when she had answered some question the others in the class had been unable to answer, she smiled happily. "See, I have done it for you," her eyes seemed to

say. "You need not bother about the matter. I will answer all
questions. For the whole class it will be easy while I am here."

In the evening after supper in the Hardy house, Albert
Hardy began to praise Louise. One of the teachers had spoken
highly of her and he was delighted. "Well, again I have heard
of it," he began, looking hard at his daughters and then turning
to smile at Louise. "Another of the teachers has told me of the
good work Louise is doing. Everyone in Winesburg is telling
me how smart she is. I am ashamed that they do not speak so of
my own girls." Arising, the merchant marched about the room
and lighted his evening cigar.

The two girls looked at each other and shook their heads
wearily. Seeing their indifference the father became angry. "I
tell you it is something for you two to be thinking about," he
cried, glaring at them. "There is a big change coming here in
America and in learning is the only hope of the coming generations. Louise is the daughter of a rich man but she is not
ashamed to study. It should make you ashamed to see what she
does."

The merchant took his hat from a rack by the door and
prepared to depart for the evening. At the door he stopped
and glared back. So fierce was his manner that Louise was
frightened and ran upstairs to her own room. The daughters
began to speak of their own affairs. "Pay attention to me,"
roared the merchant. "Your minds are lazy. Your indifference
to education is affecting your characters. You will amount to
nothing. Now mark what I say—Louise will be so far ahead of
you that you will never catch up."

The distracted man went out of the house and into the
street shaking with wrath. He went along muttering words
and swearing, but when he got into Main Street his anger
passed. He stopped to talk of the weather or the crops with
some other merchant or with a farmer who had come into
town and forgot his daughters altogether or, if he thought of
them, only shrugged his shoulders. "Oh, well, girls will be
girls," he muttered philosophically.

In the house when Louise came down into the room where the two girls sat, they would have nothing to do with her. One evening after she had been there for more than six weeks and was heartbroken because of the continued air of coldness with which she was always greeted, she burst into tears. "Shut up your crying and go back to your own room and to your books," Mary Hardy said sharply.

*

The room occupied by Louise was on the second floor of the Hardy house, and her window looked out upon an orchard. There was a stove in the room and every evening young John Hardy carried up an armful of wood and put it in a box that stood by the wall. During the second month after she came to the house, Louise gave up all hope of getting on a friendly footing with the Hardy girls and went to her own room as soon as the evening meal was at an end.

Her mind began to play with thoughts of making friends with John Hardy. When he came into the room with the wood in his arms, she pretended to be busy with her studies but watched him eagerly. When he had put the wood in the box and turned to go out, she put down her head and blushed. She tried to make talk but could say nothing, and after he had gone she was angry at herself for her stupidity.

The mind of the country girl became filled with the idea of drawing close to the young man. She thought that in him might be found the quality she had all her life been seeking in people. It seemed to her that between herself and all the other people in the world, a wall had been built up and that she was living just on the edge of some warm inner circle of life that must be quite open and understandable to others. She became obsessed with the thought that it wanted but a courageous act on her part to make all of her association with people something quite different, and that it was possible by such an act to pass into a new life as one opens a door and goes into a room. Day and night she thought of the matter, but although the thing she wanted so earnestly was something very warm and close it had as yet no conscious connection with sex. It had not become that definite, and her mind had only alighted upon the person of John Hardy because he was at hand and unlike his sisters had not been unfriendly to her.

The Hardy sisters, Mary and Harriet, were both older than Louise. In a certain kind of knowledge of the world they were years older. They lived as all of the young women of Middle Western towns lived. In those days young women did not go out of our towns to Eastern colleges and ideas in regard to social classes had hardly begun to exist. A daughter of a laborer was in much the same social position as a daughter of a farmer or a merchant, and there were no leisure classes. A girl was "nice" or she was "not nice." If a nice girl, she had a young man who came to her house to see her on Sunday and on Wednesday evenings. Sometimes she went with her young man to a dance or a church social. At other times she received him at the house and was given the use of the parlor for that purpose. No one intruded upon her. For hours the two sat behind closed doors. Sometimes the lights were turned low and the young man and woman embraced. Cheeks became hot and hair disarranged. After a year or two, if the impulse within them became strong and insistent enough, they married.

One evening during her first winter in Winesburg, Louise had an adventure that gave a new impulse to her desire to break down the wall that she thought stood between her and John Hardy. It was Wednesday and immediately after the evening meal Albert Hardy put on his hat and went away. Young John brought the wood and put it in the box in Louise's room. "You do work hard, don't you?" he said awkwardly, and then before she could answer he also went away.

Louise heard him go out of the house and had a mad desire to run after him. Opening her window she leaned out and called softly. "John, dear John, come back, don't go away." The night was cloudy and she could not see far into the darkness, but as she waited she fancied she could hear a soft little noise as of someone going on tiptoes through the trees in the orchard. She was frightened and closed the window quickly. For an hour she moved about the room trembling with excitement and when she could not longer bear the waiting, she crept into the hall and down the stairs into a closet-like room that opened off the parlor.

Louise had decided that she would perform the courageous act that had for weeks been in her mind. She was convinced that John Hardy had concealed himself in the orchard beneath her window and she was determined to find him and tell him that she wanted him to come close to her, to hold her in his arms, to tell her of his thoughts and dreams and to listen while she told him her thoughts and dreams. "In the darkness it will be easier to say things," she whispered to herself, as she stood in the little room groping for the door.

And then suddenly Louise realized that she was not alone in the house. In the parlor on the other side of the door a man's voice spoke softly and the door opened. Louise just had time to conceal herself in a little opening beneath the stairway when Mary Hardy, accompanied by her young man, came into the little dark room.

For an hour Louise sat on the floor in the darkness and listened. Without words Mary Hardy, with the aid of the man who had come to spend the evening with her, brought to the country girl a knowledge of men and women. Putting her head down until she was curled into a little ball she lay perfectly still. It seemed to her that by some strange impulse of the gods, a great gift had been brought to Mary Hardy and she could not understand the older woman's determined protest.

The young man took Mary Hardy into his arms and kissed her. When she struggled and laughed, he but held her the more tightly. For an hour the contest between them went on and then they went back into the parlor and Louise escaped up the stairs. "I hope you were quiet out there. You must not disturb the little mouse at her studies," she heard Harriet saying to her sister as she stood by her own door in the hallway above.

Louise wrote a note to John Hardy and late that night when all in the house were asleep, she crept downstairs and slipped it under his door. She was afraid that if she did not do the thing at once her courage would fail. In the note she tried to be quite definite about what she wanted. "I want someone to love me and I want to love someone," she wrote. "If you are the one for me I want you to come into the orchard at night and make a noise under my window. It will be easy for me to crawl down over the shed and come to you. I am thinking about it all the time, so if you are to come at all you must come soon."

For a long time Louise did not know what would be the outcome of her bold attempt to secure for herself a lover. In a way she still did not know whether or not she wanted him to come. Sometimes it seemed to her that to be held tightly and kissed was the whole secret of life, and then a new impulse came and she was terribly afraid. The age-old woman's desire to be possessed had taken possession of her, but so vague was her notion of life that it seemed to her just the touch of John Hardy's hand upon her own hand would satisfy. She wondered if he would understand that. At the table next day while Albert Hardy talked and the two girls whispered and laughed, she did not look at John but at the table and as soon as possible escaped. In the evening she went out of the house until she was sure he had taken the wood to her room and gone away. When after several evenings of intense listening she heard no call from the darkness in the orchard, she was half beside herself with grief and decided that for her there was no way to break through the wall that had shut her off from the joy of life.

And then on a Monday evening two or three weeks after the writing of the note, John Hardy came for her. Louise had so entirely given up the thought of his coming that for a long time she did not hear the call that came up from the orchard. On the Friday evening before, as she was being driven back to the farm for the week-end by one of the hired men, she had on an impulse done a thing that had startled her, and as John Hardy stood in the darkness below and called her name softly and insistently, she walked about in her room and wondered what new impulse had led her to commit so ridiculous an act.

The farm hand, a young fellow with black curly hair, had come for her somewhat late on that Friday evening and they drove home in the darkness. Louise, whose mind was filled with thoughts of John Hardy, tried to make talk but the country boy was embarrassed and would say nothing. Her mind began to review the loneliness of her childhood and she remembered with a pang the sharp new loneliness that had just come to her. "I hate everyone," she cried suddenly, and then broke forth into a tirade that frightened her escort. "I hate father and old man Hardy, too," she declared vehemently. "I get my lessons there in the school in town but I hate that also."

Louise frightened the farm hand still more by turning and putting her cheek down upon his shoulder. Vaguely she hoped that he like that young man who had stood in the darkness with Mary would put his arms about her and kiss her, but the country boy was only alarmed. He struck the horse with the whip and began to whistle. "The road is rough, eh?" he said loudly. Louise was so angry that reaching up she snatched his hat from his head and threw it into the road. When he jumped out of the buggy and went to get it, she drove off and left him to walk the rest of the way back to the farm.

Louise Bentley took John Hardy to be her lover. That was not what she wanted but it was so the young man had interpreted her approach to him, and so anxious was she to achieve something else that she made no resistance. When after a few months they were both afraid that she was about to become a mother, they went one evening to the county seat and were married. For a few months they lived in the Hardy house and then took a house of their own. All during the first year Louise tried to make her husband understand the vague and intangible hunger that had led to the writing of the note and that was still unsatisfied. Again and again she crept into his arms and tried to talk of it, but always without success. Filled with his own notions of love between men and women, he did not listen but began to kiss her upon the lips. That confused her so that in the end she did not want to be kissed. She did not know what she wanted.

When the alarm that had tricked them into marriage proved to be groundless, she was angry and said bitter, hurtful things. Later when her son David was born, she could not nurse him and did not know whether she wanted him or not. Sometimes she stayed in the room with him all day, walking about and occasionally creeping close to touch him tenderly with her hands, and then other days came when she did not want to see or be near the tiny bit of humanity that had come into the house. When John Hardy reproached her for her cruelty, she laughed. "It is a man child and will get what it wants anyway," she said sharply. "Had it been a woman child there is nothing in the world I would not have done for it."

TERROR

PART FOUR

WHEN David Hardy was a tall boy of fifteen, he, like his mother, had an adventure that changed the whole current of his life and sent him out of his quiet corner into the world. The shell of the circumstances of his life was broken and he was compelled to start forth. He left Winesburg and no one there ever saw him again. After his disappearance, his mother and grandfather both died and his father became very rich. He spent much money in trying to locate his son, but that is no part of this story.

It was in the late fall of an unusual year on the Bentley farms. Everywhere the crops had been heavy. That spring, Jesse had bought part of a long strip of black swamp land that lay in the valley of Wine Creek. He got the land at a low price but had spent a large sum of money to improve it. Great ditches had to be dug and thousands of tile laid. Neighboring farmers shook their heads over the expense. Some of them laughed and hoped that Jesse would lose heavily by the venture, but the old man went silently on with the work and said nothing.

When the land was drained he planted it to cabbages and onions, and again the neighbors laughed. The crop was, however, enormous and brought high prices. In the one year Jesse made enough money to pay for all the cost of preparing the land and had a surplus that enabled him to buy two more farms. He was exultant and could not conceal his delight. For the first time in all the history of his ownership of the farms, he went among his men with a smiling face.

Jesse bought a great many new machines for cutting down the cost of labor and all of the remaining acres in the strip of black fertile swamp land. One day he went into Winesburg and bought a bicycle and a new suit of clothes for David and he gave his two sisters money with which to go to a religious convention at Cleveland, Ohio.

In the fall of that year when the frost came and the trees in the forests along Wine Creek were golden brown, David spent every moment when he did not have to attend school, out in the open. Alone or with other boys he went every afternoon into the woods to gather nuts. The other boys of the countryside, most of them sons of laborers on the Bentley farms, had guns with which they went hunting rabbits and squirrels, but David did not go with them. He made himself a sling with rubber bands and a forked stick and went off by himself to gather nuts. As he went about thoughts came to him. He realized that he was almost a man and wondered what he would do in life, but before they came to anything, the thoughts passed and he was a boy again. One day he killed a squirrel that sat on one of the lower branches of a tree and chattered at him. Home he ran with the squirrel in his hand. One of the Bentley sisters cooked the little animal and he ate it with great gusto. The skin he tacked on a board and suspended the board by a string from his bedroom window.

That gave his mind a new turn. After that he never went into the woods without carrying the sling in his pocket and he spent hours shooting at imaginary animals concealed among the brown leaves in the trees. Thoughts of his coming manhood passed and he was content to be a boy with a boy's impulses.

One Saturday morning when he was about to set off for the woods with the sling in his pocket and a bag for nuts on his shoulder, his grandfather stopped him. In the eyes of the old man was the strained serious look that always a little frightened David. At such times Jesse Bentley's eyes did not look straight ahead but wavered and seemed to be looking at nothing. Something like an invisible curtain appeared to have come between the man and all the rest of the world. "I want you to come with me," he said briefly, and his eyes looked over the boy's head into the sky. "We have something important to do to-day. You may bring the bag for nuts if you wish. It does not matter and anyway we will be going into the woods."

Jesse and David set out from the Bentley farmhouse in the old phaeton that was drawn by the white horse. When they had gone along in silence for a long way they stopped at the edge of a field where a flock of sheep were grazing. Among the sheep was a lamb that had been born out of season, and this David and his grandfather caught and tied so tightly that it looked like a little white ball. When they drove on again Jesse let David hold the lamb in his arms. "I saw it yesterday and it put me in mind of what I have long wanted to do," he said, and again he looked away over the head of the boy with the wavering, uncertain stare in his eyes.

After the feeling of exaltation that had come to the farmer as a result of his successful year, another mood had taken possession of him. For a long time he had been going about feeling very humble and prayerful. Again he walked alone at night thinking of God and as he walked he again connected his own figure with the figures of old days. Under the stars he knelt on the wet grass and raised up his voice in prayer. Now he had decided that like the men whose stories filled the pages of the Bible, he would make a sacrifice to God. "I have been given these abundant crops and God has also sent me a boy who is called David," he whispered to himself. "Perhaps I should have done this thing long ago." He was sorry the idea had not come into his mind in the days before his daughter Louise had been born and thought that surely now when he had erected a pile of burning sticks in some lonely place in the woods and had offered the body of a lamb as a burnt offering, God would appear to him and give him a message.

More and more as he thought of the matter, he thought also of David and his passionate self love was partially forgotten. "It is time for the boy to begin thinking of going out into the world and the message will be one concerning him," he decided. "God will make a pathway for him. He will tell me what place

David is to take in life and when he shall set out on his journey. It is right that the boy should be there. If I am fortunate and an angel of God should appear, David will see the beauty and glory of God made manifest to man. It will make a true man of God of him also."

In silence Jesse and David drove along the road until they came to that place where Jesse had once before appealed to God and had frightened his grandson. The morning had been bright and cheerful, but a cold wind now began to blow and clouds hid the sun. When David saw the place to which they had come he began to tremble with fright, and when they stopped by the bridge where the creek came down from among the trees, he wanted to spring out of the phaeton and run away.

A dozen plans for escape ran through David's head, but when Jesse stopped the horse and climbed over the fence into the wood, he followed. "It is foolish to be afraid. Nothing will happen," he told himself as he went along with the lamb in his arms. There was something in the helplessness of the little animal, held so tightly in his arms that gave him courage. He could feel the rapid beating of the beast's heart and that made his own heart beat less rapidly. As he walked swiftly along behind his grandfather, he untied the string with which the four legs of the lamb were fastened together. "If anything happens we will run away together," he thought.

In the woods, after they had gone a long way from the road, Jesse stopped in an opening among the trees where a clearing, overgrown with small bushes, ran up from the creek. He was still silent but began at once to erect a heap of dry sticks which he presently set afire. The boy sat on the ground with the lamb in his arms. His imagination began to invest every movement of the old man with significance and he became every moment more afraid. "I must put the blood of the lamb on the head of the boy," Jesse muttered when the sticks had begun to blaze greedily, and taking a long knife from his pocket he turned and walked rapidly across the clearing toward David.

Terror seized upon the soul of the boy. He was sick with it. For a moment he sat perfectly still and then his body stiffened and he sprang to his feet. His face became as white as the fleece of the lamb, that now finding itself suddenly released, ran down the hill. David ran also. Fear made his feet fly. Over the low bushes and logs he leaped frantically. As he ran he put his hand into his pocket and took out the branched stick from which the sling for shooting squirrels was suspended. When he came to the creek that was shallow and splashed down over the stones, he dashed into the water and turned to look back, and when he saw his grandfather still running toward him with the long knife held tightly in his hand he did not hesitate but reaching down, selected a stone and put it in the sling. With all his strength he drew back the heavy rubber bands and the stone whistled through the air. It hit Jesse, who had entirely forgotten the boy and was pursuing the lamb, squarely in the head. With a groan he pitched forward and fell almost at the boy's feet. When David saw that he lay still and that he was apparently dead, his fright increased immeasurably. It became an insane panic.

With a cry he turned and ran off through the woods weeping convulsively. "I don't care—I killed him, but I don't care," he sobbed. As he ran on and on he decided suddenly that he would never go back again to the Bentley farms or to the town of Winesburg. "I have killed the man of God and now I will myself be a man and go into the world," he said stoutly as he stopped running and walked rapidly down a road that followed the windings of Wine Creek as it ran through fields and forests into the west.

On the ground by the creek Jesse Bentley moved uneasily about. He groaned and opened his eyes. For a long time he lay perfectly still and looked at the sky. When at last he got to his feet, his mind was confused and he was not surprised by the boy's disappearance. By the roadside he sat down on a log and began to talk about God. That is all they ever got out of him. Whenever David's name was mentioned he looked vaguely at the sky and said that a messenger from God had taken the boy. "It happened because I was too greedy for glory," he declared, and would have no more to say in the matter.

A MAN OF IDEAS

HE lived with his mother, a grey, silent woman with a peculiar ashy complexion. The house in which they lived stood in a little grove of trees beyond where the main street of Winesburg crossed Wine Creek. His name was Joe Welling, and his father had been a man of some dignity in the community, a lawyer and a member of the state legislature at Columbus. Joe himself was small of body and in his character unlike anyone else in town. He was like a tiny little volcano that lies silent for days and then suddenly spouts fire. No, he wasn't like that—he was like a man who is subject to fits, one who walks among his fellow men inspiring fear because a fit may come upon him suddenly and blow him away into a strange uncanny physical state in which his eyes roll and his legs and arms jerk. He was like that, only that the visitation that descended upon Joe Welling was a mental and not a physical thing. He was beset by ideas and in the throes of one of his ideas was uncontrollable. Words rolled and tumbled from his mouth. A peculiar smile came upon his lips. The edges of his teeth that were tipped with gold glistened in the light. Pouncing upon a bystander he began to talk. For the bystander there was no escape. The excited man breathed into his face, peered into his eyes, pounded upon his chest with a shaking forefinger, demanded, compelled attention.

In those days the Standard Oil Company did not deliver oil to the consumer in big wagons and motor trucks as it does now, but delivered instead to retail grocers, hardware stores, and the like. Joe was the Standard Oil agent in Winesburg and in several towns up and down the railroad that went through Winesburg. He collected bills, booked orders, and did other things. His father, the legislator, had secured the job for him.

In and out of the stores of Winesburg went Joe Welling—silent, excessively polite, intent upon his business. Men watched him with eyes in which lurked amusement tempered by alarm. They were waiting for him to break forth, preparing to flee. Although the seizures that came upon him were harmless enough, they could not be laughed away. They were overwhelming. Astride an idea, Joe was overmastering. His personality became gigantic. It overrode the man to whom he talked, swept him away, swept all away, all who stood within sound of his voice.

In Sylvester West's Drug Store stood four men who were talking of horse racing. Wesley Moyer's stallion, Tony Tip, was to race at the June meeting at Tiffin, Ohio, and there was a rumor that he would meet the stiffest competition of his career. It was said that Pop Geers, the great racing driver, would himself be there. A doubt of the success of Tony Tip hung heavy in the air of Winesburg.

Into the drug store came Joe Welling, brushing the screen door violently aside. With a strange absorbed light in his eyes he pounced upon Ed Thomas, he who knew Pop Geers and whose opinion of Tony Tip's chances was worth considering.

"The water is up in Wine Creek," cried Joe Welling with the air of Pheidippides bringing news of the victory of the Greeks in the struggle at Marathon. His finger beat a tattoo upon Ed Thomas' broad chest. "By Trunion bridge it is within eleven and a half inches of the flooring," he went on, the words coming quickly and with a little whistling noise from between his teeth. An expression of helpless annoyance crept over the faces of the four.

"I have my facts correct. Depend upon that. I went to Sinnings' Hardware Store and got a rule. Then I went back and measured. I could hardly believe my own eyes. It hasn't rained you see for ten days. At first I didn't know what to think. Thoughts rushed through my head. I thought of subterranean passages and springs. Down under the ground went my mind, delving about. I sat on the floor of the bridge and rubbed my head. There wasn't a cloud in the sky, not one. Come out into the street and you'll see. There wasn't a cloud. There isn't a cloud now. Yes, there was a cloud. I don't want to keep back any facts. There was a cloud in the west down near the horizon, a cloud no bigger than a man's hand.

"Not that I think that has anything to do with it. There it is you see. You understand how puzzled I was.

"Then an idea came to me. I laughed. You'll laugh, too. Of course it rained over in Medina County. That's interesting, eh? If we had no trains, no mails, no telegraph, we would know that it rained over in Medina County. That's where Wine Creek comes from. Everyone knows that. Little old Wine Creek brought us the news. That's interesting. I laughed. I thought I'd tell you— it's interesting, eh?"

Joe Welling turned and went out at the door. Taking a book from his pocket, he stopped and ran a finger down one of the pages. Again he was absorbed in his duties as agent of the Standard Oil Company. "Hern's Grocery will be getting low on coal oil. I'll see them," he muttered, hurrying along the street, and bowing politely to the right and left at the people walking past.

When George Willard went to work for the *Winesburg Eagle* he was besieged by Joe Welling. Joe envied the boy. It seemed to him that he was meant by Nature to be a reporter on a newspaper. "It is what I should be doing, there is no doubt of that," he declared, stopping George Willard on the sidewalk before Daugherty's Feed Store. His eyes began to glisten and his forefinger to tremble. "Of course I make more money with the Standard Oil Company and I'm only telling you," he added. "I've got nothing against you, but I should have your place. I could do the work at odd moments. Here and there I would run finding out things you'll never see."

Becoming more excited Joe Welling crowded the young reporter against the front of the feed store. He appeared to be lost in thought, rolling his eyes about and running a thin nervous hand through his hair. A smile spread over his face and his gold teeth glittered. "You get out your note book," he commanded. "You carry a little pad of paper in your pocket, don't you? I knew you did. Well, you set this down. I thought of it the other day. Let's take decay. Now what is decay? It's fire. It burns up wood and other things. You never thought of that? Of course not. This sidewalk here and this feed store, the trees down the street there—they're all on fire. They're burning up. Decay you see is always going on. It don't stop. Water and paint can't stop it. If a thing is iron, then what? It rusts, you see. That's fire, too. The world is on fire. Start your pieces in the paper that way. Just say in big letters '*The World Is On Fire.*' That will make 'em look up. They'll say you're a smart one. I don't care. I don't envy you. I just snatched that idea out of the air. I would make a newspaper hum. You got to admit that."

Turning quickly, Joe Welling walked rapidly away. When he had taken several steps he stopped and looked back. "I'm going to stick to you," he said. "I'm going to make you a regular hummer. I should start a newspaper myself, that's what I should do. I'd be a marvel. Everybody knows that."

When George Willard had been for a year on the *Winesburg Eagle*, four things happened to Joe Welling. His mother died, he came to live at the New Willard House, he became involved in a love affair, and he organized the Winesburg Baseball Club.

Joe organized the baseball club because he wanted to be a coach and in that position he began to win the respect of his townsmen. "He is a wonder," they declared after Joe's team had whipped the team from Medina County. "He gets everybody working together. You just watch him."

Upon the baseball field Joe Welling stood by first base, his whole body quivering with excitement. In spite of themselves all of the players watched him closely. The opposing pitcher became confused.

"Now! Now! Now! Now!" shouted the excited man. "Watch me! Watch me! Watch my fingers! Watch my hands! Watch my feet! Watch my eyes! Let's work together here! Watch me! In me you see all the movements of the game! Work with me! Work with me! Watch me! Watch me! Watch me!"

With runners of the Winesburg team on bases, Joe Welling became as one inspired. Before they knew what had come over them, the base runners were watching the man, edging off the bases, advancing, retreating, held as by an invisible cord. The players of the opposing team also watched Joe. They were fascinated. For a moment they watched and then as though to break a spell that hung over them, they began hurling the ball wildly about, and amid a series of fierce animal-like cries from the coach, the runners of the Winesburg team scampered home.

Joe Welling's love affair set the town of Winesburg on edge. When it began everyone whispered and shook his head. When people tried to laugh, the laughter was forced and unnatural. Joe fell in love with Sarah King, a lean, sad-looking woman who lived with her father and brother in a brick house that stood opposite the gate leading to the Winesburg Cemetery.

The two Kings, Edward the father, and Tom the son, were not popular in Winesburg. They were called proud and dangerous. They had come to Winesburg from some place in the South and ran a cider mill on the Trunion Pike. Tom King was reported to have killed a man before he came to Winesburg. He was twenty-seven years old and rode about town on a grey pony. Also he had a long yellow mustache that dropped down over his teeth, and always carried a heavy, wicked-looking walking stick in his hand. Once he killed a dog with the stick. The dog belonged to Win Pawsey, the shoe merchant, and stood on the sidewalk wagging its tail. Tom King killed it with one blow. He was arrested and paid a fine of ten dollars.

Old Edward King was small of stature and when he passed people in the street laughed a queer unmirthful laugh. When he laughed he scratched his left elbow with his right hand. The sleeve of his coat was almost worn through from the habit. As he walked along the street, looking nervously about and laughing, he seemed more dangerous than his silent, fierce looking son.

When Sarah King began walking out in the evening with Joe Welling, people shook their heads in alarm. She was tall and pale and had dark rings under her eyes. The couple looked ridiculous together. Under the trees they walked and Joe talked. His passionate eager protestations of love, heard coming out of the darkness by the cemetery wall, or from the deep shadows of the trees on the hill that ran up to the Fair Grounds from Waterworks Pond, were repeated in the stores. Men stood by the bar in the New Willard House laughing and talking of Joe's courtship. After the laughter came silence. The Winesburg baseball team, under his management, was winning game after game, and the town had begun to respect him. Sensing a tragedy, they waited, laughing nervously.

Late on a Saturday afternoon the meeting between Joe Welling and the two Kings, the anticipation of which had set the town on edge, took place in Joe Welling's room in the New Willard House. George Willard was a witness to the meeting. It came about in this way:

When the young reporter went to his room after the evening meal he saw Tom King and his father sitting in the half darkness in Joe's room. The son had the heavy walking stick in his hand and sat near the door. Old Edward King walked nervously about, scratching his left elbow with his right hand. The hallways were empty and silent.

George Willard went to his own room and sat down at his desk. He tried to write but his hand trembled so that he could not hold the pen. He also walked nervously up and down. Like the rest of the town of Winesburg he was perplexed and knew not what to do.

It was seven-thirty and fast growing dark when Joe Welling came along the station platform toward the New Willard House. In his arms he held a bundle of weeds and grasses. In spite of the terror that made his body shake, George Willard was amused at the sight of the small spry figure holding the grasses and half running along the platform.

Shaking with fright and anxiety, the young reporter lurked in the hallway outside the door of the room in which Joe Welling talked to the two Kings. There had been an oath, the nervous giggle of old Edward King, and then silence. Now the voice of Joe Welling, sharp and clear, broke forth. George Willard began to laugh. He understood. As he had swept all men before him, so now Joe Welling was carrying the two men in the room off their feet with a tidal wave of words. The listener in the hall walked up and down, lost in amazement.

Inside the room Joe Welling had paid no attention to the grumbled threat of Tom King. Absorbed in an idea he closed the door and lighting a lamp, spread the handful of weeds and grasses upon the floor. "I've got something here," he announced solemnly. "I was going to tell George Willard about it, let him make a piece out of it for the paper. I'm glad you're here. I wish Sarah were here also. I've been going to come to your house and tell you of some of my ideas. They're interesting. Sarah wouldn't let me. She said we'd quarrel. That's foolish."

Running up and down before the two perplexed men, Joe Welling began to explain. "Don't you make a mistake now," he cried. "This is something big." His voice was shrill with excitement. "You just follow me, you'll be interested. I know you will. Suppose this—suppose all of the wheat, the corn, the oats, the peas, the potatoes, were all by some miracle swept away. Now here we are, you see, in this county. There is a high fence built all around us. We'll suppose that. No one can get over the fence and all the fruits of the earth are destroyed, nothing left but these wild things, these grasses. Would we be done for? I ask you that. Would we be done for?" Again Tom King growled and for a moment there was silence in the room. Then again Joe plunged into the exposition of his idea. "Things would go hard for a time. I admit that. I've got to admit that. No getting around it. We'd be hard put to it. More than one fat stomach would cave in. But they couldn't down us. I should say not."

Tom King laughed good naturedly and the shivery, nervous laugh of Edward King rang through the house. Joe Welling hurried on. "We'd begin, you see, to breed up new vegetables and fruits. Soon we'd regain all we had lost. Mind, I don't say the new things would be the same as the old. They wouldn't. Maybe they'd be better, maybe not so good. That's interesting, eh? You can think about that. It starts your mind working, now don't it?"

In the room there was silence and then again old Edward King laughed nervously. "Say, I wish Sarah was here," cried Joe Welling. "Let's go up to your house. I want to tell her of this."

There was a scraping of chairs in the room. It was then that George Willard retreated to his own room. Leaning out at the window he saw Joe Welling going along the street with the two Kings. Tom King was forced to take extraordinary long strides to keep pace with the little man. As he strode along, he leaned over, listening—absorbed, fascinated. Joe Welling again talked excitedly. "Take milkweed now," he cried. "A lot might be done with milkweed, eh? It's almost unbelievable. I want you to think about it. I want you two to think about it. There would be a new vegetable kingdom you see. It's interesting, eh? It's an idea. Wait till you see Sarah, she'll get the idea. She'll be interested. Sarah is always interested in ideas. You can't be too smart for Sarah, now can you? Of course you can't. You know that."

ADVENTURE

ALICE HINDMAN, a woman of twenty-seven when George Willard was a mere boy, had lived in Winesburg all her life. She clerked in Winney's Dry Goods Store and lived with her mother who had married a second husband.

Alice's step-father was a carriage painter, and given to drink. His story is an odd one. It will be worth telling some day.

At twenty-seven Alice was tall and somewhat slight. Her head was large and overshadowed her body. Her shoulders were a little stooped and her hair and eyes brown. She was very quiet but beneath a placid exterior a continual ferment went on.

When she was a girl of sixteen and before she began to work in the store, Alice had an affair with a young man. The young man, named Ned Currie, was older than Alice. He, like George Willard, was employed on the *Winesburg Eagle* and for a long time he went to see Alice almost every evening. Together the two walked under the trees through the streets of the town and talked of what they would do with their lives. Alice was then a very pretty girl and Ned Currie took her into his arms and kissed her. He became excited and said things he did not intend to say and Alice, betrayed by her desire to have something beautiful come into her rather narrow life, also grew excited. She also talked. The outer crust of her life, all of her natural diffidence and reserve, was torn away and she gave herself over to the emotions of love. When, late in the fall of her sixteenth year, Ned Currie went away to Cleveland where he hoped to get a place on a city newspaper and rise in the world, she wanted to go with him. With a trembling voice she told him what was in her mind. "I will work and you can work," she said. "I do not want to harness you to a needless expense that will prevent your making progress. Don't marry me now. We will get along without that and we can be together. Even though we live in the same house no one will say anything. In the city we will be unknown and people will pay no attention to us."

Ned Currie was puzzled by the determination and abandon of his sweetheart and was also deeply touched. He had wanted the girl to become his mistress but changed his mind. He wanted to protect and care for her. "You don't know what you're talking about," he said sharply; "you may be sure I'll let you do no such thing. As soon as I get a good job I'll come back. For the present you'll have to stay here. It's the only thing we can do."

On the evening before he left Winesburg to take up his new life in the city, Ned Currie went to call on Alice. They walked about through the streets for an hour and then got a rig from Wesley Moyer's livery and went for a drive in the country. The moon came up and they found themselves unable to talk. In his sadness the young man forgot the resolutions he had made regarding his conduct with the girl.

They got out of the buggy at a place where a long meadow ran down to the bank of Wine Creek and there in the dim light became lovers. When at midnight they returned to town they were both glad. It did not seem to them that anything that could happen in the future could blot out the wonder and beauty of the thing that had happened. "Now we will have to stick to each other, whatever happens we will have to do that," Ned Currie said as he left the girl at her father's door.

The young newspaper man did not succeed in getting a place on a Cleveland paper and went west to Chicago. For a time he was lonely and wrote to Alice almost every day. Then he was caught up by the life of the city; he began to make friends and found new interests in life. In Chicago he boarded at a house where there were several women. One of them attracted his attention and he forgot Alice in Winesburg. At the end of a year he had stopped writing letters, and only once in a long time, when he was lonely or when he went into one of the city parks and saw the moon shining on the grass as it had shone that night on the meadow by Wine Creek, did he think of her at all.

In Winesburg the girl who had been loved grew to be a woman. When she was twenty-two years old her father, who owned a harness repair shop, died suddenly. The harness maker was an old soldier, and after a few months his wife received a widow's pension. She used the first money she got to buy a loom and became a weaver of carpets, and Alice got a place in Winney's store. For a number of years nothing could have induced her to believe that Ned Currie would not in the end return to her.

She was glad to be employed because the daily round of toil in the store made the time of waiting seem less long and uninteresting. She began to save money, thinking that when she had saved two or three hundred dollars she would follow her lover to the city and try if her presence would not win back his affections.

Alice did not blame Ned Currie for what had happened in the moonlight in the field, but felt that she could never marry another man. To her the thought of giving to another what she still felt could belong only to Ned seemed monstrous. When other young men tried to attract her attention she would have nothing to do with them. "I am his wife and shall remain his wife whether he comes back or not," she whispered to herself, and for all of her willingness to support herself could not have understood the growing modern idea of a woman's owning herself and giving and taking for her own ends in life.

Alice worked in the dry goods store from eight in the morning until six at night and on three evenings a week went back to the store to stay from seven until nine. As time passed and she became more and more lonely she began to practice the devices common to lonely people. When at night she went upstairs into her own room she knelt on the floor to pray and in her prayers whispered things she wanted to say to her lover. She became attached to inanimate objects, and because it was her own, could not bear to have anyone touch the furniture of her room. The trick of saving money, begun for a purpose, was carried on after the scheme of going to the city to find Ned Currie had been given up. It became a fixed habit, and when she needed new clothes she did not get them. Sometimes on rainy afternoons in the store she got out her bank book and, letting it lie open before her, spent hours dreaming impossible dreams of saving money enough so that the interest would support both herself and her future husband.

"Ned always liked to travel about," she thought. "I'll give him the chance. Some day when we are married and I can save both his money and my own, we will be rich. Then we can travel together all over the world."

In the dry goods store weeks ran into months and months into years as Alice waited and dreamed of her lover's return. Her employer, a grey old man with false teeth and a thin grey mustache that drooped down over his mouth, was not given to conversation, and sometimes, on rainy days and in the winter when a storm raged in Main Street, long hours passed when no customers came in. Alice arranged and rearranged the stock. She stood near the front window where she could look down the deserted street and thought of the evenings when she had walked with Ned Currie and of what he had said. "We will have to stick to each other now." The words echoed and re-echoed through the mind of the maturing woman. Tears came into her eyes. Sometimes when her employer had gone out and she was alone in the store she put her head on the counter and wept. "Oh, Ned, I am waiting," she whispered over and over, and all the time the creeping fear that he would never come back grew stronger within her.

In the spring when the rains have passed and before the long hot days of summer have come, the country about Winesburg is delightful. The town lies in the midst of open fields, but beyond the fields are pleasant patches of woodlands. In the wooded places are many little cloistered nooks, quiet places where lovers go to sit on Sunday afternoons. Through the trees they look out across the fields and see farmers at work about the barns or people driving up and down on the roads. In the town bells ring and occasionally a train passes, looking like a toy thing in the distance.

For several years after Ned Currie went away Alice did not go into the wood with other young people on Sunday, but one day after he had been gone for two or three years and when her loneliness seemed unbearable, she put on her best dress and set out. Finding a little sheltered place from which she could see the town and a long stretch of the fields, she sat down. Fear of age and ineffectuality took possession of her. She could not sit still, and arose. As she stood looking out over the land something, perhaps the thought of never ceasing life as it expresses itself in the flow of the seasons, fixed her mind on the passing years. With a shiver of dread, she realized that for her the beauty and freshness of youth had passed. For the first time she felt that she had been cheated. She did not blame Ned Currie and did not know what to blame. Sadness swept over her. Dropping to her knees, she tried to pray, but instead of prayers words of protest came to her lips. "It is not going to come to me. I will never find happiness. Why do I tell myself lies?" she cried, and an odd sense of relief came with this, her first bold attempt to face the fear that had become a part of her everyday life.

In the year when Alice Hindman became twenty-five two things happened to disturb the dull uneventfulness of her days. Her mother married Bush Milton, the carriage painter of Winesburg, and she herself became a member of the Winesburg Methodist Church. Alice joined the church because she had become frightened by the loneliness of her position in life. Her mother's second marriage had emphasized her isolation. "I am becoming old and queer. If Ned comes he will not want me. In the city where he is living men are perpetually young. There is so much going on that they do not have time to grow old," she told herself with a grim little smile, and went resolutely about the business of becoming acquainted with people. Every Thursday evening when the

store had closed she went to a prayer meeting in the basement
of the church and on Sunday evening attended a meeting of an
organization called The Epworth League.

When Will Hurley, a middle-aged man who clerked in a
drug store and who also belonged to the church, offered to
walk home with her she did not protest. "Of course I will not
let him make a practice of being with me, but if he comes to
see me once in a long time there can be no harm in that," she
told herself, still determined in her loyalty to Ned Currie.

Without realizing what was happening, Alice was trying
feebly at first, but with growing determination, to get a new
hold upon life. Beside the drug clerk she walked in silence, but
sometimes in the darkness as they went stolidly along she put
out her hand and touched softly the folds of his coat. When he
left her at the gate before her mother's house she did not go
indoors, but stood for a moment by the door. She wanted to
call to the drug clerk, to ask him to sit with her in the darkness
on the porch before the house, but was afraid he would not
understand. "It is not him that I want," she told herself; "I want
to avoid being so much alone. If I am not careful I will grow
unaccustomed to being with people."

*

During the early fall of her twenty-seventh year a passionate
restlessness took possession of Alice. She could not bear to be
in the company of the drug clerk, and when, in the evening, he
came to walk with her she sent him away. Her mind became
intensely active and when, weary from the long hours of
standing behind the counter in the store, she went home and
crawled into bed, she could not sleep. With staring eyes she
looked into the darkness. Her imagination, like a child awa-
kened from long sleep, played about the room. Deep within
her there was something that would not be cheated by phan-
tasies and that demanded some definite answer from life.

Alice took a pillow into her arms and held it tightly against
her breasts. Getting out of bed, she arranged a blanket so that
in the darkness it looked like a form lying between the sheets

and, kneeling beside the bed, she caressed it, whispering words over and over, like a refrain. "Why doesn't something happen? Why am I left here alone?" she muttered. Although she sometimes thought of Ned Currie, she no longer depended on him. Her desire had grown vague. She did not want Ned Currie or any other man. She wanted to be loved, to have something answer the call that was growing louder and louder within her.

And then one night when it rained Alice had an adventure. It frightened and confused her. She had come home from the store at nine and found the house empty. Bush Milton had gone off to town and her mother to the house of a neighbor. Alice went upstairs to her room and undressed in the darkness. For a moment she stood by the window hearing the rain beat against the glass and then a strange desire took possession of her. Without stopping to think of what she intended to do, she ran downstairs through the dark house and out into the rain. As she stood on the little grass plot before the house and felt the cold rain on her body a mad desire to run naked through the streets took possession of her.

She thought that the rain would have some creative and wonderful effect on her body. Not for years had she felt so full of youth and courage. She wanted to leap and run, to cry out, to find some other lonely human and embrace him. On the brick sidewalk before the house a man stumbled homeward. Alice started to run. A wild, desperate mood took possession of her. "What do I care who it is. He is alone, and I will go to him," she thought; and then without stopping to consider the possible result of her madness, called softly. "Wait!" she cried. "Don't go away. Whoever you are, you must wait."

The man on the sidewalk stopped and stood listening. He was an old man and somewhat deaf. Putting his hand to his mouth, he shouted: "What? What say?" he called.

Alice dropped to the ground and lay trembling. She was so frightened at the thought of what she had done that when the man had gone on his way she did not dare get to her feet, but crawled on hands and knees through the grass to the house. When she got to her own room she bolted the door and drew her dressing table across the doorway. Her body shook as with a chill and her hands trembled so that she had difficulty getting into her nightdress. When she got into bed she buried her face in the pillow and wept broken-heartedly. "What is the matter with me? I will do something dreadful if I am not careful," she thought, and turning her face to the wall, began trying to force herself to face bravely the fact that many people must live and die alone, even in Winesburg.

RESPECTABILITY

IF you have lived in cities and have walked in the park on a summer afternoon, you have perhaps seen, blinking in a corner of his iron cage, a huge, grotesque kind of monkey, a creature with ugly, sagging, hairless skin below his eyes and a bright purple underbody. This monkey is a true monster. In the completeness of his ugliness he achieved a kind of perverted beauty. Children stopping before the cage are fascinated, men turn away with an air of disgust, and women linger for a moment, trying perhaps to remember which one of their male acquaintances the thing in some faint way resembles.

Had you been in the earlier years of your life a citizen of the village of Winesburg, Ohio, there would have been for you no mystery in regard to the beast in his cage. "It is like Wash Williams," you would have said. "As he sits in the corner there, the beast is exactly like old Wash sitting on the grass in the station yard on a summer evening after he has closed his office for the night."

Wash Williams, the telegraph operator of Winesburg, was the ugliest thing in town. His girth was immense, his neck thin, his legs feeble. He was dirty. Everything about him was unclean. Even the whites of his eyes looked soiled.

I go too fast. Not everything about Wash was unclean. He took care of his hands. His fingers were fat, but there was something sensitive and shapely in the hand that lay on the table by the instrument in the telegraph office. In his youth Wash Williams had been called the best telegraph operator in the state, and in spite of his degradement to the obscure office at Winesburg, he was still proud of his ability.

Wash Williams did not associate with the men of the town in which he lived. "I'll have nothing to do with them," he said, looking with bleary eyes at the men who walked along the station platform past the telegraph office. Up along Main

Street he went in the evening to Ed Griffith's saloon, and after drinking unbelievable quantities of beer staggered off to his room in the New Willard House and to his bed for the night.

Wash Williams was a man of courage. A thing had happened to him that made him hate life, and he hated it whole-heartedly, with the abandon of a poet. First of all, he hated women. "Bitches," he called them. His feeling toward men was somewhat different. He pitied them. "Does not every man let his life be managed for him by some bitch or another?" he asked.

In Winesburg no attention was paid to Wash Williams and his hatred of his fellows. Once Mrs. White, the banker's wife, complained to the telegraph company, saying that the office in Winesburg was dirty and smelled abominably, but nothing came of her complaint. Here and there a man respected the operator. Instinctively the man felt in him a glowing resent-ment of something he had not the courage to resent. When Wash walked through the streets such a one had an instinct to pay him homage, to raise his hat or to bow before him. The superintendent who had supervision over the telegraph op-erators on the railroad that went through Winesburg felt that way. He had put Wash into the obscure office at Winesburg to avoid discharging him, and he meant to keep him there. When he received the letter of complaint from the banker's wife, he tore it up and laughed unpleasantly. For some reason he thought of his own wife as he tore up the letter.

Wash Williams once had a wife. When he was still a young man he married a woman at Dayton, Ohio. The woman was tall and slender and had blue eyes and yellow hair. Wash was himself a comely youth. He loved the woman with a love as absorbing as the hatred he later felt for all women.

In all of Winesburg there was but one person who knew the story of the thing that had made ugly the person and the character of Wash Williams. He once told the story to George Willard and the telling of the tale came about in this way:

George Willard went one evening to walk with Belle Car-penter, a trimmer of women's hats who worked in a millinery shop kept by Mrs. Kate McHugh. The young man was not in love with the woman, who, in fact, had a suitor who worked as bartender in Ed Griffith's saloon, but as they walked about under the trees they occasionally embraced. The night and their own thoughts had aroused something in them. As they were returning to Main Street they passed the little lawn beside the railroad station and saw Wash Williams apparently asleep on the grass beneath a tree. On the next evening the operator and George Willard walked out together. Down the railroad they went and sat on a pile of decaying railroad ties beside the tracks. It was then that the operator told the young reporter his story of hate.

Perhaps a dozen times George Willard and the strange, shapeless man who lived at his father's hotel had been on the point of talking. The young man looked at the hideous, leering face staring about the hotel dining room and was consumed with curiosity. Something he saw lurking in the staring eyes told him that the man who had nothing to say to others had nevertheless something to say to him. On the pile of railroad ties on the summer evening, he waited expectantly. When the operator remained silent and seemed to have changed his mind about talking, he tried to make conversation. "Were you ever married, Mr. Williams?" he began. "I suppose you were and your wife is dead, is that it?"

Wash Williams spat forth a succession of vile oaths. "Yes, she is dead," he agreed. "She is dead as all women are dead. She is a living-dead thing, walking in the sight of men and making the earth foul by her presence." Staring into the boy's eyes, the man became purple with rage. "Don't have fool notions in your head," he commanded. "My wife, she is dead; yes, surely. I tell you, all women are dead, my mother, your mother, that tall dark woman who works in the millinery store and with whom I saw you walking about yesterday,—all of them, they are all dead. I tell you there is something rotten about them. I was married, sure. My wife was dead before she married me, she was a foul thing come out of a woman more foul. She was a thing

sent to make life unbearable to me. I was a fool, do you see, as
you are now, and so I married this woman. I would like to see
men a little begin to understand women. They are sent to prevent men making the world worth while. It is a trick in Nature.
Ugh! They are creeping, crawling, squirming things, they with
their soft hands and their blue eyes. The sight of a woman
sickens me. Why I don't kill every woman I see I don't know."

Half frightened and yet fascinated by the light burning in
the eyes of the hideous old man, George Willard listened, afire
with curiosity. Darkness came on and he leaned forward trying
to see the face of the man who talked. When, in the gathering
darkness, he could no longer see the purple, bloated face and
the burning eyes, a curious fancy came to him. Wash Williams
talked in low even tones that made his words seem the more
terrible. In the darkness the young reporter found himself
imagining that he sat on the railroad ties beside a comely
young man with black hair and black shining eyes. There
was something almost beautiful in the voice of Wash Williams,
the hideous, telling his story of hate.

The telegraph operator of Winesburg, sitting in the darkness on the railroad ties, had become a poet. Hatred had
raised him to that elevation. "It is because I saw you kissing
the lips of that Belle Carpenter that I tell you my story," he
said. "What happened to me may next happen to you. I want to
put you on your guard. Already you may be having dreams in
your head. I want to destroy them."

Wash Williams began telling the story of his married life
with the tall blonde girl with blue eyes whom he had met when
he was a young operator at Dayton, Ohio. Here and there his
story was touched with moments of beauty intermingled with
strings of vile curses. The operator had married the daughter
of a dentist who was the youngest of three sisters. On his
marriage day, because of his ability, he was promoted to a
position as dispatcher at an increased salary and sent to an
office at Columbus, Ohio. There he settled down with his
young wife and began buying a house on the installment plan.

The young telegraph operator was madly in love. With a kind of religious fervor he had managed to go through the pitfalls of his youth and to remain virginal until after his marriage. He made for George Willard a picture of his life in the house at Columbus, Ohio, with the young wife. "In the garden back of our house we planted vegetables," he said, "you know, peas and corn and such things. We went to Columbus in early March and as soon as the days became warm I went to work in the garden. With a spade I turned up the black ground while she ran about laughing and pretending to be afraid of the worms I uncovered. Late in April came the planting. In the little paths among the seed beds she stood holding a paper bag in her hand. The bag was filled with seeds. A few at a time she handed me the seeds that I might thrust them into the warm, soft ground."

For a moment there was a catch in the voice of the man talking in the darkness. "I loved her," he said. "I don't claim not to be a fool. I love her yet. There in the dusk in the spring evening I crawled along the black ground to her feet and groveled before her. I kissed her shoes and the ankles above her shoes. When the hem of her garment touched my face I trembled. When after two years of that life I found she had managed to acquire three other lovers who came regularly to our house when I was away at work, I didn't want to touch them or her. I just sent her home to her mother and said nothing. There was nothing to say. I had four hundred dollars in the bank and I gave her that. I didn't ask her reasons. I didn't say anything. When she had gone I cried like a silly boy. Pretty soon I had a chance to sell the house and I sent that money to her."

Wash Williams and George Willard arose from the pile of railroad ties and walked along the tracks toward town. The operator finished his tale quickly, breathlessly.

"Her mother sent for me," he said. "She wrote me a letter and asked me to come to their house at Dayton. When I got there it was evening about this time."

Wash Williams' voice rose to a half scream. "I sat in the parlor of that house two hours. Her mother took me in there and left me. Their house was stylish. They were what is called respectable people. There were plush chairs and a couch in the room. I was trembling all over. I hated the men I thought had wronged her. I was sick of living alone and wanted her back. The longer I waited the more raw and tender I became. I thought that if she came in and just touched me with her hand I would perhaps faint away. I ached to forgive and forget."

Wash Williams stopped and stood staring at George Willard. The boy's body shook as from a chill. Again the man's voice became soft and low. "She came into the room naked," he went on. "Her mother did that. While I sat there she was taking the girl's clothes off, perhaps coaxing her to do it. First I heard voices at the door that led into a little hallway and then it opened softly. The girl was ashamed and stood perfectly still staring at the floor. The mother didn't come into the room. When she had pushed the girl in through the door she stood in the hallway waiting, hoping we would—well, you see—waiting."

George Willard and the telegraph operator came into the main street of Winesburg. The lights from the store windows lay bright and shining on the sidewalks. People moved about laughing and talking. The young reporter felt ill and weak. In imagination, he also became old and shapeless. "I didn't get the mother killed," said Wash Williams, staring up and down the street. "I struck her once with a chair and then the neighbors came in and took it away. She screamed so loud you see. I won't ever have a chance to kill her now. She died of a fever a month after that happened."

THE THINKER

THE house in which Seth Richmond of Winesburg lived with his mother had been at one time the show place of the town, but when young Seth lived there its glory had become somewhat dimmed. The huge brick house which Banker White had built on Buckeye Street had overshadowed it. The Richmond place was in a little valley far out at the end of Main Street. Farmers coming into town by a dusty road from the south passed by a grove of walnut trees, skirted the Fair Ground with its high board fence covered with advertisements, and trotted their horses down through the valley past the Richmond place into town. As much of the country north and south of Winesburg was devoted to fruit and berry raising, Seth saw wagon-loads of berry pickers—boys, girls, and women—going to the fields in the morning and returning covered with dust in the evening. The chattering crowd, with their rude jokes cried out from wagon to wagon, sometimes irritated him sharply. He regretted that he also could not laugh boisterously, shout meaningless jokes and make of himself a figure in the endless stream of moving, giggling activity that went up and down the road.

The Richmond house was built of limestone, and although it was said in the village to have become run down, had in reality grown more beautiful with every passing year. Already time had begun a little to color the stone, lending a golden richness to its surface and in the evening or on dark days touching the shaded places beneath the eaves with wavering patches of browns and blacks.

The house had been built by Seth's grandfather, a stone quarryman, and it, together with the stone quarries on Lake Erie eighteen miles to the north, had been left to his son, Clarence Richmond, Seth's father. Clarence Richmond, a quiet passionate man extraordinarily admired by his neighbors, had been killed in a street fight with the editor of a newspaper in Toledo, Ohio. The fight concerned the publication of Clarence Richmond's name coupled with that of a woman school teacher, and as the dead man had begun the row by firing upon the editor, the effort to punish the slayer was unsuccessful. After the quarryman's death it was found that much of the money left to him had been squandered in speculation and in insecure investments made through the influence of friends.

Left with but a small income, Virginia Richmond had settled down to a retired life in the village and to the raising of her son. Although she had been deeply moved by the death of the husband and father, she did not at all believe the stories concerning him that ran about after his death. To her mind, the sensitive, boyish man whom all had instinctively loved, was but an unfortunate, a being too fine for everyday life. "You'll be hearing all sorts of stories, but you are not to believe what you hear," she said to her son. "He was a good man, full of tenderness for everyone, and should not have tried to be a man of affairs. No matter how much I were to plan and dream of your future, I could not imagine anything better for you than that you turn out as good a man as your father."

Several years after the death of her husband, Virginia Richmond had become alarmed at the growing demands upon her income and had set herself to the task of increasing it. She had learned stenography and through the influence of her husband's friends got the position of court stenographer at the county seat. There she went by train each morning during the sessions of the court and when no court sat, spent her days working among the rosebushes in her garden. She was a tall, straight figure of a woman with a plain face and a great mass of brown hair.

In the relationship between Seth Richmond and his mother, there was a quality that even at eighteen had begun to color all of his traffic with men. An almost unhealthy respect for the youth kept the mother for the most part silent in his presence.

When she did speak sharply to him he had only to look steadily into her eyes to see dawning there the puzzled look he had already noticed in the eyes of others when he looked at them.

The truth was that the son thought with remarkable clearness and the mother did not. She expected from all people certain conventional reactions to life. A boy was your son, you scolded him and he trembled and looked at the floor. When you had scolded enough he wept and all was forgiven. After the weeping and when he had gone to bed, you crept into his room and kissed him.

Virginia Richmond could not understand why her son did not do these things. After the severest reprimand, he did not tremble and look at the floor but instead looked steadily at her, causing uneasy doubts to invade her mind. As for creeping into his room—after Seth had passed his fifteenth year, she would have been half afraid to do anything of the kind.

Once when he was a boy of sixteen, Seth in company with two other boys, ran away from home. The three boys climbed into the open door of an empty freight car and rode some forty miles to a town where a fair was being held. One of the boys had a bottle filled with a combination of whiskey and blackberry wine, and the three sat with legs dangling out of the car door drinking from the bottle. Seth's two companions sang and waved their hands to idlers about the stations of the towns through which the train passed. They planned raids upon the baskets of farmers who had come with their families to the fair. "We will live like kings and won't have to spend a penny to see the fair and horse races," they declared boastfully.

After the disappearance of Seth, Virginia Richmond walked up and down the floor of her home filled with vague alarms. Although on the next day she discovered, through an inquiry made by the town marshal, on what adventure the boys had gone, she could not quiet herself. All through the night she lay awake hearing the clock tick and telling herself that Seth, like his father, would come to a sudden and violent end. So determined was she that the boy should this time feel the weight of her wrath that, although she would not allow the marshal to interfere with his adventure, she got out pencil and paper and wrote down a series of sharp, stinging reproofs she intended to pour out upon him. The reproofs she committed to memory, going about the garden and saying them aloud like an actor memorizing his part.

And when, at the end of the week, Seth returned, a little weary and with coal soot in his ears and about his eyes, she again found herself unable to reprove him. Walking into the house he hung his cap on a nail by the kitchen door and stood looking steadily at her. "I wanted to turn back within an hour after we had started," he explained. "I didn't know what to do. I knew you would be bothered, but I knew also that if I didn't go on I would be ashamed of myself. I went through with the thing for my own good. It was uncomfortable, sleeping on wet straw, and two drunken negroes came and slept with us. When I stole a lunch basket out of a farmer's wagon I couldn't help thinking of his children going all day without food. I was sick of the whole affair, but I was determined to stick it out until the other boys were ready to come back."

"I'm glad you did stick it out," replied the mother, half resentfully, and kissing him upon the forehead pretended to busy herself with the work about the house.

On a summer evening Seth Richmond went to the New Willard House to visit his friend, George Willard. It had rained during the afternoon, but as he walked through Main Street, the sky had partially cleared and a golden glow lit up the west. Going around a corner, he turned in at the door of the hotel and began to climb the stairway leading up to his friend's room. In the hotel office the proprietor and two traveling men were engaged in a discussion of politics.

On the stairway Seth stopped and listened to the voices of the men below. They were excited and talked rapidly. Tom Willard was berating the traveling men. "I am a Democrat but your talk makes me sick," he said. "You don't understand McKinley. McKinley and Mark Hanna are friends. It is impossible perhaps for your mind to grasp that. If anyone tells you that a friendship can be deeper and bigger and more worth while than dollars and cents, or even more worth while than state politics, you snicker and laugh."

The landlord was interrupted by one of the guests, a tall grey-mustached man who worked for a wholesale grocery house. "Do you think that I've lived in Cleveland all these years without knowing Mark Hanna?" he demanded. "Your talk is piffle. Hanna is after money and nothing else. This McKinley is his tool. He has McKinley bluffed and don't you forget it."

The young man on the stairs did not linger to hear the rest of the discussion, but went on up the stairway and into a little dark hall. Something in the voices of the men talking in the hotel office started a chain of thoughts in his mind. He was lonely and had begun to think that loneliness was a part of his character, something that would always stay with him. Stepping into a side hall he stood by a window that looked into an alleyway. At the back of his shop stood Abner Groff, the town baker. His tiny bloodshot eyes looked up and down the alleyway. In his shop someone called the baker who pretended not to hear. The baker had an empty milk bottle in his hand and an angry sullen look in his eyes.

In Winesburg, Seth Richmond was called the "deep one." "He's like his father," men said as he went through the streets. "He'll break out some of these days. You wait and see."

The talk of the town and the respect with which men and boys instinctively greeted him, as all men greet silent people, had affected Seth Richmond's outlook on life and on himself. He, like most boys, was deeper than boys are given credit for being, but he was not what the men of the town, and even his mother, thought him to be. No great underlying purpose lay back of his habitual silence, and he had no definite plan for his life. When the boys with whom he associated were noisy and quarrelsome, he stood quietly at one side. With calm eyes he watched the gesticulating lively figures of his companions. He wasn't particularly interested in what was going on, and sometimes wondered if he would ever be particularly interested in anything. Now, as he stood in the half-darkness by the window watching the baker, he wished that he himself might become thoroughly stirred by something, even by the fits of sullen anger for which Baker Groff was noted. "It would be better for me if I could become excited and wrangle about politics like windy old Tom Willard," he thought, as he left the window and went again along the hallway to the room occupied by his friend, George Willard.

George Willard was older than Seth Richmond, but in the rather odd friendship between the two, it was he who was forever courting and the younger boy who was being courted. The paper on which George worked had one policy. It strove to mention by name in each issue, as many as possible of the inhabitants of the village. Like an excited dog, George Willard ran here and there, noting on his pad of paper who had gone on business to the county seat or had returned from a visit to a neighboring village. All day he wrote little facts upon the pad. "A. P. Wringlet has received a shipment of straw hats. Ed Byerbaum and Tom Marshall were in Cleveland Friday. Uncle Tom Sinnings is building a new barn on his place on the Valley Road."

The idea that George Willard would some day become a writer had given him a place of distinction in Winesburg, and to Seth Richmond he talked continually of the matter. "It's the easiest of all lives to live," he declared, becoming excited and boastful. "Here and there you go and there is no one to boss you. Though you are in India or in the South Seas in a boat, you have but to write and there you are. Wait till I get my name up and then see what fun I shall have."

In George Willard's room, which had a window looking down into an alleyway and one that looked across railroad tracks to Biff Carter's Lunch Room facing the railroad station, Seth Richmond sat in a chair and looked at the floor. George Willard, who had been sitting for an hour idly playing with a lead pencil, greeted him effusively. "I've been trying to write a love story," he explained, laughing nervously. Lighting a pipe he began walking up and down the room. "I know what I'm going to do. I'm going to fall in love. I've been sitting here and thinking it over and I'm going to do it."

As though embarrassed by his declaration, George went to a window and turning his back to his friend leaned out. "I know who I'm going to fall in love with," he said sharply. "It's Helen White. She is the only girl in town with any 'get-up' to her."

Struck with a new idea, young Willard turned and walked towards his visitor. "Look here," he said. "You know Helen White better than I do. I want you to tell her what I said. You just get to talking to her and say that I'm in love with her. See what she says to that. See how she takes it, and then you come and tell me."

Seth Richmond arose and went towards the door. The words of his comrade irritated him unbearably. "Well, good-bye," he said briefly.

George was amazed. Running forward he stood in the darkness trying to look into Seth's face. "What's the matter? What are you going to do? You stay here and let's talk," he urged.

A wave of resentment directed against his friend, the men of the town who were, he thought, perpetually talking of nothing, and most of all, against his own habit of silence, made Seth half desperate. "Aw, speak to her yourself," he burst forth and then going quickly through the door, slammed it sharply in his friend's face. "I'm going to find Helen White and talk to her, but not about him," he muttered.

Seth went down the stairway and out at the front door of the hotel muttering with wrath. Crossing a little dusty street and climbing a low iron railing, he went to sit upon the grass in the station yard. George Willard he thought a profound fool, and he wished that he had said so more vigorously. Although his acquaintanceship with Helen White, the banker's daughter, was outwardly but casual, she was often the subject of his thoughts and he felt that she was something private and personal to himself. "The busy fool with his love stories," he muttered, staring back over his shoulder at George Willard's room, "why does he never tire of his eternal talking."

It was berry harvest time in Winesburg and upon the station platform men and boys loaded the boxes of red, fragrant berries into two express cars that stood upon the siding. A June moon was in the sky, although in the west a storm threatened, and no street lamps were lighted. In the dim light the figures of the men standing upon the express truck and pitching the boxes in at the doors of the cars were but dimly discernible. Upon the iron railing that protected the station lawn sat other men. Pipes were lighted. Village jokes went back and forth. Away in the distance a train whistled and the men loading the boxes into the cars worked with renewed activity.

Seth arose from his place on the grass and went silently past the men perched upon the railing and into Main Street. He had come to a resolution. "I'll get out of here," he told himself. "What good am I here? I'm going to some city and go to work. I'll tell mother about it to-morrow."

Seth Richmond went slowly along Main Street, past Wacker's Cigar Store and the Town Hall, and into Buckeye Street. He was depressed by the thought that he was not a part of the life in his own town, but the depression did not cut deeply as he did not think of himself as at fault. In the heavy shadows of a big tree before Dr. Welling's house, he stopped and stood watching half-witted Turk Smollet, who was pushing a wheelbarrow in the road. The old man with his absurdly boyish mind had a dozen long boards on the wheelbarrow, and as he hurried along the road, balanced the load with extreme nicety. "Easy there, Turk! Steady now, old boy!" the old man shouted to himself, and laughed so that the load of boards rocked dangerously.

Seth knew Turk Smollet, the half dangerous old wood chopper whose peculiarities added so much of color to the life of the village. He knew that when Turk got into Main Street he would become the center of a whirlwind of cries and comments, that in truth the old man was going far out of his way in order to pass through Main Street and exhibit his skill in wheeling the boards. "If George Willard were here, he'd have something to say," thought Seth. "George belongs to this town. He'd shout at Turk and Turk would shout at him. They'd both be secretly pleased by what they had said. It's different with me. I don't belong. I'll not make a fuss about it, but I'm going to get out of here."

Seth stumbled forward through the half darkness, feeling himself an outcast in his own town. He began to pity himself, but a sense of the absurdity of his thoughts made him smile. In the end he decided that he was simply old beyond his years and not at all a subject for self-pity. "I'm made to go to work. I may be able to make a place for myself by steady working, and I might as well be at it," he decided.

Seth went to the house of Banker White and stood in the darkness by the front door. On the door hung a heavy brass knocker, an innovation introduced into the village by Helen White's mother, who had also organized a woman's club for the study of poetry. Seth raised the knocker and let it fall. Its heavy clatter sounded like a report from distant guns. "How awkward and foolish I am," he thought. "If Mrs. White comes to the door, I won't know what to say."

It was Helen White who came to the door and found Seth standing at the edge of the porch. Blushing with pleasure, she stepped forward, closing the door softly. "I'm going to get out of town. I don't know what I'll do, but I'm going to get out of here and go to work. I think I'll go to Columbus," he said. "Perhaps I'll get into the State University down there. Anyway, I'm going. I'll tell mother to-night." He hesitated and looked doubtfully about. "Perhaps you wouldn't mind coming to walk with me?"

Seth and Helen walked through the streets beneath the trees. Heavy clouds had drifted across the face of the moon, and before them in the deep twilight went a man with a short ladder upon his shoulder. Hurrying forward, the man stopped at the street crossing and, putting the ladder against the wooden lamp post, lighted the village lights so that their way was half lighted, half darkened, by the lamps and by the deepening shadows cast by the low-branched trees. In the tops of the trees the wind began to play, disturbing the sleeping birds so that they flew about calling plaintively. In the lighted space before one of the lamps, two bats wheeled and circled, pursuing the gathering swarm of night flies.

Since Seth had been a boy in knee trousers there had been a half expressed intimacy between him and the maiden who now for the first time walked beside him. For a time she had been beset with a madness for writing notes which she addressed to Seth. He had found them concealed in his books at school and one had been given him by a child met in the street, while several had been delivered through the village post office.

The notes had been written in a round, boyish hand and had reflected a mind inflamed by novel reading. Seth had not answered them, although he had been moved and flattered by some of the sentences scrawled in pencil upon the stationery of the banker's wife. Putting them into the pocket of his coat, he went through the street or stood by the fence in the school yard with something burning at his side. He thought it fine that he should be thus selected as the favorite of the richest and most attractive girl in town.

Helen and Seth stopped by a fence near where a low dark building faced the street. The building had once been a factory for the making of barrel staves but was now vacant. Across the street upon the porch of a house a man and woman talked of their childhood, their voices coming clearly across to the half-embarrassed youth and maiden. There was the sound of scraping chairs and the man and woman came down the gravel path to a wooden gate. Standing outside the gate, the man leaned over and kissed the woman. "For old times' sake," he said and, turning, walked rapidly away along the sidewalk.

"That's Belle Turner," whispered Helen, and put her hand boldly into Seth's hand. "I didn't know she had a fellow. I thought she was too old for that." Seth laughed uneasily. The hand of the girl was warm and a strange, dizzy feeling crept over him. Into his mind came a desire to tell her something he had been determined not to tell. "George Willard's in love with you," he said, and in spite of his agitation his voice was low and quiet. "He's writing a story, and he wants to be in love. He wants to know how it feels. He wanted me to tell you and see what you said."

Again Helen and Seth walked in silence. They came to the garden surrounding the old Richmond place and going through a gap in the hedge sat on a wooden bench beneath a bush.

On the street as he walked beside the girl new and daring thoughts had come into Seth Richmond's mind. He began to regret his decision to get out of town. "It would be something new and altogether delightful to remain and walk often through the streets with Helen White," he thought. In imagination he saw himself putting his arm about her waist and feeling her arms clasped tightly about his neck. One of those odd combinations of events and places made him connect the idea of love-making with this girl and a spot he had visited some days before. He had gone on an errand to the house of a farmer who lived on a hillside beyond the Fair Ground and had returned by a path through a field. At the foot of the hill below the farmer's house Seth had stopped beneath a sycamore tree and looked about him. A soft humming noise had greeted his ears. For a moment he had thought the tree must be the home of a swarm of bees.

And then, looking down, Seth had seen the bees everywhere all about him in the long grass. He stood in a mass of weeds that grew waist-high in the field that ran away from the hillside. The weeds were abloom with tiny purple blossoms and gave forth an overpowering fragrance. Upon the weeds the bees were gathered in armies, singing as they worked.

Seth imagined himself lying on a summer evening, buried deep among the weeds beneath the tree. Beside him, in the scene built in his fancy, lay Helen White, her hand lying in his hand. A peculiar reluctance kept him from kissing her lips, but he felt he might have done that if he wished. Instead, he lay perfectly still, looking at her and listening to the army of bees that sang the sustained masterful song of labor above his head.

On the bench in the garden Seth stirred uneasily. Releasing the hand of the girl, he thrust his hands into his trouser pockets. A desire to impress the mind of his companion with the importance of the resolution he had made came over him and he nodded his head toward the house. "Mother'll make a fuss, I suppose," he whispered. "She hasn't thought at all about what I'm going to do in life. She thinks I'm going to stay on here forever just being a boy."

Seth's voice became charged with boyish earnestness. "You see, I've got to strike out. I've got to get to work. It's what I'm good for."

Helen White was impressed. She nodded her head and a feeling of admiration swept over her. "This is as it should be," she thought. "This boy is not a boy at all, but a strong, purposeful man." Certain vague desires that had been invading her body were swept away and she sat up very straight on the bench. The thunder continued to rumble and flashes of heat lightning lit up the eastern sky. The garden that had been so mysterious and vast, a place that with Seth beside her might have become the background for strange and wonderful adventures, now seemed no more than an ordinary Winesburg back yard, quite definite and limited in its outlines.

"What will you do up there?" she whispered.

Seth turned half around on the bench, striving to see her face in the darkness. He thought her infinitely more sensible and straightforward than George Willard, and was glad he had come away from his friend. A feeling of impatience with the town that had been in his mind returned, and he tried to tell her of it. "Everyone talks and talks," he began. "I'm sick of it. I'll do something, get into some kind of work where talk don't count. Maybe I'll just be a mechanic in a shop. I don't know. I guess I don't care much. I just want to work and keep quiet. That's all I've got in my mind."

Seth arose from the bench and put out his hand. He did not want to bring the meeting to an end but could not think of anything more to say. "It's the last time we'll see each other," he whispered.

A wave of sentiment swept over Helen. Putting her hand upon Seth's shoulder, she started to draw his face down towards her own upturned face. The act was one of pure affection and cutting regret that some vague adventure that had been present in the spirit of the night would now never be realized. "I think I'd better be going along," she said, letting her hand fall heavily to her side. A thought came to her. "Don't you go with me; I want to be alone," she said. "You go and talk with your mother. You'd better do that now."

Seth hesitated and, as he stood waiting, the girl turned and ran away through the hedge. A desire to run after her came to him, but he only stood staring, perplexed and puzzled by her action as he had been perplexed and puzzled by all of the life of the town out of which she had come. Walking slowly toward the house, he stopped in the shadow of a large tree and looked at his mother sitting by a lighted window busily sewing. The feeling of loneliness that had visited him earlier in the evening returned and colored his thoughts of the adventure through which he had just passed. "Huh!" he exclaimed, turning and staring in the direction taken by Helen White. "That's how things'll turn out. She'll be like the rest. I suppose she'll begin now to look at me in a funny way." He looked at the ground and pondered this thought. "She'll be embarrassed and feel strange when I'm around," he whispered to himself. "That's how it'll be. That's how everything'll turn out. When it comes to loving some one, it won't never be me. It'll be some one else—some fool—some one who talks a lot—some one like that George Willard."

TANDY

UNTIL she was seven years old she lived in an old unpainted house on an unused road that led off Trunion Pike. Her father gave her but little attention and her mother was dead. The father spent his time talking and thinking of religion. He proclaimed himself an agnostic and was so absorbed in destroying the ideas of God that had crept into the minds of his neighbors that he never saw God manifesting himself in the little child that, half forgotten, lived here and there on the bounty of her dead mother's relatives.

A stranger came to Winesburg and saw in the child what the father did not see. He was a tall, red-haired young man who was almost always drunk. Sometimes he sat in a chair before the New Willard House with Tom Hard, the father. As Tom talked, declaring there could be no God, the stranger smiled and winked at the bystanders. He and Tom became friends and were much together.

The stranger was the son of a rich merchant of Cleveland and had come to Winesburg on a mission. He wanted to cure himself of the habit of drink, and thought that by escaping from his city associates and living in a rural community he would have a better chance in the struggle with the appetite that was destroying him.

His sojourn in Winesburg was not a success. The dullness of the passing hours led to his drinking harder than ever. But he did succeed in doing something. He gave a name rich with meaning to Tom Hard's daughter.

One evening when he was recovering from a long debauch the stranger came reeling along the main street of the town. Tom Hard sat in a chair before the New Willard House with his daughter, then a child of five, on his knees. Beside him on the board sidewalk sat young George Willard. The stranger dropped into a chair beside them. His body shook and when he tried to talk his voice trembled.

It was late evening and darkness lay over the town and over the railroad that ran along the foot of a little incline before the hotel. Somewhere in the distance, off to the west, there was a prolonged blast from the whistle of a passenger engine. A dog that had been sleeping in the roadway arose and barked. The stranger began to babble and made a prophecy concerning the child that lay in the arms of the agnostic.

"I came here to quit drinking," he said, and tears began to run down his cheeks. He did not look at Tom Hard, but leaned forward and stared into the darkness as though seeing a vision. "I ran away to the country to be cured, but I am not cured. There is a reason." He turned to look at the child who sat up very straight on her father's knee and returned the look.

The stranger touched Tom Hard on the arm. "Drink is not the only thing to which I am addicted," he said. "There is something else. I am a lover and have not found my thing to love. That is a big point if you know enough to realize what I mean. It makes my destruction inevitable, you see. There are few who understand that."

The stranger became silent and seemed overcome with sadness, but another blast from the whistle of the passenger engine aroused him. "I have not lost faith. I proclaim that. I have only been brought to the place where I know my faith will not be realized," he declared hoarsely. He looked hard at the child and began to address her, paying no more attention to the father. "There is a woman coming," he said, and his voice was now sharp and earnest. "I have missed her, you see. She did not come in my time. You may be the woman. It would be like fate to let me stand in her presence once, on such an evening as this, when I have destroyed myself with drink and she is as yet only a child."

The shoulders of the stranger shook violently, and when he tried to roll a cigarette the paper fell from his trembling fingers. He grew angry and scolded. "They think it's easy to be a woman, to be loved, but I know better," he declared. Again he turned to the child. "I understand," he cried. "Perhaps of all men I alone understand."

His glance again wandered away to the darkened street. "I know about her, although she has never crossed my path," he said softly. "I know about her struggles and her defeats. It is because of her defeats that she is to me the lovely one. Out of her defeats has been born a new quality in woman. I have a name for it. I call it Tandy. I made up the name when I was a true dreamer and before my body became vile. It is the quality of being strong to be loved. It is something men need from women and that they do not get."

The stranger arose and stood before Tom Hard. His body rocked back and forth and he seemed about to fall, but instead he dropped to his knees on the sidewalk and raised the hands of the little girl to his drunken lips. He kissed them ecstatically. "Be Tandy, little one," he pled. "Dare to be strong and courageous. That is the road. Venture anything. Be brave enough to dare to be loved. Be something more than man or woman. Be Tandy."

The stranger arose and staggered off down the street. A day or two later he got aboard a train and returned to his home in Cleveland. On the summer evening, after the talk before the hotel, Tom Hard took the girl child to the house of a relative where she had been invited to spend the night. As he went along in the darkness under the trees he forgot the babbling voice of the stranger and his mind returned to the making of arguments by which he might destroy men's faith in God. He spoke his daughter's name and she began to weep.

"I don't want to be called that," she declared. "I want to be called Tandy—Tandy Hard." The child wept so bitterly that Tom Hard was touched and tried to comfort her. He stopped beneath a tree and, taking her into his arms, began to caress her. "Be good, now," he said sharply; but she would not be quieted. With childish abandon she gave herself over to grief, her voice breaking the evening stillness of the street. "I want to be Tandy. I want to be Tandy. I want to be Tandy Hard," she cried, shaking her head and sobbing as though her young strength were not enough to bear the vision the words of the drunkard had brought to her.

THE STRENGTH OF GOD

THE REVEREND CURTIS HARTMAN was pastor of the
Presbyterian Church of Winesburg, and had been in that
position ten years. He was forty years old, and by his nature
very silent and reticent. To preach, standing in the pulpit
before the people, was always a hardship for him and from
Wednesday morning until Saturday evening he thought of
nothing but the two sermons that must be preached on Sunday. Early on Sunday morning he went into a little room called
a study in the bell tower of the church and prayed. In his
prayers there was one note that always predominated. "Give
me strength and courage for Thy work, O Lord!" he pled,
kneeling on the bare floor and bowing his head in the presence
of the task that lay before him.

The Reverend Hartman was a tall man with a brown beard.
His wife, a stout, nervous woman, was the daughter of a
manufacturer of underwear at Cleveland, Ohio. The minister
himself was rather a favorite in the town. The elders of the
church liked him because he was quiet and unpretentious and
Mrs. White, the banker's wife, thought him scholarly and
refined.

The Presbyterian Church held itself somewhat aloof from
the other churches of Winesburg. It was larger and more
imposing and its minister was better paid. He even had a
carriage of his own and on summer evenings sometimes
drove about town with his wife. Through Main Street and up
and down Buckeye Street he went, bowing gravely to the
people, while his wife, afire with secret pride, looked at him
out of the corners of her eyes and worried lest the horse
become frightened and run away.

For a good many years after he came to Winesburg things
went well with Curtis Hartman. He was not one to arouse keen
enthusiasm among the worshippers in his church but on the

other hand he made no enemies. In reality he was much in earnest and sometimes suffered prolonged periods of remorse because he could not go crying the word of God in the highways and byways of the town. He wondered if the flame of the spirit really burned in him and dreamed of a day when a strong sweet new current of power would come like a great wind into his voice and his soul and the people would tremble before the spirit of God made manifest in him. "I am a poor stick and that will never really happen to me," he mused dejectedly and then a patient smile lit up his features. "Oh well, I suppose I'm doing well enough," he added philosophically.

The room in the bell tower of the church, where on Sunday mornings the minister prayed for an increase in him of the power of God, had but one window. It was long and narrow and swung outward on a hinge like a door. On the window, made of little leaded panes, was a design showing the Christ laying his hand upon the head of a child. One Sunday morning in the summer as he sat by his desk in the room with a large Bible opened before him, and the sheets of his sermon scattered about, the minister was shocked to see, in the upper room of the house next door, a woman lying in her bed and smoking a cigarette while she read a book. Curtis Hartman went on tip-toe to the window and closed it softly. He was horror stricken at the thought of a woman smoking and trembled also to think that his eyes, just raised from the pages of the book of God, had looked upon the bare shoulders and white throat of a woman. With his brain in a whirl he went down into the pulpit and preached a long sermon without once thinking of his gestures or his voice. The sermon attracted unusual attention because of its power and clearness. "I wonder if she is listening, if my voice is carrying a message into her soul," he thought and began to hope that on future Sunday mornings he might be able to say words that would touch and awaken the woman apparently far gone in secret sin.

The house next door to the Presbyterian Church, through the windows of which the minister had seen the sight that had

so upset him, was occupied by two women. Aunt Elizabeth
Swift, a grey competent-looking widow with money in the
Winesburg National Bank, lived there with her daughter
Kate Swift, a school teacher. The school teacher was thirty
years old and had a neat trim-looking figure. She had few
friends and bore a reputation of having a sharp tongue.
When he began to think about her, Curtis Hartman remembered that she had been to Europe and had lived for two years
in New York City. "Perhaps after all her smoking means
nothing," he thought. He began to remember that when he
was a student in college and occasionally read novels, good,
although somewhat worldly women, had smoked through
the pages of a book that had once fallen into his hands. With
a rush of new determination he worked on his sermons all
through the week and forgot, in his zeal to reach the ears and
the soul of this new listener, both his embarrassment in the
pulpit and the necessity of prayer in the study on Sunday
mornings.

Reverend Hartman's experience with women had been
somewhat limited. He was the son of a wagon maker from
Muncie, Indiana, and had worked his way through college.
The daughter of the underwear manufacturer had boarded in
a house where he lived during his school days and he had
married her after a formal and prolonged courtship, carried
on for the most part by the girl herself. On his marriage day the
underwear manufacturer had given his daughter five thousand dollars and he promised to leave her at least twice that
amount in his will. The minister had thought himself fortunate
in marriage and had never permitted himself to think of other
women. He did not want to think of other women. What he
wanted was to do the work of God quietly and earnestly.

In the soul of the minister a struggle awoke. From wanting
to reach the ears of Kate Swift, and through his sermons to
delve into her soul, he began to want also to look again at the
figure lying white and quiet in the bed. On a Sunday morning
when he could not sleep because of his thoughts he arose and

went to walk in the streets. When he had gone along Main Street almost to the old Richmond place he stopped and picking up a stone rushed off to the room in the bell tower. With the stone he broke out a corner of the window and then locked the door and sat down at the desk before the open Bible to wait. When the shade of the window to Kate Swift's room was raised he could see, through the hole, directly into her bed, but she was not there. She also had arisen and had gone for a walk and the hand that raised the shade was the hand of Aunt Elizabeth Swift.

The minister almost wept with joy at this deliverance from the carnal desire to "peep" and went back to his own house praising God. In an ill moment he forgot, however, to stop the hole in the window. The piece of glass broken out at the corner of the window just nipped off the bare heel of the boy standing motionless and looking with rapt eyes into the face of the Christ.

Curtis Hartman forgot his sermon on that Sunday morning. He talked to his congregation and in his talk said that it was a mistake for people to think of their minister as a man set aside and intended by nature to lead a blameless life. "Out of my own experience I know that we, who are the ministers of God's word, are beset by the same temptations that assail you," he declared. "I have been tempted and have surrendered to temptation. It is only the hand of God, placed beneath my head, that has raised me up. As he has raised me so also will he raise you. Do not despair. In your hour of sin raise your eyes to the skies and you will be again and again saved."

Resolutely the minister put the thoughts of the woman in the bed out of his mind and began to be something like a lover in the presence of his wife. One evening when they drove out together he turned the horse out of Buckeye Street and in the darkness on Gospel Hill, above Waterworks Pond, put his arm about Sarah Hartman's waist. When he had eaten breakfast in the morning and was ready to retire to his study at the back of his house he went around the table and kissed his wife on the cheek. When thoughts of Kate Swift came into his head, he smiled and raised his eyes to the skies. "Intercede for me, Master," he muttered, "keep me in the narrow path intent on Thy work."

And now began the real struggle in the soul of the brown-bearded minister. By chance he discovered that Kate Swift was in the habit of lying in her bed in the evenings and reading a book. A lamp stood on a table by the side of the bed and the light streamed down upon her white shoulders and bare throat. On the evening when he made the discovery the minister sat at the desk in the study from nine until after eleven and when her light was put out stumbled out of the church to spend two more hours walking and praying in the streets. He did not want to kiss the shoulders and the throat of Kate Swift and had not allowed his mind to dwell on such thoughts. He did not know what he wanted. "I am God's child and he must save me from myself," he cried, in the darkness under the trees as he wandered in the streets. By a tree he stood and looked at the sky that was covered with hurrying clouds. He began to talk to God intimately and closely. "Please, Father, do not forget me. Give me power to go to-morrow and repair the hole in the window. Lift my eyes again to the skies. Stay with me, Thy servant, in his hour of need."

Up and down through the silent streets walked the minister and for days and weeks his soul was troubled. He could not understand the temptation that had come to him nor could he fathom the reason for its coming. In a way he began to blame God, saying to himself that he had tried to keep his feet in the true path and had not run about seeking sin. "Through my days as a young man and all through my life here I have gone quietly about my work," he declared. "Why now should I be tempted? What have I done that this burden should be laid on me?"

Three times during the early fall and winter of that year Curtis Hartman crept out of his house to the room in the bell tower to sit in the darkness looking at the figure of Kate Swift lying in her bed and later went to walk and pray in the streets. He could not understand himself. For weeks he would go along scarcely thinking of the school teacher and telling himself that he had conquered the carnal desire to look at her body. And then something would happen. As he sat in the study of his own house, hard at work on a sermon, he would become nervous and begin to walk up and down the room. "I will go out into the streets," he told himself and even as he let himself in at the church door he persistently denied to himself the cause of his being there. "I will not repair the hole in the window and I will train myself to come here at night and sit in the presence of this woman without raising my eyes. I will not be defeated in this thing. The Lord has devised this temptation as a test of my soul and I will grope my way out of darkness into the light of righteousness."

One night in January when it was bitter cold and snow lay deep on the streets of Winesburg Curtis Hartman paid his last visit to the room in the bell tower of the church. It was past nine o'clock when he left his own house and he set out so hurriedly that he forgot to put on his overshoes. In Main Street no one was abroad but Hop Higgins the night watchman and in the whole town no one was awake but the watchman and young George Willard, who sat in the office of the *Winesburg Eagle* trying to write a story. Along the street to the church went the minister, plowing through the drifts and thinking that this time he would utterly give way to sin. "I want to look at the woman and to think of kissing her shoulders and I am going to let myself think what I choose," he declared bitterly and tears came into his eyes. He began to think that he would get out of the ministry and try some other way of life. "I shall go to some city and get into business," he declared. "If my nature is such that I cannot resist sin, I shall give myself over to sin. At least I shall not be a hypocrite, preaching the word of God with my mind thinking of the shoulders and neck of a woman who does not belong to me."

It was cold in the room of the bell tower of the church on that January night and almost as soon as he came into the room Curtis Hartman knew that if he stayed he would be ill. His feet were wet from tramping in the snow and there was no fire. In the room in the house next door Kate Swift had not yet appeared. With grim determination the man sat down to wait. Sitting in the chair and gripping the edge of the desk on which lay the Bible he stared into the darkness thinking the blackest thoughts of his life. He thought of his wife and for the moment almost hated her. "She has always been ashamed of passion and has cheated me," he thought. "Man has a right to expect living passion and beauty in a woman. He has no right to forget that he is an animal and in me there is something that is Greek. I will throw off the woman of my bosom and seek other women. I will besiege this school teacher. I will fly in the face of all men and if I am a creature of carnal lusts I will live then for my lusts."

The distracted man trembled from head to foot, partly from cold, partly from the struggle in which he was engaged. Hours passed and a fever assailed his body. His throat began to hurt and his teeth chattered. His feet on the study floor felt like two cakes of ice. Still he would not give up. "I will see this woman and will think the thoughts I have never dared to think," he told himself, gripping the edge of the desk and waiting.

Curtis Hartman came near dying from the effects of that night of waiting in the church, and also he found in the thing that happened what he took to be the way of life for him. On other evenings when he had waited he had not been able to see, through the little hole in the glass, any part of the school teacher's room except that occupied by her bed. In the darkness he had waited until the woman suddenly appeared sitting in the bed in her white night-robe. When the light was turned up she propped herself up among the pillows and read a book. Sometimes she smoked one of the cigarettes. Only her bare shoulders and throat were visible.

On the January night, after he had come near dying with cold and after his mind had two or three times actually slipped away into an odd land of fantasy so that he had by an exercise of will power to force himself back into consciousness, Kate Swift appeared. In the room next door a lamp was lighted and the waiting man stared into an empty bed. Then upon the bed before his eyes a naked woman threw herself. Lying face downward she wept and beat with her fists upon the pillow. With a final outburst of weeping she half arose, and in the presence of the man who had waited to look and to think thoughts the woman of sin began to pray. In the lamplight her figure, slim and strong, looked like the figure of the boy in the presence of the Christ on the leaded window.

Curtis Hartman never remembered how he got out of the church. With a cry he arose, dragging the heavy desk along the floor. The Bible fell, making a great clatter in the silence. When the light in the house next door went out he stumbled down the stairway and into the street. Along the street he went and ran in at the door of the *Winesburg Eagle*. To George Willard, who was tramping up and down in the office under-going a struggle of his own, he began to talk half incoherently. "The ways of God are beyond human understanding," he cried, running in quickly and closing the door. He began to advance upon the young man, his eyes glowing and his voice ringing with fervor. "I have found the light," he cried. "After ten years in this town, God has manifested himself to me in the body of a woman." His voice dropped and he began to whisper. "I did not understand," he said. "What I took to be a trial of my soul was only a preparation for a new and more beautiful fervor of the spirit. God has appeared to me in the person of Kate Swift, the school teacher, kneeling naked on a bed. Do you know Kate Swift? Although she may not be aware of it, she is an instrument of God, bearing the message of truth."

Reverend Curtis Hartman turned and ran out of the office. At the door he stopped, and after looking up and down the deserted street, turned again to George Willard. "I am deliv-

ered. Have no fear." He held up a bleeding fist for the young
man to see. "I smashed the glass of the window," he cried.
"Now it will have to be wholly replaced. The strength of God
was in me and I broke it with my fist."

THE TEACHER

SNOW lay deep in the streets of Winesburg. It had begun to snow about ten o'clock in the morning and a wind sprang up and blew the snow in clouds along Main Street. The frozen mud roads that led into town were fairly smooth and in places ice covered the mud. "There will be good sleighing," said Will Henderson, standing by the bar in Ed Griffith's saloon. Out of the saloon he went and met Sylvester West the druggist stumbling along in the kind of heavy overshoes called arctics. "Snow will bring the people into town on Saturday," said the druggist. The two men stopped and discussed their affairs. Will Henderson, who had on a light overcoat and no overshoes, kicked the heel of his left foot with the toe of the right. "Snow will be good for the wheat," observed the druggist sagely.

Young George Willard, who had nothing to do, was glad because he did not feel like working that day. The weekly paper had been printed and taken to the post office on Wednesday evening and the snow began to fall on Thursday. At eight o'clock, after the morning train had passed, he put a pair of skates in his pocket and went up to Waterworks Pond but did not go skating. Past the pond and along a path that followed Wine Creek he went until he came to a grove of beech trees. There he built a fire against the side of a log and sat down at the end of the log to think. When the snow began to fall and the wind to blow he hurried about getting fuel for the fire.

The young reporter was thinking of Kate Swift who had once been his school teacher. On the evening before he had gone to her house to get a book she wanted him to read and had been alone with her for an hour. For the fourth or fifth time the woman had talked to him with great earnestness and he could not make out what she meant by her talk. He began to believe she might be in love with him and the thought was both pleasing and annoying.

Up from the log he sprang and began to pile sticks on the fire. Looking about to be sure he was alone he talked aloud pretending he was in the presence of the woman. "Oh, you're just letting on, you know you are," he declared. "I am going to find out about you. You wait and see."

The young man got up and went back along the path toward town leaving the fire blazing in the wood. As he went through the streets the skates clanked in his pocket. In his own room in the New Willard House he built a fire in the stove and lay down on top of the bed. He began to have lustful thoughts and pulling down the shade of the window closed his eyes and turned his face to the wall. He took a pillow into his arms and embraced it thinking first of the school teacher, who by her words had stirred something within him and later of Helen White, the slim daughter of the town banker, with whom he had been for a long time half in love.

By nine o'clock of that evening snow lay deep in the streets and the weather had become bitter cold. It was difficult to walk about. The stores were dark and the people had crawled away to their houses. The evening train from Cleveland was very late but nobody was interested in its arrival. By ten o'clock all but four of the eighteen hundred citizens of the town were in bed.

Hop Higgins, the night watchman, was partially awake. He was lame and carried a heavy stick. On dark nights he carried a lantern. Between nine and ten o'clock he went his rounds. Up and down Main Street he stumbled through the drifts trying the doors of the stores. Then he went into alleyways and tried the back doors. Finding all tight he hurried around the corner to the New Willard House and beat on the door. Through the rest of the night he intended to stay by the stove. "You go to bed. I'll keep the stove going," he said to the boy who slept on a cot in the hotel office.

Hop Higgins sat down by the stove and took off his shoes. When the boy had gone to sleep he began to think of his own affairs. He intended to paint his house in the spring and sat by the stove calculating the cost of paint and labor. That led him into other calculations. The night watchman was sixty years old and wanted to retire. He had been a soldier in the Civil War and drew a small pension. He hoped to find some new method of making a living and aspired to become a professional breeder of ferrets. Already he had four of the strangely shaped savage little creatures, that are used by sportsmen in the pursuit of rabbits, in the cellar of his house. "Now I have one male and three females," he mused. "If I am lucky by spring I shall have twelve or fifteen. In another year I shall be able to begin advertising ferrets for sale in the sporting papers."

The night watchman settled into his chair and his mind became a blank. He did not sleep. By years of practice he had trained himself to sit for hours through the long nights neither asleep nor awake. In the morning he was almost as refreshed as though he had slept.

With Hop Higgins safely stowed away in the chair behind the stove only three people were awake in Winesburg. George Willard was in the office of the *Eagle* pretending to be at work on the writing of a story but in reality continuing the mood of the morning by the fire in the wood. In the bell tower of the Presbyterian Church the Reverend Curtis Hartman was sitting in the darkness preparing himself for a revelation from God, and Kate Swift, the school teacher, was leaving her house for a walk in the storm.

It was past ten o'clock when Kate Swift set out and the walk was unpremeditated. It was as though the man and the boy, by thinking of her, had driven her forth into the wintry streets. Aunt Elizabeth Swift had gone to the county seat concerning some business in connection with mortgages in which she had money invested and would not be back until the next day. By a huge stove, called a base burner, in the living room of the house sat the daughter reading a book. Suddenly she sprang to her feet and, snatching a cloak from a rack by the front door, ran out of the house.

At the age of thirty Kate Swift was not known in Winesburg as a pretty woman. Her complexion was not good and her face was covered with blotches that indicated ill health. Alone in the night in the winter streets she was lovely. Her back was straight, her shoulders square and her features were as the features of a tiny goddess on a pedestal in a garden in the dim light of a summer evening.

During the afternoon the school teacher had been to see Dr. Welling concerning her health. The doctor had scolded her and had declared she was in danger of losing her hearing. It was foolish for Kate Swift to be abroad in the storm, foolish and perhaps dangerous.

The woman in the streets did not remember the words of the doctor and would not have turned back had she remembered. She was very cold but after walking for five minutes no longer minded the cold. First she went to the end of her own street and then across a pair of hay scales set in the ground before a feed barn and into Trunion Pike. Along Trunion Pike she went to Ned Winters' barn and turning east followed a street of low frame houses that led over Gospel Hill and into Sucker Road that ran down a shallow valley past Ike Smead's chicken farm to Waterworks Pond. As she went along, the bold, excited mood that had driven her out of doors passed and then returned again.

There was something biting and forbidding in the character of Kate Swift. Everyone felt it. In the schoolroom she was silent, cold, and stern, and yet in an odd way very close to her pupils. Once in a long while something seemed to have come over her and she was happy. All of the children in the schoolroom felt the effect of her happiness. For a time they did not work but sat back in their chairs and looked at her.

With hands clasped behind her back the school teacher walked up and down in the schoolroom and talked very rapidly. It did not seem to matter what subject came into her mind. Once she talked to the children of Charles Lamb and made up strange intimate little stories concerning the life of the dead writer. The stories were told with the air of one who had lived in a house with Charles Lamb and knew all the secrets of his private life. The children were somewhat confused, thinking Charles Lamb must be someone who had once lived in Winesburg.

On another occasion the teacher talked to the children of Benvenuto Cellini. That time they laughed. What a bragging, blustering, brave, lovable fellow she made of the old artist! Concerning him also she invented anecdotes. There was one of a German music teacher who had a room above Cellini's lodgings in the city of Milan that made the boys guffaw. Sugars McNutts, a fat boy with red cheeks, laughed so hard that he became dizzy and fell off his seat and Kate Swift laughed with him. Then suddenly she became again cold and stern.

On the winter night when she walked through the deserted snow-covered streets, a crisis had come into the life of the school teacher. Although no one in Winesburg would have suspected it, her life had been very adventurous. It was still adventurous. Day by day as she worked in the schoolroom or walked in the streets, grief, hope, and desire fought within her. Behind a cold exterior the most extraordinary events transpired in her mind. The people of the town thought of her as a confirmed old maid and because she spoke sharply and went her own way thought her lacking in all the human feeling that did so much to make and mar their own lives. In reality she was the most eagerly passionate soul among them, and more than once, in the five years since she had come back from her travels to settle in Winesburg and become a school teacher, had been compelled to go out of the house and walk half through the night fighting out some battle raging within. Once on a night when it rained she had stayed out six hours and when she came home had a quarrel with Aunt Elizabeth Swift. "I am glad you're not a man," said the mother sharply. "More than once I've waited for your father to come home, not knowing what new mess he had got into. I've had my share of uncertainty and you cannot blame me if I do not want to see the worst side of him reproduced in you."

*

Kate Swift's mind was ablaze with thoughts of George Willard. In something he had written as a school boy she thought she had recognized the spark of genius and wanted to blow on the spark. One day in the summer she had gone to the *Eagle* office and finding the boy unoccupied had taken him out Main Street to the fair ground, where the two sat on a grassy bank and talked. The school teacher tried to bring home to the mind of the boy some conception of the difficulties he would have to face as a writer. "You will have to know life," she declared, and her voice trembled with earnestness. She took hold of George Willard's shoulders and turned him about so that she could look into his eyes. A passer-by might have thought them about to embrace. "If you are to become a writer you'll have to stop fooling with words," she explained. "It would be better to give up the notion of writing until you are better prepared. Now it's time to be living. I don't want to frighten you, but I would like to make you understand the import of what you think of attempting. You must not become a mere peddler of words. The thing to learn is to know what people are thinking about, not what they say."

On the evening before that stormy Thursday night, when the Reverend Curtis Hartman sat in the bell tower of the church waiting to look at her body, young Willard had gone to visit the teacher and to borrow a book. It was then the thing happened that confused and puzzled the boy. He had the book under his arm and was preparing to depart. Again Kate Swift talked with great earnestness. Night was coming on and the light in the room grew dim. As he turned to go she spoke his name softly and with an impulsive movement took hold of his hand. Because the reporter was rapidly becoming a man something of his man's appeal, combined with the winsomeness of the boy, stirred the heart of the lonely woman. A passionate desire to have him understand the import of life, to learn to interpret it truly and honestly, swept over her. Leaning forward, her lips brushed his cheek. At the same moment he for the first time became aware of the marked beauty of her features. They were both embarrassed, and to relieve her feeling she became harsh and domineering. "What's the use? It will be ten years before you begin to understand what I mean when I talk to you," she cried passionately.

*

On the night of the storm and while the minister sat in the church waiting for her, Kate Swift went to the office of the *Winesburg Eagle*, intending to have another talk with the boy. After the long walk in the snow she was cold, lonely, and tired. As she came through Main Street she saw the light from the print shop window shining on the snow and on an impulse opened the door and went in. For an hour she sat by the stove in the office talking of life. She talked with passionate earnestness. The impulse that had driven her out into the snow poured itself out into talk. She became inspired as she sometimes did in the presence of the children in school. A great eagerness to open the door of life to the boy, who had been her pupil and who she thought might possess a talent for the understanding of life, had possession of her. So strong was her passion that it became something physical. Again her hands took hold of his shoulders and she turned him about. In the dim light her eyes blazed. She arose and laughed, not sharply as was customary with her, but in a queer, hesitating way. "I must be going," she said. "In a moment, if I stay, I'll be wanting to kiss you."

In the newspaper office a confusion arose. Kate Swift turned and walked to the door. She was a teacher but she was also a woman. As she looked at George Willard, the passionate desire to be loved by a man, that had a thousand times before swept like a storm over her body, took possession of her. In the lamplight George Willard looked no longer a boy, but a man ready to play the part of a man.

The school teacher let George Willard take her into his arms. In the warm little office the air became suddenly heavy and the strength went out of her body. Leaning against a low counter by the door she waited. When he came and put a hand on her shoulder she turned and let her body fall heavily against him. For George Willard the confusion was immediately increased. For a moment he held the body of the woman tightly against his body and then it stiffened. Two sharp little fists began to beat on his face. When the school teacher had run away and left him alone, he walked up and down in the office swearing furiously.

It was into this confusion that the Reverend Curtis Hartman protruded himself. When he came in George Willard thought the town had gone mad. Shaking a bleeding fist in the air, the minister proclaimed the woman George had only a moment before held in his arms an instrument of God bearing a message of truth.

*

George blew out the lamp by the window and locking the door of the print shop went home. Through the hotel office, past Hop Higgins lost in his dream of the raising of ferrets, he went and up into his own room. The fire in the stove had gone out and he undressed in the cold. When he got into bed the sheets were like blankets of dry snow.

George Willard rolled about in the bed on which he had lain in the afternoon hugging the pillow and thinking thoughts of Kate Swift. The words of the minister, who he thought had gone suddenly insane, rang in his ears. His eyes stared about the room. The resentment, natural to the baffled male, passed and he tried to understand what had happened. He could not make it out. Over and over he turned the matter in his mind. Hours passed and he began to think it must be time for another day to come. At four o'clock he pulled the covers up about his neck and tried to sleep. When he became drowsy and closed his eyes, he raised a hand and with it groped about in the darkness. "I have missed something. I have missed something Kate Swift was trying to tell me," he muttered sleepily. Then he slept and in all Winesburg he was the last soul on that winter night to go to sleep.

LONELINESS

HE was the son of Mrs. Al Robinson who once owned a farm on a side road leading off Trunion Pike, east of Winesburg and two miles beyond the town limits. The farmhouse was painted brown and the blinds to all of the windows facing the road were kept closed. In the road before the house a flock of chickens, accompanied by two guinea hens, lay in the deep dust. Enoch lived in the house with his mother in those days and when he was a young boy went to school at the Winesburg High School. Old citizens remembered him as a quiet, smiling youth inclined to silence. He walked in the middle of the road when he came into town and sometimes read a book. Drivers of teams had to shout and swear to make him realize where he was so that he would turn out of the beaten track and let them pass.

When he was twenty-one years old Enoch went to New York City and was a city man for fifteen years. He studied French and went to an art school, hoping to develop a faculty he had for drawing. In his own mind he planned to go to Paris and to finish his art education among the masters there, but that never turned out.

Nothing ever turned out for Enoch Robinson. He could draw well enough and he had many odd delicate thoughts hidden away in his brain that might have expressed themselves through the brush of a painter, but he was always a child and that was a handicap to his worldly development. He never grew up and of course he couldn't understand people and he couldn't make people understand him. The child in him kept bumping against things, against actualities like money and sex and opinions. Once he was hit by a street car and thrown against an iron post. That made him lame. It was one of the many things that kept things from turning out for Enoch Robinson.

In New York City, when he first went there to live and before he became confused and disconcerted by the facts of life, Enoch went about a good deal with young men. He got into a group of other young artists, both men and women, and in the evenings they sometimes came to visit him in his room. Once he got drunk and was taken to a police station where a police magistrate frightened him horribly, and once he tried to have an affair with a woman of the town met on the sidewalk before his lodging house. The woman and Enoch walked together three blocks and then the young man grew afraid and ran away. The woman had been drinking and the incident amused her. She leaned against the wall of a building and laughed so heartily that another man stopped and laughed with her. The two went away together, still laughing, and Enoch crept off to his room trembling and vexed.

The room in which young Robinson lived in New York faced Washington Square and was long and narrow like a hallway. It is important to get that fixed in your mind. The story of Enoch is in fact the story of a room almost more than it is the story of a man.

And so into the room in the evening came young Enoch's friends. There was nothing particularly striking about them except that they were artists of the kind that talk. Everyone knows of the talking artists. Throughout all of the known history of the world they have gathered in rooms and talked. They talk of art and are passionately, almost feverishly, in earnest about it. They think it matters much more than it does.

And so these people gathered and smoked cigarettes and talked and Enoch Robinson, the boy from the farm near Winesburg, was there. He stayed in a corner and for the most part said nothing. How his big blue childlike eyes stared about! On the walls were pictures he had made, crude things, half finished. His friends talked of these. Leaning back in their chairs, they talked and talked with their heads rocking from side to side. Words were said about line and values and composition, lots of words, such as are always being said.

Enoch wanted to talk too but he didn't know how. He was too excited to talk coherently. When he tried he sputtered and stammered and his voice sounded strange and squeaky to him. That made him stop talking. He knew what he wanted to say, but he knew also that he could never by any possibility say it. When a picture he had painted was under discussion, he wanted to burst out with something like this: "You don't get the point," he wanted to explain: "the picture you see doesn't consist of the things you see and say words about. There is something else, something you don't see at all, something you aren't intended to see. Look at this one over here, by the door here, where the light from the window falls on it. The dark spot by the road that you might not notice at all is, you see, the beginning of everything. There is a clump of elders there such as used to grow beside the road before our house back in Winesburg, Ohio, and in among the elders there is something hidden. It is a woman, that's what it is. She has been thrown from a horse and the horse has run away out of sight. Do you not see how the old man who drives a cart looks anxiously about? That is Thad Grayback who has a farm up the road. He is taking corn to Winesburg to be ground into meal at Comstock's mill. He knows there is something in the elders, something hidden away, and yet he doesn't quite know.

"It's a woman you see, that's what it is! It's a woman and, oh, she is lovely! She is hurt and is suffering but she makes no sound. Don't you see how it is? She lies quite still, white and still, and the beauty comes out from her and spreads over everything. It is in the sky back there and all around everywhere. I didn't try to paint the woman, of course. She is too beautiful to be painted. How dull to talk of composition and such things! Why do you not look at the sky and then run away as I used to do when I was a boy back there in Winesburg, Ohio?"

That is the kind of thing young Enoch Robinson trembled to say to the guests who came into his room when he was a young fellow in New York City, but he always ended by saying nothing. Then he began to doubt his own mind. He was afraid the things he felt were not getting expressed in the pictures he painted. In a half indignant mood he stopped inviting people into his room and presently got into the habit of locking the door. He began to think that enough people had visited him, that he did not need people any more. With quick imagination he began to invent his own people to whom he could really talk and to whom he explained the things he had been unable to explain to living people. His room began to be inhabited by the spirits of men and women among whom he went, in his turn saying words. It was as though every one Enoch Robinson had ever seen had left with him some essence of himself, something he could mould and change to suit his own fancy, something that understood all about such things as the wounded woman behind the elders in the pictures.

The mild, blue-eyed young Ohio boy was a complete egotist, as all children are egotists. He did not want friends for the quite simple reason that no child wants friends. He wanted most of all the people of his own mind, people with whom he could really talk, people he could harangue and scold by the hour, servants, you see, to his fancy. Among these people he was always self-confident and bold. They might talk, to be sure, and even have opinions of their own, but always he talked last and best. He was like a writer busy among the figures of his brain, a kind of tiny blue-eyed king he was, in a six-dollar room facing Washington Square in the city of New York.

Then Enoch Robinson got married. He began to get lonely and to want to touch actual flesh and bone people with his hands. Days passed when his room seemed empty. Lust visited his body and desire grew in his mind. At night strange fevers, burning within, kept him awake. He married a girl who sat in a chair next to his own in the art school and went to live in an apartment house in Brooklyn. Two children were born to the woman he married, and Enoch got a job in a place where illustrations are made for advertisements.

That began another phase of Enoch's life. He began to play at a new game. For a while he was very proud of himself in the role of producing citizen of the world. He dismissed the essence of things and played with realities. In the fall he voted at an election and he had a newspaper thrown on his porch each morning. When in the evening he came home from work he got off a street car and walked sedately along behind some business man, striving to look very substantial and important. As a payer of taxes he thought he should post himself on how things are run. "I'm getting to be of some moment, a real part of things, of the state and the city and all that," he told himself with an amusing miniature air of dignity. Once coming home from Philadelphia, he had a discussion with a man met on a train. Enoch talked about the advisability of the government's owning and operating the railroads and the man gave him a cigar. It was Enoch's notion that such a move on the part of the government would be a good thing, and he grew quite excited as he talked. Later he remembered his own words with pleasure. "I gave him something to think about, that fellow," he muttered to himself as he climbed the stairs to his Brooklyn apartment.

To be sure, Enoch's marriage did not turn out. He himself brought it to an end. He began to feel choked and walled in by the life in the apartment, and to feel toward his wife and even toward his children as he had felt concerning the friends who once came to visit him. He began to tell little lies about business engagements that would give him freedom to walk alone in the street at night and, the chance offering, he secretly re-rented the room facing Washington Square. Then Mrs. Al Robinson died on the farm near Winesburg, and he got eight thousand dollars from the bank that acted as trustee of her estate. That took Enoch out of the world of men altogether. He gave the money to his wife and told her he could not live in the apartment any more. She cried and was angry and threatened, but he only stared at her and went his own way. In reality the wife did not care much. She thought

Enoch slightly insane and was a little afraid of him. When it was quite sure that he would never come back, she took the two children and went to a village in Connecticut where she had lived as a girl. In the end she married a man who bought and sold real estate and was contented enough.

And so Enoch Robinson stayed in the New York room among the people of his fancy, playing with them, talking to them, happy as a child is happy. They were an odd lot, Enoch's people. They were made, I suppose, out of real people he had seen and who had for some obscure reason made an appeal to him. There was a woman with a sword in her hand, an old man with a long white beard who went about followed by a dog, a young girl whose stockings were always coming down and hanging over her shoe tops. There must have been two dozen of the shadow people, invented by the child-mind of Enoch Robinson, who lived in the room with him.

And Enoch was happy. Into the room he went and locked the door. With an absurd air of importance he talked aloud, giving instructions, making comments on life. He was happy and satisfied to go on making his living in the advertising place until something happened. Of course something did happen. That is why he went back to live in Winesburg and why we know about him. The thing that happened was a woman. It would be that way. He was too happy. Something had to come into his world. Something had to drive him out of the New York room to live out his life, an obscure, jerky little figure, bobbing up and down on the streets of an Ohio town at evening when the sun was going down behind the roof of Wesley Moyer's livery barn.

About the thing that happened. Enoch told George Willard about it one night. He wanted to talk to someone, and he chose the young newspaper reporter because the two happened to be thrown together at a time when the younger man was in a mood to understand.

Youthful sadness, young man's sadness, the sadness of a growing boy in a village at the year's end opened the lips

of the old man. The sadness was in the heart of George
Willard and was without meaning, but it appealed to Enoch
Robinson.

It rained on the evening when the two met and talked, a
drizzly wet October rain. The fruition of the year had come
and the night should have been fine with a moon in the sky and
the crisp sharp promise of frost in the air, but it wasn't that way.
It rained and little puddles of water shone under the street
lamps on Main Street. In the woods in the darkness beyond
the Fair Ground water dripped from the black trees. Beneath
the trees wet leaves were pasted against tree roots that protruded from the ground. In gardens back of houses in Winesburg dry shriveled potato vines lay sprawling on the ground.
Men who had finished the evening meal and who had planned
to go uptown to talk the evening away with other men at the
back of some store changed their minds. George Willard
tramped about in the rain and was glad that it rained. He felt
that way. He was like Enoch Robinson on the evenings when
the old man came down out of his room and wandered alone in
the streets. He was like that only that George Willard had
become a tall young man and did not think it manly to weep
and carry on. For a month his mother had been very ill and
that had something to do with his sadness, but not much. He
thought about himself and to the young that always brings
sadness.

Enoch Robinson and George Willard met beneath a
wooden awning that extended out over the sidewalk before
Voight's wagon shop on Maumee Street just off the main street
of Winesburg. They went together from there through the
rain-washed streets to the older man's room on the third floor
of the Heffner Block. The young reporter went willingly
enough. Enoch Robinson asked him to go after the two had
talked for ten minutes. The boy was a little afraid but had
never been more curious in his life. A hundred times he
had heard the old man spoken of as a little off his head and
he thought himself rather brave and manly to go at all. From

the very beginning, in the street in the rain, the old man talked in a queer way, trying to tell the story of the room in Washington Square and of his life in the room. "You'll understand if you try hard enough," he said conclusively. "I have looked at you when you went past me on the street and I think you can understand. It isn't hard. All you have to do is to believe what I say, just listen and believe, that's all there is to it."

It was past eleven o'clock that evening when Old Enoch, talking to George Willard in the room in the Heffner Block, came to the vital thing, the story of the woman and of what drove him out of the city to live out his life alone and defeated in Winesburg. He sat on a cot by the window with his head in his hand and George Willard was in a chair by a table. A kerosene lamp sat on the table and the room, although almost bare of furniture, was scrupulously clean. As the man talked George Willard began to feel that he would like to get out of the chair and sit on the cot also. He wanted to put his arms about the little old man. In the half darkness the man talked and the boy listened, filled with sadness.

"She got to coming in there after there hadn't been anyone in the room for years," said Enoch Robinson. "She saw me in the hallway of the house and we got acquainted. I don't know just what she did in her own room. I never went there. I think she was a musician and played a violin. Every now and then she came and knocked at the door and I opened it. In she came and sat down beside me, just sat and looked about and said nothing. Anyway, she said nothing that mattered."

The old man arose from the cot and moved about the room. The overcoat he wore was wet from the rain and drops of water kept falling with a soft little thump on the floor. When he again sat upon the cot George Willard got out of the chair and sat beside him.

"I had a feeling about her. She sat there in the room with me and she was too big for the room. I felt that she was driving everything else away. We just talked of little things, but I couldn't sit still. I wanted to touch her with my fingers and to kiss her. Her hands were so strong and her face was so good and she looked at me all the time."

The trembling voice of the old man became silent and his body shook as from a chill. "I was afraid," he whispered. "I was terribly afraid. I didn't want to let her come in when she knocked at the door but I couldn't sit still. 'No, no,' I said to myself, but I got up and opened the door just the same. She was so grown up, you see. She was a woman. I thought she would be bigger than I was there in that room."

Enoch Robinson stared at George Willard, his childlike blue eyes shining in the lamplight. Again he shivered. "I wanted her and all the time I didn't want her," he explained. "Then I began to tell her about my people, about everything that meant anything to me. I tried to keep quiet, to keep myself to myself, but I couldn't. I felt just as I did about opening the door. Sometimes I ached to have her go away and never come back any more."

The old man sprang to his feet and his voice shook with excitement. "One night something happened. I became mad to make her understand me and to know what a big thing I was in that room. I wanted her to see how important I was. I told her over and over. When she tried to go away, I ran and locked the door. I followed her about. I talked and talked and then all of a sudden things went to smash. A look came into her eyes and I knew she did understand. Maybe she had understood all the time. I was furious. I couldn't stand it. I wanted her to understand but, don't you see, I couldn't let her understand. I felt that then she would know everything, that I would be submerged, drowned out, you see. That's how it is. I don't know why."

The old man dropped into a chair by the lamp and the boy listened, filled with awe. "Go away, boy," said the man. "Don't stay here with me any more. I thought it might be a good thing to tell you but it isn't. I don't want to talk any more. Go away."

George Willard shook his head and a note of command came into his voice. "Don't stop now. Tell me the rest of it," he commanded sharply. "What happened? Tell me the rest of the story."

Enoch Robinson sprang to his feet and ran to the window that looked down into the deserted main street of Winesburg. George Willard followed. By the window the two stood, the tall awkward boy-man and the little wrinkled man-boy. The childish, eager voice carried forward the tale. "I swore at her," he explained. "I said vile words. I ordered her to go away and not to come back. Oh, I said terrible things. At first she pretended not to understand but I kept at it. I screamed and stamped on the floor. I made the house ring with my curses. I didn't want ever to see her again and I knew, after some of the things I said, that I never would see her again."

The old man's voice broke and he shook his head. "Things went to smash," he said quietly and sadly. "Out she went through the door and all the life there had been in the room followed her out. She took all of my people away. They all went out through the door after her. That's the way it was."

George Willard turned and went out of Enoch Robinson's room. In the darkness by the window, as he went through the door, he could hear the thin old voice whimpering and complaining. "I'm alone, all alone here," said the voice. "It was warm and friendly in my room but now I'm all alone."

AN AWAKENING

BELLE CARPENTER had a dark skin, grey eyes and thick lips. She was tall and strong. When black thoughts visited her she grew angry and wished she were a man and could fight someone with her fists. She worked in the millinery shop kept by Mrs. Kate McHugh and during the day sat trimming hats by a window at the rear of the store. She was the daughter of Henry Carpenter, bookkeeper in the First National Bank of Winesburg, and lived with him in a gloomy old house far out at the end of Buckeye Street. The house was surrounded by pine trees and there was no grass beneath the trees. A rusty tin eaves-trough had slipped from its fastenings at the back of the house and when the wind blew it beat against the roof of a small shed, making a dismal drumming noise that sometimes persisted all through the night.

When she was a young girl Henry Carpenter made life almost unbearable for Belle, but as she emerged from girlhood into womanhood he lost his power over her. The bookkeeper's life was made up of innumerable little pettinesses. When he went to the bank in the morning he stepped into a closet and put on a black alpaca coat that had become shabby with age. At night when he returned to his home he donned another black alpaca coat. Every evening he pressed the clothes worn in the streets. He had invented an arrangement of boards for the purpose. The trousers to his street suit were placed between the boards and the boards were clamped together with heavy screws. In the morning he wiped the boards with a damp cloth and stood them upright behind the dining room door. If they were moved during the day he was speechless with anger and did not recover his equilibrium for a week.

The bank cashier was a little bully and was afraid of his daughter. She, he realized, knew the story of his brutal treatment of her mother and hated him for it. One day she went home at noon and carried a handful of soft mud, taken from the road, into the house. With the mud she smeared the face of the boards used for the pressing of trousers and then went back to her work feeling relieved and happy.

Belle Carpenter occasionally walked out in the evening with George Willard. Secretly she loved another man, but her love affair, about which no one knew, caused her much anxiety. She was in love with Ed Handby, bartender in Ed Griffith's Saloon, and went about with the young reporter as a kind of relief to her feelings. She did not think that her station in life would permit her to be seen in the company of the bartender and walked about under the trees with George Willard and let him kiss her to relieve a longing that was very insistent in her nature. She felt that she could keep the younger man within bounds. About Ed Handby she was somewhat uncertain.

Handby, the bartender, was a tall, broad-shouldered man of thirty who lived in a room upstairs above Griffith's saloon. His fists were large and his eyes unusually small, but his voice, as though striving to conceal the power back of his fists, was soft and quiet.

At twenty-five the bartender had inherited a large farm from an uncle in Indiana. When sold, the farm brought in eight thousand dollars which Ed spent in six months. Going to Sandusky, on Lake Erie, he began an orgy of dissipation, the story of which afterward filled his home town with awe. Here and there he went throwing the money about, driving carriages through the streets, giving wine parties to crowds of men and women, playing cards for high stakes and keeping mistresses whose wardrobes cost him hundreds of dollars. One night at a resort called Cedar Point, he got into a fight and ran amuck like a wild thing. With his fist he broke a large mirror in the wash room of a hotel and later went about smashing windows and breaking chairs in dance halls for the joy of hearing the glass rattle on the floor and seeing the terror in the eyes of clerks who had come from Sandusky to spend the evening at the resort with their sweethearts.

The affair between Ed Handby and Belle Carpenter on the surface amounted to nothing. He had succeeded in spending but one evening in her company. On that evening he hired a horse and buggy at Wesley Moyer's livery barn and took her for a drive. The conviction that she was the woman his nature demanded and that he must get her settled upon him and he told her of his desires. The bartender was ready to marry and to begin trying to earn money for the support of his wife, but so simple was his nature that he found it difficult to explain his intentions. His body ached with physical longing and with his body he expressed himself. Taking the milliner into his arms and holding her tightly in spite of her struggles, he kissed her until she became helpless. Then he brought her back to town and let her out of the buggy. "When I get hold of you again I'll not let you go. You can't play with me," he declared as he turned to drive away. Then, jumping out of the buggy, he gripped her shoulders with his strong hands. "I'll keep you for good the next time," he said. "You might as well make up your mind to that. It's you and me for it and I'm going to have you before I get through."

One night in January when there was a new moon George Willard, who was in Ed Handby's mind the only obstacle to his getting Belle Carpenter, went for a walk. Early that evening George went into Ransom Surbeck's pool room with Seth Richmond and Art Wilson, son of the town butcher. Seth Richmond stood with his back against the wall and remained silent, but George Willard talked. The pool room was filled with Winesburg boys and they talked of women. The young reporter got into that vein. He said that women should look out for themselves, that the fellow who went out with a girl was not responsible for what happened. As he talked he looked about, eager for attention. He held the floor for five minutes and then Art Wilson began to talk. Art was learning the barber's trade in Cal Prouse's shop and already began to consider himself an authority in such matters as baseball, horse racing, drinking, and going about with women. He began to tell of a night when he with two men from Winesburg went into a house of prostitution at the county seat. The butcher's son held a cigar in the side of his mouth and as he talked spat on the floor. "The women in the place couldn't embarrass me although they tried hard enough," he boasted. "One of the girls in the house tried to get fresh, but I fooled her. As soon as she began to talk I went and sat in her lap. Everyone in the room laughed when I kissed her. I taught her to let me alone."

George Willard went out of the pool room and into Main Street. For days the weather had been bitter cold with a high wind blowing down on the town from Lake Erie, eighteen miles to the north, but on that night the wind had died away and a new moon made the night unusually lovely. Without thinking where he was going or what he wanted to do, George went out of Main Street and began walking in dimly lighted streets filled with frame houses.

Out of doors under the black sky filled with stars he forgot his companions of the pool room. Because it was dark and he was alone he began to talk aloud. In a spirit of play he reeled along the street imitating a drunken man and then imagined himself a soldier clad in shining boots that reached to the knees and wearing a sword that jingled as he walked. As a soldier he pictured himself as an inspector, passing before a long line of men who stood at attention. He began to examine the accoutrements of the men. Before a tree he stopped and began to scold. "Your pack is not in order," he said sharply. "How many times will I have to speak of this matter? Everything must be in order here. We have a difficult task before us and no difficult task can be done without order."

Hypnotized by his own words, the young man stumbled along the board sidewalk saying more words. "There is a law for armies and for men too," he muttered, lost in reflection. "The law begins with little things and spreads out until it covers everything. In every little thing there must be order, in the place where men work, in their clothes, in their thoughts. I myself must be orderly. I must learn that law. I must get myself into touch with something orderly and big that swings through the night like a star. In my little way I must begin to learn something, to give and swing and work with life, with the law."

George Willard stopped by a picket fence near a street lamp and his body began to tremble. He had never before thought such thoughts as had just come into his head and he wondered where they had come from. For the moment it seemed to him that some voice outside of himself had been talking as he walked. He was amazed and delighted with his own mind and when he walked on again spoke of the matter with fervor. "To come out of Ransom Surbeck's pool room and think things like that," he whispered. "It is better to be alone. If I talked like Art Wilson the boys would understand me but they wouldn't understand what I've been thinking down here."

In Winesburg, as in all Ohio towns of twenty years ago, there was a section in which lived day laborers. As the time of factories had not yet come, the laborers worked in the fields or were section hands on the railroads. They worked twelve hours a day and received one dollar for the long day of toil. The houses in which they lived were small cheaply constructed wooden affairs with a garden at the back. The more comfortable among them kept cows and perhaps a pig, housed in a little shed at the rear of the garden.

With his head filled with resounding thoughts, George Willard walked into such a street on the clear January night. The street was dimly lighted and in places there was no sidewalk. In the scene that lay about him there was something that excited his already aroused fancy. For a year he had been devoting all of his odd moments to the reading of books and now some tale he had read concerning life in old world towns of the middle ages came sharply back to his mind so that he stumbled forward with the curious feeling of one revisiting a place that had been a part of some former existence. On an impulse he turned out of the street and went into a little dark alleyway behind the sheds in which lived the cows and pigs.

For a half hour he stayed in the alleyway, smelling the strong smell of animals too closely housed and letting his mind play with the strange new thoughts that came to him. The very rankness of the smell of manure in the clear sweet air awoke something heady in his brain. The poor little houses lighted by kerosene lamps, the smoke from the chimneys mounting straight up into the clear air, the grunting of pigs, the women clad in cheap calico dresses and washing dishes in the kitchens, the footsteps of men coming out of the houses and going off to the stores and saloons of Main Street, the dogs barking and the children crying—all of these things made him seem, as he lurked in the darkness, oddly detached and apart from all life.

The excited young man, unable to bear the weight of his own thoughts, began to move cautiously along the alleyway. A dog attacked him and had to be driven away with stones, and a man appeared at the door of one of the houses and swore at the dog. George went into a vacant lot and throwing back his head looked up at the sky. He felt unutterably big and remade by the simple experience through which he had been passing and in a kind of fervor of emotion put up his hands, thrusting them into the darkness above his head and muttering words. The desire to say words overcame him and he said words without meaning, rolling them over on his tongue and saying them because they were brave words, full of meaning. "Death," he muttered, "night, the sea, fear, loveliness."

George Willard came out of the vacant lot and stood again on the sidewalk facing the houses. He felt that all of the people in the little street must be brothers and sisters to him and he wished he had the courage to call them out of their houses and to shake their hands. "If there were only a woman here I would take hold of her hand and we would run until we were both tired out," he thought. "That would make me feel better." With the thought of a woman in his mind he walked out of the street and went toward the house where Belle Carpenter lived. He thought she would understand his mood and that he could achieve in her presence a position he had long been wanting to achieve. In the past when he had been with her and had kissed her lips he had come away filled with anger at himself. He had felt like one being used for some obscure purpose and had not enjoyed the feeling. Now he thought he had suddenly become too big to be used.

When George got to Belle Carpenter's house there had already been a visitor there before him. Ed Handby had come to the door and calling Belle out of the house had tried to talk to her. He had wanted to ask the woman to come away with him and to be his wife, but when she came and stood by the door he lost his self-assurance and became sullen. "You stay away from that kid," he growled, thinking of George Willard, and then, not knowing what else to say, turned to go away. "If I catch you together I will break your bones and his too," he added. The bartender had come to woo, not to threaten, and was angry with himself because of his failure.

When her lover had departed Belle went indoors and ran hurriedly upstairs. From a window at the upper part of the house she saw Ed Handby cross the street and sit down on a horse block before the house of a neighbor. In the dim light the man sat motionless holding his head in his hands. She was made happy by the sight, and when George Willard came to the door she greeted him effusively and hurriedly put on her hat. She thought that, as she walked through the streets with young Willard, Ed Handby would follow and she wanted to make him suffer.

For an hour Belle Carpenter and the young reporter walked about under the trees in the sweet night air. George Willard was full of big words. The sense of power that had come to him during the hour in the darkness in the alleyway remained with him and he talked boldly, swaggering along and swinging his arms about. He wanted to make Belle Carpenter realize that he was aware of his former weakness and that he had changed.

"You'll find me different," he declared, thrusting his hands into his pockets and looking boldly into her eyes. "I don't know why but it is so. You've got to take me for a man or let me alone. That's how it is."

Up and down the quiet streets under the new moon went the woman and the boy. When George had finished talking they turned down a side street and went across a bridge into a path that ran up the side of a hill. The hill began at Waterworks Pond and climbed upwards to the Winesburg Fair Grounds. On the hillside grew dense bushes and small trees and among the bushes were little open spaces carpeted with long grass, now stiff and frozen.

As he walked behind the woman up the hill George Willard's heart began to beat rapidly and his shoulders straightened. Suddenly he decided that Belle Carpenter was about to surrender herself to him. The new force that had manifested itself in him had, he felt, been at work upon her and had led to her conquest. The thought made him half drunk with the sense of masculine power. Although he had been annoyed that as they walked about she had not seemed to be listening to his words, the fact that she had accompanied him to this place took all his doubts away. "It is different. Everything has become different," he thought and taking hold of her shoulder turned her about and stood looking at her, his eyes shining with pride.

Belle Carpenter did not resist. When he kissed her upon the lips she leaned heavily against him and looked over his shoulder into the darkness. In her whole attitude there was a suggestion of waiting. Again, as in the alleyway, George Willard's mind ran off into words and, holding the woman tightly he whispered the words into the still night. "Lust," he whispered, "lust and night and women."

George Willard did not understand what happened to him that night on the hillside. Later, when he got to his own room, he wanted to weep and then grew half insane with anger and hate. He hated Belle Carpenter and was sure that all his life he would continue to hate her. On the hillside he had led the woman to one of the little open spaces among the bushes and had dropped to his knees beside her. As in the vacant lot, by the laborers' houses, he had put up his hands in gratitude for the new power in himself and was waiting for the woman to speak when Ed Handby appeared.

The bartender did not want to beat the boy, who he thought had tried to take his woman away. He knew that beating was unnecessary, that he had power within himself to accomplish his purpose without using his fists. Gripping George by the shoulder and pulling him to his feet, he held him with one hand while he looked at Belle Carpenter seated on the grass. Then with a quick wide movement of his arm he sent the younger man sprawling away into the bushes and began to bully the woman, who had risen to her feet. "You're no good," he said roughly. "I've half a mind not to bother with you. I'd let you alone if I didn't want you so much."

On his hands and knees in the bushes George Willard stared at the scene before him and tried hard to think. He prepared to spring at the man who had humiliated him. To be beaten seemed to be infinitely better than to be thus hurled ignominiously aside.

Three times the young reporter sprang at Ed Handby and each time the bartender, catching him by the shoulder, hurled him back into the bushes. The older man seemed prepared to keep the exercise going indefinitely but George Willard's head struck the root of a tree and he lay still. Then Ed Hanby took Belle Carpenter by the arm and marched her away.

George heard the man and woman making their way through the bushes. As he crept down the hillside his heart was sick within him. He hated himself and he hated the fate that had brought about his humiliation. When his mind went back to the hour alone in the alleyway he was puzzled and stopping in the darkness listened, hoping to hear again the voice outside himself that had so short a time before put new courage into his heart. When his way homeward led him again into the street of frame houses he could not bear the sight and began to run, wanting to get quickly out of the neighborhood that now seemed to him utterly squalid and commonplace.

"QUEER"

FROM his seat on a box in the rough board shed that stuck like a burr on the rear of Cowley & Son's store in Winesburg, Elmer Cowley, the junior member of the firm, could see through a dirty window into the printshop of the *Winesburg Eagle*. Elmer was putting new shoelaces in his shoes. They did not go in readily and he had to take the shoes off. With the shoes in his hand he sat looking at a large hole in the heel of one of his stockings. Then looking quickly up he saw George Willard, the only newspaper reporter in Winesburg, standing at the back door of the *Eagle* printshop and staring absent-mindedly about. "Well, well, what next!" exclaimed the young man with the shoes in his hand, jumping to his feet and creeping away from the window.

A flush crept into Elmer Cowley's face and his hands began to tremble. In Cowley & Son's store a Jewish traveling sales-man stood by the counter talking to his father. He imagined the reporter could hear what was being said and the thought made him furious. With one of the shoes still held in his hand he stood in a corner of the shed and stamped with a stockinged foot upon the board floor.

Cowley & Son's store did not face the main street of Wines-burg. The front was on Maumee Street and beyond it was Voight's wagon shop and a shed for the sheltering of farmers' horses. Beside the store an alleyway ran behind the main street stores and all day drays and delivery wagons, intent on bringing in and taking out goods, passed up and down. The store itself was indescribable. Will Henderson once said of it that it sold everything and nothing. In the window facing Maumee Street stood a chunk of coal as large as an apple barrel, to indicate that orders for coal were taken, and beside the black mass of the coal stood three combs of honey grown brown and dirty in their wooden frames.

The honey had stood in the store window for six months. It was for sale as were also the coat hangers, patent suspender buttons, cans of roof paint, bottles of rheumatism cure and a substitute for coffee that companioned the honey in its patient willingness to serve the public.

Ebenezer Cowley, the man who stood in the store listening to the eager patter of words that fell from the lips of the traveling man, was tall and lean and looked unwashed. On his scrawny neck was a large wen partially covered by a grey beard. He wore a long Prince Albert coat. The coat had been purchased to serve as a wedding garment. Before he became a merchant Ebenezer was a farmer and after his marriage he wore the Prince Albert coat to church on Sundays and on Saturday afternoons when he came into town to trade. When he sold the farm to become a merchant he wore the coat constantly. It had become brown with age and was covered with grease spots, but in it Ebenezer always felt dressed up and ready for the day in town.

As a merchant Ebenezer was not happily placed in life and he had not been happily placed as a farmer. Still he existed. His family, consisting of a daughter named Mabel and the son, lived with him in rooms above the store and it did not cost them much to live. His troubles were not financial. His unhappiness as a merchant lay in the fact that when a traveling man with wares to be sold came in at the front door he was afraid. Behind the counter he stood shaking his head. He was afraid, first that he would stubbornly refuse to buy and thus lose the opportunity to sell again; second that he would not be stubborn enough and would in a moment of weakness buy what could not be sold.

In the store on the morning when Elmer Cowley saw George Willard standing and apparently listening at the back door of the *Eagle* printshop, a situation had arisen that always stirred the son's wrath. The traveling man talked and Ebenezer listened, his whole figure expressing uncertainty. "You see how quickly it is done," said the traveling man who had for sale a small flat metal substitute for collar buttons. With one hand he quickly unfastened a collar from his shirt and then fastened it on again. He assumed a flattering wheedling tone. "I tell you what, men have come to the end of all this fooling with collar buttons and you are the man to make money out of the change that is coming. I am offering you the exclusive agency for this town. Take twenty dozen of these fasteners and I'll not visit any other store. I'll leave the field to you."

The traveling man leaned over the counter and tapped with his finger on Ebenezer's breast. "It's an opportunity and I want you to take it," he urged. "A friend of mine told me about you. 'See that man Cowley,' he said. 'He's a live one.'"

The traveling man paused and waited. Taking a book from his pocket he began writing out the order. Still holding the shoe in his hand Elmer Cowley went through the store, past the two absorbed men, to a glass show case near the front door. He took a cheap revolver from the case and began to wave it about. "You get out of here!" he shrieked. "We don't want any collar fasteners here." An idea came to him. "Mind, I'm not making any threat," he added. "I don't say I'll shoot. Maybe I just took this gun out of the case to look at it. But you better get out. Yes sir, I'll say that. You better grab up your things and get out."

The young storekeeper's voice rose to a scream and going behind the counter he began to advance upon the two men. "We're through being fools here!" he cried. "We ain't going to buy any more stuff until we begin to sell. We ain't going to keep on being queer and have folks staring and listening. You get out of here!"

The traveling man left. Raking the samples of collar fasteners off the counter into a black leather bag, he ran. He was a small man and very bow-legged and he ran awkwardly. The black bag caught against the door and he stumbled and fell. "Crazy, that's what he is—crazy!" he sputtered as he arose from the sidewalk and hurried away.

In the store Elmer Cowley and his father stared at each other. Now that the immediate object of his wrath had fled, the younger man was embarrassed. "Well, I meant it. I think we've been queer long enough," he declared, going to the showcase and replacing the revolver. Sitting on a barrel he pulled on and fastened the shoe he had been holding in his hand. He was waiting for some word of understanding from his father but when Ebenezer spoke his words only served to reawaken the wrath in the son and the young man ran out of the store without replying. Scratching his grey beard with his long dirty fingers, the merchant looked at his son with the same wavering uncertain stare with which he had confronted the traveling man. "I'll be starched," he said softly. "Well, well, I'll be washed and ironed and starched!"

Elmer Cowley went out of Winesburg and along a country road that paralleled the railroad track. He did not know where he was going or what he was going to do. In the shelter of a deep cut where the road, after turning sharply to the right, dipped under the tracks he stopped and the passion that had been the cause of his outburst in the store began to again find expression. "I will not be queer—one to be looked at and listened to," he declared aloud. "I'll be like other people. I'll show that George Willard. He'll find out. I'll show him!"

The distraught young man stood in the middle of the road and glared back at the town. He did not know the reporter George Willard and had no special feeling concerning the tall boy who ran about town gathering the town news. The reporter had merely come, by his presence in the office and in the printshop of the *Winesburg Eagle*, to stand for something in the young merchant's mind. He thought the boy who passed and repassed Cowley & Son's store and who stopped to talk to people in the street must be thinking of him and perhaps laughing at him. George Willard, he felt, belonged to the town, typified the town, represented in his person the spirit of the town. Elmer Cowley could not have believed that George Willard had also his days of unhappiness, that vague hungers and secret unnamable desires visited also his mind. Did he not represent public opinion and had not the public opinion of Winesburg condemned the Cowleys to queerness? Did he not walk whistling and laughing through Main Street? Might not one by striking his person strike also the greater enemy—the thing that smiled and went its own way—the judgment of Winesburg?

Elmer Cowley was extraordinarily tall and his arms were long and powerful. His hair, his eyebrows, and the downy beard that had begun to grow upon his chin, were pale almost to whiteness. His teeth protruded from between his lips and his eyes were blue with the colorless blueness of the marbles called "aggies" that the boys of Winesburg carried in their pockets. Elmer had lived in Winesburg for a year and had made no friends. He was, he felt, one condemned to go through life without friends and he hated the thought.

Sullenly the tall young man tramped along the road with his hands stuffed into his trouser pockets. The day was cold with a raw wind, but presently the sun began to shine and the road became soft and muddy. The tops of the ridges of frozen mud that formed the road began to melt and the mud clung to Elmer's shoes. His feet became cold. When he had gone several miles he turned off the road, crossed a field and entered a wood. In the wood he gathered sticks to build a fire by which he sat trying to warm himself, miserable in body and in mind.

For two hours he sat on the log by the fire and then, arising and creeping cautiously through a mass of underbrush, he went to a fence and looked across fields to a small farmhouse surrounded by low sheds. A smile came to his lips and he began making motions with his long arms to a man who was husking corn in one of the fields.

In his hour of misery the young merchant had returned to the farm where he had lived through boyhood and where there was another human being to whom he felt he could explain himself. The man on the farm was a half-witted old

fellow named Mook. He had once been employed by Ebenezer Cowley and had stayed on the farm when it was sold. The
old man lived in one of the unpainted sheds back of the farmhouse and puttered about all day in the fields.

Mook the half-wit lived happily. With childlike faith he
believed in the intelligence of the animals that lived in the
sheds with him, and when he was lonely held long conversa-
tions with the cows, the pigs, and even with the chickens that
ran about the barnyard. He it was who had put the expression
regarding being "laundered" into the mouth of his former
employer. When excited or surprised by anything he smiled
vaguely and muttered: "I'll be washed and ironed. Well, well,
I'll be washed and ironed and starched."

When the half-witted old man left his husking of corn and
came into the wood to meet Elmer Cowley, he was neither
surprised nor especially interested in the sudden appearance
of the young man. His feet also were cold and he sat on the log
by the fire, grateful for the warmth and apparently indifferent
to what Elmer had to say.

Elmer talked earnestly and with great freedom, walking up
and down and waving his arms about. "You don't understand
what's the matter with me so of course you don't care," he
declared. "With me it's different. Look how it has always been
with me. Father is queer and mother was queer, too. Even the
clothes mother used to wear were not like other people's
clothes, and look at that coat in which father goes about
there in town, thinking he's dressed up, too. Why don't he
get a new one? It wouldn't cost much. I'll tell you why. Father
doesn't know and when mother was alive she didn't know
either. Mabel is different. She knows but she won't say anything. I will, though. I'm not going to be stared at any longer.
Why look here, Mook, father doesn't know that his store there
in town is just a queer jumble, that he'll never sell the stuff he
buys. He knows nothing about it. Sometimes he's a little
worried that trade doesn't come and then he goes and buys
something else. In the evenings he sits by the fire upstairs and

says trade will come after a while. He isn't worried. He's queer. He doesn't know enough to be worried."

The excited young man became more excited. "He don't know but I know," he shouted, stopping to gaze down into the dumb, unresponsive face of the half-wit. "I know too well. I can't stand it. When we lived out here it was different. I worked and at night I went to bed and slept. I wasn't always seeing people and thinking as I am now. In the evening, there in town, I go to the post office or to the depot to see the train come in, and no one says anything to me. Everyone stands around and laughs and they talk but they say nothing to me. Then I feel so queer that I can't talk either. I go away. I don't say anything. I can't."

The fury of the young man became uncontrollable. "I won't stand it," he yelled, looking up at the bare branches of the trees. "I'm not made to stand it."

Maddened by the dull face of the man on the log by the fire, Elmer turned and glared at him as he had glared back along the road at the town of Winesburg. "Go on back to work," he screamed. "What good does it do me to talk to you?" A thought came to him and his voice dropped. "I'm a coward too, eh?" he muttered. "Do you know why I came clear out here afoot? I had to tell some one and you were the only one I could tell. I hunted out another queer one, you see. I ran away, that's what I did. I couldn't stand up to some one like that George Willard. I had to come to you. I ought to tell him and I will."

Again his voice arose to a shout and his arms flew about. "I will tell him. I won't be queer. I don't care what they think. I won't stand it."

Elmer Cowley ran out of the woods leaving the half-wit sitting on the log before the fire. Presently the old man arose and climbing over the fence went back to his work in the corn. "I'll be washed and ironed and starched," he declared. "Well, well, I'll be washed and ironed." Mook was interested. He went along a lane to a field where two cows stood nibbling at a straw stack. "Elmer was here," he said to the cows. "Elmer is crazy. You better get behind the stack where he don't see you. He'll hurt someone yet, Elmer will."

At eight o'clock that evening Elmer Cowley put his head in at the front door of the office of the *Winesburg Eagle* where George Willard sat writing. His cap was pulled down over his eyes and a sullen determined look was on his face. "You come on outside with me," he said, stepping in and closing the door. He kept his hand on the knob as though prepared to resist anyone else coming in. "You just come along outside. I want to see you."

George Willard and Elmer Cowley walked through the main street of Winesburg. The night was cold and George Willard had on a new overcoat and looked very spruce and dressed up. He thrust his hands into the overcoat pockets and looked inquiringly at his companion. He had long been wanting to make friends with the young merchant and find out what was in his mind. Now he thought he saw a chance and was delighted. "I wonder what he's up to? Perhaps he thinks he has a piece of news for the paper. It can't be a fire because I haven't heard the fire bell and there isn't anyone running," he thought.

In the main street of Winesburg, on the cold November evening, but few citizens appeared and these hurried along bent on getting to the stove at the back of some store. The windows of the stores were frosted and the wind rattled the tin sign that hung over the entrance to the stairway leading to Doctor Welling's office. Before Hern's Grocery a basket of apples and a rack filled with new brooms stood on the sidewalk. Elmer Cowley stopped and stood facing George Willard. He tried to talk and his arms began to pump up and down. His face worked spasmodically. He seemed about to shout. "Oh, you go on back," he cried. "Don't stay out here with me. I ain't got anything to tell you. I don't want to see you at all."

For three hours the distracted young merchant wandered through the resident streets of Winesburg blind with anger, brought on by his failure to declare his determination not to be queer. Bitterly the sense of defeat settled upon him and he wanted to weep. After the hours of futile sputtering at nothingness that had occupied the afternoon and his failure in the presence of the young reporter, he thought he could see no hope of a future for himself.

And then a new idea dawned for him. In the darkness that surrounded him he began to see a light. Going to the now darkened store, where Cowley & Son had for over a year waited vainly for trade to come, he crept stealthily in and felt about in a barrel that stood by the stove at the rear. In the barrel beneath shavings lay a tin box containing Cowley & Son's cash. Every evening Ebenezer Cowley put the box in the barrel when he closed the store and went upstairs to bed. "They wouldn't never think of a careless place like that," he told himself, thinking of robbers.

Elmer took twenty dollars, two ten dollar bills, from the little roll containing perhaps four hundred dollars, the cash left from the sale of the farm. Then replacing the box beneath the shavings he went quietly out at the front door and walked again in the streets.

The idea that he thought might put an end to all of his unhappiness was very simple. "I will get out of here, run away from home," he told himself. He knew that a local freight train passed through Winesburg at midnight and went on to Cleveland where it arrived at dawn. He would steal a ride on the local and when he got to Cleveland would lose himself in the crowds there. He would get work in some shop and become friends with the other workmen. Gradually he would become like other men and would be indistinguishable. Then he could talk and laugh. He would no longer be queer and would make friends. Life would begin to have warmth and meaning for him as it had for others.

The tall awkward young man, striding through the streets, laughed at himself because he had been angry and had been half afraid of George Willard. He decided he would have his talk with the young reporter before he left town, that he would tell him about things, perhaps challenge him, challenge all of Winesburg through him.

Aglow with new confidence Elmer went to the office of the New Willard House and pounded on the door. A sleep-eyed boy slept on a cot in the office. He received no salary but was fed at the hotel table and bore with pride the title of "night clerk." Before the boy Elmer was bold, insistent. "You wake him up," he commanded. "You tell him to come down by the depot. I got to see him and I'm going away on the local. Tell him to dress and come on down. I ain't got much time."

The midnight local had finished its work in Winesburg and the trainsmen were coupling cars, swinging lanterns and preparing to resume their flight east. George Willard, rubbing his eyes and again wearing the new overcoat, ran down to the station platform afire with curiosity. "Well, here I am. What do you want? You've got something to tell me, eh?" he said.

Elmer tried to explain. He wet his lips with his tongue and looked at the train that had begun to groan and get under way. "Well, you see," he began, and then lost control of his tongue. "I'll be washed and ironed. I'll be washed and ironed and starched," he muttered half incoherently.

Elmer Cowley danced with fury beside the groaning train in the darkness on the station platform. Lights leaped into the air and bobbed up and down before his eyes. Taking the two ten dollar bills from his pocket he thrust them into George Willard's hand. "Take them," he cried. "I don't want them. Give them to father. I stole them." With a snarl of rage he turned and his long arms began to flay the air. Like one struggling for release from hands that held him he struck out, hitting George Willard blow after blow on the breast, the neck, the mouth. The young reporter rolled over on the platform half unconscious, stunned by the terrific force of the blows. Springing aboard the passing train and running over the tops of cars, Elmer sprang down to a flat car and lying on his face looked back, trying to see the fallen man in the darkness. Pride surged up in him. "I showed him," he cried. "I guess I showed him. I ain't so queer. I guess I showed him I ain't so queer."

THE UNTOLD LIE

RAY PEARSON and Hal Winters were farm hands employed on a farm three miles north of Winesburg. On Saturday afternoons they came into town and wandered about through the streets with other fellows from the country.

Ray was a quiet, rather nervous man of perhaps fifty with a brown beard and shoulders rounded by too much and too hard labor. In his nature he was as unlike Hal Winters as two men can be unlike.

Ray was an altogether serious man and had a little sharp featured wife who had also a sharp voice. The two, with half a dozen thin legged children, lived in a tumble-down frame house beside a creek at the back end of the Wills farm where Ray was employed.

Hal Winters, his fellow employee, was a young fellow. He was not of the Ned Winters family, who were very respectable people in Winesburg, but was one of the three sons of the old man called Windpeter Winters who had a sawmill near Unionville, six miles away, and who was looked upon by everyone in Winesburg as a confirmed old reprobate.

People from the part of Northern Ohio in which Winesburg lies will remember old Windpeter by his unusual and tragic death. He got drunk one evening in town and started to drive home to Unionville along the railroad tracks. Henry Brattenburg, the butcher, who lived out that way, stopped him at the edge of the town and told him he was sure to meet the down train but Windpeter slashed at him with his whip and drove on. When the train struck and killed him and his two horses a farmer and his wife who were driving home along a nearby road saw the accident. They said that old Windpeter stood up on the seat of his wagon, raving and swearing at the onrushing locomotive, and that he fairly screamed with delight when the team, maddened by his incessant slashing at them, rushed straight ahead to certain death. Boys like young George Willard and Seth Richmond will remember the incident quite vividly because, although everyone in our town said that the old man would go straight to hell and that the community was better off without him, they had a secret conviction that he knew what he was doing and admired his foolish courage. Most boys have seasons of wishing they could die gloriously instead of just being grocery clerks and going on with their humdrum lives.

But this is not the story of Windpeter Winters nor yet of his son Hal who worked on the Wills farm with Ray Pearson. It is Ray's story. It will, however, be necessary to talk a little of young Hal so that you will get into the spirit of it.

Hal was a bad one. Everyone said that. There were three of the Winters boys in that family, John, Hal, and Edward, all broad shouldered big fellows like old Windpeter himself and all fighters and woman-chasers and generally all-around bad ones.

Hal was the worst of the lot and always up to some devilment. He once stole a load of boards from his father's mill and sold them in Winesburg. With the money he bought himself a suit of cheap, flashy clothes. Then he got drunk and when his father came raving into town to find him, they met and fought with their fists on Main Street and were arrested and put into jail together.

Hal went to work on the Wills farm because there was a country school teacher out that way who had taken his fancy. He was only twenty-two then but had already been in two or three of what were spoken of in Winesburg as "women scrapes." Everyone who heard of his infatuation for the school teacher was sure it would turn out badly. "He'll only get her into trouble, you'll see," was the word that went around.

And so these two men, Ray and Hal, were at work in a field on a day in the late October. They were husking corn and occasionally something was said and they laughed. Then came silence. Ray, who was the more sensitive and always minded things more, had chapped hands and they hurt. He put them into his coat pockets and looked away across the fields. He was in a sad distracted mood and was affected by the beauty of the country. If you knew the Winesburg country in the fall and how the low hills are all splashed with yellows and reds you would understand his feeling. He began to think of the time, long ago when he was a young fellow living with his father, then a baker in Winesburg, and how on such days he had wandered away to the woods to gather nuts, hunt rabbits, or just to loaf about and smoke his pipe. His marriage had come about through one of his days of wandering. He had induced a girl who waited on trade in his father's shop to go with him and something had happened. He was thinking of that afternoon and how it had affected his whole life when a spirit of protest awoke in him. He had forgotten about Hal and muttered words. "Tricked by Gad, that's what I was, tricked by life and made a fool of," he said in a low voice.

As though understanding his thoughts, Hal Winters spoke up. "Well, has it been worth while? What about it, eh? What about marriage and all that?" he asked and then laughed. Hal tried to keep on laughing but he too was in an earnest mood. He began to talk earnestly. "Has a fellow got to do it?" he asked. "Has he got to be harnessed up and driven through life like a horse?"

Hal didn't wait for an answer but sprang to his feet and began to walk back and forth between the corn shocks. He was getting more and more excited. Bending down suddenly he picked up an ear of the yellow corn and threw it at the fence. "I've got Nell Gunther in trouble," he said. "I'm telling you, but you keep your mouth shut."

Ray Pearson arose and stood staring. He was almost a foot shorter than Hal, and when the younger man came and put his two hands on the older man's shoulders they made a picture. There they stood in the big empty field with the quiet corn shocks standing in rows behind them and the red and yellow hills in the distance, and from being just two indifferent work-men they had become all alive to each other. Hal sensed it and because that was his way he laughed. "Well, old daddy," he said awkwardly, "come on, advise me. I've got Nell in trouble. Perhaps you've been in the same fix yourself. I know what every one would say is the right thing to do, but what do you say? Shall I marry and settle down? Shall I put myself into the harness to be worn out like an old horse? You know me, Ray. There can't any one break me but I can break myself. Shall I do it or shall I tell Nell to go to the devil? Come on, you tell me. Whatever you say, Ray, I'll do."

Ray couldn't answer. He shook Hal's hands loose and turning walked straight away toward the barn. He was a sensitive man and there were tears in his eyes. He knew there was only one thing to say to Hal Winters, son of old Windpeter Winters, only one thing that all his own training and all the beliefs of the people he knew would approve, but for his life he couldn't say what he knew he should say.

At half-past four that afternoon Ray was puttering about the barnyard when his wife came up the lane along the creek and called him. After the talk with Hal he hadn't returned to the corn field but worked about the barn. He had already done the evening chores and had seen Hal, dressed and ready for a roistering night in town, come out of the farmhouse and go into the road. Along the path to his own house he trudged behind his wife, looking at the ground and thinking. He couldn't make out what was wrong. Every time he raised his eyes and saw the beauty of the country in the failing light he wanted to do something he had never done before, shout or scream or hit his wife with his fists or something equally unex-pected and terrifying. Along the path he went scratching his head and trying to make it out. He looked hard at his wife's back but she seemed all right.

She only wanted him to go into town for groceries and as soon as she had told him what she wanted began to scold. "You're always puttering," she said. "Now I want you to hustle.

There isn't anything in the house for supper and you've got to get to town and back in a hurry."

Ray went into his own house and took an overcoat from a hook back of the door. It was torn about the pockets and the collar was shiny. His wife went into the bedroom and presently came out with a soiled cloth in one hand and three silver dollars in the other. Somewhere in the house a child wept bitterly and a dog that had been sleeping by the stove arose and yawned. Again the wife scolded. "The children will cry and cry. Why are you always puttering?" she asked.

Ray went out of the house and climbed the fence into a field. It was just growing dark and the scene that lay before him was lovely. All the low hills were washed with color and even the little clusters of bushes in the corners by the fences were alive with beauty. The whole world seemed to Ray Pearson to have become alive with something just as he and Hal had suddenly become alive when they stood in the corn field staring into each other's eyes.

The beauty of the country about Winesburg was too much for Ray on that fall evening. That is all there was to it. He could not stand it. Of a sudden he forgot all about being a quiet old farm hand and throwing off the torn overcoat began to run across the field. As he ran he shouted a protest against his life, against all life, against everything that makes life ugly. "There was no promise made," he cried into the empty spaces that lay about him. "I didn't promise my Minnie anything and Hal hasn't made any promise to Nell. I know he hasn't. She went into the woods with him because she wanted to go. What he wanted she wanted. Why should I pay? Why should Hal pay? Why should any one pay? I don't want Hal to become old and worn out. I'll tell him. I won't let it go on. I'll catch Hal before he gets to town and I'll tell him."

Ray ran clumsily and once he stumbled and fell down. "I must catch Hal and tell him," he kept thinking and although his breath came in gasps he kept running harder and harder. As he ran he thought of things that hadn't come into his mind for years—how at the time he married he had planned to go west to his uncle in Portland, Oregon—how he hadn't wanted to be a farm hand, but had thought when he got out west he would go to sea and be a sailor or get a job on a ranch and ride a horse into western towns, shouting and laughing and waking the people in the houses with his wild cries. Then as he ran he remembered his children and in fancy felt their hands clutching at him. All of his thoughts of himself were involved with the thoughts of Hal and he thought the children were clutching at the younger man also. "They are the accidents of life, Hal," he cried. "They are not mine or yours. I had nothing to do with them."

Darkness began to spread over the fields as Ray Pearson ran on and on. His breath came in little sobs. When he came to the fence at the edge of the road and confronted Hal Winters, all dressed up and smoking a pipe as he walked jauntily along, he could not have told what he thought or what he wanted.

Ray Pearson lost his nerve and this is really the end of the story of what happened to him. It was almost dark when he got to the fence and he put his hands on the top bar and stood staring. Hal Winters jumped a ditch and coming up close to Ray put his hands into his pockets and laughed. He seemed to have lost his own sense of what had happened in the corn field and when he put up a strong hand and took hold of the lapel of Ray's coat he shook the old man as he might have shaken a dog that had misbehaved.

"You came to tell me, eh?" he said. "Well, never mind telling me anything. I'm not a coward and I've already made up my mind." He laughed again and jumped back across the ditch. "Nell ain't no fool," he said. "She didn't ask me to marry her. I want to marry her. I want to settle down and have kids."

Ray Pearson also laughed. He felt like laughing at himself and all the world.

As the form of Hal Winters disappeared in the dusk that lay over the road that led to Winesburg, he turned and walked slowly back across the fields to where he had left his torn overcoat. As he went some memory of pleasant evenings spent with the thin-legged children in the tumble-down house by the creek must have come into his mind, for he muttered words. "It's just as well. Whatever I told him would have been a lie," he said softly, and then his form also disappeared into the darkness of the fields.

DRINK

TOM FOSTER came to Winesburg from Cincinnati when he was still young and could get many new impressions. His grandmother had been raised on a farm near the town and as a young girl had gone to school there when Winesburg was a village of twelve or fifteen houses clustered about a general store on the Trunion Pike.

What a life the old woman had led since she went away from the frontier settlement and what a strong, capable little old thing she was! She had been in Kansas, in Canada, and in New York City, traveling about with her husband, a mechanic, before he died. Later she went to stay with her daughter who had also married a mechanic and lived in Covington, Kentucky, across the river from Cincinnati.

Then began the hard years for Tom Foster's grandmother. First her son-in-law was killed by a policeman during a strike and then Tom's mother became an invalid and died also. The grandmother had saved a little money, but it was swept away by the illness of the daughter and by the cost of the two funerals. She became a half worn-out old woman worker and lived with the grandson above a junk shop on a side street in Cincinnati. For five years she scrubbed the floors in an office building and then got a place as dish washer in a restaurant. Her hands were all twisted out of shape. When she took hold of a mop or a broom handle the hands looked like the dried stems of an old creeping vine clinging to a tree.

The old woman came back to Winesburg as soon as she got the chance. One evening as she was coming home from work she found a pocket-book containing thirty-seven dollars, and that opened the way. The trip was a great adventure for the boy. It was past seven o'clock at night when the grandmother came home with the pocket-book held tightly in her old hands and she was so excited she could scarcely speak. She insisted on leaving Cincinnati that night, saying that if they stayed until morning the owner of the money would be sure to find them out and make trouble. Tom, who was then sixteen years old, had to go trudging off to the station with the old woman bearing all of their earthly belongings done up in a worn-out blanket and slung across his back. By his side walked the grandmother urging him forward. Her toothless old mouth twitched nervously, and when Tom grew weary and wanted to put the pack down at a street crossing she snatched it up and if he had not prevented would have slung it across her own back. When they got into the train and it had run out of the city she was as delighted as a girl and talked as the boy had never heard her talk before.

All through the night as the train rattled along, the grandmother told Tom tales of Winesburg and of how he would enjoy his life working in the fields and shooting wild things in the wood there. She could not believe that the tiny village of fifty years before had grown into a thriving town in her absence, and in the morning when the train came to Winesburg did not want to get off. "It isn't what I thought. It may be hard for you here," she said, and then the train went on its way and the two stood confused, not knowing where to turn, in the presence of Albert Longworth, the Winesburg baggage master.

But Tom Foster did get along all right. He was one to get along anywhere. Mrs. White, the banker's wife, employed his grandmother to work in the kitchen and he got a place as stable boy in the banker's new brick barn.

In Winesburg servants were hard to get. The woman who wanted help in her housework employed a "hired girl" who insisted on sitting at the table with the family. Mrs. White was sick of hired girls and snatched at the chance to get hold of the old city woman. She furnished a room for the boy Tom upstairs in the barn. "He can mow the lawn and run errands when the horses do not need attention," she explained to her husband.

Tom Foster was rather small for his age and had a large head covered with stiff black hair that stood straight up. The hair emphasized the bigness of his head. His voice was the softest thing imaginable, and he was himself so gentle and quiet that he slipped into the life of the town without attracting the least bit of attention.

One could not help wondering where Tom Foster got his gentleness. In Cincinnati he had lived in a neighborhood where gangs of tough boys prowled through the streets, and all through his early formative years he ran about with tough boys. For a while he was messenger for a telegraph company and delivered messages in a neighborhood sprinkled with houses of prostitution. The women in the houses knew and loved Tom Foster and the tough boys in the gangs loved him also.

He never asserted himself. That was one thing that helped him escape. In an odd way he stood in the shadow of the wall of life, was meant to stand in the shadow. He saw the men and women in the houses of lust, sensed their casual and horrible love affairs, saw boys fighting and listened to their tales of thieving and drunkenness unmoved and strangely unaffected.

Once Tom did steal. That was while he still lived in the city. The grandmother was ill at the time and he himself was out of work. There was nothing to eat in the house, and so he went into a harness shop on a side street and stole a dollar and seventy-five cents out of the cash drawer.

The harness shop was run by an old man with a long mustache. He saw the boy lurking about and thought nothing of it. When he went out into the street to talk to a teamster Tom opened the cash drawer and taking the money walked away. Later he was caught and his grandmother settled the matter by offering to come twice a week for a month and scrub the shop. The boy was ashamed, but he was rather glad, too. "It is all right to be ashamed and makes me understand new things," he said to the grandmother, who didn't know what the boy was talking about but loved him so much that it didn't matter whether she understood or not.

For a year Tom Foster lived in the banker's stable and then lost his place there. He didn't take very good care of the horses and he was a constant source of irritation to the banker's wife. She told him to mow the lawn and he forgot. Then she sent him to the store or to the post office and he did not come back but joined a group of men and boys and spent the whole afternoon with them, standing about, listening and occasionally, when addressed, saying a few words. As in the city in the houses of prostitution and with the rowdy boys running through the streets at night, so in Winesburg among its citizens he had always the power to be a part of and yet distinctly apart from the life about him.

After Tom lost his place at Banker White's he did not live with his grandmother, although often in the evening she came to visit him. He rented a room at the rear of a little frame building belonging to old Rufus Whiting. The building was on Duane Street, just off Main Street, and had been used for years as a law office by the old man who had become too feeble and forgetful for the practice of his profession but did not realize his inefficiency. He liked Tom and let him have the room for a dollar a month. In the late afternoon when the lawyer had gone home the boy had the place to himself and spent hours lying on the floor by the stove and thinking of things. In the evening the grandmother came and sat in the lawyer's chair to smoke a pipe while Tom remained silent, as he always did in the presence of every one.

Often the old woman talked with great vigor. Sometimes she was angry about some happening at the banker's house and scolded away for hours. Out of her own earnings she bought a mop and regularly scrubbed the lawyer's office. Then when the place was spotlessly clean and smelled clean she lighted her clay pipe and she and Tom had a smoke together. "When you get ready to die then I will die also," she said to the boy lying on the floor beside her chair.

Tom Foster enjoyed life in Winesburg. He did odd jobs, such as cutting wood for kitchen stoves and mowing the grass before houses. In late May and early June he picked strawberries in the fields. He had time to loaf and he enjoyed loafing. Banker White had given him a cast-off coat which was too large for him, but his grandmother cut it down, and he had also an overcoat, got at the same place, that was lined with fur. The fur was worn away in spots, but the coat was warm and in the winter Tom slept in it. He thought his method of getting along good enough and was happy and satisfied with the way life in Winesburg had turned out for him.

The most absurd little things made Tom Foster happy. That, I suppose, was why people loved him. In Hern's grocery they would be roasting coffee on Friday afternoon, preparatory to the Saturday rush of trade, and the rich odor invaded lower Main Street. Tom Foster appeared and sat on a box at the rear of the store. For an hour he did not move but sat perfectly still, filling his being with the spicy odor that made him half drunk with happiness. "I like it," he said gently. "It makes me think of things far away, places and things like that."

One night Tom Foster got drunk. That came about in a curious way. He never had been drunk before, and indeed in all his life had never taken a drink of anything intoxicating, but he felt he needed to be drunk that one time and so went and did it.

In Cincinnati, when he lived there, Tom had found out many things, things about ugliness and crime and lust. Indeed, he knew more of these things than any one else in Winesburg. The matter of sex in particular had presented itself to him in a quite horrible way and had made a deep impression on his mind. He thought, after what he had seen of the women standing before the squalid houses on cold nights and the look he had seen in the eyes of the men who stopped to talk to them, that he would put sex altogether out of his own life. One of the women of the neighborhood tempted him once and he went into a room with her. He never forgot the smell of the room nor the greedy look that came into the eyes of the woman. It sickened him and in a very terrible way left a scar on

his soul. He had always before thought of women as quite
innocent things, much like his grandmother, but after that one
experience in the room he dismissed women from his mind.
So gentle was his nature that he could not hate anything and
not being able to understand he decided to forget.

And Tom did forget until he came to Winesburg. After he
had lived there for two years something began to stir in him.
On all sides he saw youth making love and he was himself a
youth. Before he knew what had happened he was in love also.
He fell in love with Helen White, daughter of the man for
whom he had worked, and found himself thinking of her at
night.

That was a problem for Tom and he settled it in his own way.
He let himself think of Helen White whenever her figure
came into his mind and only concerned himself with the
manner of his thoughts. He had a fight, a quiet determined
little fight of his own, to keep his desires in the channel where
he thought they belonged, but on the whole he was victorious.

And then came the spring night when he got drunk. Tom
was wild on that night. He was like an innocent young buck of
the forest that has eaten of some maddening weed. The thing
began, ran its course, and was ended in one night, and you may
be sure that no one in Winesburg was any the worse for Tom's
outbreak.

In the first place, the night was one to make a sensitive
nature drunk. The trees along the residence streets of the
town were all newly clothed in soft green leaves, in the gardens behind the houses men were puttering about in vegetable gardens, and in the air there was a hush, a waiting kind of
silence very stirring to the blood.

Tom left his room on Duane Street just as the young night
began to make itself felt. First he walked through the streets,
going softly and quietly along, thinking thoughts that he tried
to put into words. He said that Helen White was a flame
dancing in the air and that he was a little tree without leaves
standing out sharply against the sky. Then he said that she was

a wind, a strong terrible wind, coming out of the darkness of a stormy sea and that he was a boat left on the shore of the sea by a fisherman.

That idea pleased the boy and he sauntered along playing with it. He went into Main Street and sat on the curbing before Wacker's tobacco store. For an hour he lingered about listening to the talk of men, but it did not interest him much and he slipped away. Then he decided to get drunk and went into Willy's saloon and bought a bottle of whiskey. Putting the bottle into his pocket, he walked out of town, wanting to be alone to think more thoughts and to drink the whiskey.

Tom got drunk sitting on a bank of new grass beside the road about a mile north of town. Before him was a white road and at his back an apple orchard in full bloom. He took a drink out of the bottle and then lay down on the grass. He thought of mornings in Winesburg and of how the stones in the graveled driveway by Banker White's house were wet with dew and glistened in the morning light. He thought of the nights in the barn when it rained and he lay awake hearing the drumming of the rain drops and smelling the warm smell of horses and of hay. Then he thought of a storm that had gone roaring through Winesburg several days before and, his mind going back, he relived the night he had spent on the train with his grandmother when the two were coming from Cincinnati. Sharply he remembered how strange it had seemed to sit quietly in the coach and to feel the power of the engine hurling the train along through the night.

Tom got drunk in a very short time. He kept taking drinks from the bottle as the thoughts visited him and when his head began to reel got up and walked along the road going away from Winesburg. There was a bridge on the road that ran out of Winesburg north to Lake Erie and the drunken boy made his way along the road to the bridge. There he sat down. He tried to drink again, but when he had taken the cork out of the bottle he became ill and put it quickly back. His head was rocking back and forth and so he sat on the stone approach to the bridge and sighed. His head seemed to be flying about like a pin wheel and then projecting itself off into space and his arms and legs flopped helplessly about.

At eleven o'clock Tom got back into town. George Willard found him wandering about and took him into the *Eagle* printshop. Then he became afraid that the drunken boy would make a mess on the floor and helped him into the alleyway.

The reporter was confused by Tom Foster. The drunken boy talked of Helen White and said he had been with her on the shore of a sea and had made love to her. George had seen Helen White walking in the street with her father during the evening and decided that Tom was out of his head. A sentiment concerning Helen White that lurked in his own heart flamed up and he became angry. "Now you quit that," he said. "I won't let Helen White's name be dragged into this. I won't let that happen." He began shaking Tom's shoulder, trying to make him understand. "You quit it," he said again.

For three hours the two young men, thus strangely thrown together, stayed in the printshop. When he had a little recovered George took Tom for a walk. They went into the country and sat on a log near the edge of a wood. Something in the still night drew them together and when the drunken boy's head began to clear they talked.

"It was good to be drunk," Tom Foster said. "It taught me something. I won't have to do it again. I will think more clearly after this. You see how it is."

George Willard did not see, but his anger concerning Helen White passed and he felt drawn towards the pale, shaken boy as he had never before been drawn towards any one. With motherly solicitude, he insisted that Tom get to his feet and walk about. Again they went back to the printshop and sat in silence in the darkness.

The reporter could not get the purpose of Tom Foster's action straightened out in his mind. When Tom spoke again of Helen White he again grew angry and began to scold. "You quit that," he said sharply. "You haven't been with her. What makes you say you have? What makes you keep saying such things? Now you quit it, do you hear?"

Tom was hurt. He couldn't quarrel with George Willard because he was incapable of quarreling, so he got up to go away. When George Willard was insistent he put out his hand, laying it on the older boy's arm, and tried to explain.

"Well," he said softly, "I don't know how it was. I was happy. You see how that was. Helen White made me happy and the night did too. I wanted to suffer, to be hurt somehow. I thought that was what I should do. I wanted to suffer, you see, because every one suffers and does wrong. I thought of a lot of things to do, but they wouldn't work. They all hurt some one else."

Tom Foster's voice arose, and for once in his life he became almost excited. "It was like making love, that's what I mean," he explained. "Don't you see how it is? It hurt me to do what I did and made everything strange. That's why I did it. I'm glad, too. It taught me something, that's it, that's what I wanted. Don't you understand? I wanted to learn things, you see. That's why I did it."

DEATH

THE stairway leading up to Doctor Reefy's office, in the Heffner Block above the Paris Dry Goods Store, was but dimly lighted. At the head of the stairway hung a lamp with a dirty chimney that was fastened by a bracket to the wall. The lamp had a tin reflector, brown with rust and covered with dust. The people who went up the stairway followed with their feet the feet of many who had gone before. The soft boards of the stairs had yielded under the pressure of feet and deep hollows marked the way.

At the top of the stairway a turn to the right brought you to the doctor's door. To the left was a dark hallway filled with rubbish. Old chairs, carpenter's horses, step ladders and empty boxes lay in the darkness waiting for shins to be barked. The pile of rubbish belonged to the Paris Dry Goods Co. When a counter or a row of shelves in the store became useless, clerks carried it up the stairway and threw it on the pile.

Doctor Reefy's office was as large as a barn. A stove with a round paunch sat in the middle of the room. Around its base was piled sawdust, held in place by heavy planks nailed to the floor. By the door stood a huge table that had once been a part of the furniture of Herrick's Clothing Store and that had been used for displaying custom-made clothes. It was covered with books, bottles and surgical instruments. Near the edge of the table lay three or four apples left by John Spaniard, a tree nurseryman who was Doctor Reefy's friend, and who had slipped the apples out of his pocket as he came in at the door.

At middle age Doctor Reefy was tall and awkward. The grey beard he later wore had not yet appeared, but on the upper lip grew a brown mustache. He was not a graceful man, as when he grew older, and was much occupied with the problem of disposing of his hands and feet.

On summer afternoons, when she had been married many years and when her son George was a boy of twelve or fourteen, Elizabeth Willard sometimes went up the worn steps to Doctor Reefy's office. Already the woman's naturally tall figure had begun to droop and to drag itself listlessly about. Ostensibly she went to see the doctor because of her health, but on the half dozen occasions when she had been to see him the outcome of the visits did not primarily concern her health. She and the doctor talked of that but they talked most of her life, of their two lives and of the ideas that had come to them as they lived their lives in Winesburg.

In the big empty office the man and the woman sat looking at each other and they were a good deal alike. Their bodies were different as were also the color of their eyes, the length of their noses and the circumstances of their existence, but something inside them meant the same thing, wanted the same release, would have left the same impression on the memory of an onlooker. Later, and when he grew older and married a young wife, the doctor often talked to her of the hours spent with the sick woman and expressed a good many things he had been unable to express to Elizabeth. He was almost a poet in his old age and his notion of what happened took a poetic turn. "I had come to the time in my life when prayer became necessary and so I invented gods and prayed to them," he said. "I did not say my prayers in words nor did I kneel down but sat perfectly still in my chair. In the late afternoon when it was hot and quiet on Main Street or in the winter when the days were gloomy, the gods came into the office and I thought no one knew about them. Then I found that this woman Elizabeth knew, that she worshipped also the same gods. I have a notion that she came to the office because she thought the gods would be there but she was happy to find herself not alone just the same. It was an experience that cannot be explained, although I suppose it is always happening to men and women in all sorts of places."

*

On the summer afternoons when Elizabeth and the doctor sat in the office and talked of their two lives they talked of other lives also. Sometimes the doctor made philosophic epigrams. Then he chuckled with amusement. Now and then after a period of silence, a word was said or a hint given that strangely illuminated the life of the speaker, a wish became a desire, or a dream, half dead, flared suddenly into life. For the most part the words came from the woman and she said them without looking at the man.

Each time she came to see the doctor the hotel keeper's wife talked a little more freely and after an hour or two in his presence went down the stairway into Main Street feeling renewed and strengthened against the dullness of her days. With something approaching a girlhood swing to her body she walked along, but when she had got back to her chair by the window of her room and when darkness had come on and a girl from the hotel dining room brought her dinner on a tray, she let it grow cold. Her thoughts ran away to her girlhood with its passionate longing for adventure and she remembered the arms of men that had held her when adventure was a possible thing for her. Particularly she remembered one who had for a time been her lover and who in the moment of his passion had cried out to her more than a hundred times, saying the same words madly over and over: "You dear! You dear! You lovely dear!" The words she thought expressed something she would have liked to have achieved in life.

In her room in the shabby old hotel the sick wife of the hotel keeper began to weep and putting her hands to her face rocked back and forth. The words of her one friend, Doctor Reefy, rang in her ears. "Love is like a wind stirring the grass beneath trees on a black night," he had said. "You must not try to make love definite. It is the divine accident of life. If you try to be definite and sure about it and to live beneath the trees, where soft night winds blow, the long hot day of disappointment comes swiftly and the gritty dust from passing wagons gathers upon lips inflamed and made tender by kisses."

Elizabeth Willard could not remember her mother who had died when she was but five years old. Her girlhood had been lived in the most haphazard manner imaginable. Her father was a man who had wanted to be let alone and the affairs of the hotel would not let him alone. He also had lived and died a sick man. Every day he arose with a cheerful face, but by ten o'clock in the morning all the joy had gone out of his heart. When a guest complained of the fare in the hotel dining room or one of the girls who made up the beds got married and went away, he stamped on the floor and swore. At night when he went to bed he thought of his daughter growing up among the stream of people that drifted in and out of the hotel and was overcome with sadness. As the girl grew older and began to walk out in the evening with men he wanted to talk to her, but when he tried was not successful. He always forgot what he wanted to say and spent the time complaining of his own affairs.

In her girlhood and young womanhood Elizabeth had tried to be a real adventurer in life. At eighteen life had so gripped her that she was no longer a virgin but, although she had a half dozen lovers before she married Tom Willard, she had never entered upon an adventure prompted by desire alone. Like all the women in the world, she wanted a real lover. Always there was something she sought blindly, passionately, some hidden wonder in life. The tall beautiful girl with the swinging stride who had walked under the trees with men was forever putting out her hand into the darkness and trying to get hold of some other hand. In all the babble of words that fell from the lips of the men with whom she adventured she was trying to find what would be for her the true word.

Elizabeth had married Tom Willard, a clerk in her father's hotel, because he was at hand and wanted to marry at the time when the determination to marry came to her. For a while, like most young girls, she thought marriage would change the face of life. If there was in her mind a doubt of the outcome of the marriage with Tom she brushed it aside. Her father was ill and near death at the time and she was perplexed because of the meaningless outcome of an affair in which she had just been involved. Other girls of her age in Winesburg were marrying men she had always known, grocery clerks or young farmers. In the evening they walked in Main Street with their husbands and when she passed they smiled happily. She began to think that the fact of marriage might be full of some hidden significance. Young wives with whom she talked spoke softly and shyly. "It changes things to have a man of your own," they said.

On the evening before her marriage the perplexed girl had a talk with her father. Later she wondered if the hours alone with the sick man had not led to her decision to marry. The father talked of his life and advised the daughter to avoid being led into another such muddle. He abused Tom Willard, and that led Elizabeth to come to the clerk's defense. The sick man became excited and tried to get out of bed. When she would not let him walk about he began to complain. "I've never been let alone," he said. "Although I've worked hard I've not made the hotel pay. Even now I owe money at the bank. You'll find that out when I'm gone."

The voice of the sick man became tense with earnestness. Being unable to arise, he put out his hand and pulled the girl's head down beside his own. "There's a way out," he whispered. "Don't marry Tom Willard or any one else here in Winesburg. There is eight hundred dollars in a tin box in my trunk. Take it and go away."

Again the sick man's voice became querulous. "You've got to promise," he declared. "If you won't promise not to marry, give me your word that you'll never tell Tom about the money. It is mine and if I give it to you I've the right to make that demand. Hide it away. It is to make up to you for my failure as a father. Some time it may prove to be a door, a great open door to you. Come now, I tell you I'm about to die, give me your promise."

*

In Doctor Reefy's office, Elizabeth, a tired gaunt old woman at forty-one, sat in a chair near the stove and looked at the floor.

By a small desk near the window sat the doctor. His hands played with a lead pencil that lay on the desk. Elizabeth talked of her life as a married woman. She became impersonal and forgot her husband, only using him as a lay figure to give point to her tale. "And then I was married and it did not turn out at all," she said bitterly. "As soon as I had gone into it I began to be afraid. Perhaps I knew too much before and then perhaps I found out too much during my first night with him. I don't remember.

"What a fool I was. When father gave me the money and tried to talk me out of the thought of marriage, I would not listen. I thought of what the girls who were married had said of it and I wanted marriage also. It wasn't Tom I wanted, it was marriage. When father went to sleep I leaned out of the window and thought of the life I had led. I didn't want to be a bad woman. The town was full of stories about me. I even began to be afraid Tom would change his mind."

The woman's voice began to quiver with excitement. To Doctor Reefy, who without realizing what was happening had begun to love her, there came an odd illusion. He thought that as she talked the woman's body was changing, that she was becoming younger, straighter, stronger. When he could not shake off the illusion his mind gave it a professional twist. "It is good for both her body and her mind, this talking," he muttered.

The woman began telling of an incident that had happened one afternoon a few months after her marriage. Her voice became steadier. "In the late afternoon I went for a drive alone," she said. "I had a buggy and a little grey pony I kept in Moyer's Livery. Tom was painting and repapering rooms in the hotel. He wanted money and I was trying to make up my mind to tell him about the eight hundred dollars father had given to me. I couldn't decide to do it. I didn't like him well enough. There was always paint on his hands and face during those days and he smelled of paint. He was trying to fix up the old hotel, make it new and smart."

The excited woman sat up very straight in her chair and made a quick girlish movement with her hand as she told of the drive alone on the spring afternoon. "It was cloudy and a storm threatened," she said. "Black clouds made the green of the trees and the grass stand out so that the colors hurt my eyes. I went out Trunion Pike a mile or more and then turned into a side road. The little horse went quickly along up hill and down. I was impatient. Thoughts came and I wanted to get away from my thoughts. I began to beat the horse. The black clouds settled down and it began to rain. I wanted to go at a terrible speed, to drive on and on forever. I wanted to get out of town, out of my clothes, out of my marriage, out of my body, out of everything. I almost killed the horse, making him run, and when he could not run any more I got out of the buggy and ran afoot into the darkness until I fell and hurt my side. I wanted to run away from everything but I wanted to run towards something too. Don't you see, dear, how it was?"

Elizabeth sprang out of the chair and began to walk about in the office. She walked as Doctor Reefy thought he had never seen any one walk before. To her whole body there was a swing, a rhythm that intoxicated him. When she came and knelt on the floor beside his chair he took her into his arms and began to kiss her passionately. "I cried all the way home," she said, as she tried to continue the story of her wild ride, but he did not listen. "You dear! You lovely dear! Oh you lovely dear!" he muttered and thought he held in his arms, not the tired-out woman of forty-one but a lovely and innocent girl who had been able by some miracle to project herself out of the husk of the body of the tired-out woman.

Doctor Reefy did not see the woman he had held in his arms again until after her death. On the summer afternoon in the office when he was on the point of becoming her lover a half grotesque little incident brought his love-making quickly to an end. As the man and woman held each other tightly heavy feet came tramping up the office stairs. The two sprang to their feet and stood listening and trembling. The noise on the stairs

was made by a clerk from the Paris Dry Goods Store Co. With
a loud bang he threw an empty box on the pile of rubbish in
the hallway and then went heavily down the stairs. Elizabeth
followed him almost immediately. The thing that had come to
life in her as she talked to her one friend died suddenly. She
was hysterical, as was also Doctor Reefy, and did not want to
continue the talk. Along the street she went with the blood still
singing in her body, but when she turned out of Main Street
and saw ahead the lights of the New Willard House, she began
to tremble and her knees shook so that for a moment she
thought she would fall in the street.

The sick woman spent the last few months of her life hungering for death. Along the road of death she went, seeking,
hungering. She personified the figure of death and made him,
now a strong black-haired youth running over hills, now a
stern quiet man marked and scarred by the business of living.
In the darkness of her room she put out her hand, thrusting it
from under the covers of her bed, and she thought that death
like a living thing put out his hand to her. "Be patient, lover," she
whispered. "Keep yourself young and beautiful and be patient."

On the evening when disease laid its heavy hand upon her
and defeated her plans for telling her son George of the eight
hundred dollars hidden away, she got out of bed and crept half
across the room pleading with death for another hour of life.
"Wait, dear! The boy! The boy! The boy!" she pleaded as she
tried with all of her strength to fight off the arms of the lover
she had wanted so earnestly.

*

Elizabeth died one day in March in the year when her son
George became eighteen, and the young man had but little
sense of the meaning of her death. Only time could give him
that. For a month he had seen her lying white and still and
speechless in her bed, and then one afternoon the doctor
stopped him in the hallway and said a few words.

The young man went into his own room and closed the door.
He had a queer empty feeling in the region of his stomach. For

a moment he sat staring at the floor and then jumping up went for a walk. Along the station platform he went, and around through residence streets past the high school building, thinking almost entirely of his own affairs. The notion of death could not get hold of him and he was in fact a little annoyed that his mother had died on that day. He had just received a note from Helen White, the daughter of the town banker, in answer to one from him. "Tonight I could have gone to see her and now it will have to be put off," he thought half angrily.

Elizabeth died on a Friday afternoon at three o'clock. It had been cold and rainy in the morning but in the afternoon the sun came out. Before she died she lay paralyzed for six days unable to speak or move and with only her mind and her eyes alive. For three of the six days she struggled, thinking of her boy, trying to say some few words in regard to his future, and in her eyes there was an appeal so touching that all who saw it kept the memory of the dying woman in their minds for years. Even Tom Willard who had always half resented his wife forgot his resentment and the tears ran out of his eyes and lodged in his mustache. The mustache had begun to turn grey and Tom colored it with dye. There was oil in the preparation he used for the purpose and the tears, catching in the mustache and being brushed away by his hand, formed a fine mist-like vapor. In his grief Tom Willard's face looked like the face of a little dog that has been out a long time in bitter weather.

George came home along Main Street at dark on the day of his mother's death and, after going to his own room to brush his hair and clothes, went along the hallway and into the room where the body lay. There was a candle on the dressing table by the door and Doctor Reefy sat in a chair by the bed. The doctor arose and started to go out. He put out his hand as though to greet the younger man and then awkwardly drew it back again. The air of the room was heavy with the presence of the two self-conscious human beings, and the man hurried away.

The dead woman's son sat down in a chair and looked at the floor. He again thought of his own affairs and definitely decided he would make a change in his life, that he would leave Winesburg. "I will go to some city. Perhaps I can get a job on some newspaper," he thought and then his mind turned to the girl with whom he was to have spent this evening and again he was half angry at the turn of events that had prevented his going to her.

In the dimly lighted room with the dead woman the young man began to have thoughts. His mind played with thoughts of life as his mother's mind had played with the thought of death. He closed his eyes and imagined that the red young lips of Helen White touched his own lips. His body trembled and his hands shook. And then something happened. The boy sprang to his feet and stood stiffly. He looked at the figure of the dead woman under the sheets and shame for his thoughts swept over him so that he began to weep. A new notion came into his mind and he turned and looked guiltily about as though afraid he would be observed.

George Willard became possessed of a madness to lift the sheet from the body of his mother and look at her face. The thought that had come into his mind gripped him terribly. He became convinced that not his mother but some one else lay in the bed before him. The conviction was so real that it was almost unbearable. The body under the sheets was long and in death looked young and graceful. To the boy, held by some strange fancy, it was unspeakably lovely. The feeling that the body before him was alive, that in another moment a lovely woman would spring out of the bed and confront him, became so overpowering that he could not bear the suspense. Again and again he put out his hand. Once he touched and half lifted the white sheet that covered her, but his courage failed and he, like Doctor Reefy, turned and went out of the room. In the hallway outside the door he stopped and trembled so that he had to put a hand against the wall to support himself. "That's not my mother. That's not my mother in there," he whispered to himself and again his body shook with fright and uncertainty. When Aunt Elizabeth Swift, who had come to watch over the body, came out of an adjoining room he put his hand into hers and began to sob, shaking his head from side to side, half blind with grief. "My mother is dead," he said, and then forgetting the woman he turned and stared at the door through which he had just come. "The dear, the dear, oh the lovely dear," the boy, urged by some impulse outside himself, muttered aloud.

*

As for the eight hundred dollars, the dead woman had kept hidden so long and that was to give George Willard his start in the city, it lay in the tin box behind the plaster by the foot of his mother's bed. Elizabeth had put it there a week after her marriage, breaking the plaster away with a stick. Then she got one of the workmen her husband was at that time employing about the hotel to mend the wall. "I jammed the corner of the bed against it," she had explained to her husband, unable at the moment to give up her dream of release, the release that after all came to her but twice in her life, in the moments when her lovers Death and Doctor Reefy held her in their arms.

SOPHISTICATION

IT was early evening of a day in the late fall and the Winesburg County Fair had brought crowds of country people into town. The day had been clear and the night came on warm and pleasant. On the Trunion Pike, where the road after it left town stretched away between berry fields now covered with dry brown leaves, the dust from passing wagons arose in clouds. Children, curled into little balls, slept on the straw scattered on wagon beds. Their hair was full of dust and their fingers black and sticky. The dust rolled away over the fields and the departing sun set it ablaze with colors.

In the main street of Winesburg crowds filled the stores and the sidewalks. Night came on, horses whinnied, the clerks in the stores ran madly about, children became lost and cried lustily, an American town worked terribly at the task of amusing itself.

Pushing his way through the crowds in Main Street, young George Willard concealed himself in the stairway leading to Doctor Reefy's office and looked at the people. With feverish eyes he watched the faces drifting past under the store lights. Thoughts kept coming into his head and he did not want to think. He stamped impatiently on the wooden steps and looked sharply about. "Well, is she going to stay with him all day? Have I done all this waiting for nothing?" he muttered.

George Willard, the Ohio village boy, was fast growing into manhood and new thoughts had been coming into his mind. All that day, amid the jam of people at the Fair, he had gone about feeling lonely. He was about to leave Winesburg to go away to some city where he hoped to get work on a city newspaper and he felt grown up. The mood that had taken possession of him was a thing known to men and unknown to boys. He felt old and a little tired. Memories awoke in him. To his mind his new sense of maturity set him apart, made of him a half-tragic figure. He wanted someone to understand the feeling that had taken possession of him after his mother's death.

There is a time in the life of every boy when he for the first time takes the backward view of life. Perhaps that is the moment when he crosses the line into manhood. The boy is walking through the street of his town. He is thinking of the future and of the figure he will cut in the world. Ambitions and regrets awake within him. Suddenly something happens; he stops under a tree and waits as for a voice calling his name. Ghosts of old things creep into his consciousness; the voices outside of himself whisper a message concerning the limitations of life. From being quite sure of himself and his future he becomes not at all sure. If he be an imaginative boy a door is torn open and for the first time he looks out upon the world, seeing, as though they marched in procession before him, the countless figures of men who before his time have come out of nothingness into the world, lived their lives and again disappeared into nothingness. The sadness of sophistication has come to the boy. With a little gasp he sees himself as merely a leaf blown by the wind through the streets of his village. He knows that in spite of all the stout talk of his fellows he must live and die in uncertainty, a thing blown by the winds, a thing destined like corn to wilt in the sun. He shivers and looks eagerly about. The eighteen years he has lived seem but a moment, a breathing space in the long march of humanity. Already he hears death calling. With all his heart he wants to come close to some other human, touch someone with his hands, be touched by the hand of another. If he prefers that the other be a woman, that is because he believes that a woman will be gentle, that she will understand. He wants, most of all, understanding.

When the moment of sophistication came to George Willard his mind turned to Helen White, the Winesburg banker's daughter. Always he had been conscious of the girl growing into womanhood as he grew into manhood. Once on a summer night when he was eighteen, he had walked with her on a country road and in her presence had given way to an impulse to boast, to make himself appear big and significant in her eyes. Now he wanted to see her for another purpose. He wanted to tell her of the new impulses that had come to him. He had tried to make her think of him as a man when he knew nothing of manhood and now he wanted to be with her and to try to make her feel the change he believed had taken place in his nature.

As for Helen White, she also had come to a period of change. What George felt, she in her young woman's way felt also. She was no longer a girl and hungered to reach into the grace and beauty of womanhood. She had come home from Cleveland, where she was attending college, to spend a day at the Fair. She also had begun to have memories. During the day she sat in the grand-stand with a young man, one of the instructors from the college, who was a guest of her mother's. The young man was of a pedantic turn of mind and she felt at once he would not do for her purpose. At the Fair she was glad to be seen in his company as he was well dressed and a stranger. She knew that the fact of his presence would create an impression. During the day she was happy, but when night came on she began to grow restless. She wanted to drive the instructor away, to get out of his presence. While they sat together in the grand-stand and while the eyes of former schoolmates were upon them, she paid so much attention to her escort that he grew interested. "A scholar needs money. I should marry a woman with money," he mused.

Helen White was thinking of George Willard even as he wandered gloomily through the crowds thinking of her. She remembered the summer evening when they had walked together and wanted to walk with him again. She thought that the months she had spent in the city, the going to theatres and the seeing of great crowds wandering in lighted thorough-fares, had changed her profoundly. She wanted him to feel and be conscious of the change in her nature.

The summer evening together that had left its mark on the memory of both the young man and woman had, when looked at quite sensibly, been rather stupidly spent. They had walked out of town along a country road. Then they had stopped by a fence near a field of young corn and George had taken off his coat and let it hang on his arm. "Well, I've stayed here in Winesburg—yes—I've not yet gone away but I'm growing up," he had said. "I've been reading books and I've been thinking. I'm going to try to amount to something in life.

"Well," he explained, "that isn't the point. Perhaps I'd better quit talking."

The confused boy put his hand on the girl's arm. His voice trembled. The two started to walk back along the road toward town. In his desperation George boasted, "I'm going to be a big man, the biggest that ever lived here in Winesburg," he declared. "I want you to do something, I don't know what. Perhaps it is none of my business. I want you to try to be different from other women. You see the point. It's none of my business I tell you. I want you to be a beautiful woman. You see what I want."

The boy's voice failed and in silence the two came back into town and went along the street to Helen White's house. At the gate he tried to say something impressive. Speeches he had thought out came into his head, but they seemed utterly pointless. "I thought—I used to think—I had it in my mind you would marry Seth Richmond. Now I know you won't," was all he could find to say as she went through the gate and toward the door of her house.

On the warm fall evening as he stood in the stairway and looked at the crowd drifting through Main Street, George thought of the talk beside the field of young corn and was ashamed of the figure he had made of himself. In the street the people surged up and down like cattle confined in a pen. Buggies and wagons almost filled the narrow thoroughfare. A band played and small boys raced along the sidewalk, diving between the legs of men. Young men with shining red faces walked awkwardly about with girls on their arms. In a room above one of the stores, where a dance was to be held, the fiddlers tuned their instruments. The broken sounds floated down through an open window and out across the murmur of voices and the loud blare of the horns of the band. The medley of sounds got on young Willard's nerves. Everywhere, on all sides, the sense of crowding, moving life closed in about him. He wanted to run away by himself and think. "If she wants to stay with that fellow she may. Why should I care? What difference does it make to me?" he growled and went along Main Street and through Hern's grocery into a side street.

George felt so utterly lonely and dejected that he wanted to weep but pride made him walk rapidly along, swinging his arms. He came to Wesley Moyer's livery barn and stopped in the shadows to listen to a group of men who talked of a race Wesley's stallion, Tony Tip, had won at the Fair during the afternoon. A crowd had gathered in front of the barn and before the crowd walked Wesley, prancing up and down and boasting. He held a whip in his hand and kept tapping the ground. Little puffs of dust arose in the lamplight. "Hell, quit your talking," Wesley exclaimed. "I wasn't afraid, I knew I had 'em beat all the time. I wasn't afraid."

Ordinarily George Willard would have been intensely interested in the boasting of Moyer, the horseman. Now it made him angry. He turned and hurried away along the street. "Old windbag," he sputtered. "Why does he want to be bragging? Why don't he shut up?"

George went into a vacant lot and as he hurried along, fell over a pile of rubbish. A nail protruding from an empty barrel tore his trousers. He sat down on the ground and swore. With a pin he mended the torn place and then arose and went on. "I'll go to Helen White's house, that's what I'll do. I'll walk right in. I'll say that I want to see her. I'll walk right in and sit down, that's what I'll do," he declared, climbing over a fence and beginning to run.

*

On the veranda of Banker White's house Helen was restless and distraught. The instructor sat between the mother and daughter. His talk wearied the girl. Although he had also been raised in an Ohio town, the instructor began to put on the airs of the city. He wanted to appear cosmopolitan. "I like the chance you have given me to study the background out of which most of our girls come," he declared. "It was good of you, Mrs. White, to have me down for the day." He turned to Helen and laughed. "Your life is still bound up with the life of this town?" he asked. "There are people here in whom you are interested?" To the girl his voice sounded pompous and heavy.

Helen arose and went into the house. At the door leading to a garden at the back she stopped and stood listening. Her mother began to talk. "There is no one here fit to associate with a girl of Helen's breeding," she said.

Helen ran down a flight of stairs at the back of the house and into the garden. In the darkness she stopped and stood trembling. It seemed to her that the world was full of meaningless people saying words. Afire with eagerness she ran through a garden gate and turning a corner by the banker's barn, went into a little side street. "George! Where are you, George?" she cried, filled with nervous excitement. She stopped running, and leaned against a tree to laugh hysterically. Along the dark little street came George Willard, still saying words. "I'm going to walk right into her house. I'll go right in and sit down," he declared as he came up to her. He stopped and stared stupidly. "Come on," he said and took hold of her hand. With hanging heads they walked away along the street under the trees. Dry leaves rustled under foot. Now that he had found her George wondered what he had better do and say.

*

At the upper end of the fair ground, in Winesburg, there is a half decayed old grand-stand. It has never been painted and the boards are all warped out of shape. The fair ground stands on top of a low hill rising out of the valley of Wine Creek and from the grand-stand one can see at night, over a cornfield, the lights of the town reflected against the sky.

George and Helen climbed the hill to the fair ground, coming by the path past Waterworks Pond. The feeling of loneliness and isolation that had come to the young man in the crowded streets of his town was both broken and intensified by the presence of Helen. What he felt was reflected in her.

In youth there are always two forces fighting in people. The warm unthinking little animal struggles against the thing that reflects and remembers, and the older, the more sophisticated thing had possession of George Willard. Sensing his mood, Helen walked beside him filled with respect. When they got to the grand-stand they climbed up under the roof and sat down on one of the long bench-like seats.

There is something memorable in the experience to be had by going into a fair ground that stands at the edge of a Middle Western town on a night after the annual fair has been held. The sensation is one never to be forgotten. On all sides are ghosts, not of the dead, but of living people. Here, during the day just passed, have come the people pouring in from the town and the country around. Farmers with their wives and children and all the people from the hundreds of little frame houses have gathered within these board walls. Young girls have laughed and men with beards have talked of the affairs of their lives. The place has been filled to overflowing with life. It has itched and squirmed with life and now it is night and the life has all gone away. The silence is almost terrifying. One conceals oneself standing silently beside the trunk of a tree and what there is of a reflective tendency in his nature is intensified. One shudders at the thought of the meaninglessness of life while at the same instant, and if the people of the town are his people, one loves life so intensely that tears come into the eyes.

In the darkness under the roof of the grand-stand, George Willard sat beside Helen White and felt very keenly his own insignificance in the scheme of existence. Now that he had come out of town where the presence of the people stirring about, busy with a multitude of affairs, had been so irritating the irritation was all gone. The presence of Helen renewed and refreshed him. It was as though her woman's hand was assisting him to make some minute readjustment of the machinery of his life. He began to think of the people in the town where he had always lived with something like reverence. He had reverence for Helen. He wanted to love and to be loved by her, but he did not want at the moment to be confused by her womanhood. In the darkness he took hold of her hand and when she crept close put a hand on her shoulder. A wind began to blow and he shivered. With all his strength he tried to hold and to understand the mood that had come upon him. In that high place in the darkness the two oddly sensitive human atoms held each other tightly and waited. In the mind of each was the same thought. "I have come to this lonely place and here is this other," was the substance of the thing felt.

In Winesburg the crowded day had run itself out into the long night of the late fall. Farm horses jogged away along lonely country roads pulling their portion of weary people. Clerks began to bring samples of goods in off the sidewalks and lock the doors of stores. In the Opera House a crowd had gathered to see a show and further down Main Street the fiddlers, their instruments tuned, sweated and worked to keep the feet of youth flying over a dance floor.

In the darkness in the grand-stand Helen White and George Willard remained silent. Now and then the spell that held them was broken and they turned and tried in the dim light to see into each other's eyes. They kissed but that impulse did not last. At the upper end of the fair ground a half dozen men worked over horses that had raced during the afternoon. The men had built a fire and were heating kettles of water. Only their legs could be seen as they passed back and forth in the light. When the wind blew the little flames of the fire danced crazily about.

George and Helen arose and walked away into the darkness. They went along a path past a field of corn that had not yet been cut. The wind whispered among the dry corn blades. For a moment during the walk back into town the spell that held them was broken. When they had come to the crest of Waterworks Hill they stopped by a tree and George again put his hands on the girl's shoulders. She embraced him eagerly and then again they drew quickly back from that impulse. They stopped kissing and stood a little apart. Mutual respect grew big in them. They were both embarrassed and to relieve their embarrassment dropped into the animalism of youth. They laughed and began to pull and haul at each other. In some way chastened and purified by the mood they had been in they became, not man and woman, not boy and girl, but excited little animals.

It was so they went down the hill. In the darkness they played like two splendid young things in a young world. Once, running swiftly forward, Helen tripped George and he fell. He squirmed and shouted. Shaking with laughter, he rolled down the hill. Helen ran after him. For just a moment she stopped in the darkness. There is no way of knowing what woman's thoughts went through her mind but, when the bottom of the hill was reached and she came up to the boy, she took his arm and walked beside him in dignified silence. For some reason they could not have explained they had both got from their silent evening together the thing needed. Man or boy, woman or girl, they had for a moment taken hold of the thing that makes the mature life of men and women in the modern world possible.

DEPARTURE

YOUNG George Willard got out of bed at four in the morning. It was April and the young tree leaves were just coming out of their buds. The trees along the residence streets in Winesburg are maple and the seeds are winged. When the wind blows they whirl crazily about, filling the air and making a carpet underfoot.

George came down stairs into the hotel office carrying a brown leather bag. His trunk was packed for departure. Since two o'clock he had been awake thinking of the journey he was about to take and wondering what he would find at the end of his journey. The boy who slept in the hotel office lay on a cot by the door. His mouth was open and he snored lustily. George crept past the cot and went out into the silent deserted main street. The east was pink with the dawn and long streaks of light climbed into the sky where a few stars still shone.

Beyond the last house on Trunion Pike in Winesburg there is a great stretch of open fields. The fields are owned by farmers who live in town and drive homeward at evening along Trunion Pike in light creaking wagons. In the fields are planted berries and small fruits. In the late afternoon in the hot summers when the road and the fields are covered with dust, a smoky haze lies over the great flat basin of land. To look across it is like looking out across the sea. In the spring when the land is green the effect is somewhat different. The land becomes a wide green billiard table on which tiny human insects toil up and down.

All through his boyhood and young manhood George Willard had been in the habit of walking on Trunion Pike. He had been in the midst of the great open place on winter nights when it was covered with snow and only the moon looked down at him; he had been there in the fall when bleak winds blew and on summer evenings when the air vibrated with the song of insects. On the April morning he wanted to go there again, to walk again in the silence. He did walk to where the road dipped down by a little stream two miles from town and then turned and walked silently back again. When he got to Main Street clerks were sweeping the sidewalks before the stores. "Hey, you George. How does it feel to be going away?" they asked.

The west bound train leaves Winesburg at seven forty-five in the morning. Tom Little is conductor. His train runs from Cleveland to where it connects with a great trunk line railroad with terminals in Chicago and New York. Tom has what in railroad circles is called an "easy run." Every evening he returns to his family. In the fall and spring he spends his Sundays fishing in Lake Erie. He has a round red face and small blue eyes. He knows the people in the towns along his railroad better than a city man knows the people who live in his apartment building.

George came down the little incline from the New Willard House at seven o'clock. Tom Willard carried his bag. The son had become taller than the father.

On the station platform everyone shook the young man's hand. More than a dozen people waited about. Then they talked of their own affairs. Even Will Henderson, who was lazy and often slept until nine, had got out of bed. George was embarrassed. Gertrude Wilmot, a tall thin woman of fifty who worked in the Winesburg post office, came along the station platform. She had never before paid any attention to George. Now she stopped and put out her hand. In two words she voiced what everyone felt. "Good luck," she said sharply and then turning went on her way.

When the train came into the station George felt relieved. He scampered hurriedly aboard. Helen White came running along Main Street hoping to have a parting word with him, but he had found a seat and did not see her. When the train started Tom Little punched his ticket, grinned and, although he knew George well and knew on what adventure he was just setting

out, made no comment. Tom had seen a thousand George
Willards go out of their towns to the city. It was a commonplace enough incident with him. In the smoking car there was
a man who had just invited Tom to go on a fishing trip to
Sandusky Bay. He wanted to accept the invitation and talk
over details.

George glanced up and down the car to be sure no one was
looking then took out his pocketbook and counted his money.
His mind was occupied with a desire not to appear green.
Almost the last words his father had said to him concerned the
matter of his behavior when he got to the city. "Be a sharp
one," Tom Willard had said. "Keep your eyes on your money.
Be awake. That's the ticket. Don't let any one think you're a
greenhorn."

After George counted his money he looked out of the
window and was surprised to see that the train was still in
Winesburg.

The young man, going out of his town to meet the adventure
of life, began to think but he did not think of anything very big
or dramatic. Things like his mother's death, his departure from
Winesburg, the uncertainty of his future life in the city, the
serious and larger aspects of his life did not come into his
mind.

He thought of little things—Turk Smollet wheeling boards
through the main street of his town in the morning, a tall
woman, beautifully gowned, who had once stayed over night
at his father's hotel, Butch Wheeler the lamp lighter of Winesburg hurrying through the streets on a summer evening and
holding a torch in his hand, Helen White standing by a window in the Winesburg post office and putting a stamp on an
envelope.

The young man's mind was carried away by his growing
passion for dreams. One looking at him would not have
thought him particularly sharp. With the recollection of little
things occupying his mind he closed his eyes and leaned back
in the car seat. He stayed that way for a long time and when he

aroused himself and again looked out of the car window the town of Winesburg had disappeared and his life there had become but a background on which to paint the dreams of his manhood.

The End

The Oxford World's Classics Website

www.worldsclassics.co.uk

- Browse the full range of Oxford World's Classics online

- Sign up for our monthly e-alert to receive information on new titles

- Read extracts from the Introductions

- Listen to our editors and translators talk about the world's greatest literature with our Oxford World's Classics audio guides

- Join the conversation, follow us on Twitter at OWC_Oxford

- Teachers and lecturers can order inspection copies quickly and simply via our website

www.worldsclassics.co.uk

American Literature

British and Irish Literature

Children's Literature

Classics and Ancient Literature

Colonial Literature

Eastern Literature

European Literature

Gothic Literature

History

Medieval Literature

Oxford English Drama

Poetry

Philosophy

Politics

Religion

The Oxford Shakespeare

A complete list of Oxford World's Classics, including Authors in Context, Oxford English Drama, and the Oxford Shakespeare, is available in the UK from the Marketing Services Department, Oxford University Press, Great Clarendon Street, Oxford OX2 6DP, or visit the website at www.oup.com/uk/worldsclassics.

In the USA, visit www.oup.com/us/owc for a complete title list.

Oxford World's Classics are available from all good bookshops. In case of difficulty, customers in the UK should contact Oxford University Press Bookshop, 116 High Street, Oxford OX1 4BR.